BCNECOLOGIA

20 YEARS OF THE URBAN ECOLOGY AGENCY OF BARCELONA

BCN ECOLOGIA
Agència d'Ecologia Urbana de Barcelona

BR BARCELONA REGIONAL

Ajuntament de Barcelona

Arquine

BCNECOLOGIA

BCNECOLOGIA'S LEGACY

Janet Sanz
Second Deputy Mayor of Barcelona City Council
and President of Barcelona Regional

In its twenty years of existence, the Urban Ecology Agency of Barcelona (BCNecologia) has undoubtedly been an essential participant in the definition of Barcelona's new urban model. During this time, the Agency and its team of professionals have led a series of initiatives that have placed the city at the forefront of the international urban transformation scene.

Personally, I believe that BCNecologia has made three main contributions to the city that we must not forget.

The first – and this is surely what the Agency will be remembered for – is the incorporation of ecology into the city's urban planning. Back in 2000, when the Agency was created, something that now seems so basic was a radical change and an innovation in the way cities were made, urban planning was approached and mobility was viewed. We owe this to brave, left-wing, green governments that understood the importance of environmentalism and showed that urban planning could be carried out from an environmental perspective. They provided responses to some of the effects of the climate crisis that were beginning to impact the city, its functioning and the lives of its residents. Twenty-one years later, the terms *urbanism* and *environment* are inextricably linked. Now, thanks in part to the Agency, we are lucky to live in a city that is ready to lead the way in sustainable urbanism for the twenty-first century.

The second way in which the Urban Ecology Agency of Barcelona has contributed to the city is by providing a space for reflection on and planning of cross-cutting public policies for the medium and long term. It has been highly useful for the Administration to have a space linked to it but that exists separately, so that urban issues can be tackled without being affected by political terms. Proof of the success of the Agency providing this space to develop models and proposals is the fact that this knowledge has been exported to other cities, both nationally and internationally.

BCNecologia's third contribution — and the most important one, in my eyes — is its adaptation to challenges faced by the city over the years. The Agency was created at the turn of the twenty-first century, ready to overcome all the challenges this new era would bring, and has always stayed one step ahead when tackling the most significant urban issues. Looking back at the major transformations that have taken place in the city in recent years, the Agency has clearly played a key role in defining them. The main urban innovations that have redefined the city are the superblock model and the orthogonal bus network. These new models, designed around a decade ago, are precursors to a new way of viewing the city that puts pedestrians, greenery and public transport first.

This legacy and accumulated knowledge will live on within Barcelona Regional, which the Agency team has recently joined. All in all, it is clear that, thanks to this work, ecology is here to stay in Barcelona. Because without ecology, there can be no life.

LEARNING FROM THE AGENCY

Josep Bohigas
Architect. Director of Barcelona Regional
and of the Urban Ecology Agency of Barcelona

Over the Urban Ecology Agency of Barcelona's 20 years of existence, I have been lucky enough to work with the team on three different occasions. The first was in 2003, when Salvador Rueda called the studio where I worked, asking us to help him to imagine urbanistic scenarios that could emerge from applying the 'superblock' strategy. The second came in 2015, when a group of students and staff from various schools of architecture, of which I was part, put forward a proposal to implement the first tactical superblock in El Poblenou. The third occasion was recently, between 2020 and 2021, during which time I led the delicate process of transferring the Agency to Barcelona Regional (BR). From now on, the latter will inherit the former's enormous amount of intellectual and human capital, which has played a key role in the changes to Barcelona's urban planning model over recent years.

A NEW PLAN

In 2003, the city was busy putting the final touches on the festivities and huge urban transformations for the 2004 Universal Forum of Cultures. This pioneering event was intended to foster major improvements, in the wake of Barcelona's successful Olympic Games, with a view to keeping the city on the competitive global map of places to visit and invest in, while showing it as the beacon of social urbanism it once was. But behind this lavish event, the city was already showing worrying signs of exhaustion from a model based on major transformative projects which, for funding purposes, offered certain perks that were incongruous with their initial aims. There was a desire to improve the city, but at the same time, parts of it were being sold to the highest bidder, thus aggravating serious social and environmental inequalities. In this contradictory, vulnerable situation, the new the Urban Ecology Agency of Barcelona proposed a change of course based on the ecosystemic urbanism theory and the radical yet viable superblock plan.

When, in 2003, Salvador Rueda recruited us to join the cause, the only superblocks we had heard of were Le Corbusier's grouping proposals in the Macià Plan of 1932 – in which a significant part of the city was demolished and a residential network of 400x400 m units was created – and the ones built by MBM Arquitectes in the Olympic Village for 1992, which tentatively brought together various blocks on the post-industrial coast of El Poblenou. The Agency put forward a very different plan: although it used the same number of superblocks and aimed to hierarchise the streets in the Eixample district, it also tackled more complex, contemporary issues. The plan did not involve demolishing part of the existing city to build a new, exemplary neighbourhood (as planned in the Macià Plan and carried out in the Olympic Village). Instead, it reinterpreted the built-up city and directed it towards a new ecosystemic model.

The Agency's plan opened up a world of new approaches, starting with quantifying urban complexity beyond the simple transformation of urban planning zones. For years, urban planning entities in Barcelona had been focusing on transforming unfinished or forgotten sites, monumentalising public spaces, and building symbolic buildings and robust infrastructures. The strategy adopted followed the old phrase 'one bad apple can spoil the barrel', but in reverse: the idea was that one flagship project, placed in a strategic location, could positively influence the surrounding area. This is how the 'Barcelona Model' came together and how many of the regeneration initiatives in the city were allocated, including the squares of the 1980s, the Olympic areas of the '90s, La Sagrera station and the Fòrum (2004). In hindsight, the decisions made were well-intentioned, but the results were not always as positive as had been hoped. Indeed, on many occasions, blind faith in *transformation* led to spectacular investments without any meaningful social improvements.

Meanwhile, Salvador Rueda's plan proposed a paradigm shift. Instead of singling out specific places, it suggested making systemic improvements to several aspects that we (and most urban planners in Barcelona) had deemed less decisive when imagining and planning the city: noise pollution, air quality, health, biodiversity, socio-spatial justice, green infrastructure, urban complexity. But, above all, the plan focused on urban recycling, indicating that the priority should not be to build iconic, supposedly sustainable buildings and overambitious territorial infrastructures. Salvador concentrated on more urgent subjects, linked to the right to the city and the need to improve quality of life in neighbourhoods without damaging the planet (not much to ask!). And he wanted to do all of this without designing an 'ideal city' on a blank piece of paper. Instead, the aim was to recycle the existing complex, contradictory city.

At the same time – and perhaps somewhat arrogantly – we found that the systemic theory of the superblock plan lacked the atmosphere, tone and emotion of a project applied in a concrete area. We thought the proposal was still too diagrammatic and could not be 'industrialised', meaning it could not be repeated over and over until reaching the edges of the city. The bold plan to roll out the model needed to incorporate management of the interim situation and constantly adjust to each place's specific needs, before the possibilities inherent in the new system could be deployed.

What came next would still be remembered seventeen years later as one of the most exciting designs the studio had worked on. What came next would still be remembered seventeen years later as one of the most exciting designs the studio had worked on.We made the most of the radical nature of the superblock layout to propose a series of scenarios, convinced that they were compatible with the Agency's original idea: new functions for new squares and streets, new materialities, better permeability with buildings, scaling up to connect superblocks and civic and green axes, new types of business and housing connected to the public space, more greenery, greater density – through storeys added to buildings for social housing – ephemeral urbanism initiatives (the term 'tactical urbanism' did not exist yet), and more. We even proposed a

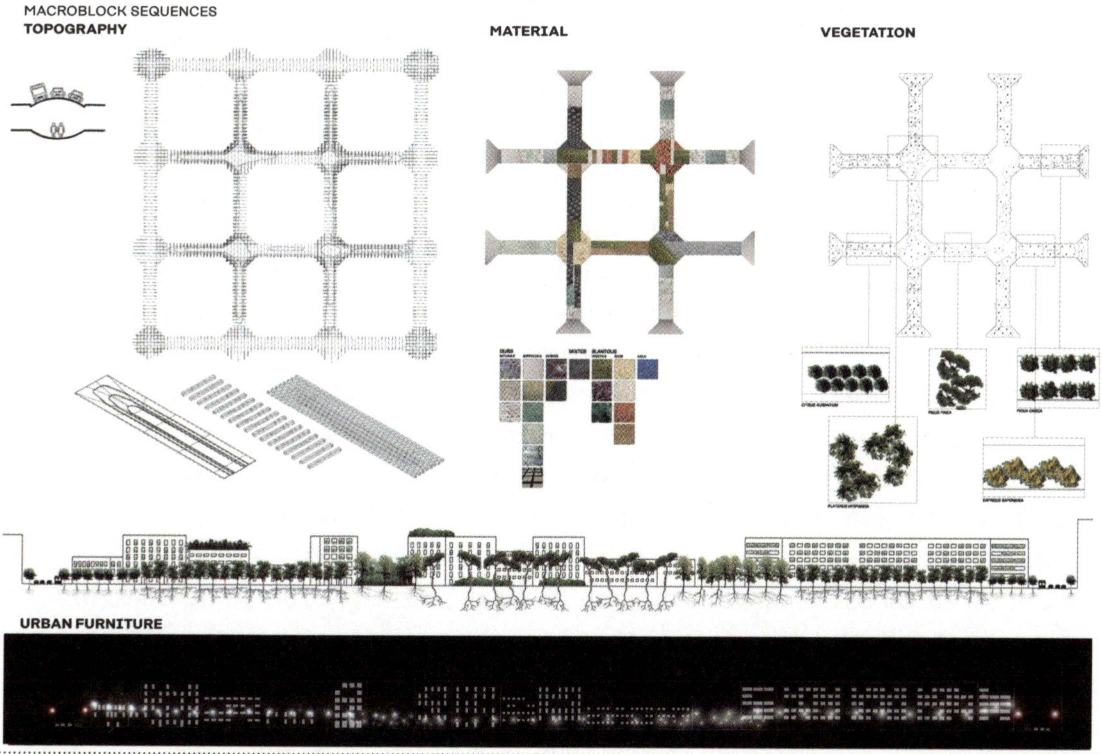

2002-2003. Various urbanisation strategies for a superblock in El Poblenou: topography, materials, permeability, trees and lighting.
Source: Bopbaa Arquitectes

pilot superblock in El Poblenou, where the model could be trialled and corrected during the 2004 Universal Forum of Cultures. These ideas brought the original design to life, incorporating new social perspectives beyond the hierarchisation of mobility and significantly improved environmental sustainability.

I remember blurting all of this out to Salvador Rueda, as passionately has he had explained his plan to us months before. But we quickly realised that our contributions did not match with his requirements, as they involved ideas that went beyond the mere urbanisation of freed-up space and that could frighten, rather than seduce, the municipal government and the public. We had gone too far.

Salvador got his point across with a rather cruel yet illustrative story:

> "Do you know how to boil a frog? If you stick a frog in a pan of boiling water, it jumps right out. But if you put it in cool water then heat it up, it doesn't get scared off. No one's stopping it from jumping out, but it just sits there as the temperature rises, getting more and more dazed, until it's boiled to death".

Many years and municipal governments have passed since 2003, and our frog (the superblock plan) is still yet to be boiled, though we have seen the water – and the atmosphere – heat up over the last few years, with tactical initiatives, pilot projects and tenders accelerating the strategy. The city is starting to change profoundly, and debates are taking place in the street, in bars, in taxis and in the media. In recent years, we have seen more and more complaints from various groups who are resisting this change in model, as it harms their interests or because they are sceptical about the promised results. But they are not the only ones complaining. Simultaneously, criticism is coming from the other direction: people are calling for bolder, faster policies to change the current, outdated city model that is monopolised by private vehicles and threatening the planet and people's health.

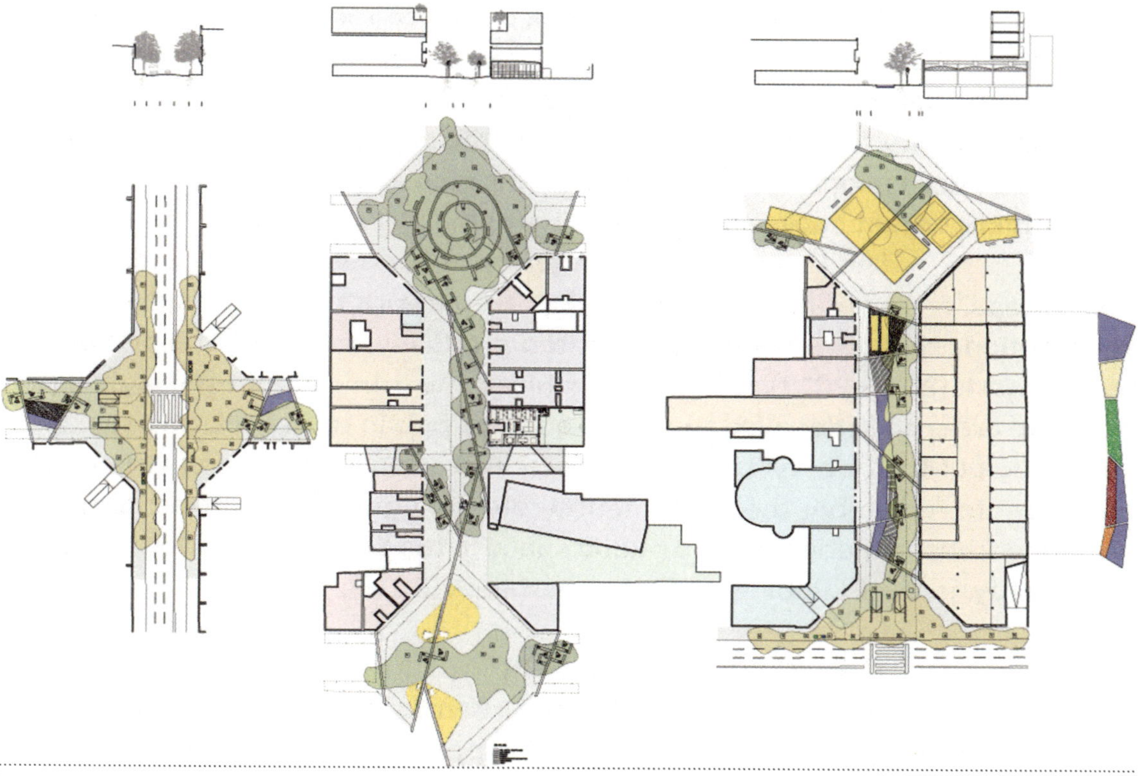

Internal and perimeter chamfered corner urbanisation proposals for a superblock in El Poblenou.
Source: Bopbaa Arquitectes

2

1

3

Radical occupation of the public space: 1. Buildings for community use and additional storeys for public housing. 2. Neighbourhood/school zoo. 3. Community swimming pool.
Source: Bopbaa Arquitectes

For some, the superblock plan is too small a step, and for others, it is too giant a leap. Either way, the 'city model' has been put back at the centre of the debate. This time, it is not about striving for the model – or even supermodel – city. It is not about 'dolling up' the city (like the famous campaign 'Barcelona posa't guapa' claimed). Instead, the plan aims to make the city healthy and mitigate urgent socio-spatial and environmental injustices.

The Urban Ecology Agency of Barcelona is behind many of these steps, from defining the theoretical framework for the plan, to offering key solutions that have been implemented gradually, including the orthogonal bus network (2012–2018), which hierarchised the urban layout through superblocks in order to rationalise the city's surface public transport, and the initial application of the new system in the historic areas of El Born and Gràcia. It is important to remember the fundamental role the Agency has played in the first effective transformations of the public space in the Eixample district and, more specifically, in the El Poblenou pilot superblock (2016).

THE PILOT SUPERBLOCK

In September 2016, the Urban Ecology Agency of Barcelona joined forces with the CTPA collective (Corporation of Architectural Design Workshops), made up of more than 200 students and staff from various schools of architecture. Together, we put forward a proposal to the Councillor for Mobility, Mercedes Vidal, and the Councillor for Sant Martí, Josep Maria Montaner: the first ever tactical superblock, applied during the annual festival in the neighbourhood of El Poblenou.

The City Council quickly and efficiently did the groundwork for this project, implementing basic initiatives that aimed to reorganise the traffic hierarchy in the streets affected, freeing up the superblock for civic use. Once this preparation was complete, the universities, the Agency

Pilot Superblock Workshop.
Source: UIC

and various residents' groups came along to make temporary, reversible, tactical changes that required little or no budget and served to put the model to the test. These changes were radical in their objective but minor in terms of the physical transformation of roadways and pavements. No significant construction work was carried out; instead, the transformation took place through management measures, urban furniture, paint, art installations, and community use of the freed-up space.

The main action during the course of the neighbourhood festival took place on the four intersections within the superblock. Each intersection was themed by a group of students and brought to life by community groups. These themes were linked to four fundamental civic rights: culture, leisure, participation and exchange.

One of the most memorable – and controversial – initiatives was the 'Parliament' space installed on the intersection between Carrer dels Almogàvers and Carrer de la Ciutat de Granada, where various heated debates took place throughout the week. Political representatives, technicians, collectives, local residents, students and experts met in the middle of an intersection, through which cars had been passing just a few days before, to present and examine the systemic ideas inherent in the superblock model. From here, a great debate emerged, which later moved on to all of the city's and the country's media outlets, before occupying key spaces in the international media. This was also the point at which groups began to position themselves for and against the plan and corrections started to be made to the model itself.

The idea continued to evolve from this initial experimental superblock. Its results were assessed and design and participation criteria were defined to establish an action plan and prioritisation hierarchy for work on the rest of the superblocks planned in the city.

The first bold decision was not reverting the superblock to its original state and

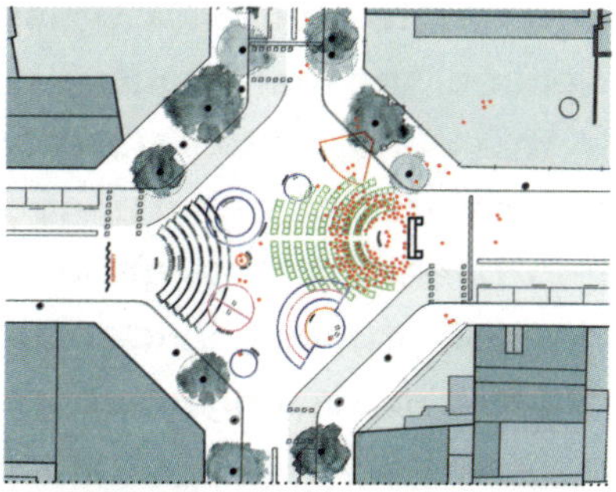

BARCELONA. POBLENOU. 2016. Pilot Superblock. Floor Plan of the intersection between Carrer dels Almogàvers and Carrer de la Ciutat de Granada, dedicated to participation.
Source: CTPA

maintaining the overall calming idea, while adapting it to different groups' needs and wishes. Slowly but surely, this 'daring' first superblock in the Eixample district, designed by Ildefons Cerdà, was moulded and, to some extent, moved away from the ideal, radical original plan. But at the same time, it became a key laboratory for various studies linked to mobility and the environment and a test bench for new community uses.

The next superblock implemented was in Sant Antoni (2019). Although this was a very different case (in terms of dimensions, impact, density and design technique), it incorporated many of the lessons learned from the El Poblenou pilot superblock. Its immediate success, partly down to the more radical 'dirty work' done by its predecessor, represents the consolidation of certain strategies to reprogramme the urban space on the basis of social and environmental criteria.

BARCELONA. POBLENOU. 2016.
Some snapshots taken during the inauguration of the superblock.
Pictures: CTPA and Josep Bohigas

Despite the positive readings of the results of these two initial experiences, the main doubts that have emerged in this debate are connected to a very 'Barcelona' risk of being a victim of its own success and to the fact that this clear improvement to neighbourhoods may cause or accelerate an unwanted gentrification process. Evidence of this danger has already been seen, with slight increases in housing and commercial rent prices, though interpretations of figures may be distorted by the recent effects of the pandemic.

BARCELONA. POBLENOU. 2016. Pilot Superblock. Junction between Carrer de Sancho de Ávila and Carrer de Roc Boronat, dedicated to leisure.
Picture: CPTA

But one of the most recurrent criticisms of the original superblock plan is that it is based on creating calm areas with low permeability and poor urban continuity. Salvador Rueda has had to defend himself against this kind of accusation innumerable times, arguing that the whole plan should be applied all at the same time, like in Vitoria, thus avoiding the danger of creating a '*gated community*' that lives happily ever after, closed off in an area that is more privileged than the rest of the city. His argument is faultless, as applying the whole plan at once ensures continuity in the streets with calming measures and makes its success less noteworthy, thus preventing the aforementioned unwanted gentrification.

But applying the whole plan simultaneously is at odds with a more gradual, possibilist, attentive approach where lessons are learned from events and the model is improved and adapted according to the place's needs. Furthermore, Salvador Rueda's solution of applying the plan in one fell swoop contradicts his frog metaphor: applied quickly, the plan could be rejected by the public and the frog and the proposal could be thrown up in the air. A glance at newspapers from the last few years shows that the plan needs to be rewritten and refined at every step and that, in spite of its important, enormously relevant aims, it still has a long way to go before convincing everyone.

So, faced with the challenge of redistributing the initiatives the municipal budget can cover, the proposal is to adapt the original plan, creating a new version where the superblock makes way for what could be called 'superaxes and supercrossroads'. These would make up a network of streets and squares with calming measures, turning the whole Eixample district into one big superblock undergoing constant transformation. It would be a clever pivot and another step towards the superblock plan, navigating an 'interim' period where, instead of continuing to create a series of calm blocks, we apply calming measures to the continuous axes that connect them and build a new network of more liveable streets.

This new theory shifts the focus but provides continuity to the projects already implemented. Deputy Mayor for Urban Planning Janet Sanz and her Urban Model teams – previously led by Ton Salvador, now by Chief Architect Xavi Matilla – have persevered and moulded a plan now at the crucial stage of its execution as a system: it is being scaled up so that it covers the whole expanded city area.

Many have been involved in implementing this plan and helping it to evolve, from the daring politicians representing us to the city's increasingly exacting citizens. But, above all, it is important to acknowledge (and pay tribute to) the essential role played by the Agency in this process. With their talent and tenacity, the BCNecologia team have enabled us to keep on 'boiling the frog' to recycle the city and really improve the lives of those who live in it.

THE TRANSFER

In December 2019, Salvador Rueda retired and I took his place at the head of the Agency. I was then tasked with transferring all of its assets and liabilities to Barcelona Regional, the big sister of the strategic planning agencies in the city and the Barcelona Metropolitan Area (AMB). This complex, delicate transfer will culminate in 2021. As well as inheriting a vast accumulation of innovative ideas and experience, BR will acquire a team of twenty talented professionals who have grown intellectually in a special space at a unique time.

BR was created in 1993 as a multidisciplinary agency that enabled the city to take on projects on a metropolitan and regional scale, at a time when the Metropolitan Area had not yet been redefined. Its first projects were related to infrastructure and major urban transformations left pending after the Olympics, but BR quickly incorporated the environmental dimension into its work, until forming the environmental department with the most assets and greatest ability to work with a cross-cutting approach in the city. This gradual progress is both a sign of the times and the result of healthy competition with the Urban Ecology Agency of Barcelona, which accelerated changes to the structure of many municipal bodies and helped to build a new vision for urban planning in the city.

The Agency will be no more after twenty jam-packed years, during which it has more than fulfilled its original aims. This book reflects the huge impact of its projects and the challenges yet to be overcome. A constant set of criteria underlies all of these projects, driving and connecting them, and generating a holistic theory based on ecosystemic urbanism where superblocks are the prototype for all applications and theoretical speculations.

This legacy and its ambitious intent have influenced and will continue to influence the city and the world, through the lessons it has taught a legion of collaborators and followers (myself included). Barcelona Regional, now stronger than ever, has the opportunity and the duty to take on this legacy and continue to work towards a change in model that puts people and the planet at the heart of all urban planning decisions.

OSTAN

SUPERBLOCK IN GRÀCIA, BARCELONA

Picture: Marta Torrent

NYC

SUPERBLOCK IN EL POBLENOU, BARCELONA

Picture: Marta Torrent

SUPERBLOCK IN SANT ANTONI, BARCELONA

Picture: Marta Torrent

MISSION

Throughout its history, the Urban Ecology Agency of Barcelona (BCNecologia) has promoted an ecosystemic urbanism approach that offers sustainable solutions and alternatives to tackle the challenges faced by cities and other human settlements in any context all over the world.

Ecologist Salvador Rueda has spearheaded this movement, firmly believing that another future for metropolises is possible. He maintains that anything can be reformulated, without any kind of professional prejudice, as long as people's fundamental rights – including health, liveability, equal development opportunities and system functionality – are guaranteed. This is how the BCNecologia team has always imagined, created, analysed and quantified its projects.

Superblock in El Poblenou. 2016
Picture: School of Architecture. International University of Catalonia (UIC)

Its mission has materialised in the form of active participation in seminars, conferences, events and publications, through which the organisation has strived to spread its ideas: ideas designed to inspire other entities to facilitate change. The creation of synergies with other public institutions and involvement in the educational and academic sector have long been two of the Agency's main aims.

IDEAS

The Urban Ecology Agency of Barcelona's contribution has been clear in terms of analysing cities and formulating proposals that foster urban planning projects based on sustainability, resilience and complexity criteria.

One of the Agency's main achievements is its definition of a **more sustainable urban model for the Information and Knowledge Age**: a socially cohesive model with a compact morphology, a complex organisation (mixed in terms of uses, with rich biodiversity) and an efficient metabolism. These are four inextricably linked areas that interact synergistically to provide integrated responses to urban realities undergoing rehabilitation and regeneration processes and to support planners of new urban developments.

- **Compactness** is one of the main ways of guaranteeing proximity between urban functions and uses, while balanced density fundamentally ensures efficient use of resources. This is the concept that defines the system's functionality and the mobility and public space scenario.
- **Urban complexity** looks at urban organisation and assesses the density of the area's legal persons (businesses, associations, facilities and institutions) and how mixed they are. This concept also covers biodiversity, as the expression of the biological complexity that lives alongside humans in the urban ecosystem.

- **Urban metabolism** seeks efficiency in the material, water and energy flows that support urban systems, while fostering metabolic circularity and establishing the conditions needed to create a renewable, decentralised model for resource generation and use of waste flows. This way, the city's own resources are optimised and a rational balance is established with the surrounding areas.

Superblock in El Poblenou, Barcelona. 2016
Picture: BCNecologia

- **Social cohesion** refers to the coexistence between people living in the urban space (of varying incomes, cultures and ages) and the relationships between them. Local provision of basic services and facilities and access to housing in more sustainable buildings are key goals in this area.

These four pillars of the urban model are detailed in the book *Barcelona, ciutat mediterrània, compacta i complexa. Una visió de futur més sostenible* (2002),[1] (Barcelona, a compact and complex meditarranean city. A more sustainable vision for the future, 2007), produced as a result of the agreement between Barcelona City Council and the Agency as part of the Agenda 21. The publication offers a prospective, integrated, systemic view of a desirable, more sustainable future for Barcelona. It brings together the principles that were developed over the years through the Agency's projects and that would later constitute the ecosystemic urbanism approach.

1 Rueda, Salvador. *Barcelona, a compact and complex meditarranean city. A more sustainable vision for the future*. Barcelona: Barcelona City Council. Maintenance and Services Sector. Environmental Education and Participation, 2007. (Catalan version, 2002; English/Spanish version, 2007).

ECOLOGY: THE BASIS OF A THEORETICAL FRAMEWORK

The Agency has adopted a systemic approach to redirect urban ecosystem management towards a more sustainable urban model and to provide mobility, energy, urbanism, waste, climate change, biodiversity and social cohesion solutions. To strive for sustainability, the prevailing goal in all its work has been to reduce energy use (consumption of resources) and to maintain or improve urban organisation, in a quest for efficiency. This translates as maintaining or improving quality of life and complexity in cities while reducing humans' impact on the area.

A multi-scale logic and cross-discipline planning approach have also been key tools for successfully tackling the challenges faced, in the form of projects. It has been important to think big, with large-scale strategies, to then work on more local areas at a steadier speed. To this end, **superblocks** have had a far-reaching impact. Through this more sustainable mobility and public space model for the city, a local, sustainable, 'slow' urbanism has been consolidated.

Three-level urban planning (surface, underground and roofs) has been an essential concept in the Agency's work, as it ensures system functionality. Many of the challenges faced and solutions provided have required an understanding of land as a living entity and greater efficiency in the occupation of roofs and underground space to achieve maximum self-sufficiency in metabolic flows.

THREE-LEVEL URBANISM

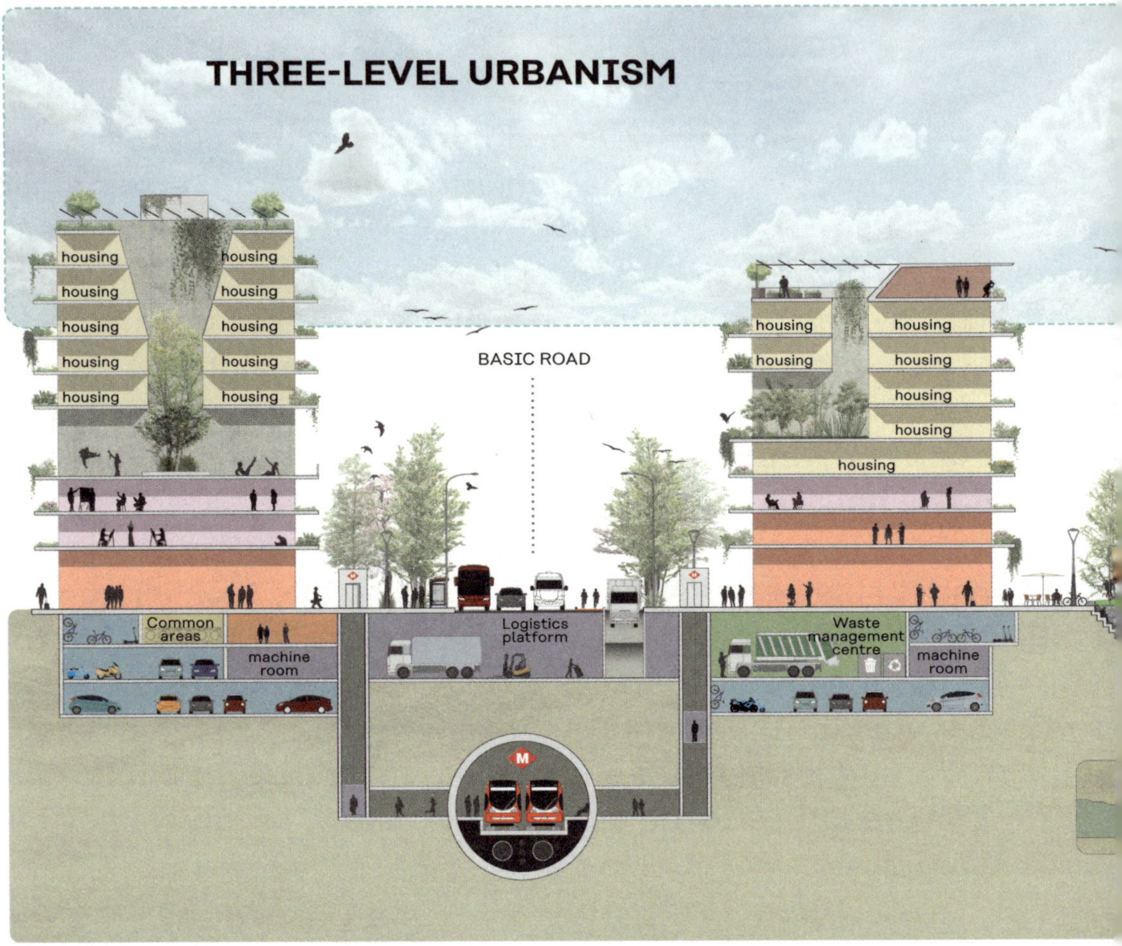

ENVIRONMENTAL AND BIODIVERSITY SERVICES
Urban allotments and community composting
Recycling point, Waste management facility
Seasonal thermal energy storage tank

HOUSING
Private housing
Social housing
Common areas

KNOWLEDGE-INTENSIVE SERVICES
Cultural activities
Education and research centres
Fab Lab, Coworking

LOCAL SERVICES
Social services
Basic facilities
Shops

LOGISTICS SERVICES
Logistics services (MaaS)[1]
Logistics platform UFD[2]
Machine room

PARKING AND CHARGING SERVICES
Charging station for electric vehicle
PRM[3] parking
PMV[4] and bicycle parking
Public parking
Private parking

1 MaaS: Mobility as a Service
2 UFD: Urban Freight Distribution
3 PRM: Persons with Reduced Mobility
4 PMV: Personal Mobility Vehicle

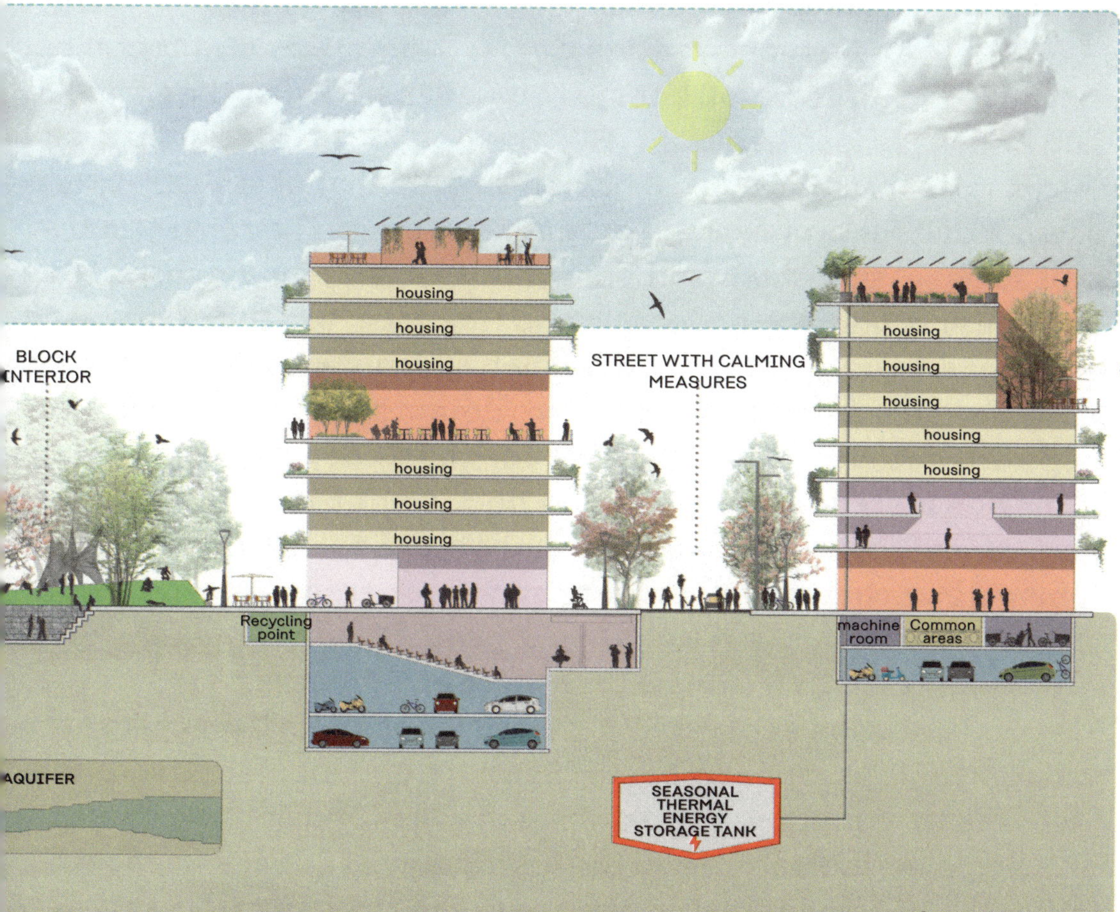

Source: BCNecologia

Three-level urbanism – one of the instruments offered by ecosystemic urbanism–based planning – examines three plans with the same amount of detail and same scale as an ordinary surface plan. This reveals the variables involved in current urbanism challenges. Furthermore, it offers a series of solutions that boost each level's potential to contribute to more self-sufficiency, functionality and liveability in the urban environment.

Each level is designed in its totality and connected to the other levels. This interconnection comes from buildings (on three levels), mobility, services, biodiversity, material cycles, water and energy.

Roofs are linked to biodiversity, energy and water. The underground space is associated with services, urban distribution, parking, mass mobility, the water cycle, energy management and underground waste management. The surface, meanwhile, is related to uses, functionality and the public space. These three levels pave the way for urbanism at a height, on the surface and underground.

As well as creating a new theoretical and technical framework, in the form of **ecosystemic urbanism** and its fifteen guiding principles (see pages 34–35), the Agency has designed a new methodology consisting of a set of instruments that give shape to and act as a conduit for proposals, in order to make sure they are effective. As well as assessment instruments (**the system of indicators**), this set includes regulatory, economic and financial, organisational and governance, and educational and training instruments. The principles of ecosystemic urbanism and the instruments that accompany the concept are detailed in the **Charter for the Ecosystemic Planning of Cities and Metropolises** (2018),[2] a document that brings together the Agency's conceptual legacy and other specific directives for designing new urban developments and regenerating existing ones.

ECOSYSTEMIC URBANISM

Urban ecosystems' degree of complexity requires the formulation of intentional models that both encapsulate the fundamental axes that support the planning process and act as a mould in which principles, indicators and the instrumental apparatus must fit.

Ecosystemic urbanism is the construction of a new urbanism, with ecological foundations, that promotes a more sustainable city model for the Information and Knowledge Age. Through a systemic approach, the basic principles of this new urbanism were defined, so that it could be fully applied to an urban model and the problems inherent in a linear, sectoral method could be avoided.

This type of urbanism is founded upon fifteen basic principles and brought to life through flexible tools that can adapt to the dynamics and context of each territory. With the system of

2 Rueda, Salvador. *Carta para la planificación ecosistémica de ciudades y metrópolis. [Charter for the Ecosystemic Planning of Cities and Metropolises]*, 2018. Digital edition available until 2019.

indicators that characterises this new urbanism, urban planning and recycling proposals can be monitored and assessed. Complying with the ideas and goals inherent in these indicators results in systemic balances that ensure that current urban challenges are tackled.

So, with a view to measuring the extent to which the intentional principles, and therefore the urban model, are implemented, three technical instruments were proposed. Together, they articulate the conceptual basis, strategy and proposal for planning and implementation.

First, the minimum urban ecosystem, measuring around 16-20 hectares, was designed: the superblock. As a management unit, it constitutes part of an urban mosaic and emerges as the basic unit of the functional and urban planning model. It includes most variables involved in the new urbanism and solves the problems inherent in the current urban reality. From an urban planning point of view, three levels are proposed: underground, surface and roofs. These three levels can include all the variables in the eco-integrative approach, while current urbanism, with just one level, cannot.

In parallel, a system of indicators was established to define the determining, or restricting, factors that set the rules of the game, numerically speaking. The Agency has put a great deal of intellectual effort into developing enough expertise to identify both the suitable variables that encapsulate each of these determining factors – and set goals and reference values as accurately as possible – and the planning criteria and strategic solutions for implementing the urban model.

THE PRINCIPLES OF ECOSYSTEMIC URBANISM

1 COMPACTNESS VS. SPRAWL

This principle focuses on compactness to achieve a more sustainable city. Consumption of land, energy and materials must be reduced, through an increase in the density and proximity of legal persons in the area, which generate a civic kind of critical mass.

2 DECOMPRESSION VS. COMPRESSION

Urban balance must be achieved by designing cities with sufficient public space, in order to reach the ideal ratio between these spaces and private spaces and to improve quality of life.

3 ACCESSIBILITY VS. PRIVATE MOBILITY

Forms of mobility other than cars must be prioritised, with a focus on walking, cycling and efficient public transport. This way, access to any point in the city is guaranteed for the whole population.

4 CITIZENS VS. PEDESTRIANS

Urban space currently dedicated to private mobility must be freed up for various uses and citizens' rights. Most of the public space in cities must become an egalitarian, democratic place where everyone can walk around, enjoy themselves, interact, share, express themselves and debate.

5 LIVEABILITY IN THE PUBLIC SPACE

A liveable space that takes care of people must be created. Urban planning proposals should provide comfort, ergonomics, greenery and access to services for the whole population.

6 COMPLEXITY VS. SIMPLIFICATION

The ideal conditions must be created for different people to meet in one place so that they interact. Urban complexity increases when the economic, associative and cultural fabrics are strengthened. In sparse fabrics, there are fewer interactions and civic life is worse off.

7 HYPERCONNECTIVITY

The incorporation of ICT into the social and productive body has boosted contact and the flow of useful information between people and organisations.

8 GREENERY VS. CONCRETE

Urban biodiversity and greenery must be improved to create urban centres that maintain a connection with the natural environment.

9 **SELF-SUFFICIENCY VS. DEPENDENCY**

Energy consumption must be reduced in conurbations and renewable energy must be produced locally to achieve energy self-sufficiency.

10 **WATER SELF-SUFFICIENCY WITH LOCAL, RENEWABLE RESOURCES**

Cities must reduce their water consumption and use local, renewable resources to be self-sufficient and preserve the water cycle.

11 **REDUCE, REUSE AND RECYCLE VS. WASTE**

It is important to reduce waste and incorporate waste management as a fundamental part of the circular economy, as this is essential in city regeneration.

12 **CLIMATE CHANGE ADAPTATION AND MITIGATION**

To mitigate the effects of climate change, there must be a review of the production of the city, its population's lifestyles, and the management of energy and material flows (water, food, waste, etc.). Cities must adapt their public and private spaces to accommodate a population that is increasingly exposed to global warming.

13 **SOCIAL COHESION VS. SOCIAL EXCLUSION**

Social cohesion must be achieved through coexistence between people of different ages, incomes and origins. Nobody should be excluded from the city.

14 **UNIVERSAL ACCESS TO HOUSING IN MORE SUSTAINABLE BUILDINGS**

Urban planning initiatives must guarantee the universal right to housing, while reducing the amount of energy and materials consumed in the construction or refurbishment of buildings.

15 **BALANCED ALLOCATION AND DISTRIBUTION OF FACILITIES**

The whole population, regardless of sociodemographic characteristics, must have access to adequate public services.

CONCEPTUAL MAP OF ECOSYSTEMIC URBANISM

A More Sustainable City Model

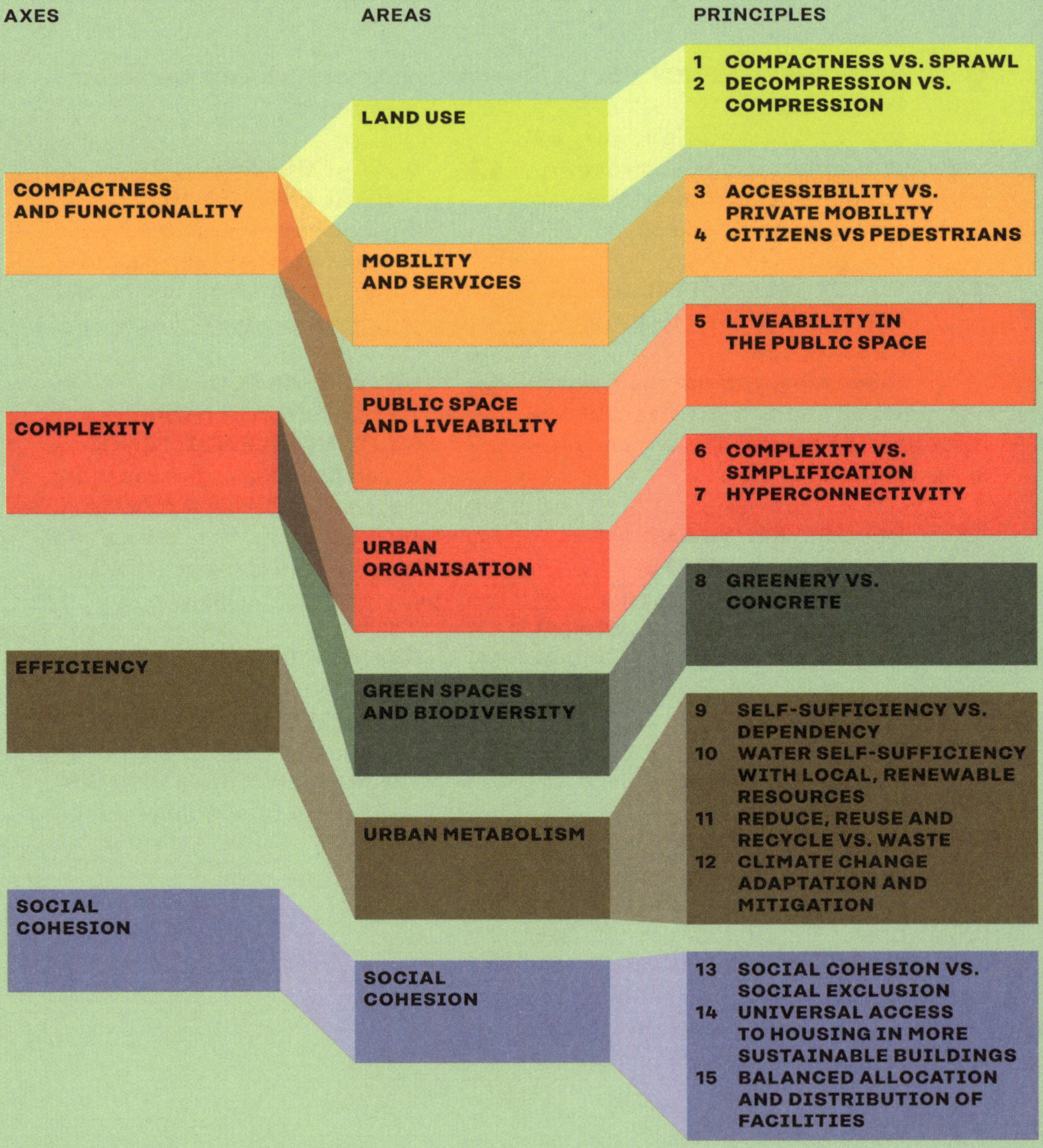

Source: BCNecologia

Evaluation

WEIGHT	No.	Indicator	INDICATORS
25%	01	Housing density	100 dwel./inh
	02	Absolute compactness	5 m
	03	Corrected compactness	10 m · 50 m
	04	Public open spaces per inhabitant	10 m^2/inh. · 15 m^2/inh.
	05	Mode of transport of population	Private car journeys · < 15% · < 25%
	06	Proximity to alternative transport networks	Population served · 75% · 100%
	07	Pedestrians area and spaces for coexistence	60% · 75%
	08	Proximity to bicycle parking	Population served · 75% · 100%
	09	Off-street parking for vehicles	Off-street parking places · 75% · 90%
	10	Charging station for electric vehicle	Off-street stations · 75% · 90%
	11	Labour market self-containment	50% · 75%
	12	Air quality	< 40 $\mu g/m^3$
	13	Acoustic comfort	< 65 dB(A)
	14	Thermal comfort	-50 W/m^2 · 50 W/m^2
	15	Road accessibility	Pavements > 1.8 m · Pavements > 2.5 m
	16	Liveability index in public space	> 65 points · > 85 points
25%	17	Urban diversity index	4 bits · 5 bits
	18	Density of legal persons	25 activ./ha · 50 activ./ha
	19	Mix of uses	Non-residential surface · 20% · 25%
	20	Knowledge-dense activities	10% · 20%
	21	Spatial and functional continuity of the street	Stretches with high interaction · 25% · 50%
	22	Biotic index of soil	15% · 30%
	23	Green space per inhabitant	5 m^2/inh. · 10 m^2/inh.
	24	Proximity to green spaces	Population served · 75% · 100%
	25	Density of trees lining streets	Adequately endowed stretches · 75% · 100%
25%	26	Residential energy consumption	kWh/m^2/year · < 55 · < 65
	27	Services energy consumption	kWh/m^2/year · < 105 · < 210
	28	Public lighting energy consumption	kWh/m^2/year · < 4 · < 2.5
	29	Energy self-sufficiency. Renewables	50% · 100%
	30	Greenhouse gas emissions	Reduction 2050 · 100% · 80-95%
	31	Drinking water consumption	Domestic use · < 70 lpd · < 100 lpd
	32	Treated Wastewater	Volume treated in plant · 75% · 100%
	33	Water sufficiency	20% · 40%
	34	Waste generated per capita	kg/inh/day · < 1.35 · < 1.5
	35	Gross separate collection	50% · 65%
	36	Closure of the organic material cycle	30% · 50%
25%	37	Segregation index of the older population	< 10% · < 25%
	38	Segregation index of the foreign born population	< 10% · < 25%
	39	Segregation index of tertiary graduates	< 10% · < 25%
	40	Spatial/gender distribution of disposable household income	< 10% · < 25% · Population deviation > 25 % from the city average
	41	Social inequalities rate	< 10% · < 25% · Population deviation > 25 % from the city average
	42	Proximity to basic facilities	Population served · 75% · 100%
	43	Allocation of basic facilities	Allocation (m^2/inh.) · 75% · 100%
	44	Social housing	15% · 30%
	45	The guiding function of urban sustainability	Urban efficiency (E/nH) · < 10 · < 20

SUPERBLOCKS

Inspired by the urban fabric designed by Ildefons Cerdà, BCNecologia has invented a new paradigm: the superblock. This unit of urban planning and management coordinates and organises the different areas involved in urbanistic activity: mobility networks, public space planning, biodiversity conservation, economic activity, energy efficiency, waste management, water cycle management, and the provision of services to encourage harmonious coexistence and social cohesion.

The dimensions of this urban unit are approximately 16-20 hectares, or 400x400 m, which is equivalent to nine blocks in Barcelona's Eixample neighbourhood (the superblock archetype). The superblock is the starting point for reorganising mobility networks and is defined by a structure of peripheral routes (basic roads) on which surface transport networks circulate and the maximum speed is 50 km/h. Inside the superblocks (local roads), the vehicle speed limit is 10 km/h: a measure that calms traffic, makes the space compatible with citizens' uses and rights, and prioritises pedestrians and cyclists.

Superblocks offer an ultra-efficient way of integrating transport networks while guaranteeing the city's functionality and organisation, and in turn, free up a significant amount of public space currently dedicated to transit. In the city of Barcelona, if the number of vehicles on the road were reduced by 13%, 70% of the public space could be freed up. This reorganisation of mobility opens up a host of options that are not viable when motor vehicles occupy the streets. The freed-up space can then be used for urban uses that would be unimaginable otherwise.

Before... / Superblock

Road hierarchy

Basic network

Motorised transport can pass through all the streets in the superblock.

Maximum speed: 50

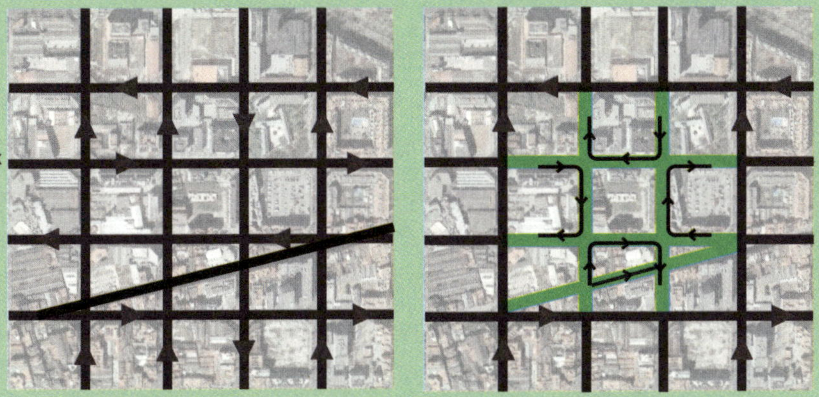

Withing the superblock

A new mobility configuration is designed to prevent traffic within the superblock. Traffic cannot pass through in a straight line.

Maximum speed: 10

Pedestrians

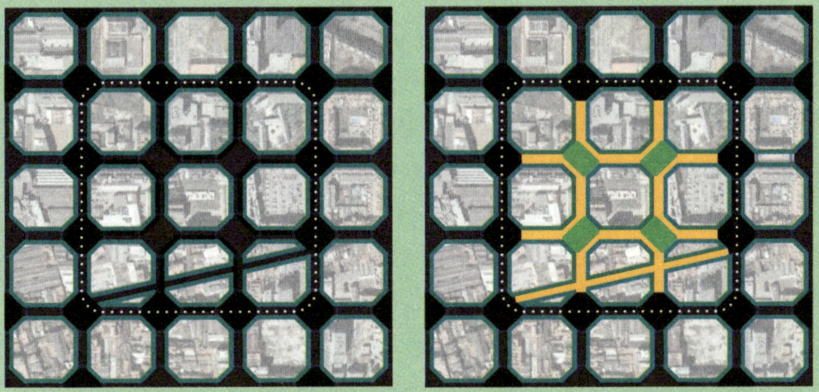

- Space for pedestrian movement (pavements)
- Space for motorised traffic
- Space for shared uses, with priority for pedestrians
- New square

Cyclists

Main cycling network. Separate lane on the basic road network (peripheral routes around the superblock).

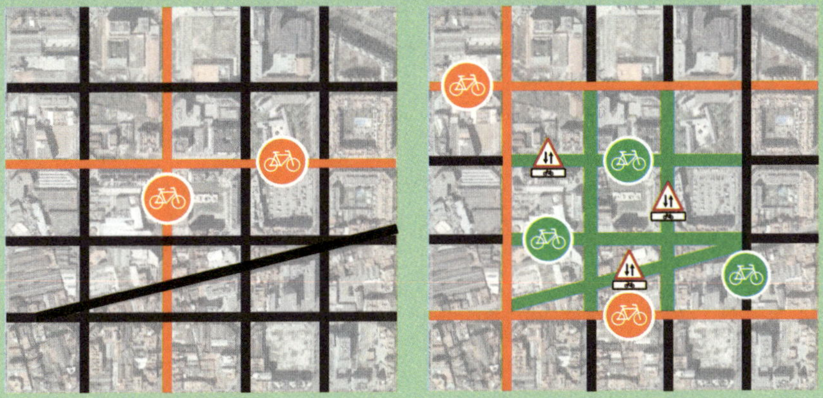

There are no cycle lanes within the superblock. Cyclists can move in both directions and adapt to the uses of the public space at any given time.

Source: BCNecologia

Streets inside superblocks offer a new perspective of public space planning. Thanks to this new road hierarchy, urban functions can be organised at the intersections between streets and new hubs can be created: intermodal hubs between basic roads, service hubs between basic roads and interior streets, and traffic-free hubs for residents, mainly dedicated to citizens' uses.

The space created can be used to provide more urban greenery, through green corridors and the replacement of tarmac with permeable surfaces and vegetation. It also enables citizens to use the public space in a more diverse range of ways. The speed limit is a key tool in calming these spaces.

This mobility transformation – and the resulting transformation of the public space – provides the conditions needed for action, but the superblock concept goes much further than that. Superblocks become miniature cities with an average population of around 6,000, enough affordable housing and all the basic services their residents need: a medical centre, nursery and primary schools, a secondary school, a community space, local green spaces and a diverse business fabric. The human dimension of superblocks makes them the ideal context for providing public services on a local, community scale. For example, the superblock can take on a role as a territorial unit for the deployment of primary social services, as proposed in Barcelona.

Furthermore, the superblock offers a new structure where the city's provisions and future changes can be planned comprehensively in advance. It could be described as the element that structures urban transformations, that facilitates dialogue between sectors and departments, and that organises, executes and manages with sustainability criteria in mind.

It is worth noting that this model is applicable to any kind of fabric, whether it is an already built-up urban space or a new development. When inserted into low-density fabrics, it acts as a stimulus for urban development, expanding to produce a compact, complex city. Alternatively, it can be inserted into a mid-density development, to regenerate the urban fabric, or into a dense conurbation to create a network that spreads across the whole city. In this case, the superblock is repeated and becomes the building block of the urban planning model. Scaling up the implementation of the superblock generates various advantages. Creating a single superblock is viable and leads to considerable changes to the urban space, but the impact of a network of superblocks across a city is larger than just the additive effect. The general reduction in the use of private vehicles, the creation of continuous pedestrian routes and the optimisation of public transport networks, for example, are profound changes that can only take place if the model is applied to the whole city.

URBAN SUSTAINABILITY INDICATORS

The system of indicators developed by BCNecologia objectively assesses the degree to which each of the principles of ecosystemic urbanism is fulfilled. It is structured around four axes: compactness, complexity, efficiency and social cohesion; subdivided into seven specific areas of assessment.

1. Morphology and land use
2. Public space and liveability
3. Mobility services and networks
4. Biodiversity and urban green spaces
5. Urban complexity
6. Urban metabolism, energy, water and material cycle
7. Social cohesion

This system of indicators is accompanied by an initial set of determining factors dictated by the context in which the urban development takes place. Any development of land generates reversible, partially reversible or irreversible impacts and transformations to the natural and urban environment. The spatial context and elements that define the environmental profile therefore determine the viability and coherence of ecosystemic urbanism goals. For this reason, a series of determining factors, which aim to preserve the area's distinctive features and mitigate the impacts of the urbanisation process, are taken into account.

One of the characteristics of the proposed system is that, to assess it, the results obtained are compared with maximum or minimum values, or reference ranges, which indicate whether or not the system is balanced. This way, anyone can see how far the results differ from the reference values that constitute the system of restrictions for ecosystemic planning.

Urban realities require interpretation of results. For this reason, studies aim to define these reference values in accordance with urban development typologies – whether new or already consolidated – types of urban fabric and even demographic composition. Furthermore, a decision is made regarding which indicators are the most appropriate depending on the scale of analysis (municipality, neighbourhood or superblock).

The reference area for reference values established for the indicators is the superblock, as it is the smallest urban ecosystem that can integrate all of the proposed principles. Urban planning initiatives tend to be accompanied by a regulatory document that sets the parameters and determining factors that guide the land transformation.

Standards and determining factors come from regulatory frameworks of different kinds and based on different scales, with variables of an eminently social and economic nature. To take on new challenges, there must be new approach and reference parameters that, while retaining some traditional urbanism variables, focus on sustainability criteria in the Information Age.

Superblock in Sant Antoni
Picture: BCNecologia

The system of urban sustainability indicators is detailed in a publication written by BCNecologia for the Ministry of Development (2012): the *Methodological Guide for Quality and Sustainability Auditing, Certification and Accreditation in the Urban Environment*,[3] aimed at all the parties involved in urban planning. The certification process objectively assesses urban fabrics and municipalities with a population of over 50,000. The guide is methodological, in that it establishes the necessary information requirements, indicators and steps for calculating them, and minimum and ideal reference values.

CHARTER FOR THE ECOSYSTEMIC PLANNING OF CITIES AND METROPOLISES[4]

The Barcelona Charter for the Ecosystemic Planning of Cities and Metropolises is a document for the design of new developments and the regeneration of existing urban fabrics, produced with a view to tackling the future challenges faced by cities from an urban ecology point of view.

3 Rueda, Salvador. *Guía Metodológica para los Sistemas de Auditoría, Certificación o Acreditación de la Calidad y Sostenibilidad en el Medio Urbano. [Methodological Guide for Quality and Sustainability Auditing, Certification and Accreditation in the Urban Environment]*. Madrid: Ministry of Development. General Directorate for Architecture, Housing and Land. General Technical Secretariat. Publications Centre, 2012.

4 Rueda. *Carta para la planificación ecosistémica de ciudades y metrópolis. Op. cit.*

It is aimed at all institutions, cities, regions, universities, non-profit organisations and professionals from various disciplines involved in the management of planning of urban systems, whether their role is to maintain them or to transform them. It is an open charter that has been amended with suggestions and contributions made by its members. Today, over 100 institutions and 400 members are involved in the Charter, including Vitoria-Gasteiz, Madrid and Málaga city councils.

From 22 to 24 May 2018, the international conference 'Post Habitat III. The challenges faced by metropolises beyond Habitat III: a contribution to the new urban agenda' took place in Barcelona, as the culmination of a journey started in 2016 in Quito, with the United Nations Habitat III conference. In this space for reflection and exchange, the Charter was presented and disseminated, with the aim of promoting change in cities based on sustainability criteria.

This document was an initiative of the Urban Ecology Agency of Barcelona and sought to drive a global movement that brought together cities everywhere, regardless of their social and cultural reality, to take on the great challenges of the twenty-first century: the climate emergency (which is forcing millions to flee their homes), the social emergency (a third of the inhabitants of the world's cities are living in conditions of extreme poverty, according to the UN), the demographic emergency (according to the UN, in 2050, the percentage of the world's population living in urban areas will reach 68%, with 2.5 billion additional city dwellers) and the challenge of new technologies and artificial intelligence, which could jeopardise the urban balance. The world is being urbanised at an unstoppable rate. The question is whether cities are ready to deal with this.

The Barcelona Charter proposes a pioneering, sustainable, environmentally-friendly urban model shaped by ecosystemic urbanism and its principles that meets the UN's 2030 Agenda Sustainable Development Goals, approved on 25 September 2015.[3]

Ecosystemic urbanism defines fifteen principles that bulk out the four axes of the sustainable urban model (compactness, complexity, urban metabolism and social cohesion). The Charter develops every one of these principles and sets out a list of minimum requirements and criteria to achieve the goals established for each of them. It acts as a kind of communal navigation chart that provides a direction for the work carried out by everyone involved in the design, construction and recycling of cities and their metropolitan areas.

The superblock is the smallest urban ecosystem that can integrate and maximise the principles of ecosystemic urbanism. This area of between 16 and 20 hectares transforms into a miniature city and a building block for a new urban planning model that, when repeated, becomes a module for the regeneration of any urban fabric or the planning of a new urban development.

A new urbanism can only be applied if it is accompanied by a series of organisational conditions and instruments that make it viable. The Charter also looks at these instruments, which guarantee that ecosystemic urbanism principles materialise and changing scenarios adapt. It details a set of organisational, management and governance, regulatory, financial, educational and training instruments.

5 UN. *2030 Agenda for Sustainable Development*. United Nations General Assembly, 25 September 2015.

HOW

WE WORK

AREAS

The conceptual framework developed by BCNecologia over the last twenty years has materialised as almost three hundred projects, plans and studies for municipalities and councils in Spain and beyond. These local administrations have trusted in the Agency to develop strategies for transitioning to an urban model based on the principles of ecosystemic urbanism.

Training and education have also made up a significant part of the organisation's activities. By exchanging experiences regarding how different urban management models work, through the implementation of education and training programmes, environmental campaigns, publications, conferences and exhibitions, the Agency's team members have grown as professionals and as people.

THE EVOLUTION OF OUR PROJECTS

The Agency's principles of sustainability and ecosystemic approach were established during its formative stage. Its first relevant projects were the Water Plan for the Barcelona Metropolitan Region, the first city waste management plans and the mobility plans for El Prat de Llobregat and the district of Gràcia in Barcelona. Looking from another angle, if the Agency's projects were a tree, there would be five main branches structuring the evolution of the content, methodologies and tools it has developed.

Despite this classification into five main themes, many of the projects mentioned feed off each other and could span two or more areas of knowledge. The Agency's work has constantly crossed disciplines and boundaries, reflecting its status as an urban laboratory studying complex systems.

The first branch consists of **urban sustainability indicators**. It represents the Agency's compilation of instruments and their application to ecosystemic planning in various urban initiatives, in towns and cities, as a tool for analysis and assessment. From the very beginning, BCNecologia's work has been characterised by the definition of quantitative indicators for assessing the complexity of urban systems. Through applied research and the development of its own technology for various fields of work, the Agency has been able to identify regularities in how urban systems work, thus increasing cities' ability to anticipate uncertainties and future challenges.

The second branch is formed by the evolution of the urban model based on superblocks and by all the **urban regeneration strategies** developed within the Agency. These projects defined the key elements that would characterise superblocks as a basic unit of ecosystemic urbanism. Furthermore, the strategies applied ensured cross-disciplinary consistency in the planning, organisation and implementation of the superblock urban model, in biodiversity, and in urban and social metabolism.

The third branch – which could even be considered the trunk – consists of **mobility and public space** projects. The Agency has been catapulted around the world by its vision of a more sustainable mobility and public space model, in which the city is reorganised to give the pedestrian priority, followed by the cyclist and public transport, and to improve environmental conditions and make more, high-quality public space available for people. Superblocks have been designed and approved in cities of all kinds, such as Vitoria-Gasteiz – the European Green Capital 2012, whose Sustainable Mobility and Public Space Plan, based on superblocks, has been recognised as Best Practice by UN-Habitat – A Coruña, Ferrol, Buenos Aires, Havana and Barcelona, among others. The superblocks in Vila de Gràcia won the BMW Initiative award in 2011 and were named as Best Practice by UN-Habitat in 2010.

The fourth branch – **the environment** – brings together projects that directly deal with the analysis of energy flows, the water cycle, noise and air pollution, and biodiversity. The Agency's environmental areas have evolved continuously over time and participated with an active, cross-cutting approach in the development of superblock projects, urban regeneration strategies and sustainability indicators.

The Waste and Material Cycle Area, previously known as the Waste Area and driven by the Citizens' Centre for Waste Prevention and Recycling (CCMRR), represents the fifth branch: the **circular economy**. This branch covers a host of significant projects, plans and other tools promoting the development of innovative waste management models – especially those focusing on encouraging prevention and new collection models – which have led BCNecologia to adopt a circular economy perspective in recent years.

These branches make up the tree of knowledge accumulated by the Urban Ecology Agency of Barcelona over the years, thanks to the work of the different teams that have been part of the institution, partners, and the beneficiary organisations behind the projects carried out. All of these people have built BCNecologia's legacy.

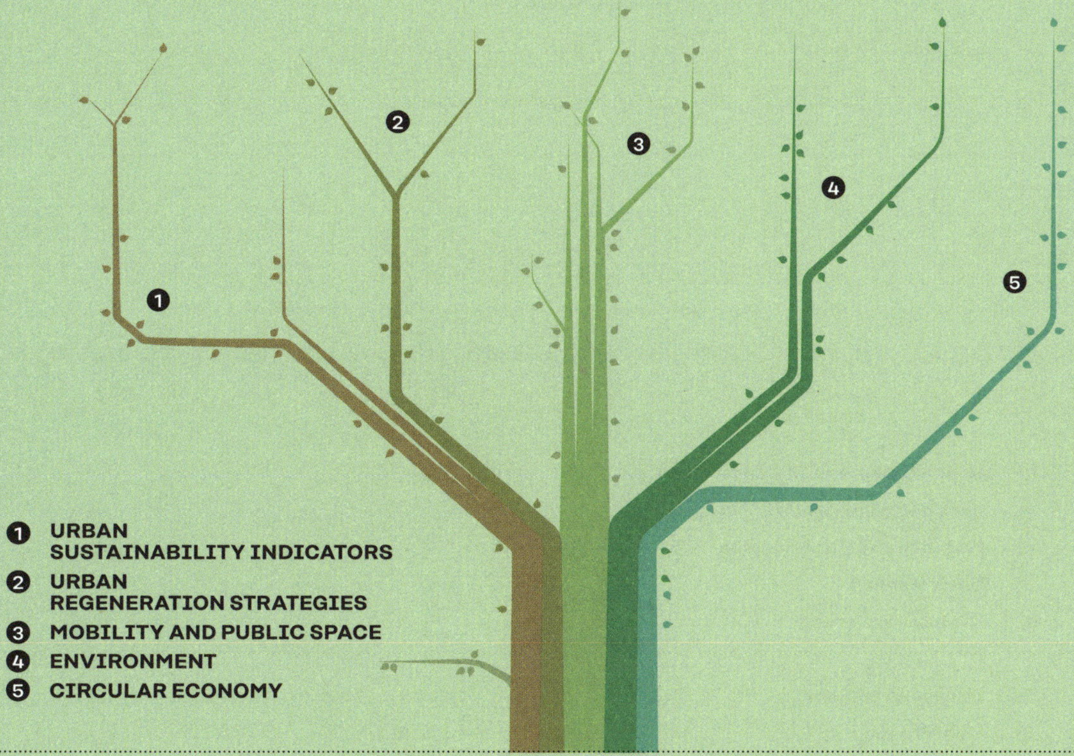

THE AGENCY WORLDWIDE

The principles and methodologies developed by the Agency have been enriched by extensive international experience. This knowledge has been shared and exchanged through talks, workshops and conferences in more than one hundred cities all over the world.

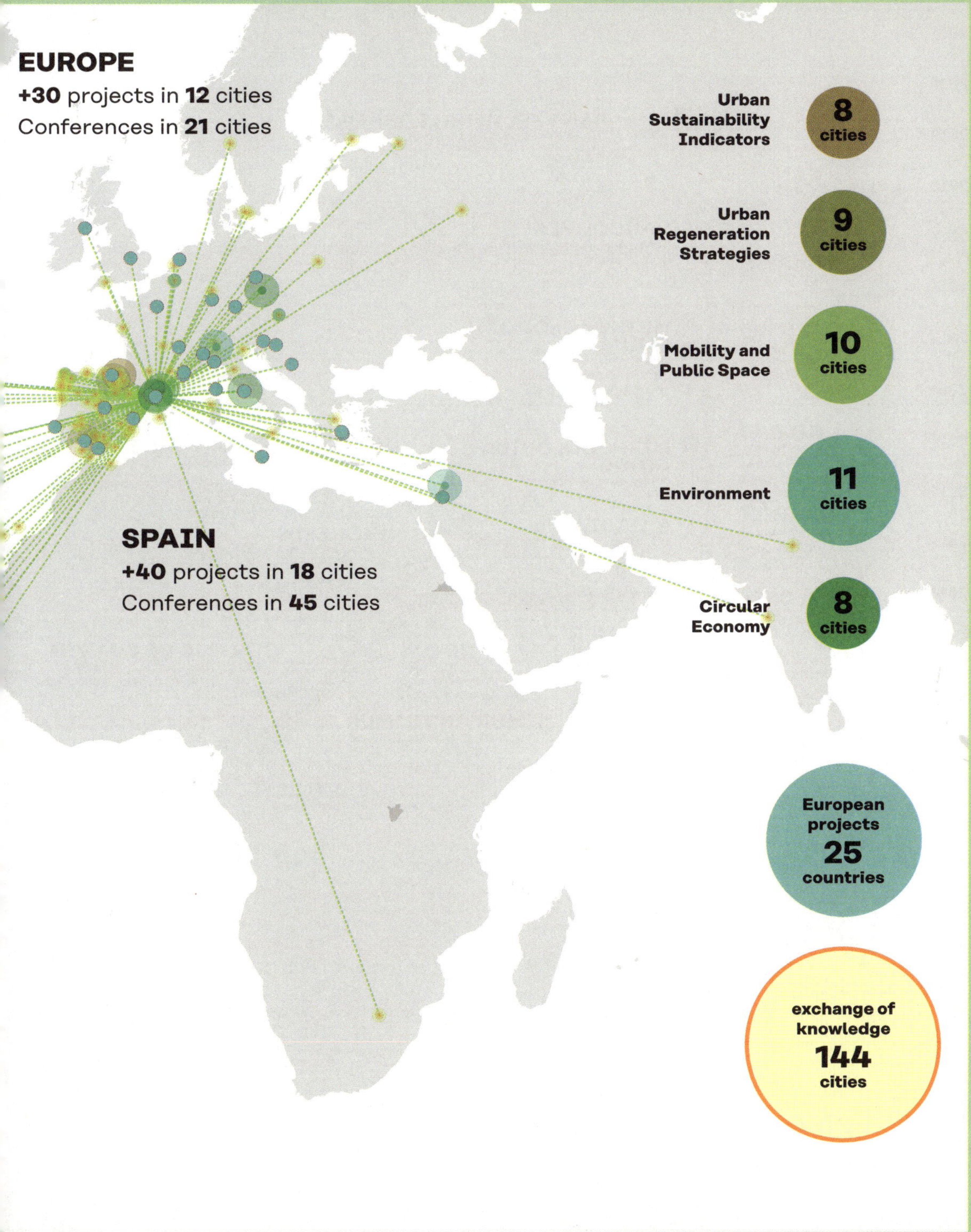
EUROPE
+30 projects in 12 cities
Conferences in 21 cities
SPAIN
+40 projects in 18 cities
Conferences in 45 cities
Urban Sustainability Indicators
8 cities
Urban Regeneration Strategies
9 cities
Mobility and Public Space
10 cities
Environment
11 cities
Circular Economy
8 cities
European projects 25 countries
exchange of knowledge 144 cities

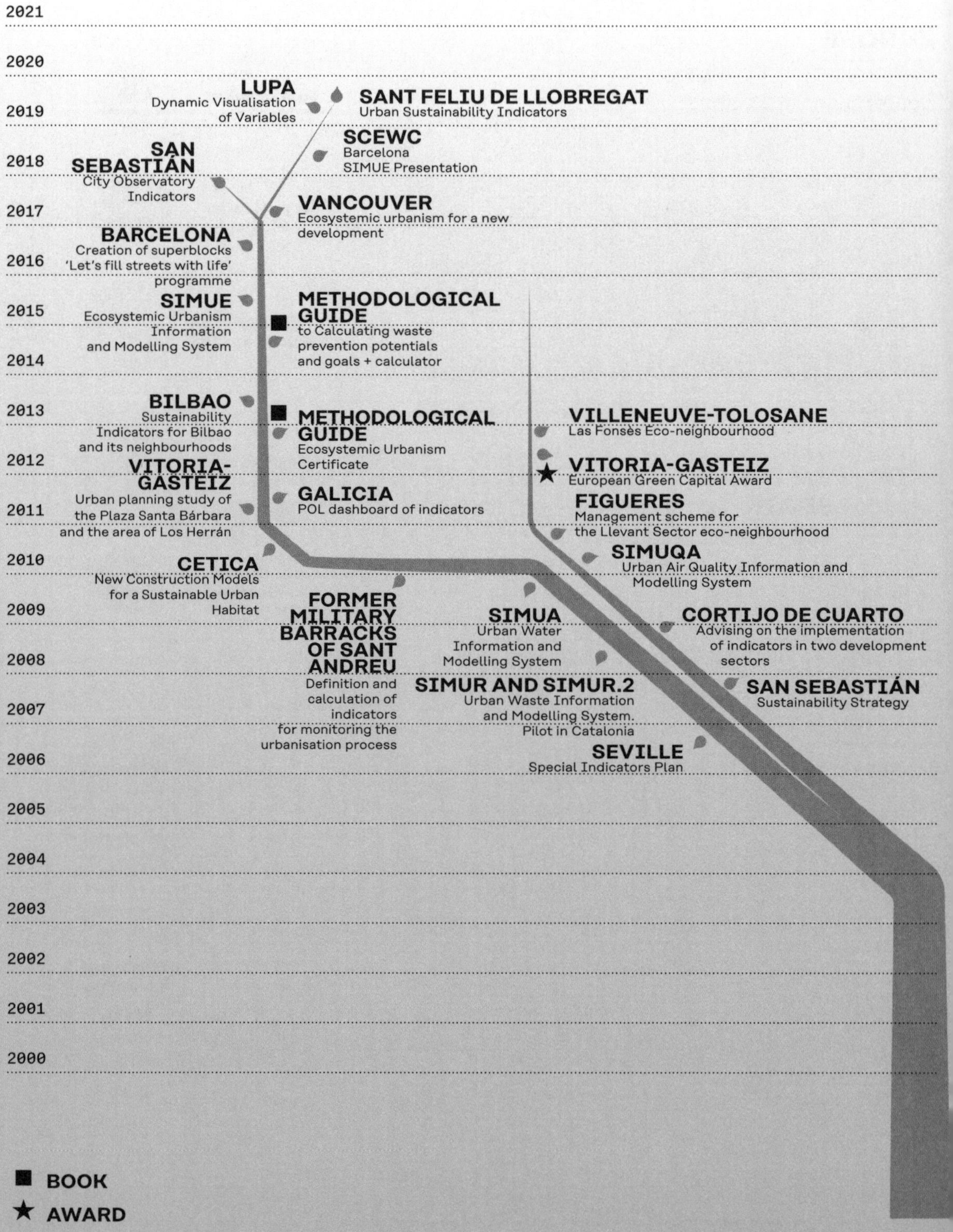
2021
2020
2019
2018
2017
2016
2015
2014
2013
2012
2011
2010
2009
2008
2007
2006
2005
2004
2003
2002
2001
2000
LUPA
Dynamic Visualisation of Variables
SANT FELIU DE LLOBREGAT
Urban Sustainability Indicators
SCEWC
Barcelona
SIMUE Presentation
SAN SEBASTIÁN
City Observatory Indicators
VANCOUVER
Ecosystemic urbanism for a new development
BARCELONA
Creation of superblocks
'Let's fill streets with life' programme
SIMUE
Ecosystemic Urbanism Information and Modelling System
METHODOLOGICAL GUIDE
to Calculating waste prevention potentials and goals + calculator
BILBAO
Sustainability Indicators for Bilbao and its neighbourhoods
METHODOLOGICAL GUIDE
Ecosystemic Urbanism Certificate
VILLENEUVE-TOLOSANE
Las Fonsès Eco-neighbourhood
VITORIA-GASTEIZ
Urban planning study of the Plaza Santa Bárbara and the area of Los Herrán
VITORIA-GASTEIZ
European Green Capital Award
GALICIA
POL dashboard of indicators
FIGUERES
Management scheme for the Llevant Sector eco-neighbourhood
CETICA
New Construction Models for a Sustainable Urban Habitat
SIMUQA
Urban Air Quality Information and Modelling System
FORMER MILITARY BARRACKS OF SANT ANDREU
Definition and calculation of indicators for monitoring the urbanisation process
SIMUA
Urban Water Information and Modelling System
CORTIJO DE CUARTO
Advising on the implementation of indicators in two development sectors
SIMUR AND SIMUR.2
Urban Waste Information and Modelling System. Pilot in Catalonia
SAN SEBASTIÁN
Sustainability Strategy
SEVILLE
Special Indicators Plan
BOOK
AWARD

URBAN SUSTAIN ABILITY INDI CA TORS

In a context where the concept of sustainability has been trivialised, scientific research and its dissemination have become a necessity. Over the last twenty years, BCNecologia's work has consisted of developing and delving into the concept of sustainability, and not in the natural environment – with which it is more often associated – but within urban systems. For the Agency, fleshing out this concept has inevitably required a quantification of the different aspects of sustainability and its systematisation within the theory of ecosystemic urbanism.

This section includes an analysis of the work done to develop, design, systematise and apply a system of sustainability indicators in various urban contexts. First, the chapter 'Methodological guide to the system of indicators' analyses the evolution of the most theoretical projects, linked to the definition of a complete dashboard of indicators. The aim was to define a sufficiently explanatory yet concise system of indicators that included all aspects of urban sustainability.

This work has been carried out in parallel to the application of the system of indicators to the area under analysis, whether it be a municipality or an urban renovation project of any size and in any location. The most representative examples can be found in the chapters 'Applying the system of indicators to regions and cities' and 'Applying the system of indicators to urban projects'. The indicators' adaptability has been proven in each urban context. The theoretical system has developed from the practical experience provided by the application of the indicators, thus becoming sounder and gaining scientific rigour.

A final chapter examines the work leading to the automation of part of the indicator calculation process, as well as the graphic and visual representation of the indicators: key steps in ensuring project results are understood properly and in spreading the Agency's philosophy.

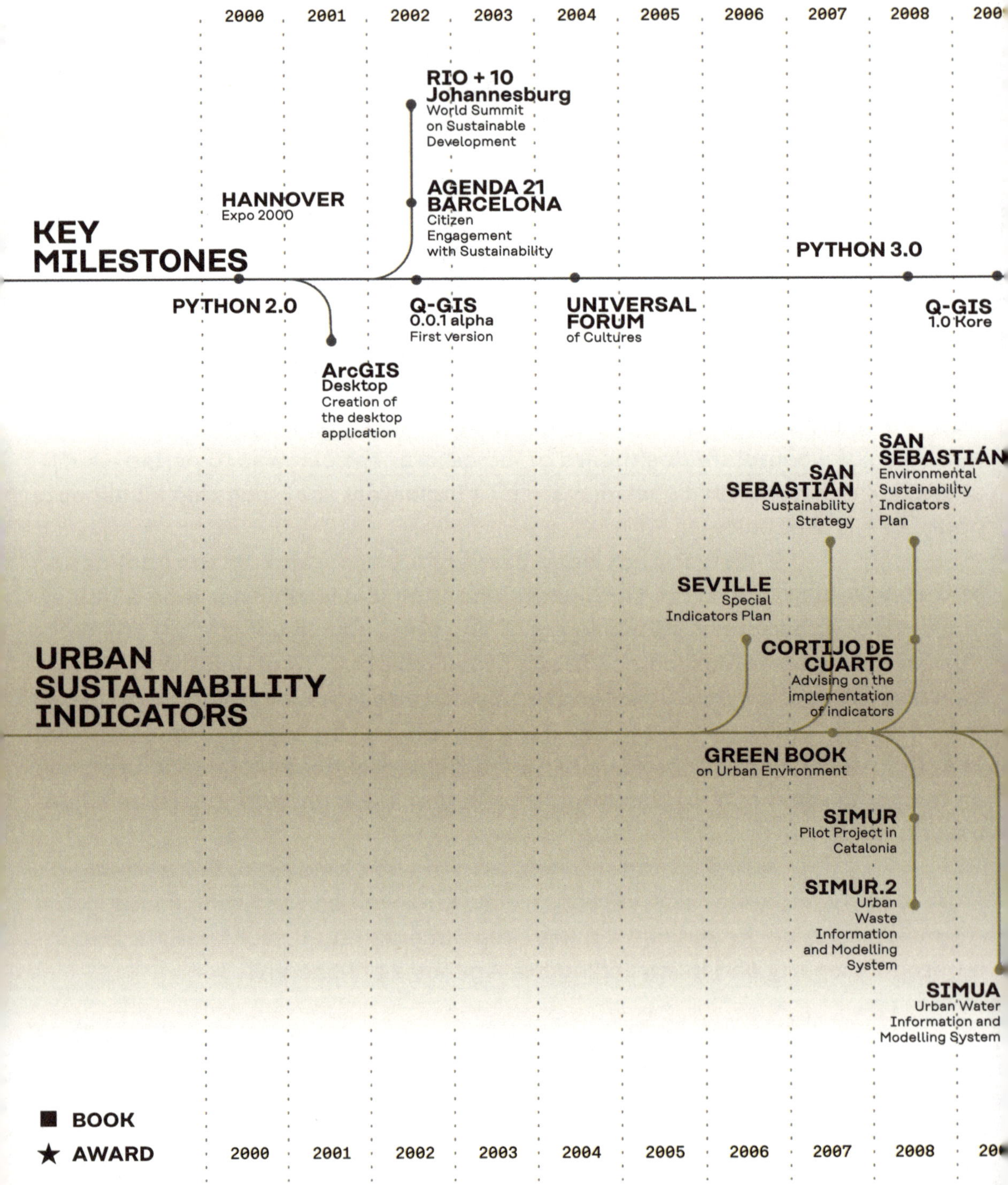
2000
2001
2002
2003
2004
2005
2006
2007
2008
KEY MILESTONES
HANNOVER
Expo 2000
PYTHON 2.0
ArcGIS
Desktop
Creation of the desktop application
RIO + 10
Johannesburg
World Summit on Sustainable Development
AGENDA 21
BARCELONA
Citizen Engagement with Sustainability
Q-GIS
0.0.1 alpha
First version
UNIVERSAL FORUM
of Cultures
PYTHON 3.0
Q-GIS
1.0 Kore
URBAN SUSTAINABILITY INDICATORS
SEVILLE
Special Indicators Plan
SAN SEBASTIÁN
Sustainability Strategy
SAN SEBASTIÁN
Environmental Sustainability Indicators Plan
CORTIJO DE CUARTO
Advising on the implementation of indicators
GREEN BOOK
on Urban Environment
SIMUR
Pilot Project in Catalonia
SIMUR.2
Urban Waste Information and Modelling System
SIMUA
Urban Water Information and Modelling System
BOOK
AWARD
2000
2001
2002
2003
2004
2005
2006
2007
2008

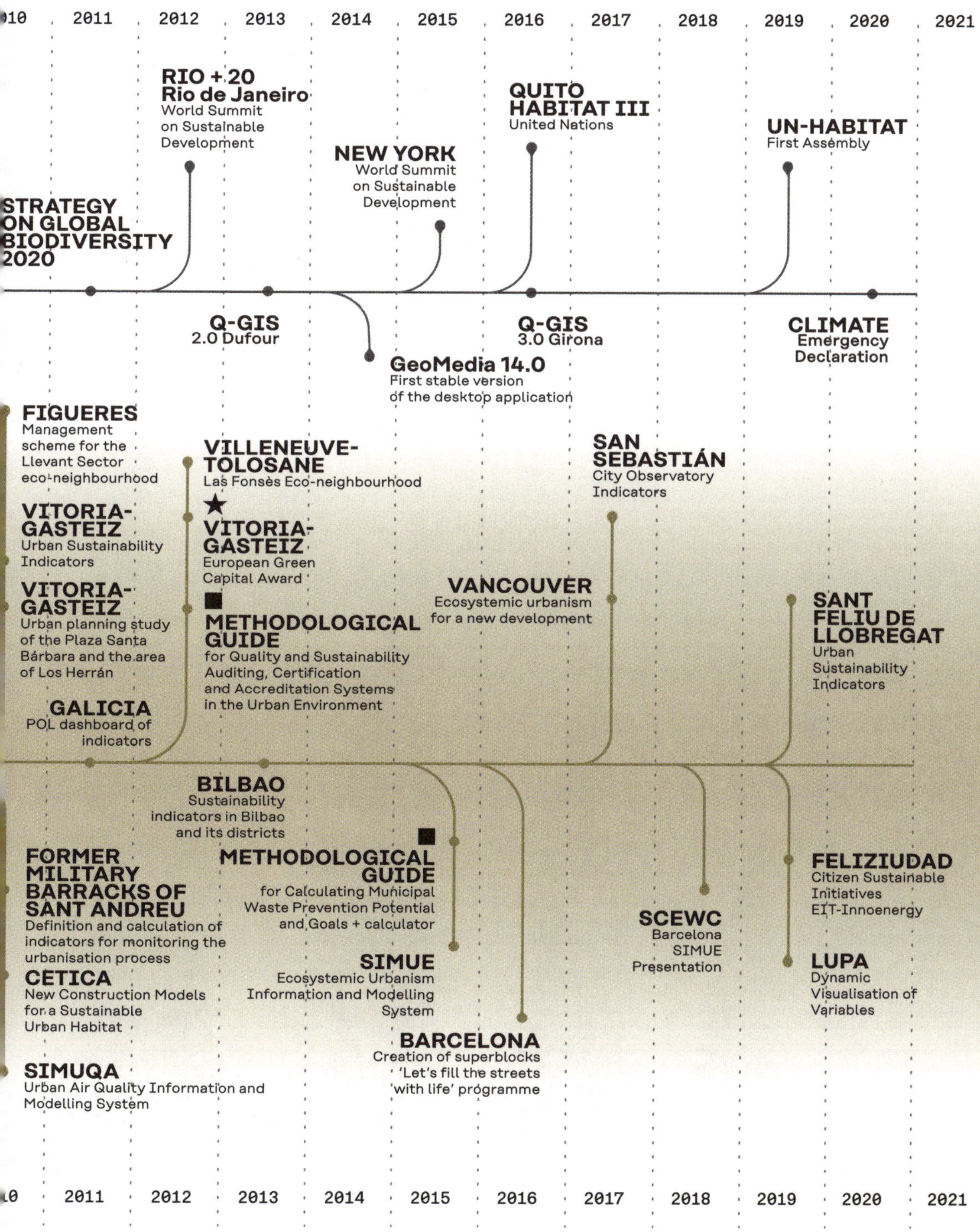
2010
2011
2012
2013
2014
2015
2016
2017
2018
2019
2020
2021
RIO + 20
Rio de Janeiro
World Summit
on Sustainable
Development
QUITO
HABITAT III
United Nations
UN-HABITAT
First Assembly
NEW YORK
World Summit
on Sustainable
Development
STRATEGY
ON GLOBAL
BIODIVERSITY
2020
Q-GIS
2.0 Dufour
Q-GIS
3.0 Girona
CLIMATE
Emergency
Declaration
GeoMedia 14.0
First stable version
of the desktop application
FIGUERES
Management
scheme for the
Llevant Sector
eco-neighbourhood
VILLENEUVE-
TOLOSANE
Las Fonsès Eco-neighbourhood
SAN
SEBASTIÁN
City Observatory
Indicators
VITORIA-
GASTEIZ
Urban Sustainability
Indicators
VITORIA-
GASTEIZ
European Green
Capital Award
VITORIA-
GASTEIZ
Urban planning study
of the Plaza Santa
Bárbara and the area
of Los Herrán
VANCOUVER
Ecosystemic urbanism
for a new development
METHODOLOGICAL
GUIDE
for Quality and Sustainability
Auditing, Certification
and Accreditation Systems
in the Urban Environment
SANT
FELIU DE
LLOBREGAT
Urban
Sustainability
Indicators
GALICIA
POL dashboard of
indicators
BILBAO
Sustainability
indicators in Bilbao
and its districts
FORMER
MILITARY
BARRACKS OF
SANT ANDREU
Definition and calculation of
indicators for monitoring the
urbanisation process
METHODOLOGICAL
GUIDE
for Calculating Municipal
Waste Prevention Potential
and Goals + calculator
FELIZIUDAD
Citizen Sustainable
Initiatives
EIT-Innoenergy
SCEWC
Barcelona
SIMUE
Presentation
CETICA
New Construction Models
for a Sustainable
Urban Habitat
SIMUE
Ecosystemic Urbanism
Information and Modelling
System
LUPA
Dynamic
Visualisation of
Variables
BARCELONA
Creation of superblocks
'Let's fill the streets
with life' programme
SIMUQA
Urban Air Quality Information and
Modelling System
2010
2011
2012
2013
2014
2015
2016
2017
2018
2019
2020
2021

'The Agency has been a pioneer in the creation of quantified indicators. It is characterised by this "obsession" around quantifying and looking for limit or reference values in the areas of mobility, water, energy, urban greenery and soil.'

BETTINA SCHAEFER
Architect. Public Space Project Coordinator 2002–2006. BCNecologia.

Picture: Marta Torrent

METHODO LOGICAL GUIDE TO THE SYSTEM OF INDI CATORS

2021

2020

2019

2018

2017

2016

2015

2014

2013

2012 — **METHODOLOGICAL GUIDE** for Quality and Sustainability Auditing, Certification and Accreditation Systems in the Urban Environment

2011

2010 — **CETICA** New Construction Models for a Sustainable Urban Habitat

2009

2008

2007

2006 — **SEVILLE** Special Indicators Plan

2005

2004

2003

2002

2001

2000

The design, systematisation and application of sustainability indicators is one of the most characteristic features of the Urban Ecology Agency of Barcelona. This trait is displayed in all its work, from projects that focus exclusively on producing a dashboard of indicators for a certain urban reality, to initiatives where designing sustainability strategies in any field (energy, mobility, waste, etc.) is accompanied by various indicators to measure the degree to which goals are achieved. Viewing sustainability as a quantifiable concept, by combining it with a reference urban model and attaching strict requirements to it, is a way of giving scientific substance to the analysis of urban fabrics.

The development of a system of indicators has been carried out in parallel to its application to the municipalities or urban projects under analysis, in order for theory to feed off the practical experience offered by the observation, study and analysis of different realities. This has allowed the Agency to accumulate knowledge, which, in turn, has been displayed in its different projects.

This chapter includes some of the Agency's most significant projects in which the systematisation of a dashboard of indicators plays a leading role. This process may be applied, like the case of the system of indicators accompanying the General Urban Development Plan for Seville (PGOU); theoretical (and construction-oriented), as in the CETICA project (The Eco-Techno-Logical City: New Construction Models for a Sustainable Urban Habitat) – commissioned by the Ministry of Development – or comprehensive, as seen through the Methodological Guide. This Guide was another commission from the Ministry and aimed to certify the degree of overall sustainability of urban development initiatives.

THE SYSTEM OF INDICATORS: A METHODOLOGY TO BENEFIT THE CITY

The CETICA project (2007–2010) and the PGOU 2005–2007 for Seville are the most significant projects in the lead-up to the Agency's creation of a complete dashboard of indicators. As well as analysing different urban contexts, these projects brought together the most relevant indicators needed to quantify an urban fabric's degree of overall sustainability. They therefore represent the first attempts at systematising a series of tools to be used in all of the Agency's projects, though they had not yet been gathered together as an assessment method.

The Seville project centred around urban planning. At that time, the City Council was putting together the new PGOU for Seville (2006). In a project of this scope, in which a city's whole urban planning system was being reviewed, there was an opportunity to accompany this reflection process with a series of indicators that could quantify the sustainability of different areas of the planning system. In this context, the Urban Planning Department at Seville City Council commissioned the Agency to carry out this task.

This study took the form of an environmental sustainability indicators plan for urban development activity in Seville: a preliminary tool for the formulation of the planning rules included in the new PGOU. The plan defined a sustainability framework in the knowledge society for Seville's urban and territorial transformation process. It established a set of indicators to condition the urban development process, based on a city model with a compact layout, efficient metabolic flows and good social cohesion.

The CETICA project, meanwhile, focused on construction. The project intended to develop a system of sustainability indicators linked to the construction and urbanisation process, as the concept of sustainability had been neglected during the building boom of the preceding years. At the tail end of the real-estate frenzy occurring all over the world, but especially in Spain, reflections on its social and environmental impact were starting to emerge.

The aim of the project was to outline future scenarios and to develop urban design proposals from the perspective of industrial construction techniques, which use construction, structural and design criteria to offer new environmental opportunities. In parallel, the project was to develop a sustainability assessment method for urban spaces while exploring the legal framework for proposing the creation of an urban quality stamp. The project's main contributions to the Agency's system of indicators were research into and a review of existing certification processes, on both a national and an international scale. These would later

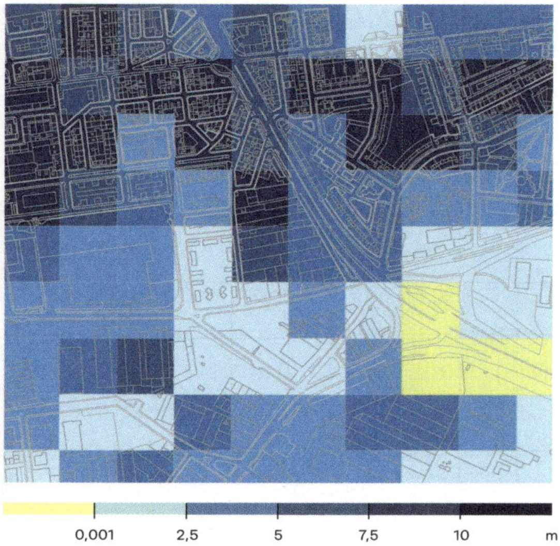

Absolute compactness in Gijón in 2007
Built volume (m³) /
Grid surface 100 m x 100 m (m²)

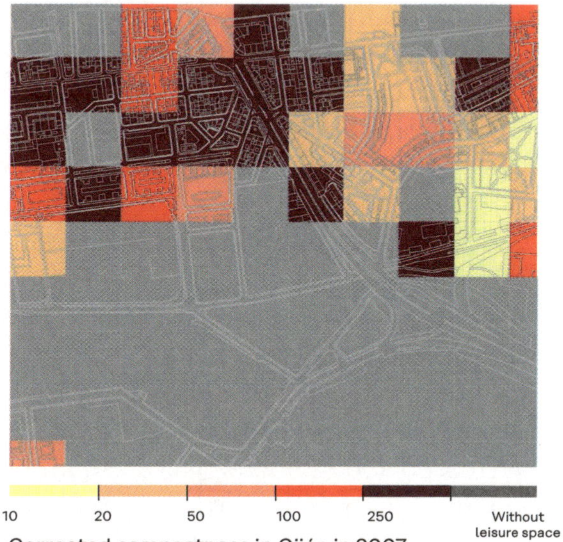

Corrected compactness in Gijón in 2007
Built volume (m³) / leisure surface (m²) in 100 x 100 m grid

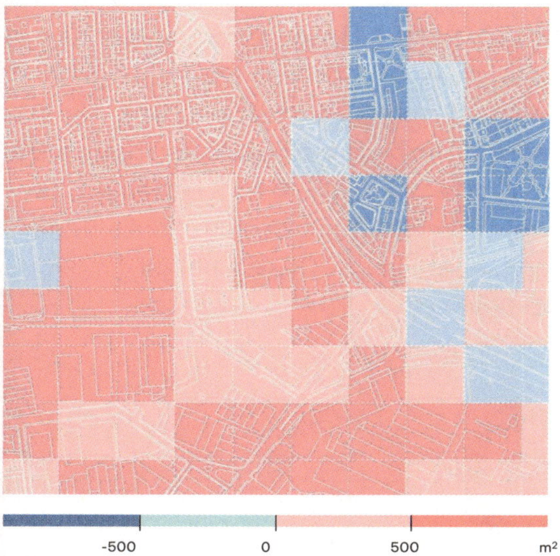

Leisure space requirements
Current built volume (m³)
Current leisure surface (m²)
m² in 100 x 100 m grid

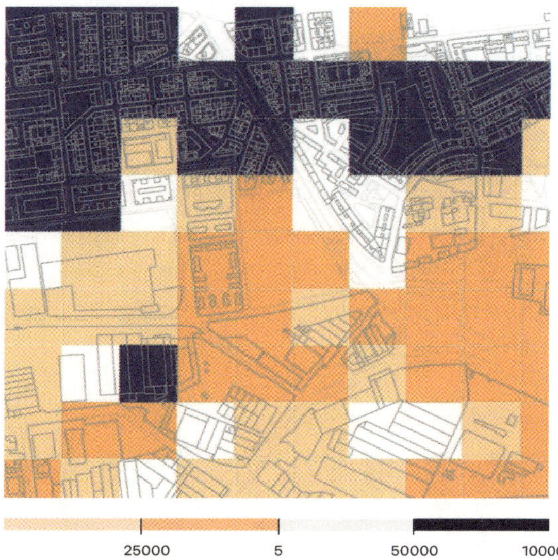

Densification potential
Built volume to be densified (m³)
Built volume to be decompressed (m³)

GIJÓN. 2007–2010. CETICA Project. Examples of indicator calculations. Mapping the calculation of some of the indicators analysed in the Gijón case study.
Source: BCNecologia

be included in the *Methodological Guide for Quality and Sustainability Auditing, Certification and Accreditation Systems in the Urban Environment*,[6] drawn up by BCNecologia and commissioned by the Ministry of Development.

The project was led by Arcelor Spain and brought together a host of companies linked to the world of construction and various research institutions.

For Seville, a dashboard of 35 indicators was established, across 7 fields: urban morphology, public space and comfort, mobility, complexity, urban metabolism, biodiversity and social cohesion. In each, a calculation methodology and a threshold were established. As for the CETICA project, the dashboard was made up of 41 indicators across 4 areas: decompression, metabolic efficiency, infrastructures and resources, and revitalisation and organisation.

This dashboard was applied to various Spanish cities, with a scope limited to each of them. These cities, including Gijón, Sagunto and Madrid, became case studies for the project.

SYSTEMATISING THE PROCESS: THE METHODOLOGICAL GUIDE

Establishing this kind of dashboard necessitates choosing the most relevant indicators that can best assess an urban fabric's degree of sustainability. The list must strike a balance between the different aspects that make up a sustainable urban model. Nonetheless, it must be as concise as possible, leaving out any indicators that offer a level of information that is not appropriate for a general dashboard assessing sustainability from an overall perspective, even though they may be useful when examining a single aspect (energy, social cohesion, etc.). Once the right indicators are chosen, each of them must be defined in the same way, including elements such as the basic information it requires, its calculation process and the information the result offers. Finally, in an assessment process, the indicator's thresholds to denote an adequate level of sustainability must be established.

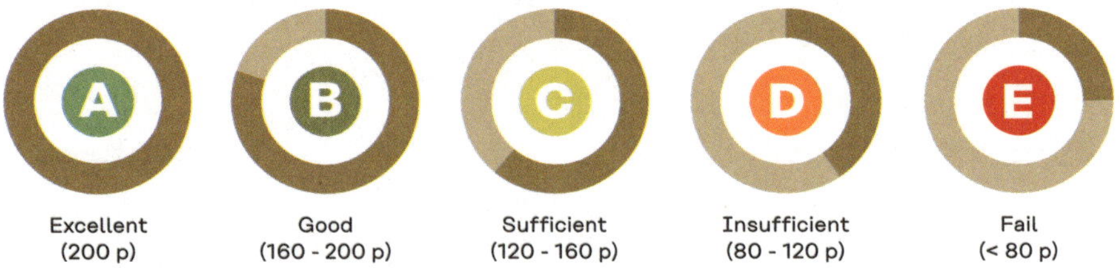

CETICA. 2007–2010. Proposal for the assessment of urban fabrics. Assessment on the basis of the score obtained for the indicators in the four areas of analysis.
Source: BCNecologia

6 Rueda. *Methodological Guide for Quality and Sustainability Auditing, Certification and Accreditation Systems in the Urban Environment. Op. cit.*

Though this work was also carried out in projects prior to the Methodological Guide, the degree of maturity reached through all projects up to this point – with the application of different indicators to multiple projects and different urban realities, and the research associated with each of them – enabled the Agency to do a more exhaustive job, resulting in a well-thought-out choice of indicators based on a more solid wealth of experience. All the theoretical and practical work done up to then in all areas of the Agency was condensed into the Methodological Guide for certifying sustainability, commissioned by the Ministry of Development in 2012.

This Guide includes a summary of the reference urban model (applied to the specific case of the compact, complex, efficient, cohesive city), comprehensive definitions of each indicator in the form of information sheets – which make up the bulk of the Guide – and the assessment (certification process).

Each sheet details the indicator's goal, definition and description. The scale of analysis delineates the scope of each indicator, while the calculation parameter shows the formula or criterion followed to assess the indicator and its calculation unit. The assessment parameter defines the minimum and desirable targets for each indicator, and justification of the choice of indicator and assessment parameter is provided. In addition, indication of which maps, studies and results must be presented to receive certification is given.

The indicators are defined in the Guide to assess two realities: an existing urban fabric or a planned urban development. In the case of existing urban fabrics, the requirements are different, according to whether it is a city, a neighbourhood or a smaller urban area. They also depend on whether the fabric is residential, an urban core or somewhere between the two.

Meanwhile, for urban development assessments, it is important to consider the type of project being carried out and the ground being used. This latter element is a fundamental issue for urban sustainability and is rarely considered. The pre-existing conditions for the urban development must be taken into account, so that, as well as the project itself, the context into which it is inserted and which it aims to transform may be assessed. The suitability of any given urban development can only be evaluated if these two factors are examined.

Defining a reference urban development model is paramount. The Guide, intended to be a set of instructions, is explicit and strict with what it considers sustainability in an urban context. Indicators are not neutral: they quantify how close an urban fabric is to ecological urbanism parameters.

THEMATIC AREA	CERTIFICATION	URBAN MODEL AXES
Compactness and Functionality		
A1. LAND USE	Maximum score: **20** Score achieved: ... R. achieved: **...%**	**Axis 1** Proportion of this axis: **20%**
A2. PUBLIC SPACE AND LIVEABILITY	Maximum score: **90** Score achieved: ... R. achieved: **... %**	
A3. MOBILITY AND SERVICES	Maximum score: **80** Score achieved: ... R. achieved: ... %	
Complexity		
A4. URBAN COMPLEXITY	Maximum score: **50** Score achieved: ... R. achieved: ... %	**Axis 2** Proportion of this axis: **20%**
A5. GREEN SPACES AND BIODIVERSITY	Maximum score: **50** Score achieved: ... R. achieved: ... %	
Efficiency		
A6. URBAN METABOLISM	Maximum score: **130** Score achieved: ... R. achieved: ... %	**Axis 3** Proportion of this axis: **20%**
Cohesion		
A7. SOCIAL COHESION	Maximum score: **70** Score achieved: ... R. achieved: ... %	**Axis 4** Proportion of this axis: **20%**
A8. MANAGEMENT AND GOVERNANCE	Maximum score: **30** Score achieved: ... R. achieved: ... %	**Axis 5** Proportion of this axis: **20%**
URBAN MODEL + MANAGEMENT AXES	**Axis 1 + Axis 2 + Axis 3 + Axis 4 + Axis 5** = **520** points (52 indicators)	

METHODOLOGICAL GUIDE. 2012. Methodological guide, in the case of existing urban fabrics.
First step: Assessment on the basis of indicators in each thematic area.
Source: BCNecologia

FINAL SCORE

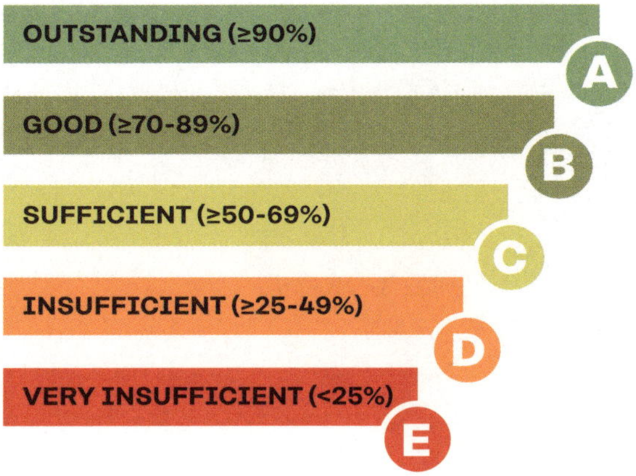

Second step. Final score: Integration of the score obtained in each area.

CERTIFYING ECOSYSTEMIC URBANISM

The Methodological Guide's certification section is based on an assessment system made up of 52 indicators from the perspective of 8 strategic areas, grouped into 5 axes: 1) Land use, public space and liveability, and mobility; 2) Urban complexity, green spaces and biodiversity; 3) Urban metabolism; 4) Social cohesion; and 5) Management and governance. The assessment procedure looks at the characteristics of the urban fabric in terms of scale (from city to neighbourhood) and type of fabric (from urban core to residential).

For each indicator, a maximum of 10 points can be awarded: 5 denotes the minimum satisfactory threshold for the indicator, while 10 denotes a score of 100%, meaning that the desirable target has been reached. The assessment takes place axis by axis: regardless of the number of indicators it contains, each one is weighted 20% in the final certification result. This results in a standardised procedure that strikes a balance between all the aspects that make up a sustainable urban model, in which the sum of the percentages achieved in each axis is the final score of the urban fabric under analysis. A score above 90% is excellent, while a result below 50% is unsatisfactory.

The Guide also defines the certification process for cases where an urban development is being assessed, rather than an existing urban fabric.

A. URBAN PLANNING

*Mainly residential use

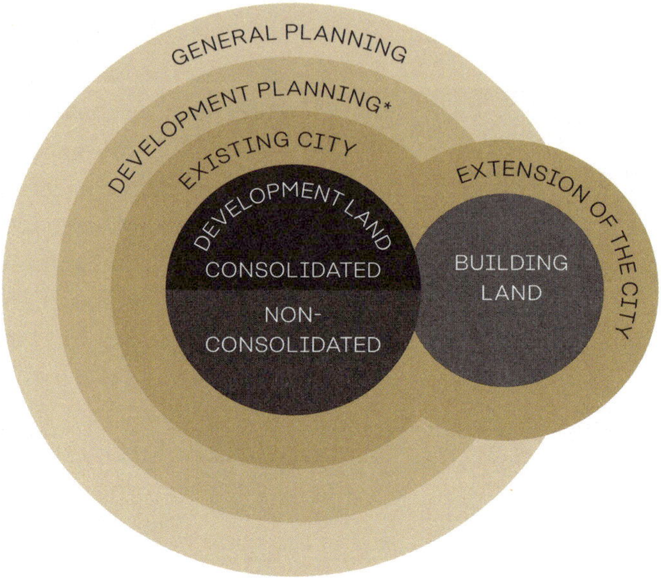

B. EXISTING FABRICS

** > 50,000 inhabitants

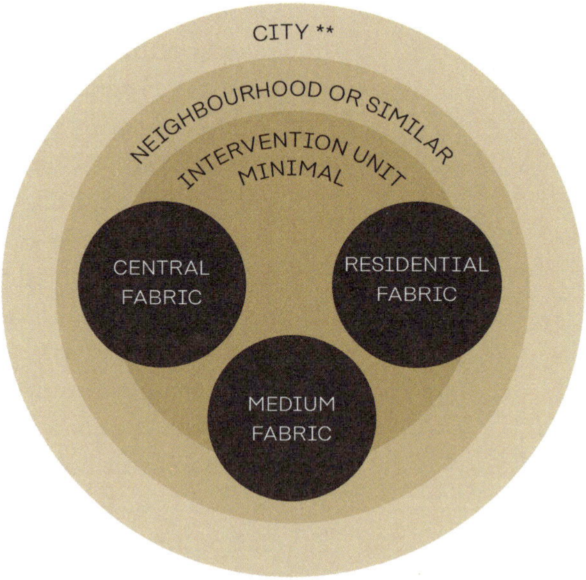

**METHODOLOGICAL GUIDE 2012. Subject matter of the methodological guide:
A. Analysis of urban planning; and B. Analysis of existing urban fabrics.**
Source: BCNecologia

Conclusions

The use of indicators has been part of the Agency's methodology from its very beginnings in the early 2000s: a time when the quantification of these aspects was uncommon outside the purely academic sphere.

The Agency's history has been marked by the selection of the most illuminating indicators that provide the most information to decide whether an urban fabric is sustainable or not in terms of urban ecology, by the definition of a methodology, by the formulation of a calculation, and by the systematisation of all of this to create an analytical tool. Early on, the Agency worked on projects in which one of the goals was to put together a dashboard of indicators summarising its accumulated knowledge. However, it was not until the publication of the Methodological Guide in 2012 that this systematisation process was complete, establishing a reference system for future projects.

The use of geographical information systems (GIS) has had a significant influence on this process. Information mapping has been key from the beginning, and GIS tools, which also originated in academia, have evolved alongside indicator calculation.

The Agency's analytical processes have developed constantly. From these projects onwards, they have continued to evolve, incorporating new methodologies into the indicators as new graphic and calculation tools have become available.

APPLYING THE SYSTEM OF INDICATORS TO REGIONS AND CITIES

2021

2020

2019

SANT FELIU DE LLOBREGAT
Urban Sustainability Indicators

2018

2017

2016

2015

2014

2013

BILBAO
Sustainability Indicators for Bilbao and its neighbourhoods

2012

2011

GALICIA
POL dashboard of indicators

2010

VITORIA-GASTEIZ
Urban Sustainability Indicators

2009

2008

SAN SEBASTIÁN
Special Plan for Environmental Sustainability Indicators

2007

SAN SEBASTIÁN
Sustainability Strategy

2006

2005

2004

2003

2002

2001

2000

The proposed indicators system allows to determine the degree of eco-systemic balance in the established territory, in samples of urban fabric, cities or metropolises. This system quantifies and sets the guiding principles for ecosystemic urbanism, and determines whether the system is balanced, or if it is close to the adequate proportion system or not.

The analysis can be performed at different scales, including the whole city or just small areas such as the superblocks. In fact, superblocks are the reference for the values established for the assessment of the indicators, since superblocks are the minimum urban ecosystem can integrate the set of principles proposed. Superblocks can emerge as the urban cell that initiates and serves as a catalyst for the transformation of urban fabric that need to regenerate. Superblocks act as small cities where it is possible to implement a more sustainable urban model: application of new measures to improve urban habitability, metabolic efficiency or social cohesion.

In this sense, the application of the indicators' system to the local area has been the main source of experience and learning while working with this methodology, which is constantly evolving in the Agency. These type of projects allowed the analysis of much different urban realities, from the location to size matters, urban sprawl, land use, metabolic fluxes or social characterization. With time, this has allowed to refine the indicators system, their kind, representation or their optimal and desirable value. The use of indicators to perform a quantitative evaluation of the different sustainability aspects is one of the main traits from BCNecologia.

Projects in this chapter cover more than one decade of indicators' calculation in different municipalities and respond to diverse realities. The most contemporary one (2019) is associated with a concrete urban transformation: the burying of the railway tracks and the urbanization of the free space at Sant Feliu de Llobregat. The rest of them are a global municipal analysis, in a concrete municipality, such as Vitoria-Gasteiz, San Sebastián and Bilbao, or in a wider territory, such as the Galician coast.

EVALUATING A WHOLE MUNICIPALITY USING INDICATORS VITÒRIA-GASTEIZ, SAN SEBASTIÁN AND BILBAO

The projects to establish a strategy for San Sebastián and sustainability indicators for Vitoria-Gasteiz and Bilbao are good examples of how to use indicators to make a comprehensive assessment of a municipal reality. These projects also show how this analysis tool has evolved. In the case of San Sebastián, the indicators were used in every step of the creation of a sustainability strategy for the city. In Vitoria-Gasteiz, calculating indicators and assessing the municipality's overall sustainability were the main focus of the project. Lastly, in Bilbao, the Agency's indicators accompanied the content of the urban strategy in the process to put together the new General Plan for Urban Planning in Bilbao.

Soon after the first major project for Vitoria-Gasteiz (the Sustainable Mobility and Public Space Plan of 2006–2007), San Sebastián City Council commissioned the Agency to formulate a sustainability strategy for the municipality (2007–2009), accompanied by a specific indicator analysis for Altza, one of the city's peripheral neighbourhoods. This was a project in which indicators were integrated – in a quantified, mapped fashion – into the various aspects of the urban analysis, namely compactness, complexity, efficiency and social cohesion. Indeed, the indicators played an essential role in characterising these aspects' degree of sustainability, though an overall numerical assessment of all the aspects was not carried out yet. The project involved a great deal of information gathering and unification, indicator calculation and variable mapping, prior to the reflection process and proposals of future scenarios.

The strategy for San Sebastián put forward a new layout for the city's public space, based on superblocks, which would increase the proportion of space designated for pedestrians from 43% to 73%. It also analysed the available energy sources to improve the city's energy self-sufficiency through local resources. Wave power, in particular, was a good potential energy source, given the municipality's characteristics. Calculations showed that 86% of the municipality's energy needs could be covered with local renewable sources, once demand was reduced with various energy-saving measures. The project also included an interesting issue that tends to be absent in the Agency's urban analyses: food sovereignty. For some food groups, 100% of demand could be covered by local production. Furthermore, this project was the first in which social cohesion indicators – especially those related to housing – were developed and characterised more extensively, at a time when ensuring access to this fundamental

SCENARIO 0

2009

Current scenario (diagnosis). It assesses the degree to which Vitoria-Gasteiz is adapted to the model of a more sustainable city.

Inhabitants: **236,525**
Dwellings: **103,808**

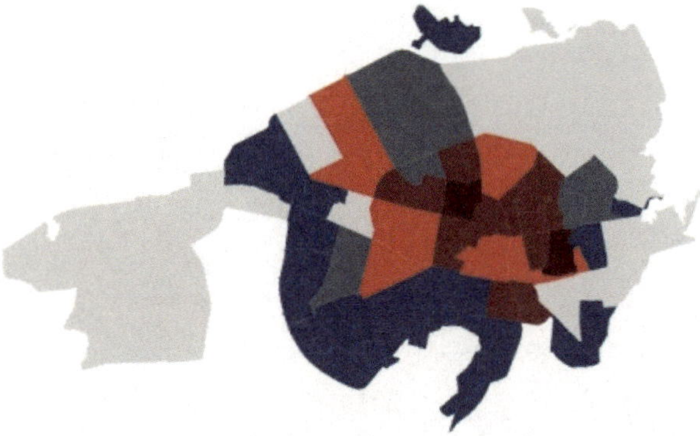

SCENARIO 1

2020

Future scenario integrating and applyling actions and plans (on approval or execution phase) coordinated by the Vitoria-Gasteiz City Council for this horizon.

Inhabitants: **256,485**
Dwellings: **122,976**

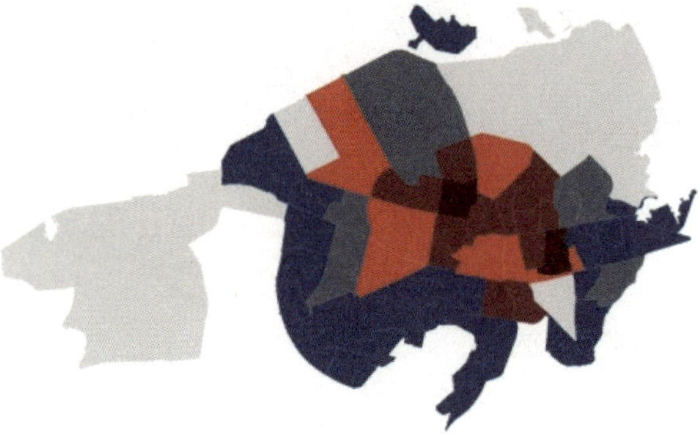

SCENARIO 2

2050

Future scenario integrating and applying specific actions to turn Vitoria-Gasteiz into a carbon-neutral city.

Inhabitants: **276,046**
Dwellings: **135,435**

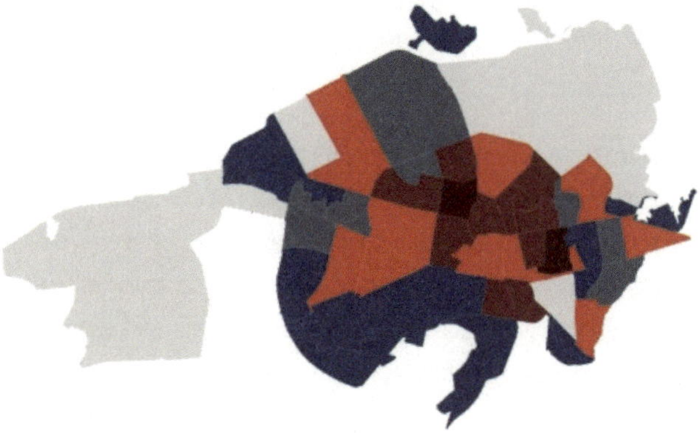

VITORIA-GASTEIZ. 2009–2010. Scenario analyses. Urban Sustainability Indicators Plan.
Source: Vitoria-Gasteiz City Council, BCNecologia

Population density inhabitants/ha

100 200 300 400

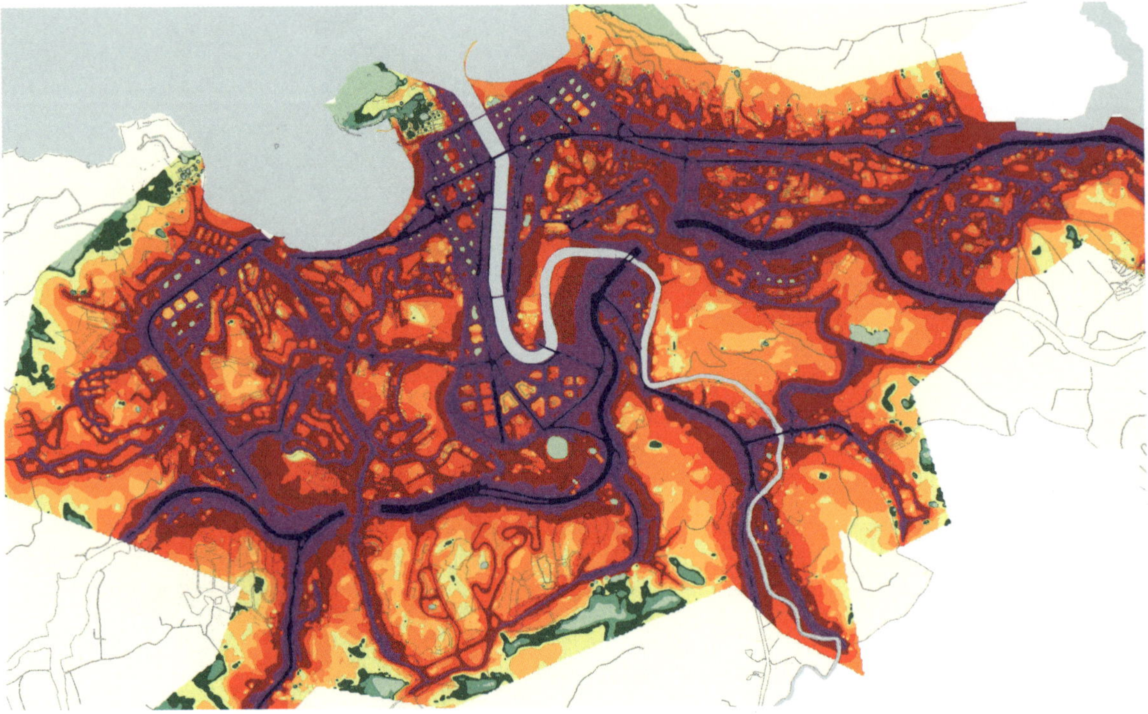

2007 SCENARIO

SAN SEBASTIÁN. 2007–2009. Strategic Sustainability Plan. Noise pollution in the 2007 scenario and in the superblock proposal.
Source: BCNecologia

right was difficult across Spain. Prices had hit all-time highs. They would start to fall for the first time in decades as the property bubble burst, but this drop had not been felt yet and was only documented through property websites (a source that was still rarely used).

The Vitoria-Gasteiz project, meanwhile, involved an assessment using a dashboard of indicators. When the project was put together (2009–2010), urban ecology interventions were being planned in various areas of the municipality. The Agency was tasked with the waste strategy, the climate change strategy and the implementation of the 'central superblock', all at the same time. In addition, the Agency had just worked on another large-scale project – the

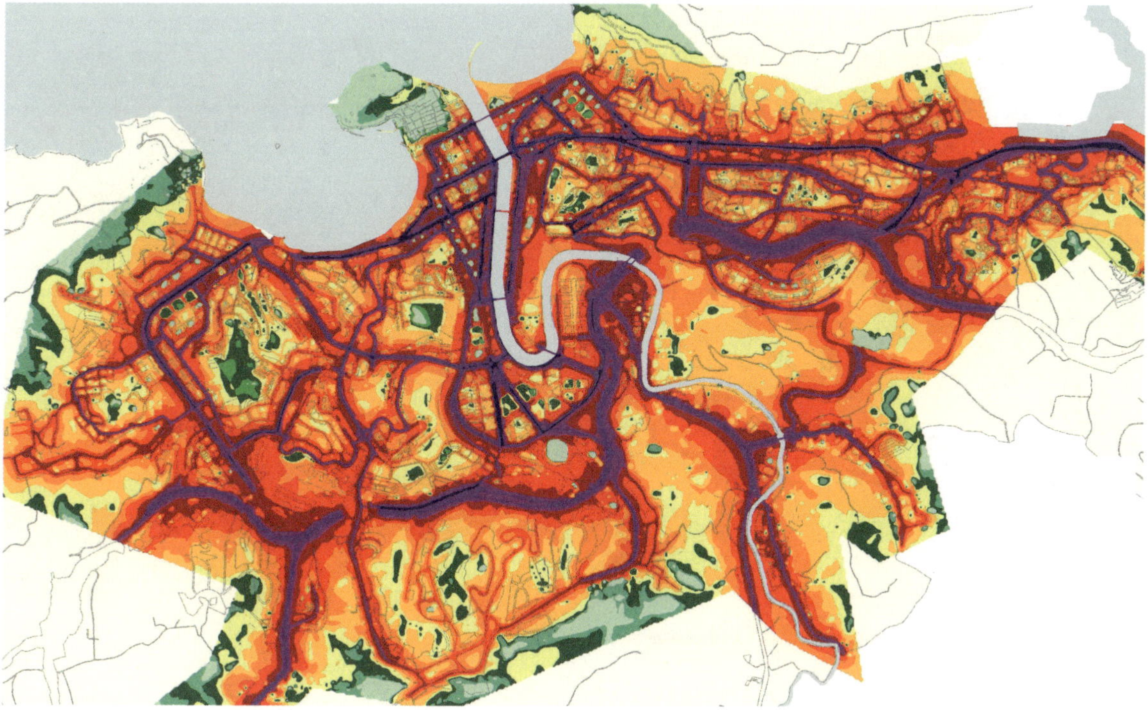

PROPOSAL WITH SUPERBLOCKS

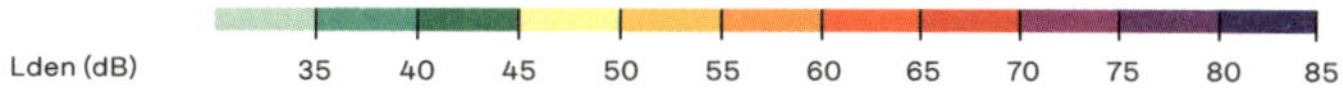

Vitoria-Gasteiz Sustainable Mobility and Public Space Plan (2006–2007) – and the subsequent expansion into the old town, and at that time, other urban interventions were being considered in the municipality. In this context, the indicators project was needed to systematise and evaluate what all these planned activities would entail for the city. This was a time of widespread urban development and adoption of different environmental strategies that had long been in the works, which were met with political consensus: a distinctive trait that has always characterised this municipality.

The dashboard of fifty indicators assessed three scenarios: 2007, the near future (2020) – with planned action in place – and a third scenario (2050), where all the

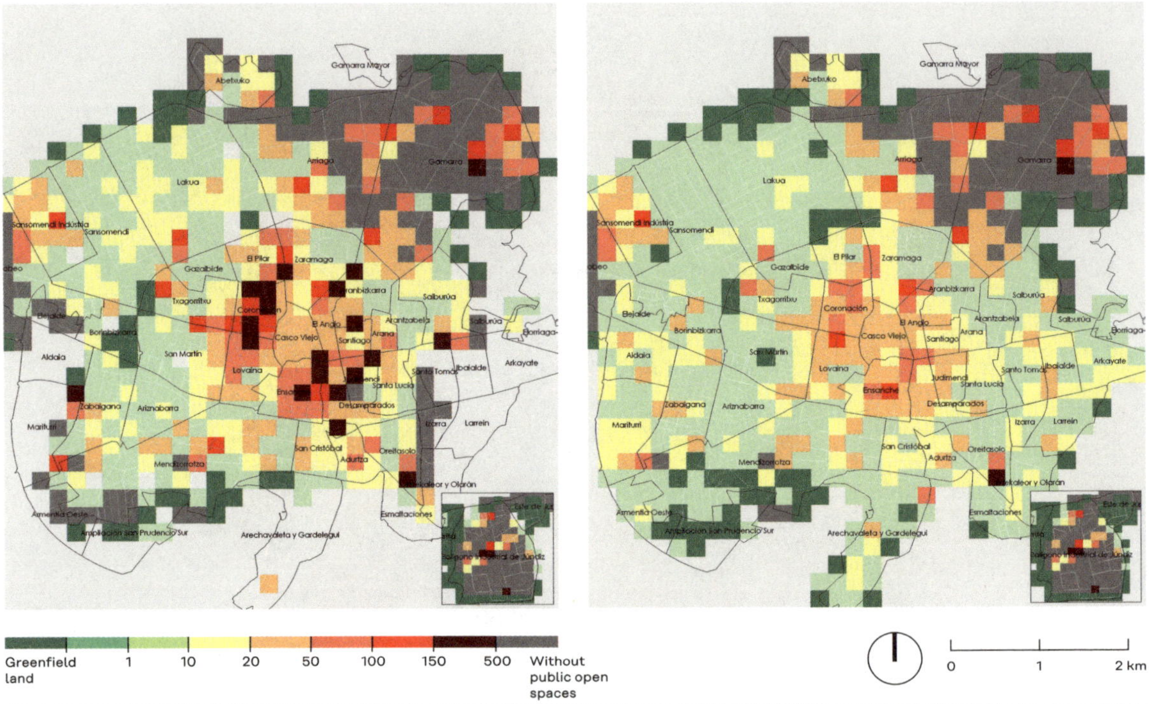

VITORIA-GASTEIZ. 2009–2020. Comparative analysis between two scenarios. Assessment of the corrected compactness indicator. This indicator provides information on the degree of balance between buildings and public spaces.
Source: BCNecologia

developments proposed in the General Plan for Urban Planning were implemented and all environmental improvement plans under examination were in effect, with a view to making Vitoria-Gasteiz a carbon-neutral city. In this project, a numerical assessment was given for each scenario, constituting the sum of the values of the different indicators according to how much they have been fulfilled.

The city achieved desirable figures in urban complexity and green spaces, but not in land use, as the indicators showed an urban reality that was not very compact, which would have consequences on urban metabolism. The existing scenario scored 37.2/100, while scenario 1 boosted urban sustainability to 53.6, especially in terms of public space and urban metabolism, which underwent improvements as part of the plans envisaged. Scenario 3, meanwhile, achieved an excellent score.

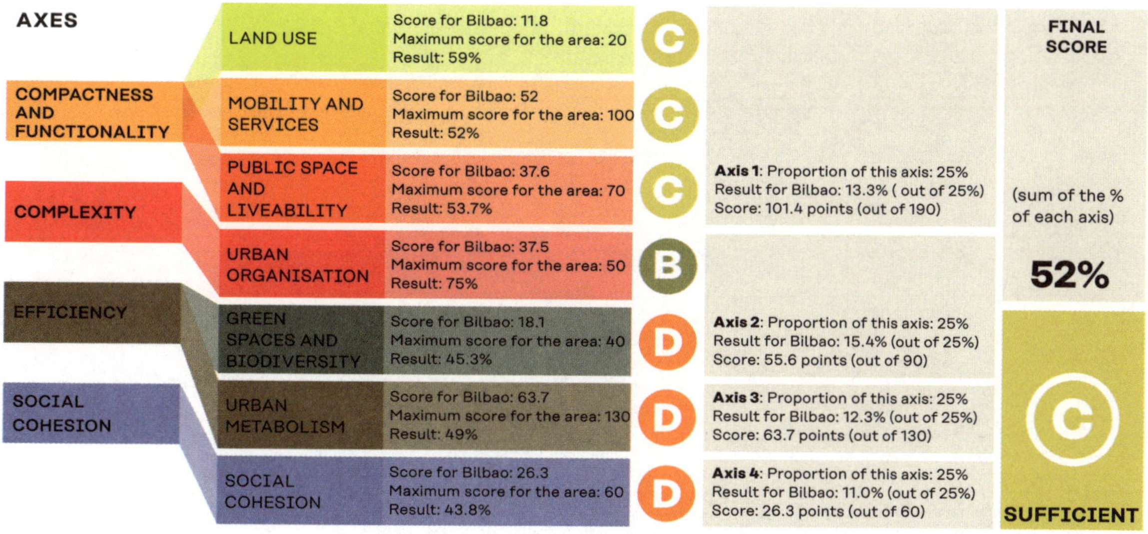

BILBAO. 2013. Sustainability Indicators. Base situation.
Source: BCNecologia

In the Bilbao case, the Office of the General Plan for Urban Planning commissioned the Agency to diagnose the city's state, so that it could be incorporated into the Proposed General Plan for Urban Planning in Bilbao. The city model of the time was deemed obsolete. The aim was therefore to rethink the future through a suitable urban reconfiguration, with sustainability criteria in mind.

The technical document written up using the system of indicators was an in-depth examination of the city, offering opportunities, solving problems, identifying shortcomings and contemplating a balance between uses and urban functions (housing, work, business, public space, mobility, services and resources). It analysed the planned urban initiatives and characterised current points of focus and those predicted for the future, based on various developments. The urban diversity study reinforced this view of the city's economic activity and incorporated proposals regarding sustainable mobility (cycling or public transport).

The last part of the document lists a series of strategic lines of action that must be included in the proposal report for the General Plan for Urban Planning in Bilbao.

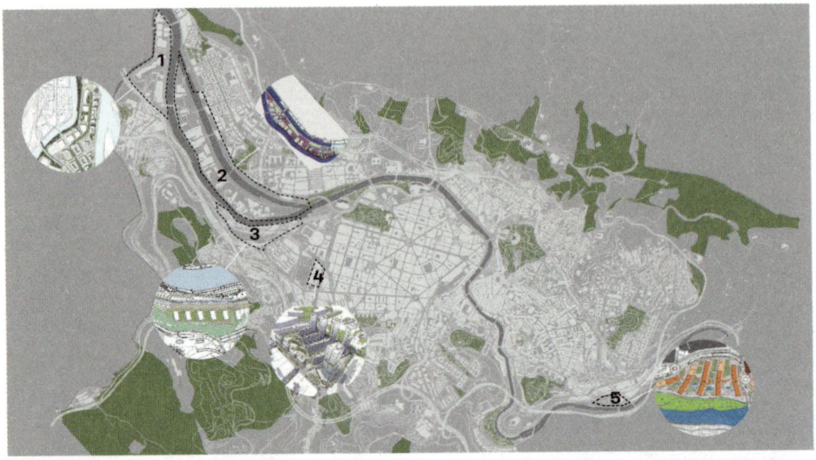

NEW URBAN DEVELOPMENT INITIATIVES

1 Puerta de Zorroza
2 Zorrotzaure
3 Olabeaga
4 Garellano
5 Bolueta

NETWORK OF CYCLE LANES

- Base situation
- Under construction
- Planned

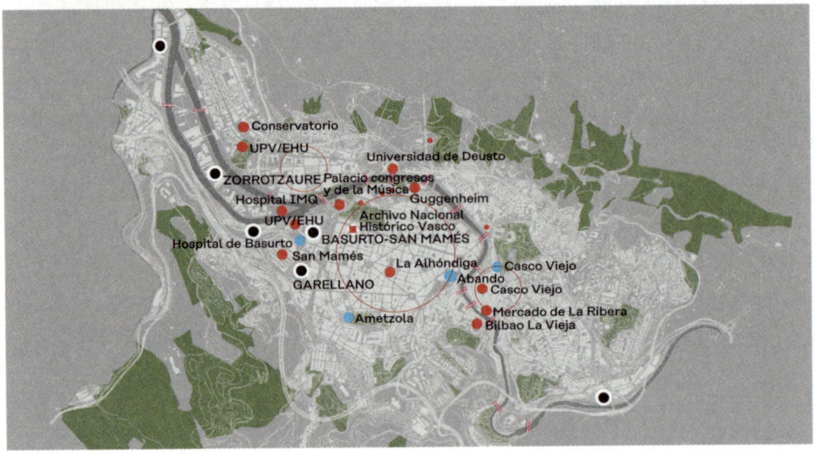

URBAN ACTIVITY AREAS

INITIAL HUBS / AREAS OF ATTRACTION

- Area of high urban diversity
- Facilities/hub of attraction
- Intermodal station
- Pedestrian connection

FUTURE HUBS / AREAS OF ATTRACTION

- Urban renewal area
- Facilities/hub of attraction
- Pedestrian connection

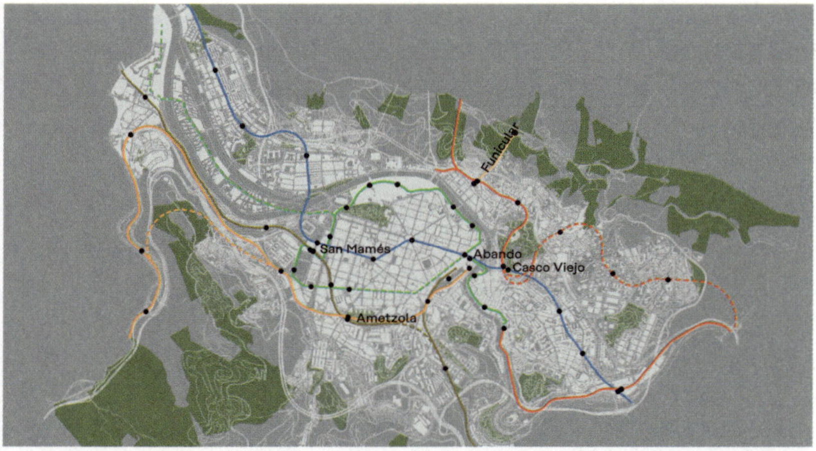

PUBLIC TRANSPORT WITH FIXED INFRASTRUCTURE

FUTURE NETWORKS
(planned, under construction)

- Eusko Tran (Tramway)
- Eusko Tren
- FEVE
- RENFE
- Future tram station

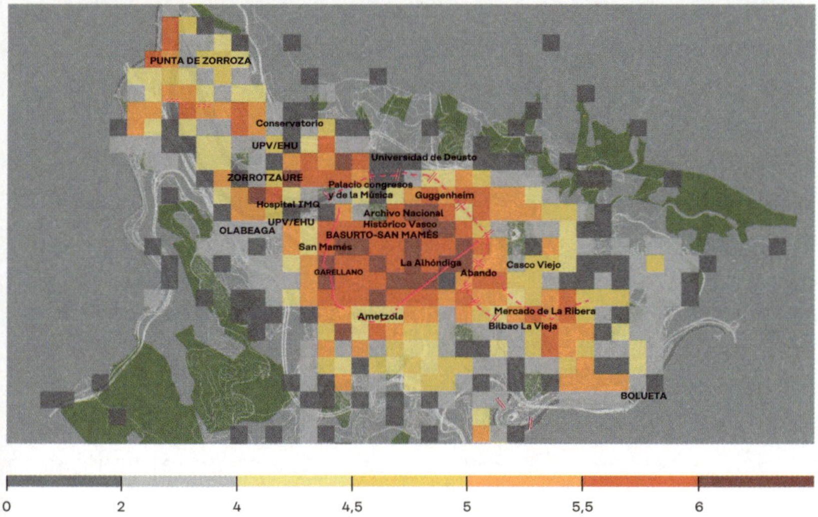

URBAN DIVERSITY INDEX + ACTIVITY CONNECTORS

- Current and/or planned activity connector in the business-as-usual scenario
- Planned activity connector

BILBAO. 2012–2013. Summary of urban actions in the Sustainability Indicators Plan.
Source: BCNecologia

ASSESSMENT WITH INDICATORS OF REALITIES FROM ABOVE THE MUNICIPAL SCALE OR IN THE MUNICIPALITY GALICIA AND SANT FELIU DE LLOBREGAT

Unlike previous projects, the Galician Coastal Management Plan (POL) and the Sant Feliu de Llobregat project are not strictly municipal-scale assessments. Nonetheless, analysis of the municipal reality is still a defining characteristic of both projects: in the first, it occurs as part of an assessment of the Galician coast above the municipal scale, and in the second, it takes the form of an urban project – moving the railway in Sant Feliu de Llobregat underground – which, due to its scope, has consequences on the whole municipality.

In the POL formulation process, the Autonomous Government of Galicia – the Xunta – commissioned the Agency to develop sustainability indicators to accompany this planning initiative, which were then brought together in the document 'Instruments for dynamic territorial management and the application of the Coastal Management Plan' (2011).

As the POL has a very specific natural and rural environment component, the indicators relating to these aspects of the project were extended and developed, while the indicators that were more relevant to an urban environment were rethought (compactness, etc.). The result was not simply a theoretical dashboard of indicators. It was tested and mapped in different 'landscape units', selected by the Xunta and the Agency in order to guarantee a diverse range of urban fabrics, in accordance with the available data they had started to gather to put the plan together. From east to west along the coast, the first landscape unit corresponded to the municipality of Barreiros; the second, to Mañón; the third, to Oleiros and Sada; and the fourth, to Cangas and Moaña.

The POL indicators were also used to analyse each landscape unit's sensitivity to future urban growth, which is a key issue in any general urban planning. The limitations posed by the municipalities were evaluated, and depending on the results from the indicators (whether urban or natural), the possibility of carrying out a new development in each municipality or landscape unit was assessed. In addition, the land was categorised on a scale where, on one end, development was prohibited, and on the other, densification could take place.

MOVING THE RAILWAY UNDERGROUND IN SANT FELIU DE LLOBREGAT

In Sant Feliu de Llobregat, the Committee for Moving the Railway Underground is the organisation that covers participation in and deliberations around issues that affect

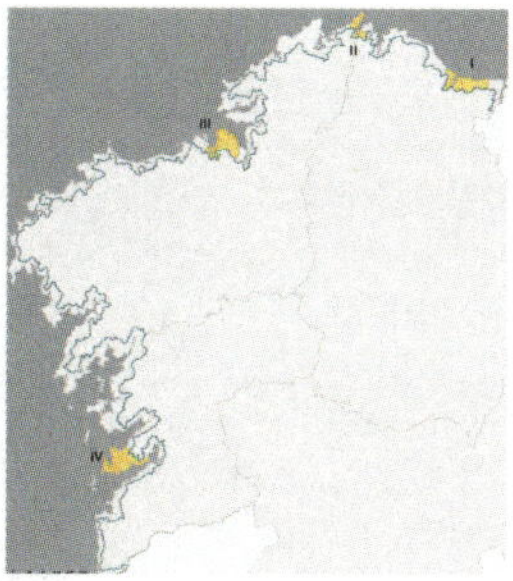

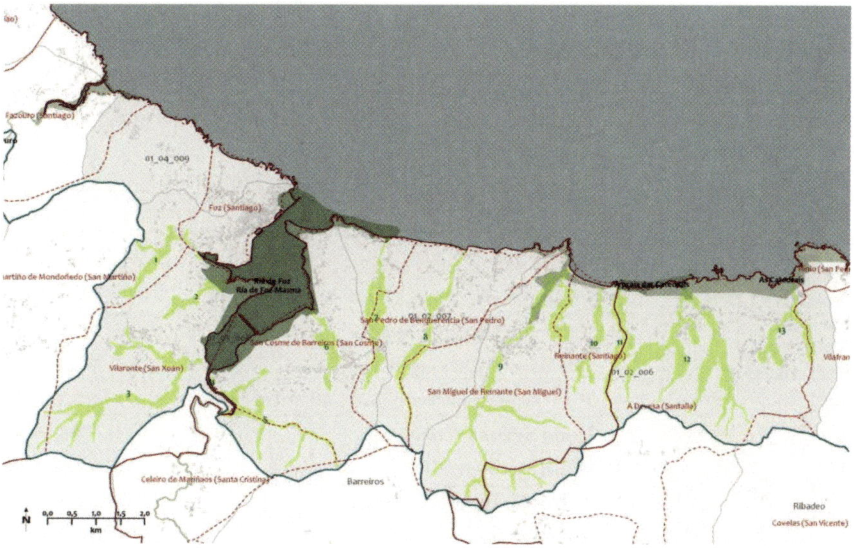

POL area
Landscape units
Parishes
Municipalities
Protected areas
River corridors

GALICIA. 2011. Management area of the Coastal Management Plan (POL) with the four landscape units chosen for the indicators' analysis. Detail of the Barreiros unit.
Source: BCNecologia

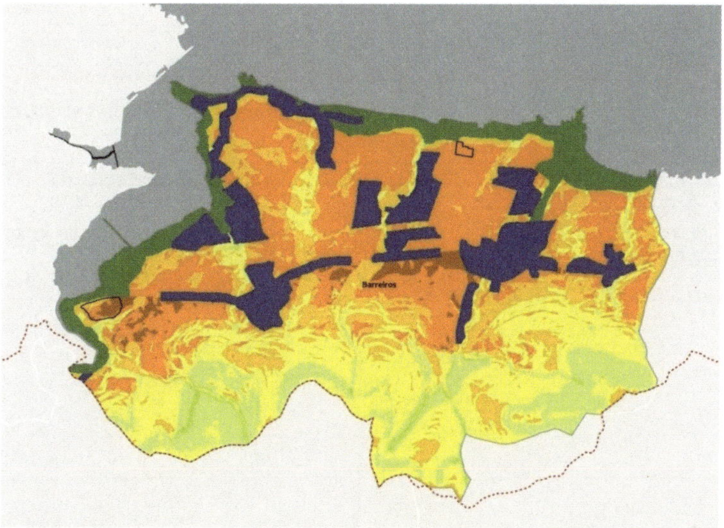

Development land
Building land

Area under study
in the municipality of Barreiros
POL area

0 2 km

BARREIROS. 2011. Coastal Management Plan. Soil sensitivity and growth limitations map.
Source: BCNecologia

Building land, sensitivity

0 min. | 2 | 5 | 10 | 15 | 20 | 25 | 100 | > 100 (protected land)

AREA		INDICATORS	RESULTS VALUE	UNIT	POINTS
1 URBAN MORPHOLOGY AND STRUCTURE	1.1	Housing density	**52.8**	% surf. (>80 dwel.)	**5.3**
	1.2	Urban compactness	**42.9**	% surf. (>5 m)	**4.3**
	1.3	Corrected compactness	**37.9**	% surf. (10-50 m)	**3.8**
	1.4	Surface area of public spaces per capita	**10.3**	m²/inh.	**7.6**
2 SUSTAINABLE MOBILITY AND CITIZENS' RIGHTS	2.1	Proximity to alternative transport networks	**87.8**	% population	**3.8**
	2.2	Motorised road space	**49.2**	% road space	**4.2**
	2.3	Proximity to bicycle parking	**24.6**	% population	**1.6**
	2.4	Provision of bicycle parking	**5.3**	places/1,000 inh.	**1.7**
	2.5	Off-street parking for vehicles	**77.2**	% parking places	**5.7**
	2.6	Provision of parking (infrastructure deficit)	**89.1**	% places covered	**7.8**
3 LIVEABLE PUBLIC SPACE	3.1	Road accessibility	**68**	% linear m	**4.5**
	3.2	Road distribution	**42.9**	% linear m	**4.3**
	3.3	Acoustic comfort (day)	**89**	% population	**7.8**
	3.4	Thermal comfort	**82.6**	% linear m	**10**
	3.5	Liveability index in public space	**57.8**	% m² road space	**6.6**
4 URBAN COMPLEXITY	4.1	Density of legal persons	**8.8**	act./ha	**2.9**
	4.2	Urban diversity index	**20.8**	% urban surface	**2.1**
	4.3	Balance of uses	**17.6**	% m² tertiary	**4.4**
	4.4	Spatial and functional continuity of the street	**15.2**	% linear m	**3.0**
5 GREEN SPACES AND BIO-DIVERSITY	5.1	Green space per inhabitant	**6.1**	m²/inh.	**6.1**
	5.2	Biotic index of soil	**26.6**	%	**9.2**
	5.3	Simultaneous proximity to green spaces	**99.4**	% population	**9.9**
	5.4	Normalised difference vegetation index (NDVI)	**32.9**	%	**10**
	5.5	Density of trees lining streets	**120.7**	%	**10**
6 SOCIAL COHESION	6.1	Simultaneous proximity to basic facilities	**76.6**	% population	**5.3**
	6.2	Ageing Index	**111.7**	%	**8.8**
	6.3	Segregation index of the older population	**12.6**	%	**7.5**
	6.4	Segregation index of the foreign born population	**18.2**	%	**6.4**

0 1 2 3 4 5 6 7 8 9 10

SANT FELIU DE LLOBREGAT. 2019. Analysis and creation of urban indicators.
Summary of assessment results with indicators and by area.
Source: BCNecologia

AREA	POINTS ACHIEVED	MAX.POINTS AREA	RESULT AREA (%)	SCORE
1	21.0	40	**52.5%**	C
2	24.8	60	**41.3%**	D
3	33.2	50	**66.4%**	C
4	12.4	40	**31.0%**	D
5	45.2	50	**90.4%**	A
6	28.0	40	**70.0%**	B

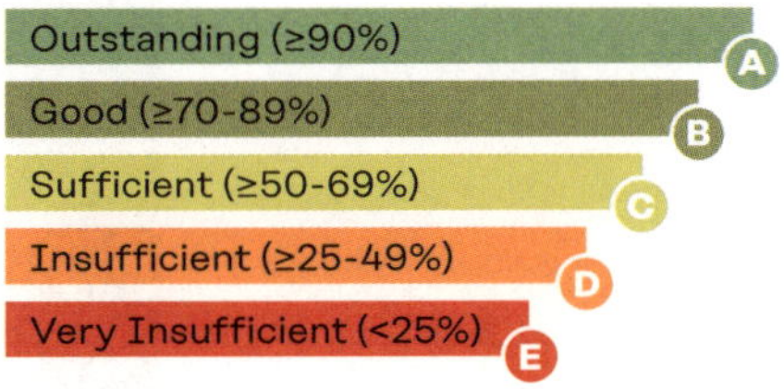

Results by area

the execution of the project and the subsequent urban development of the surface. The Agency was commissioned by this body to carry out a study, applying a system of indicators to analyse and assess Sant Feliu de Llobregat's urban fabrics with a systematic, comprehensive approach.

This report provided a theoretical and instrumental framework for regenerating existing urban fabrics adjacent to where the railway would be moved underground and for the whole city. Through the use of indicators, a quantified, aggregate assessment was made of different aspects of the project's sustainability. The dashboard used was made up of 28 indicators grouped into 6 areas of analysis: urban morphology, sustainable mobility and citizens' rights, liveable public space, urban complexity, green spaces and biodiversity, and social cohesion.

Moving a railway underground can affect the whole municipality, not just the specific area where the works take place. It could be seen as a unique opportunity in a fairly built-up municipality to move towards a sustainable city model based on the principles of ecosystemic urbanism. Therefore, the analysis was not limited to the intervention area; instead, the whole municipality's current situation was analysed to reveal all the ways in which the project could improve the city. To reach a suitable understanding of the existing realities and the opportunities for transformation as part of more sustainable urban planning, the study considered three territorial scales: the underground environment, the residential environment and the urban environment.

Conclusions were drawn from every indicator on the three territorial scales, the situation was represented through maps and graphics, and recommendations for improvement were made for each of the aspects studied. Finally, a score was obtained for

Floor area required to achieve a balance in density between housing and tertiary activities.

RESULTS
RESIDENTIAL URBAN AREA

Determining factors:
1) Achieve an optimal density of 100 dwellings/ha
2) Achieve an optimal density of 25 dwellings/ha
3) Achieve a good balance of uses: 20-40% non-residential uses

UNDERGROUND AREA
Residential floor area: 81,700 m²
Tertiary floor area (commerce and offices): 41,250 m²

SELECTED
CELLS
TRANSFORMATION AREA

Underground Area
100 Residential floor area (new)
100 Tertiary floor area (new)

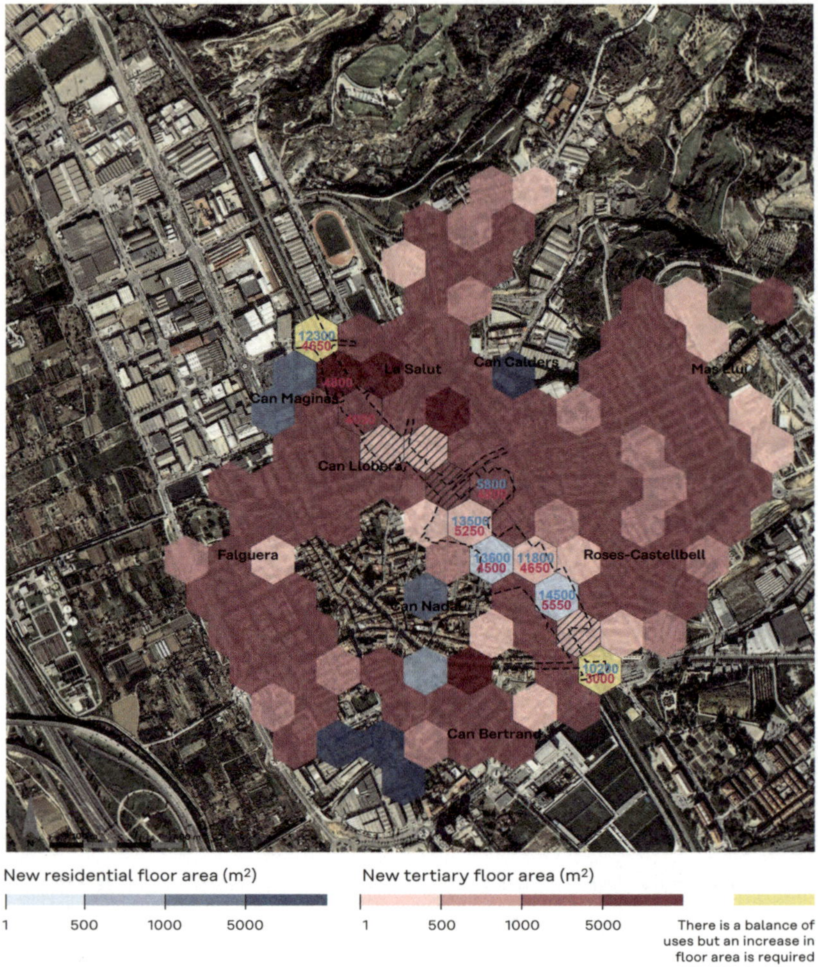

SANT FELIU DE LLOBREGAT. 2019. Analysis and creation of urban indicators.
Example map of indicator calculation (required floor area, deriving from the compactness calculation).
Source: BCNecologia

each indicator, which was then converted to a scale of 1–10, to rate the situation in the residential environment. Sant Feliu de Llobregat's situation is very positive in terms of green space, biodiversity and social cohesion, and satisfactory regarding its urban morphology, urban structure and liveable public space. Meanwhile, it needs to improve in the areas of sustainable mobility, citizens' rights and urban complexity.

Conclusions

The application of indicators to the municipal reality offers a theoretical and instrumental framework for regenerating urban fabrics and conserving the natural environment. Urban ecology adapts urban transformation processes to a more sustainable urban model for the Information Age, the four pillars of which are compactness, urban complexity, metabolic efficiency and social cohesion.

The city is made up of a set of proportions. The system of indicators used can determine its degree of ecosystemic balance on a basis of intentions. Indicators and their use are based on an urban model that promotes a fairer, more cohesive, more functional, more liveable and more balanced city. All in all, they encourage a city model that guarantees its residents' quality of life within a healthy environment. Compliance with each of the principles in the theoretical model can be assessed by creating a system of indicators that quantifies and objectifies the intentions expressed.

On a municipal level, analysis through a dashboard of indicators, accompanied by a demanding theoretical model in terms of sustainability, offers an in-depth diagnosis that helps to identify an area's specific strengths and weaknesses. When working with sustainability policies, municipalities must be aware of where their main shortcomings are and which policies are most effective for improving sustainability in the area, in order to maximise the Administration's efforts. They must also identify which aspects are already a success, so that resources are not wasted on fixing what is working well.

Despite the differences between the municipal projects to which the indicators have been applied, the outcomes show that the methodology used by the Urban Ecology Agency of Barcelona to calculate them constitutes a flexible tool for producing useful results for making decisions in the context of any kind of urban reality.

APPLYING THE SYSTEM OF INDICATORS TO URBAN PROJECTS

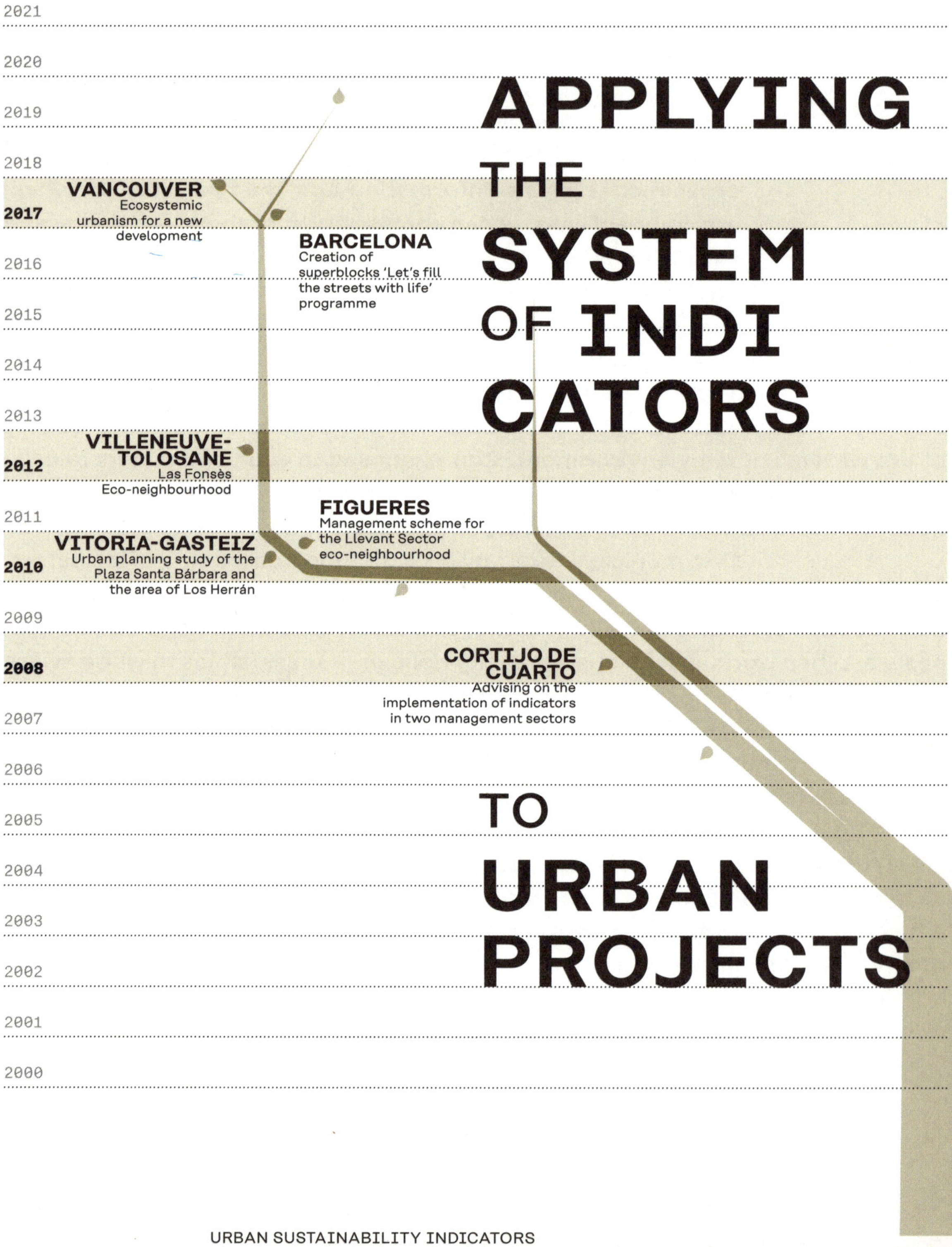

The projects in this chapter cover almost a decade of urban transformations (2010–2017), which have been assessed in terms of ecosystemic urbanism criteria through sustainability indicators.

A wide variety of projects are analysed here, from new, cross-cutting urban developments, like the construction of eco-neighbourhoods in Figueres and Villeneuve-Tolosane (Toulouse, France) or the project for the University of British Columbia-UBC (Vancouver, Canada), to smaller urban renovation projects, like those carried out in Santa Bárbara and Los Herrán (Vitoria-Gasteiz), or even large-scale initiatives on consolidated urban centres, like the superblocks in Barcelona. An ecosystemic urbanism perspective can be adopted on both new urbanisation projects and urban renovations on existing built environments. The superblock phenomenon is a clear example of how much an existing, consolidated urban area's overall sustainability can be improved.

In this case, indicators can assess the state of the urban space before and after its transformation, according to the principles of ecosystemic urbanism. But that is not all they can do. Often, these projects do not only deal with evaluating a specific urban transformation; as well as that, they examine its design as a piece within a greater ecosystemic urbanism puzzle.

For sustainability criteria to be reflected in a completed urban transformation, they must be considered from the very beginning of the design process. In this scenario, indicators can certify to what extent this has been achieved, while taking into account the determining factors in each project: the natural environment and urban fabrics around it, the potential for self-sufficiency, etc. When it comes to tackling sustainability strategies, the project's context is key and heavily influences the path to follow to improve its overall degree of sustainability. It indicates which strategies should be applied and which should be ruled out.

SEVILLE. CORTIJO DE CUARTO. 2008. A strategy for surface planning.
Ecosystemic urbanism is a three-layer planning aproach: underground, surface and roofs.
Source: BCNecologia

SUSTAINABILITY INDICATORS THAT TRANSCEND BORDERS CORTIJO DE CUARTO. SEVILLE

The Cortijo de Cuarto project (located on municipal land belonging to Seville and Dos Hermanas) marked the first time ecosystemic urbanism principles and indicators were applied comprehensively to a new urban development.

In 2008, the Andalusian Public Land Company commissioned the Agency to analyse an urban planning proposal and determine its compatibility with ecosystemic urban criteria, using the system of indicators. The proposal was to create 5,500 new dwellings and develop 1,360,531 m^2 of land, located to the south of the city and adjacent to major territorial infrastructures. The lower part of the development would create a north-south link between natural areas that constitute a large green area, which must be strengthened.

As well as the analysis, an alternative development proposal was presented and assessed with the same system of indicators. The result was a set of measures and lines of action that guaranteed an integrated, systematic urban organisation model for Cortijo de Cuarto. Two comprehensive reports on energy and water cycle management in the area under analysis were also provided.

With this work as a starting point, a comparative study between the two development proposals was carried out, assessing the efficiency of the layouts, urban forms and systems put forward in the context of a compact, complex, integrated city model. The resulting set of recommendations included proposals such as modifying land use and floor area ratio, removing gated communities, integrating service industry space into residential plots, and creating green roofs, as well as spaces for composting and urban allotments.

When the property bubble burst, this urban development plan was aborted.

LLEVANT SECTOR. FIGUERES

When it was launched in 2010, the Llevant Sector project in Figueres aimed to lead the way in the design of eco-neighbourhoods in Catalonia. For the Agency, it constituted an excellent laboratory in which an urban area could be designed in accordance with ecosystemic urbanism criteria. As well as the Agency, architectural offices (Rafael de Cáceres and Lluís Brau) participated in the project, and a book was published through the CAT-MED European project: *El urbanismo ecológico. Su aplicación en el diseño de un ecobarrio en Figueres* (2012, *Ecological Urbanism. Its application in the design of an eco-neighbourhood in Figueres*).[7]

The area in question was located in an urban fabric typical of the periphery,

7 Rueda, Salvador *[et al.]*. *El urbanismo ecológico. Su aplicación en el diseño de un ecobarrio en Figueres. [Ecological Urbanism. Its application in the design of an eco-neighbourhood in Figueres]*. Barcelona: Urban Ecology Agency of Barcelona, 2012.

FIGUERES. 2010.
A strategy for height planning.
Source: BCNecologia

Buildings 4 m
Buildings 7.5 to 11 m
Buildings 14.5 m
Buildings 18 m
Buildings 21.5 m
Buildings 25 m
Buildings 28.5 m

Small crown tree (A1)
Medium crown tree (A2)
Large crown tree (A3)
% of the roof reserved for:
ST = Thermal collection of solar energy / SF = Photo-voltaic collection of solar energy / Uso = Roof's uses

with some existing buildings, but the project would transform it completely. Despite its proximity to the centre of Figueres, the neighbourhood presented the usual symptoms of semi-urban fabrics that have grown with their back to the city, with little or no planning, dictated by its location on the other side of the train tracks, which acted as a barrier. The neighbourhood was close to other urban areas with social marginalisation issues. Therefore, its new design had to ensure it was well integrated, along with its adjacent areas, in a sustainable, balanced way.

The project offered sustainable answers on two scales: it provided solutions to problems specific to the neighbourhood, and it took on city-wide challenges and needs.

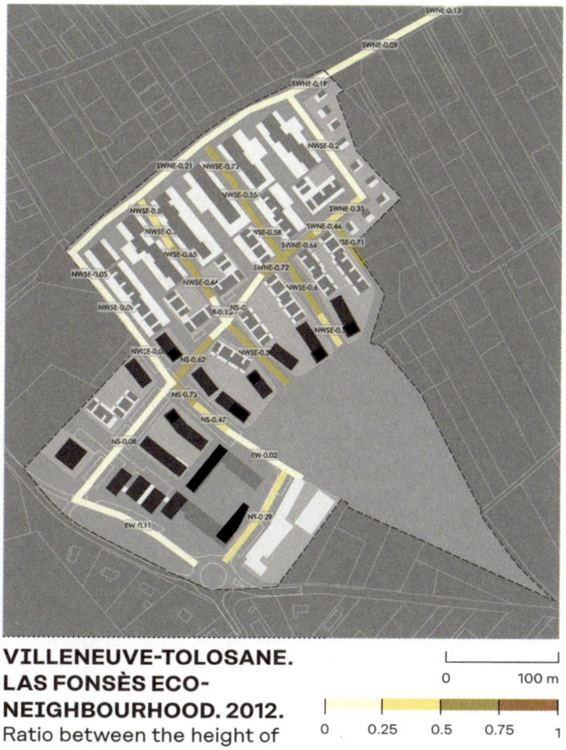

VILLENEUVE-TOLOSANE. LAS FONSÈS ECO-NEIGHBOURHOOD. 2012.
Ratio between the height of the buildings and the distance between the planned facades.
Source: BCNecologia

Furthermore, this study dealt with issues like land use, the importance of public space and mobility organisation in superblocks. It proposed innovative solutions for offering parking space, reducing water and energy consumption, ensuring self-sufficiency with local resources, managing waste more effectively, strengthening the local biodiversity (the neighbourhood is home to a typically Mediterranean watercourse), providing adequate social housing and facilities, following sustainable construction patterns, and promoting social cohesion and territorial balance in terms of activities and services.

LAS FONSÈS. VILLENEUVE-TOLOSANE. FRANCE

The Master Plan for Las Fonsès (Villeneuve-Tolosane) is another eco-neighbourhood project, this time located in the Toulouse metropolitan area, in the town of Villeneuve-Tolosane.

The planned development broadly consisted of a residential area, a commercial centre and an urban park. The total number of dwellings planned was 513, classified into four categories: single-family, multi-family, mixed and cohousing, which were consistent with their surroundings. Social housing was planned to take up 30% of these dwellings.

One of the project's environmental factors was its location next to a system of wetlands designated a Special Protection Area (SPA) for wild birds. The new park was to function as the town's major green public space, thus relieving pressure on the existing natural enclave.

The team that put together the proposal was made up of a group of companies coordinated by Forges Arquitectes and Llop-Jornet-Pastor Arquitectes. BCNecologia took care of the study's environmental elements. The main areas in which the Agency participated were biodiversity; energy, water and waste management; and sustainable public space configuration. The proposal fulfilled 67% of ecosystemic urbanism aims, later reaching 83% with the application of improvements to facilities and energy and water self-sufficiency.

ECOSYSTEMIC URBANISM ON THE UBC CAMPUS. CANADA

The aim of this assessment report was to test the programme for ecosystemic modelling on the University of British Columbia campus (UBC) in Vancouver. Work was carried out on two scales: there was a complete analysis of the whole campus and an assessment of different urban planning alternatives to develop a new area, the Stadium Neighbourhood, on strategic land

VANCOUVER. CANADA. University of British Columbia's campus.
Picture: UBC

that would create a functional connection between different residential areas on the campus.

The UBC's original vision was to develop housing to provide funding for the university: a leader in teaching and research. Almost 12,000 students and 11,000 non-students live on campus.

The UBC sustainability programme, SEEDS, supports academic research projects led by students on the UBC campus in Vancouver, with a view to linking this research to the university's operations and using the campus as a living laboratory for moving forward with its sustainability policies and plans. Thanks to SEEDS, the Urban Ecology Agency of Barcelona worked with a group of recent graduates from the UBC's School of Community and Regional Planning (SCARP) to test and assess the merits of the university's Ecosystem Programme and to inform and guide the development of community plans, thus improving environmental, economic and social well-being at UBC and in Canada more generally.

Traditionally, the Agency's set of indicators is designed for a Mediterranean context characterised by a compact, diverse urban model, but a preliminary study showed that it also suited a modern Canadian environment.

RENOVATION PROJECTS SANTA BÁRBARA AND LOS HERRÁN

While other, previously mentioned projects were being carried out in the municipality of Vitoria-Gasteiz, work on the Santa Bárbara and Los Herrán areas of the city offered the opportunity to examine the ecosystemic urbanism strategies being used on the municipality as a whole on a smaller scale. BCNecologia's indicators were a useful tool for assessing the impact of the small yet significant urban transfor-

BASE SITUATION

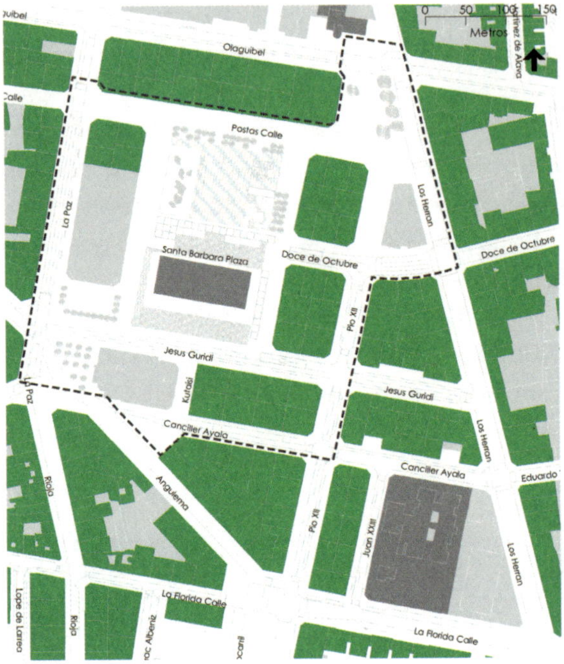

PROPOSAL

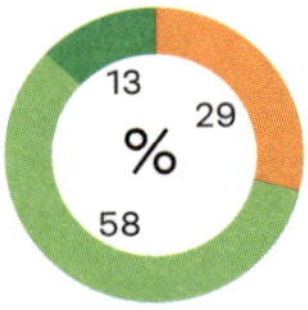

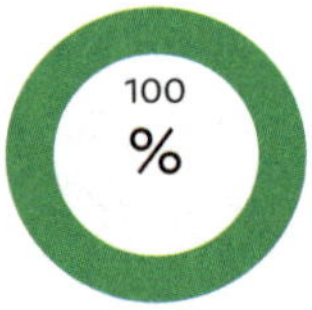

Number of types of facilities with simultaneous proximity

- 1
- 2
- 3
- 4
- Nearby public facilities

Simultaneous proximity to facilities
Minimum target: Three different types at 300 metres for 100% of the population.

Base situation: **71%** population of the superblock
Proposal: **100%** population of the superblock

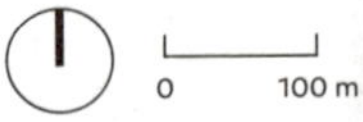

VITORIA-GASTEIZ. PLAZA SANTA BÁRBARA. 2010.
Simultaneous proximity to basic facilities according to walking distances.
Source: BCNecologia

mations carried out in these two areas as part of this model, in accordance with the Vitoria-Gasteiz Urban Sustainability Indicators Plan, which had just been written up by the Agency.

In the case of Santa Bárbara, the square of the same name and Plaza de Abastos were to be renovated, in an attempt to reclaim the public space, make it uniform and valuable for residents, and extend the transformation to the roads that converged in this area. As well as interacting with their immediate environment, these squares worked as transition spaces between the medieval old town and the wider city's fabrics, thus holding the power to exert a positive influence on day-to-day life in these areas.

The proposal assessment highlighted substantial improvements in terms of the liveability of the public space and energy efficiency. Mobility in the area also improved, thanks to the superblock system.

In the Los Herrán project, the aim was to provide a description and a basic assessment of the base situation and a development proposal for the area around this road, in the vicinity of Vitoria-Gasteiz bus station.

The planning proposal sought a new sense of centrality by converting the bus station into an indoor market. The most significant modification in the plan involved reducing the amount of public space and land for facilities to use it for public housing, within an ambitious social housing acquirement strategy being applied in the municipality – the first of its kind in any Spanish regional capital. It also aimed to renovate the existing boulevard and enact changes to mobility flows.

The proposal was evaluated according to the following criteria: land use, public space and liveability, mobility, complexity, green spaces and biodiversity, urban metabolism and social cohesion. An analysis using the Agency's indicators showed that applying the proposal would improve sustainability levels considerably from 64.9% to 82.6%, especially in aspects relating to urban metabolism (water and energy).

BARCELONA'S SUPERBLOCKS

The 2015–2019 municipal term saw the beginning of a new boost to the superblock model in Barcelona. In May 2016, the Full Municipal Council Meeting approved the creation of superblocks in the city, and the Council launched the 'Let's fill the streets with life' programme. This initiative was part of the management shift needed to adapt the city, in line with new environmental challenges and opportunities to improve its residents' quality of life.

The superblock project is the strategy that has been chosen to fill Barcelona's streets with life again: streets that must be responsible for bringing vitality to the urban layout, creating opportunities to spread greenery and facilitating harmonious

BARCELONA. 2018. Superblock in El Poblenou neighbourhood.
Picture: BCNecologia

co-existence among residents of all ages and origins.

One of the goals of the programme is to monitor all urban development initiatives, whether tactical or organisational, through regular assessment of the improvements they achieve, both in their early implementation stages and as they evolve over time.

This project therefore establishes the methodological framework for calculating the selected indicators in order to monitor and assess the process of creating superblocks in the city. The indicators were defined by consensus within the working groups that took place during the superblock execution and public participation process.

Conclusions

Through the use of a system of indicators to assess the design of new urban developments and the regeneration of existing structures, an optimal working environment has been created for the experimentation involved in ecosystemic urbanism, which includes innovative proposals, some of which are instrumental.

The application of ecosystemic urbanism to urban projects requires solutions that break away from the most traditional forms of urbanism. Cross-disciplinary planning, new management and governance instruments and development on three levels to make the most of underground space and roofs (to harvest rainwater, build green roofs or install seasonal thermal energy storage) are just some ideas to incorporate when putting together more sustainable urban development projects.

The context of the project has also been analysed in great detail. Pre-existing conditions and the desired outcome have been taken into account to deal with the most problematic aspects of each urban fabric and strengthen the most positive elements. In each case, it is important to assess the shortcomings of nearby urban fabrics (for example, their services or facilities) and the opportunities presented to build optimal strategies for the urban area as a whole (stitching together urban fabrics, connecting green spaces, etc.).

The methodology, designed by a large team of specialists, has created a dynamic working environment, separating every aspect of the project in a feedback process that incorporates the criteria and aims behind the indicators. The result is a comprehensive project that, to be executed, requires participation from all of those involved in the urban planning process (developer and construction companies, politicians, technicians, etc.) and from the public (by adopting new, more sustainable lifestyles). Only this way can fully functional, self-sufficient, economically viable eco-neighbourhoods be built.

All in all, the Agency team has learned a huge amount from these types of project. They have taken away the obstacles to designing innovative proposals and moving forward towards new, more flexible scenarios in order to deal with future challenges, one of which is sustainability in the Information Age.

AUTOMATION TOOLS

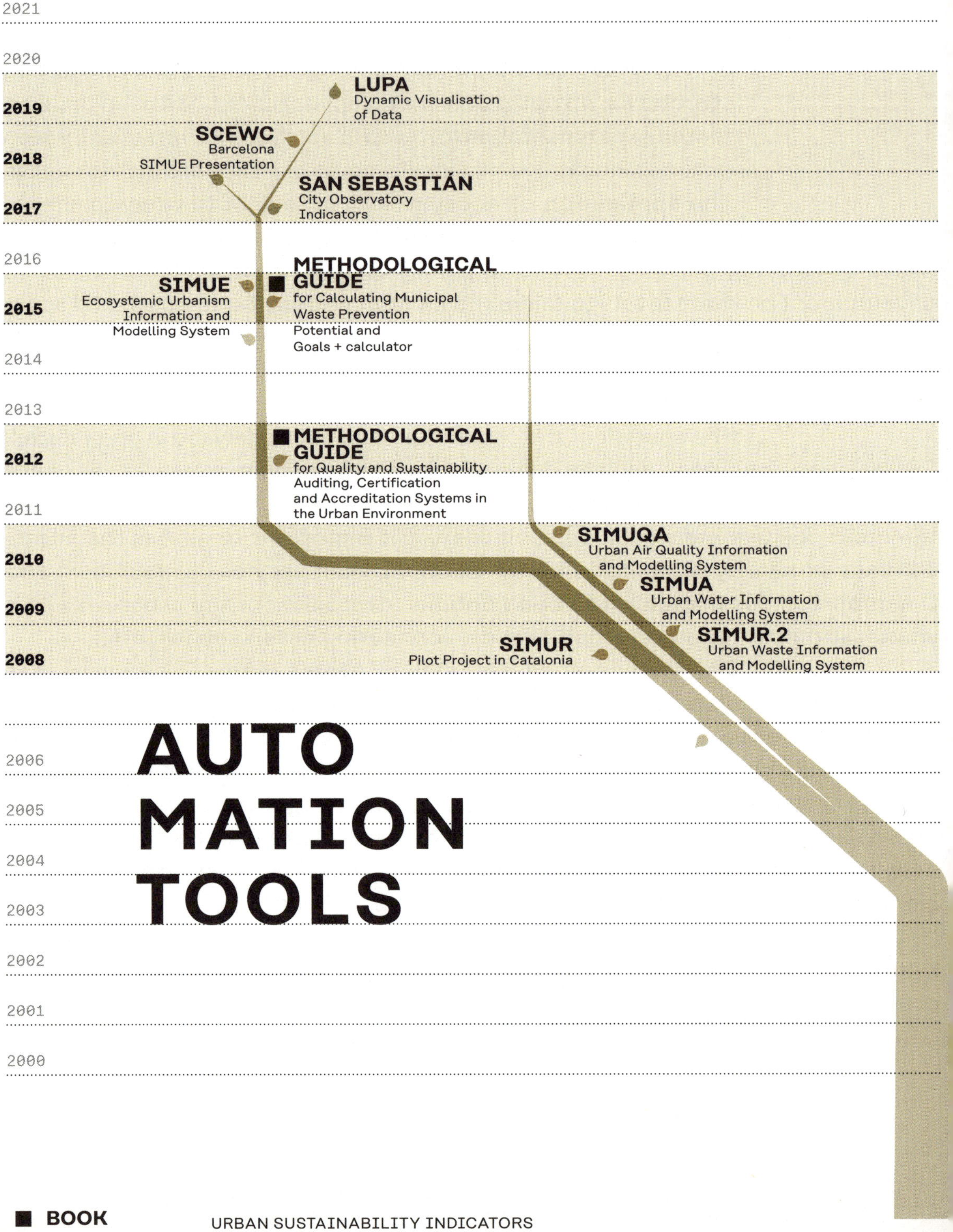

In the scientific sphere, the Agency's main contribution has been its adaptation of applied mathematics models from information theory – used by ecologist Ramon Margalef in his examinations of animal and plant communities – to the study of urban diversity and its location, and of metabolic flows of matter and energy in the urban environment. This translation has materialised as the systematisation of a set of urban indicators that allow these concepts to be applied to the built environment, thus making it easier to analyse.

To offer graphic explanations of a comparable quality to Margalef's proposals, the Agency has developed its activity in line with a series of constantly evolving representation systems. These tools are based on geographic information systems (GIS), but they are not limited to standardised solutions. On many occasions, the Agency has had to create and automate its own calculation and representation tools.

At BCNecologia, the urban phenomenon is studied using a set of urban indicators, which are calculated to give accurate, interconnected information on the different aspects that influence cities' sustainability. With every new commission, the Agency reconfigures this system of indicators and creates its own tools that make the calculation process more agile and automate the processing of results using databases.

The most direct influence on the Agency's representation methodology is undoubtedly *Urban Atlas: 20 American Cities* (1966),[8] intended to offer 'visual systems of programming information for metropolitan-scale design'. Its data visualisation is based on the standardisation of the whole map, with a standard cell size that stores multiple basic statistical information variables for each territorial unit.

Over the years, the Agency has combined its renewal and creation of tools to manage big data with the adoption of open source languages and methodologies. In this area, Python has become a highly flexible and widely used tool for collaborative work.

8 Wurman, R. S.; Passonneau, J. R. *Urban Atlas: 20 American Cities*. Cambridge: MIT Press, 1966.

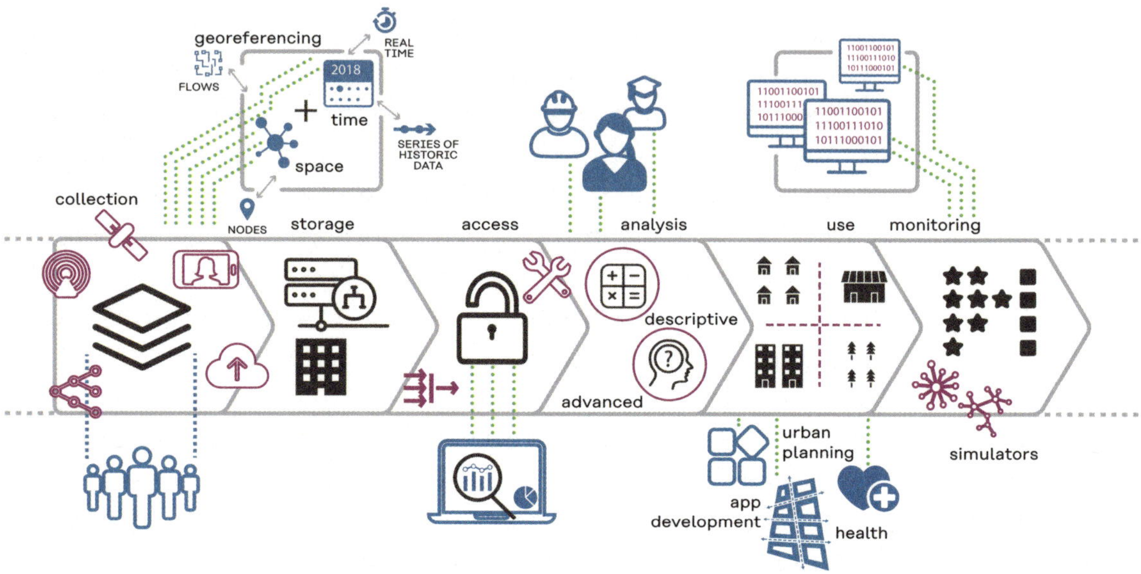

SAN SEBASTIÁN. 2017. Data life cycle for the Observatory project.
Source: BCNecologia

CARTOGRAPHIC REPRESENTATION: DATA CELLS

The Urban Ecology Agency of Barcelona's studies of the urban fabric are set in a physical context that depends on human beings' ability to move. This environment is defined within the limits of the neighbourhood, which, by definition, is the ecosystem where citizens move most efficiently and where the use of exogenous energy is minimised.

From the theories developed by BCNecologia, the superblock emerges as the minimum urban unit where a person can fulfil most of their daily needs in their immediate environment. The dimensions of this model fluctuate between 300x300 m and 500x500 m.

In the Agency's representation of a 200x200 m grid cell, the best way of representing the information from this minimum urban cell is a colour gradation for the different variables involved in urban sustainability indicators. For this reason, this type of graphic, combined with basic cartography, has been the leading system throughout the Agency's years of cartographic production.

Automating these processes can save time and increase efficiency. What is more, having been freed from the repetitive (and to some extent, manual) task of calculating indicators, team members can use the time saved to attempt to improve the proposed solutions. This can be achieved by iterating calculation processes until an optimal result is achieved for the goal set. These goals are achieved either through the programming of tools designed to be specific applications for final indicator calculation – as is the case for SIMUE, SIMUR and LUPA – or through

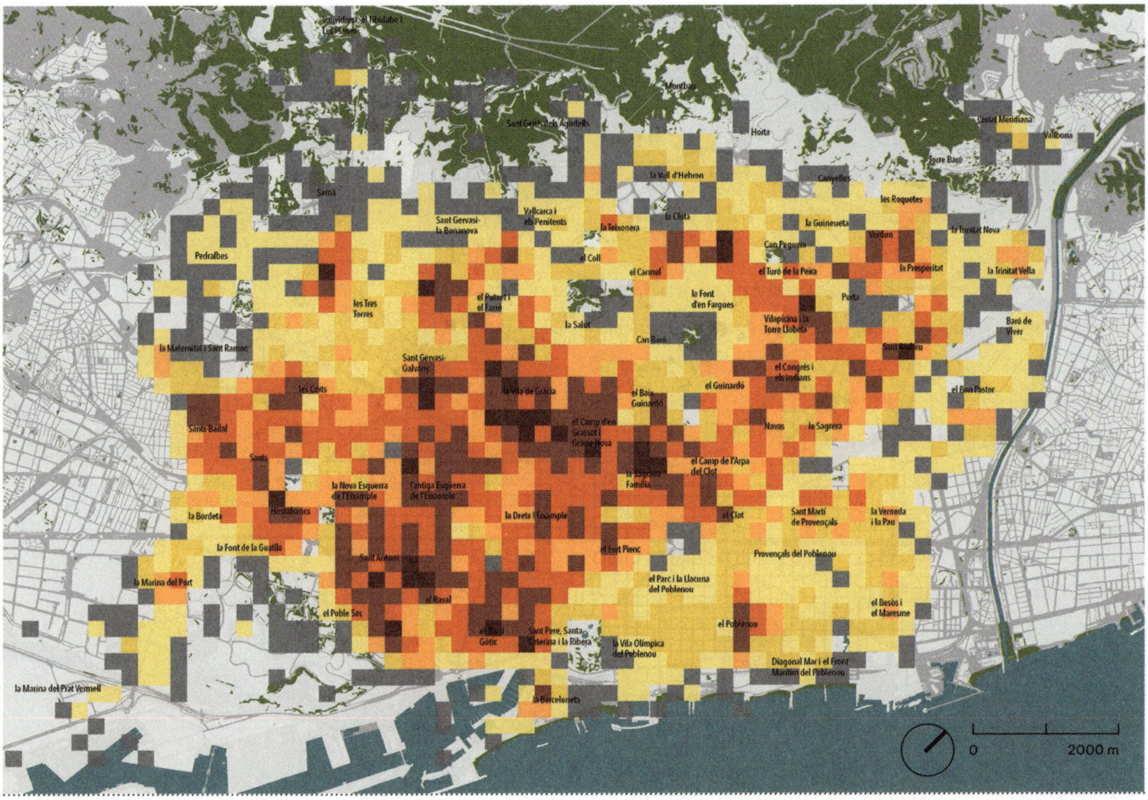

BARCELONA. Urban diversity index.
Source: BCNecologia

2 4 5 5,5 6 6,5
information bits

the generation of short programming code *scripts* that have a specific purpose according to the characteristics and requirements of the project in question.

NEW TOOLS

Studying and analysing the different areas and activities of the world around us (the urban cycle of materials and water, urban mobility, air quality, etc.) from the perspective of scientific methodology is a complex task. Difficulties can arise when obtaining series of historic data or continuously monitoring certain variables, as they are conditioned by the multiple, diverse interrelations between them. BCNecologia has constructed analytical models as an alternative for studying these fields and incorporating new simulators into its work methodology.

The Agency has thought up and developed new tools to answer questions about a complex reality or system, making it more understandable and its behaviour easier to study. These systems include:

- SIMUR (Urban Waste Information and Modelling System)
- SIMUA (Urban Water Information and Modelling System)
- SIMUQA (Urban Air Quality Information and Modelling System)
- SIMUE (Ecosystemic Urbanism Information and Modelling System)

BCNecologia has also implemented new instruments to accompany urban strategy projects, such as the Barcelona Sports Facilities Plan (2008), the CO_2 Emissions Calculator (2010), the Methodological Guide and Urban Waste Prevention Calculator (2015) and LUPA (2020). The main simulators are detailed in the following paragraphs.

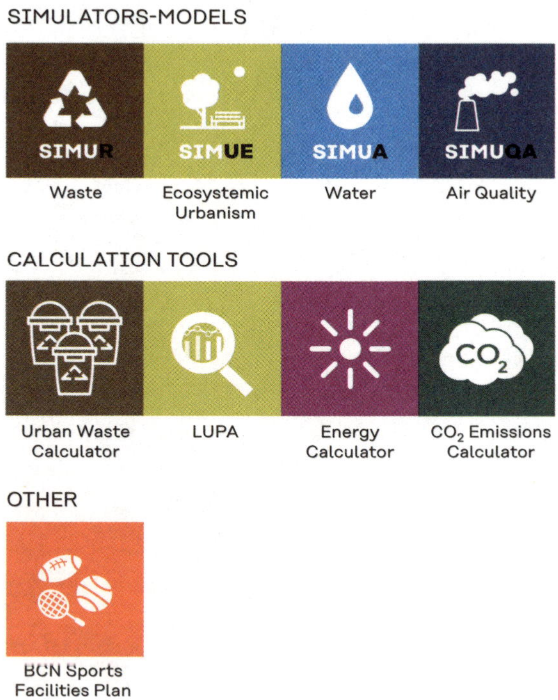

Main tools developed by BCNecologia

ENVIRONMENTAL TOOLS

SIMUR

SIMUR (Urban Waste Information and Modelling System) stemmed from the environmental impact calculation methodologies in the 1996 Metropolitan Waste Programme, which offered an analysis of the life cycle of materials using a matrix of indicators designed to build a methodology applicable to any inventory system.

SIMUR can evaluate a current management model using real data and identify management changes that could be made, as well as assessing the potential results. This way, it can assess hypothetical management scenarios, incorporate standard data and design a future management model that takes all possible environmental advantages into account.

Its main applications include generating an exhaustive analysis of the results of a waste management system in terms of mass balance, energy balance and environmental impacts; calculating indicators like the gross and net amounts of sorted waste, materials recovered, energy efficiency, greenhouse gas emissions, etc.; monitoring any changes in the collection system; comparing different management systems, thanks to a common analysis language and methodology; and checking for progress towards the goals set in the applicable waste management programmes or proposed during the design of the management model.

SIMUA

In recent years, the Urban Ecology Agency of Barcelona has created sustainable solutions for water cycle management in urban development projects, as well as alternative solutions to transferring water from the Ebre River. A result of this work has been the creation of a bank of knowledge and experience in a wide spectrum of situations, enriched with research that has led to the development of mathematical and IT tools. The systematisation and organisation of this mass of knowledge is the main goal and purpose of the Urban Water Information and Modelling System (SIMUA).

SIMUA is a suite of applications designed to offer solutions to the variety of tasks involved in optimising water management and adapting to climate change in a current or future scenario.

Its main goal is to achieve a water management model oriented towards sustainable urban systems and water self-sufficiency, through water saving, reuse, reclamation and the integration of water of different qualities and origins, while maintaining viability in terms of construction and finances. It also aims to estimate an area's water sustainability index and design systems to bioregenerate polluted waters and improve natural water.

SIMUQA

SIMUQA (Urban Air Quality Information and Modelling System), meanwhile, is a computer application that provides information on air quality. It is based on three basic pillars: a mesoscale meteorological model, an emissions model with a high resolution in space and time, and a chemical transport model. The program defines an area's quality with a temporal resolution of 1 h and a spatial resolution of 1 km^2.

Furthermore, scenarios can be personalised with a view to improving air quality in the area being studied, adjusting the characteristics of the pollution emissions by sector, and even examining specific episodes of high pollution in detail.

SIMUE. Ecosystemic Urbanism Information and Modelling System.
Source: BCNecologia

URBAN REGENERATION TOOLS

SIMUE

SIMUE (Ecosystemic Urbanism Information and Modelling System) analyses how much an urban fabric – an existing city or a new urban development – resembles a reference sustainable city model designed with ecosystemic urbanism goals in mind.

Ecosystemic urbanism is built on four fundamental pillars: compactness, complexity, urban efficiency and social cohesion. In terms of an integrated methodology, these pillars represent a new way of seeing the city and its intrinsic functions.

Created in 2015 and presented during the Smart City Expo World Congress (SCEWC) in Barcelona in 2018, the SIMUE project is a tool developed from a powerful geographic information system that calculates large volumes of data, displays them in an attractive and easily understandable way, and assesses the geospatial indicators that make up the Ecosystemic Urbanism Certificate automatically and efficiently.[9]

In short, this application aims to turn information into knowledge. The main challenge faced when working with urban data is the scattered nature of sources and storage, as they are decentralised across

9 Rueda. *Methodological Guide for Quality and Sustainability Auditing, Certification and Accreditation Systems in the Urban Environment. Op. cit.*

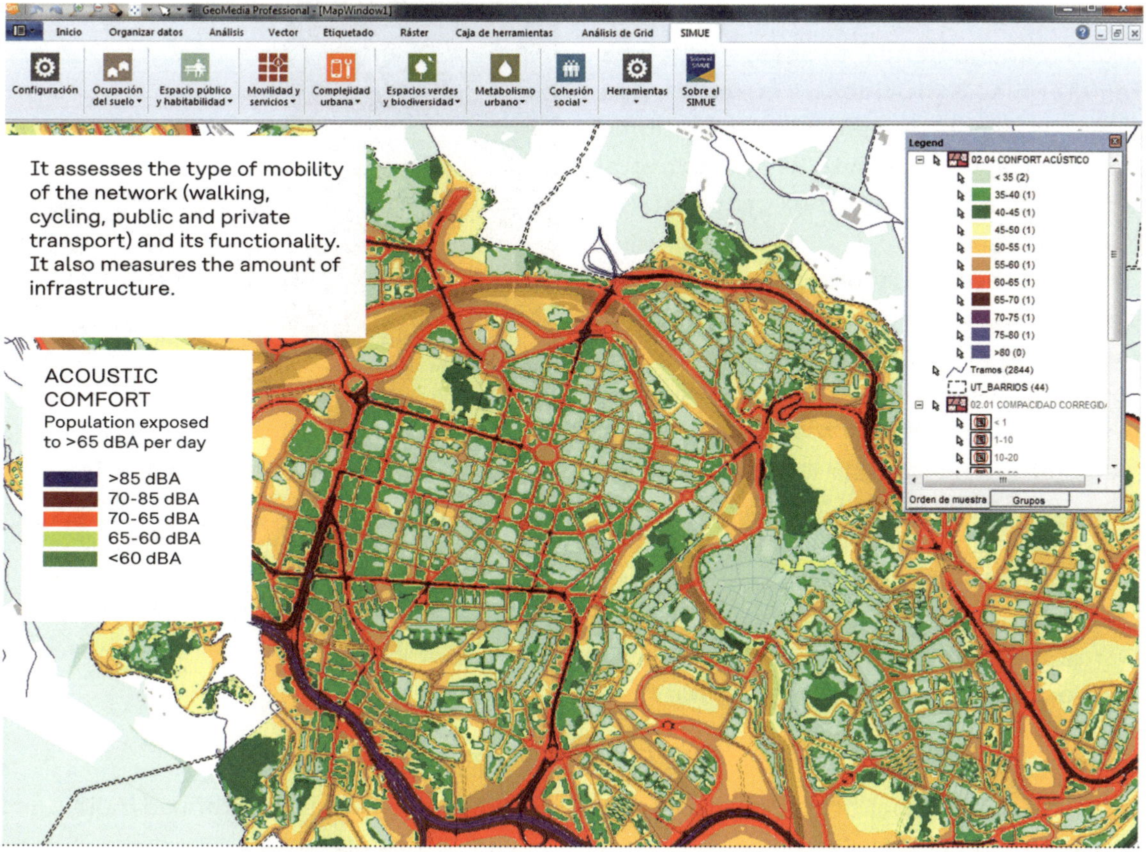

SIMUE. Acoustic comfort calculation.
Source: BCNecologia

various municipal departments. This situation makes it much more difficult to integrate data into an overall knowledge management methodology. SIMUE is designed to integrate these databases into a single environment, where they can be processed to obtain information with added value. Through verified, consistent indicators, logics and methods, it contributes towards building a more sustainable city model.

This cutting-edge instrument makes it easier for users – working in the fields of spatial planning, urbanism, politics or urban management – to assess urban parameters, as it provides an in-depth, geographically contextualised examination of the city. They can use it to formulate overall strategies or put together proposals for specific areas.

In the field of urban studies, everyone agrees that the city as a system is calling more and more for its functional structures to be renewed, with a view to building a more sustainable city model and, at the same time, a knowledge city model. This is why the goal envisioned by the Agency is to improve land organisation and the potential for information exchange, while reducing the consumption of local resources. In other words, the ultimate aim is to make the urban environment as efficient as possible.

LUPA. Tool for dynamic visualisation of data and indicators. It can display up to 100 variables and carry out a multiple-criteria analysis to search for areas that fit the criteria established by the user (ranges of values, minimum value, maximum value, etc.).
Source: BCNecologia

LUPA

LUPA is a tool prototype developed by the Urban Ecology Agency of Barcelona over the last few years for viewing and exploring primary urban data and indicators in real time. This application and SIMUE are interconnected.

With this tool, the user can consult spatial data by defining a circular or rectangular geometric observation field, called the service area. The service area varies according to the distances reachable by various methods of urban transport, whether active (walking or cycling) or motorised (public and private transport).

The observation field moves with the cursor, so the data is updated as the person moves across the map, in accordance with the urban parameters applicable to the area encompassed by the selected geometric shape.

LUPA can scan and analyse over one hundred variables and indicators and display them graphically, using the system's databases.

Conclusions

The Urban Ecology Agency of Barcelona's work in data representation and indicator calculation is constantly being reviewed and integrating new concepts and methodologies.

As part of this process, a variety of tools – both software and devices – have been incorporated into the Agency's assets as they have become available, improving and creating new spaces for opportunity.

Nowadays, users of virtual platforms are generating more and more information more frequently with every move they make. This has opened up an unprecedented opportunity for data analysis.

The latest additions to the Agency's study tools are data mining methodologies, the product of which is then analysed with open source software.

The open source concept has led to the constant and collaborative evolution of analytical ICT tools, including both their source code and their analysis methodologies, thus creating a collective shared knowledge movement that is undoubtedly accelerating the world's ability to grasp the complex phenomena happening around us.

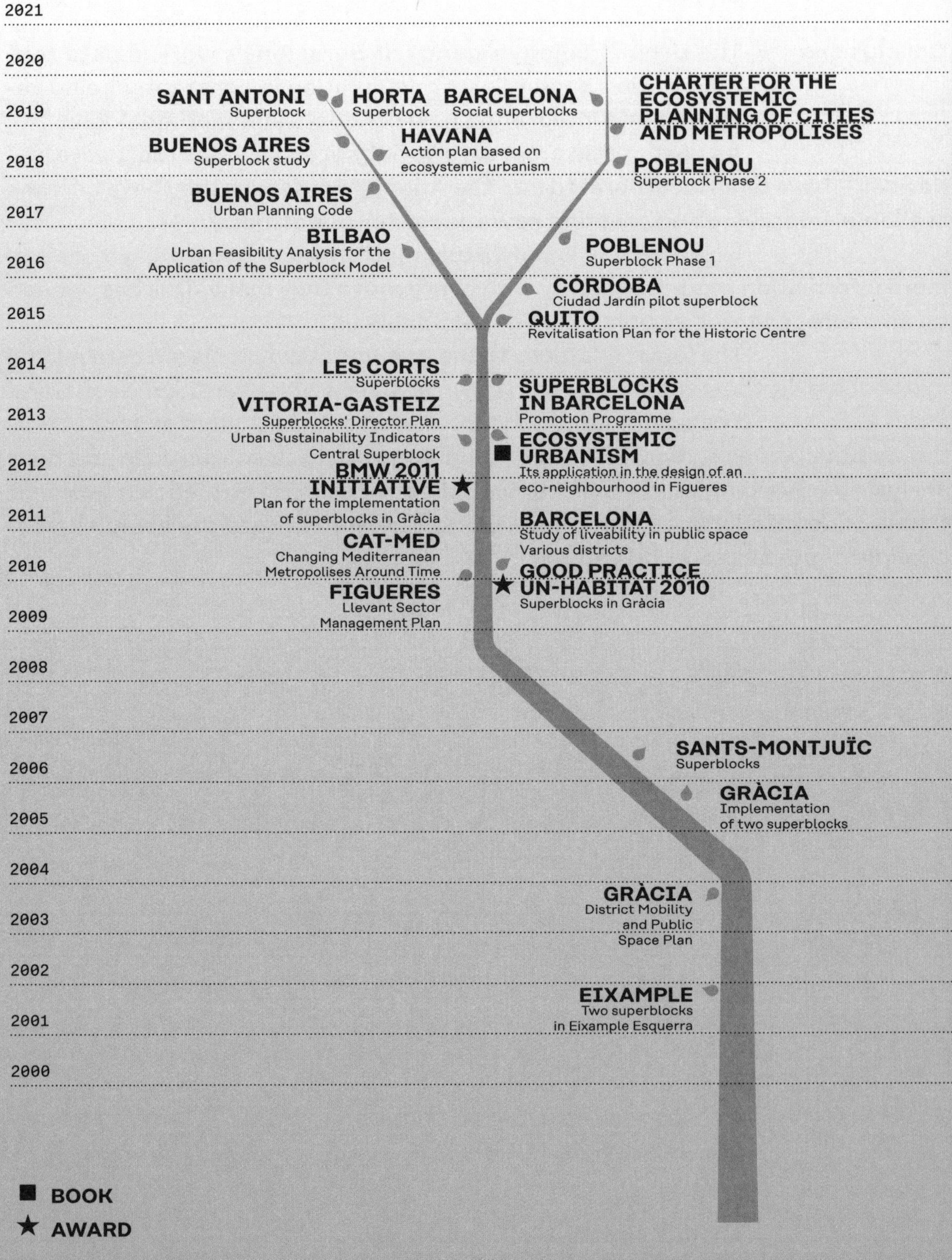
2021
2020
2019
2018
2017
2016
2015
2014
2013
2012
2011
2010
2009
2008
2007
2006
2005
2004
2003
2002
2001
2000
SANT ANTONI
Superblock
HORTA
Superblock
BARCELONA
Social superblocks
CHARTER FOR THE ECOSYSTEMIC PLANNING OF CITIES AND METROPOLISES
BUENOS AIRES
Superblock study
HAVANA
Action plan based on ecosystemic urbanism
POBLENOU
Superblock Phase 2
BUENOS AIRES
Urban Planning Code
BILBAO
Urban Feasibility Analysis for the Application of the Superblock Model
POBLENOU
Superblock Phase 1
CÓRDOBA
Ciudad Jardín pilot superblock
QUITO
Revitalisation Plan for the Historic Centre
LES CORTS
Superblocks
SUPERBLOCKS IN BARCELONA
Promotion Programme
VITORIA-GASTEIZ
Superblocks' Director Plan
Urban Sustainability Indicators
Central Superblock
ECOSYSTEMIC URBANISM
Its application in the design of an eco-neighbourhood in Figueres
BMW 2011 INITIATIVE
Plan for the implementation of superblocks in Gràcia
BARCELONA
Study of liveability in public space
Various districts
CAT-MED
Changing Mediterranean Metropolises Around Time
GOOD PRACTICE UN-HABITAT 2010
Superblocks in Gràcia
FIGUERES
Llevant Sector Management Plan
SANTS-MONTJUÏC
Superblocks
GRÀCIA
Implementation of two superblocks
GRÀCIA
District Mobility and Public Space Plan
EIXAMPLE
Two superblocks in Eixample Esquerra
BOOK
AWARD

URBAN REGENERATION STRATEGIES

The Agency has long been a think tank for redesigning urban areas with sustainability and knowledge city principles in mind. The application of innovative criteria as part of an ecosystemic urbanism approach to both new developments and regeneration projects has always been at the heart of its work.

Another fundamental influence on the Agency's expertise has been the opportunity to experiment with proposals and initiatives in pilot research areas. With open regulations and parameters – subject to fulfilling goals to achieve a more sustainable city model – and collaboration from technical and political teams, new forms of urban management and functionality have been outlined and trialled on buildings and in public spaces in Barcelona's urban fabrics and all over the world.

This area includes the most relevant projects linked to urban regeneration and revitalisation. The superblock model, based on ecosystemic urbanism, has been applied to different urban environments and realities (Barcelona, Vitoria-Gasteiz, Buenos Aires, Vancouver, etc.) to improve cities and their residents' quality of life.

The first chapter focuses on Barcelona and describes the experience of implementing the superblock model in different neighbourhoods to create a local, community-based urbanism model.

The second and third chapters look at projects elsewhere in Spain and beyond. The three Basque cities mentioned here, especially Vitoria-Gasteiz, entrusted the Agency with the task of changing their urban fabric and putting together urban regeneration strategies to reduce social and territorial inequalities. The Agency's international projects (Quito, Havana, Buenos Aires, among others), meanwhile, have been an enriching experience, in terms of both exchanging experiences and solving problems to create more liveable, more self-sufficient and, ultimately, more organised cities.

Finally, the concept of urban liveability is explored, with an emphasis on the social superblock project: the first initiative to seek ways of improving social cohesion through Home Care Services (SAD).

2000 | 2001 | 2002 | 2003 | 2004 | 2005 | 2006 | 2007 | 2008 | 20

KEY MILESTONES

Studies
ORTHOGONAL NETWORK

RIO + 10 Johannesburg
World Summit on Sustainable Development

AGENDA 21 BARCELONA
Citizen Engagement with Sustainability

Universal
FORUM
of Cultures

WHO
Recommended limits for health-harmful concentrations of key air pollutants

DECREE 226/2006
Special Atmospheric ProtectionZones

CREAL
Study on annual deaths due to air pollution in the AMB

URBAN REGENERATION STRATEGIES

EIXAMPLE
Two superblocks in Esquerra de l'Eixample

GRÀCIA
Implementation of two superblocks

SANTS-MONTJUÏC
Superblocks

SAN SEBASTIÁN
Strategy on Sustainability

■ **BARCELONA, A COMPACT AND COMPLEX MEDITERRANEAN CITY**
A more sustainable vision for the future

BARCELONA
Study of liveability in public space Various districts

■ **BOOK**
★ **AWARD**

2000 | 2001 | 2002 | 2003 | 2004 | 2005 | 2006 | 2007 | 2008 | 20

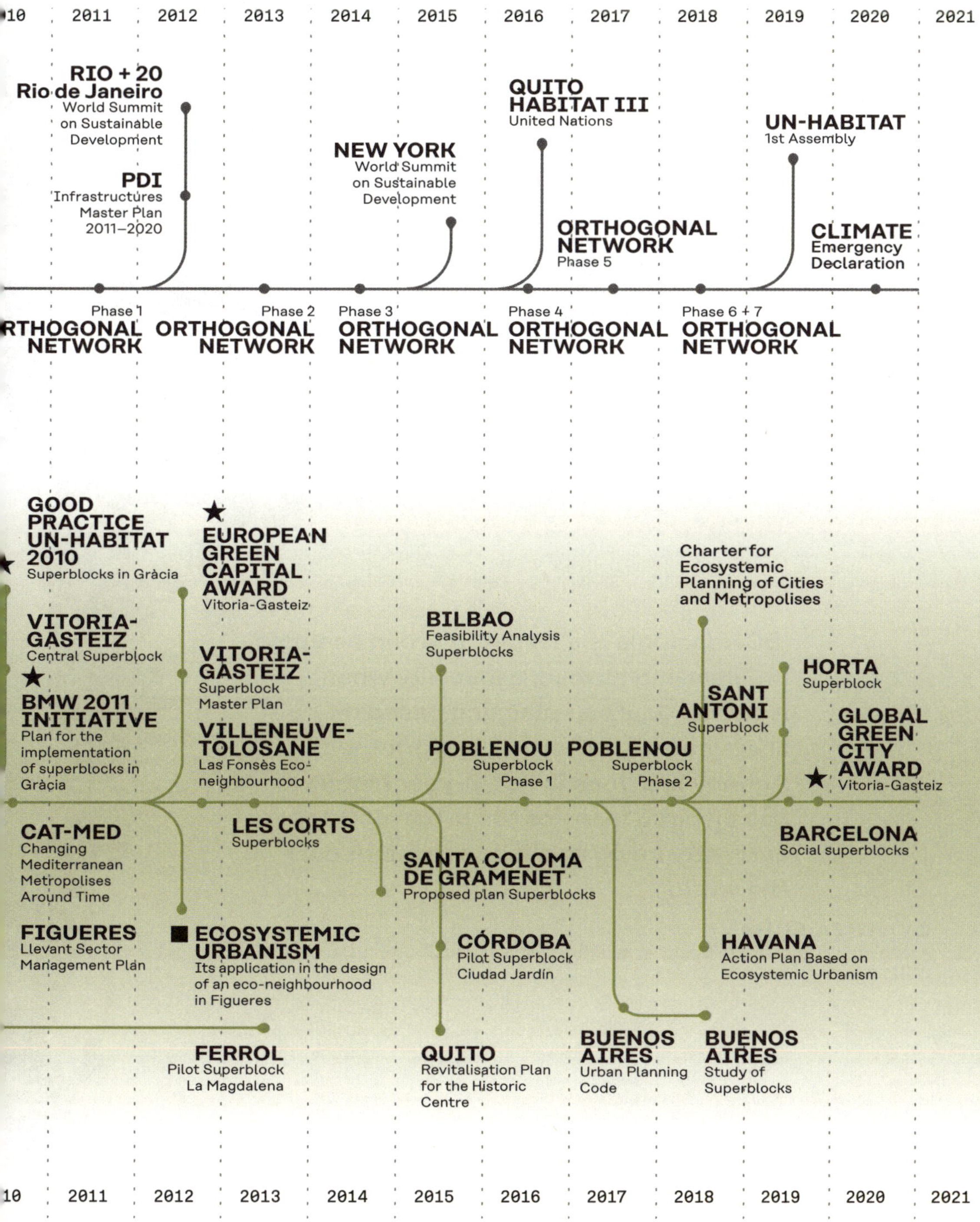
10
2011
2012
2013
2014
2015
2016
2017
2018
2019
2020
2021
RIO + 20
Rio de Janeiro
World Summit on Sustainable Development
PDI
Infrastructures Master Plan 2011–2020
NEW YORK
World Summit on Sustainable Development
QUITO
HABITAT III
United Nations
ORTHOGONAL NETWORK
Phase 5
UN-HABITAT
1st Assembly
CLIMATE
Emergency Declaration
Phase 1
RTHOGONAL NETWORK
Phase 2
ORTHOGONAL NETWORK
Phase 3
ORTHOGONAL NETWORK
Phase 4
ORTHOGONAL NETWORK
Phase 6 + 7
ORTHOGONAL NETWORK
GOOD PRACTICE UN-HABITAT 2010
Superblocks in Gràcia
EUROPEAN GREEN CAPITAL AWARD
Vitoria-Gasteiz
Charter for Ecosystemic Planning of Cities and Metropolises
VITORIA-GASTEIZ
Central Superblock
BILBAO
Feasibility Analysis Superblocks
VITORIA-GASTEIZ
Superblock Master Plan
HORTA
Superblock
BMW 2011 INITIATIVE
Plan for the implementation of superblocks in Gràcia
SANT ANTONI
Superblock
GLOBAL GREEN CITY AWARD
Vitoria-Gasteiz
VILLENEUVE-TOLOSANE
Las Fonsès Eco-neighbourhood
POBLENOU
Superblock Phase 1
POBLENOU
Superblock Phase 2
CAT-MED
Changing Mediterranean Metropolises Around Time
LES CORTS
Superblocks
BARCELONA
Social superblocks
SANTA COLOMA DE GRAMENET
Proposed plan Superblocks
FIGUERES
Llevant Sector Management Plan
ECOSYSTEMIC URBANISM
Its application in the design of an eco-neighbourhood in Figueres
CÓRDOBA
Pilot Superblock Ciudad Jardín
HAVANA
Action Plan Based on Ecosystemic Urbanism
FERROL
Pilot Superblock La Magdalena
QUITO
Revitalisation Plan for the Historic Centre
BUENOS AIRES
Urban Planning Code
BUENOS AIRES
Study of Superblocks
10
2011
2012
2013
2014
2015
2016
2017
2018
2019
2020
2021

'BCNecologia is a leader in urban ecology in Spain and abroad, especially when it comes to urban planning based on sustainability criteria. The work the Agency has done in its 20-year history has inspired many of the urban policies currently being applied to cities all over the world'.

CYNTHIA ECHAVE
Architect. Head of Urban Planning and Public Space Unit 2006–2020. BCNecologia.

Picture: Marta Torrent

BARCELONA'S SUPERBLOCKS: THE BASIC UNIT OF ECOSYSTEMIC URBANISM

2021	
2020	
2019	**SANT ANTONI** Superblock **HORTA** Superblock
2018	**POBLENOU** Superblock second phase
2017	
2016	**POBLENOU** Superblock first phase
2015	
2014	**BARCELONA'S SUPERBLOCKS:** Promotion Programme
2013	**LES CORTS** Superblock
2012	
2011	
2010	
2009	**BARCELONA** Study of liveability in public space Various districts
2008	
2007	
2006	**SANTS-MONTJUÏC** Superblocks
2005	**GRÀCIA** Implementation of two superblocks
2004	
2003	**GRÀCIA** Gràcia District Mobility and Public Space Plan
2002	
2001	
2000	

The superblock urban model was developed in Barcelona, and much of its conceptual basis is closely linked to the successful aspects of its application to the city and the lessons learnt from it. The link between Barcelona and superblocks is therefore clear and takes on special meaning within the Urban Ecology Agency of Barcelona's trajectory.

Current limitations have created a need to formulate a new kind of urbanism, based on ecological criteria, with a broader focus that deals with key issues to tackle the problems generated by urban systems. These problems include loss of biodiversity, increased CO_2 emissions, high concentrations of particulate matter and nitrogen dioxide in the air, dependency on external energy sources, intensive use of private vehicles and the urban heat island effect. Ecosystemic urbanism establishes a new theoretical and instrumental framework for designing new developments and, above all, regenerating existing ones.

This chapter aims to summarise the history of superblocks in the city of Barcelona and how they went from a theoretical structure to implementation as part of pilot projects in some of the city's neighbourhoods, like Vila de Gràcia (included in the Gràcia District Mobility and Public Space Plan, drawn up by BCNecologia).

Since then, other districts in the city have analysed the possibility of introducing this model in their neighbourhoods, inspiring the subsequent creation of superblock programmes linked to the Barcelona Sustainable Urban Mobility Plan: 'Promoting superblocks' and 'Let's fill the streets with life' (ongoing). The latter programme's great impact has led to the superblock concept being integrated into the municipality's strategy.

Superblocks are part of the Agency's DNA. Developing this model through projects has enriched the criteria and parameters that define ecosystemic urbanism and that structure preliminary considerations in different methods of qualitative and quantitative analysis and assessment.

PILOT SUPERBLOCKS

Barcelona is one of the most iconic cases of the application of the superblock model, especially in terms of mobility and public space. The Agency, in its role as the main institution promoting an urban model based on superblocks as the basic unit of public space organisation, has developed various solutions and strategies relating to energy, biodiversity, water and waste management, and social cohesion.

FIRST PHASE: SUPERBLOCKS IN VILA DE GRÀCIA

The history of superblocks in Barcelona up to the present day can be split into three phases, the first of which is linked to the early calming measures in the city and the Gràcia District Mobility and Public Space Plan of 2003. In this period, significant efforts were made to define the sustainability criteria that should guide the city. The Agenda 21 Action Plan for Barcelona, driven by Txema Castiella and Teresa Franquesa, was the key instrument of the time. The Gràcia District Mobility and Public Space Plan opened the door to a new dimension of public space, and showed that this neighbourhood was the best stage for implementing the first pilot superblocks. Rather than a whole-city-initiative, the creation of the first superblock was the work of the district authorities in Gràcia, led by councillor Ricard Martínez at the time. The Agency designed the first ecological map, identifying the activities and services connected to the district's sustainability. Around the same time, a strategic study was developed in the district of Sants-Montjuïc, and included improvement proposals based on superblocks. The proposed pilot area was around the Parc de l'Espanya Industrial in the neighbourhoods of Hostafrancs and Sants.

SECOND PHASE: EXPANSION TO FIVE PILOT AREAS

The second phase began almost nine years after the Gràcia project. Once Barcelona's new orthogonal bus network was approved in 2012, the issue of superblocks re-emerged in the city's political debates. This time, the process was entirely different. Xavier Trias (of the CiU party) was leading the municipal government at the time, and the city was making a move towards the technology and solutions characteristic of so-called smart cities. In this case, Barcelona City Council's Urban Habitat Area promoted the creation of superblocks, through a whole-city programme that defined five pilot areas from the strategic initiatives on the municipal government's political agenda, which included the Glòries project and the urban transformation of the Pere IV Axis.

The challenge was to transform the urban fabric designed by Ildefons Cerdà, so the pilot areas were mainly located in the Eixample, Sant Martí and Les Corts districts.

During this term, work only began on the Les Corts superblock. In this period, the Agency carried out two studies for the Les Corts and Sant Martí districts. They considered future scenarios with gradual implementation, as well as cross-cutting solutions in the mobility, public space, energy, biodiversity, water and waste management spheres.

Meanwhile, the city's Department of Urban Planning commissioned the Agency to formulate five more studies on various solutions to develop the pilot areas. From then on, the Agency supported the programme by writing up diagnosis and indicator analysis documents. At the end of this phase, the Urban Mobility Plan 2013–2018 was approved. This was the first plan to formalise the need to implement superblocks across the city in order to meet emissions reduction targets.

THIRD PHASE: THE EL POBLENOU SUPERBLOCK

The third phase started with the implementation of the El Poblenou superblock and the 'Let's fill the streets with life' programme, driven by Ada Colau's government.

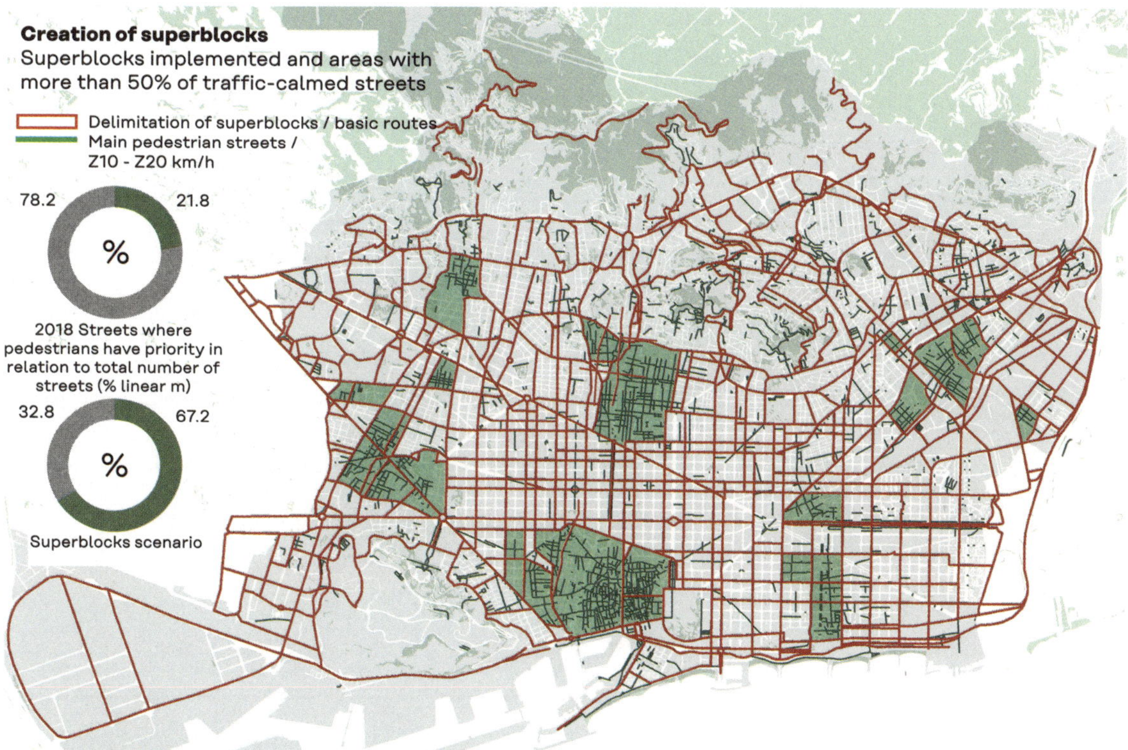

BARCELONA. 2018. Areas of pilot superblocks implemented in the city until 2019.
Source: BCNecologia

In September 2016, Barcelona saw the creation of another superblock, this time – and for the first time – in the now-iconic format made up of 3 x 3 blocks of Cerdà's original fabric. This phase entailed a significant change of direction in the execution process for subsequent pilot areas, as it incorporated tactical urbanism as a key tool. The city's schools of architecture were involved, even in the execution phase. It was an unprecedented process, with highly attainable urban development tools. The application of the functional superblock model turned the pilot area into an experimentation space for calming measures. Slowly, activity developed there and, most importantly, an identity was fostered among the neighbours. A unique characteristic of this case was the

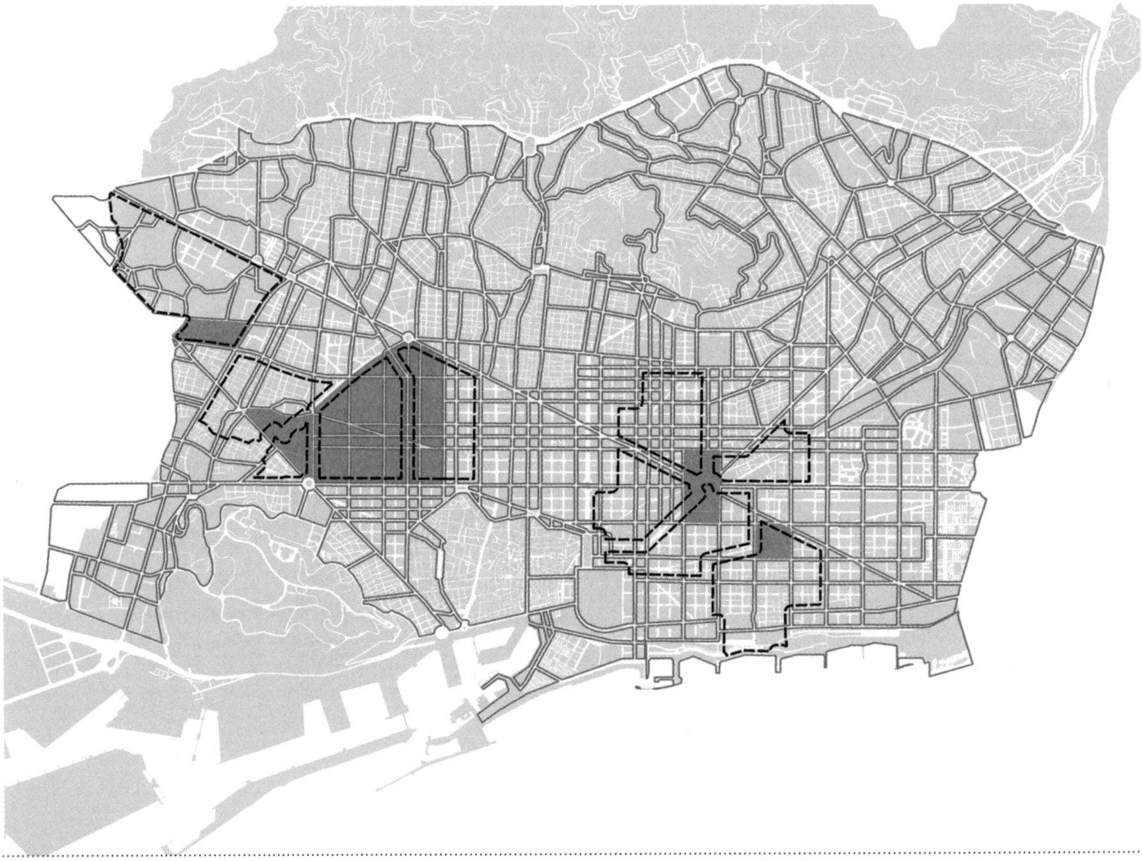

BARCELONA. Pilot Areas Map 2013–2015.
Source: BCNecologia

emergence of the Superblock P9 Collective: a group created by residents in favour of the superblock. This collective has played a key role in the continuity of the pilot area and the programme, as it has collaborated, and continues to do so, with the district of Sant Martí to create solutions and activities for the public space.

The superblock in the Sant Antoni neighbourhood was created a year after the one in El Poblenou. Lessons were learnt from the previous implementation process, and spaces were modified through tactical solutions with a definitive design based on prior experience. The initial calming measures did not affect an area as big as the El Poblenou superblock; they mainly consisted of the transformation of the junction between Carrer de Tamarit and Carrer del Comte Borrell. This was then expanded from the point between these two axes. In this phase, the Agency continued in its role of carrying out technical analyses of the areas and monitoring them through indicators, in parallel to its participation in the review of the Barcelona Sustainable Urban Mobility Plan. Other areas at the participation or execution stage in the process of having superblocks implemented are Horta (Horta-Guinardó), Hostafrancs (Sants-Montjuïc), Carrer del Consell de Cent-Germanetes and Carrer de Girona and the surrounding area (Eixample), and Sant Gervasi de Cassoles (Sarrià-Sant Gervasi).

MAIN RESULTS

Since the very beginning, the Agency's projects have been accompanied by synthetic evaluation through indicators. The superblock projects have been no exception. Below, there is a final assessment of the pilot superblock in Les Corts, in the neighbourhood of La Maternitat i Sant Ramon, using the system of ecosystemic urbanism indicators. The urban transformation proposals put forward in the district of Les Corts involved calming interior streets, reorganising mobility networks in accordance with the guidelines in the Barcelona Sustainable Urban Mobility Plan (PMUS), improving energy self-sufficiency through solar energy, and strengthening urban greenery infrastructure and biodiversity.

The results show that, before the transformation, the area scored 53%, in terms of its fulfilment of the indicator satisfactory values. The assessment of the future scenario, with improvement proposals put in place, raises this level of fulfilment to 74.9%.

EVALUATION OF THE BASE SITUATION
Certification of the Urban Sustainability Level

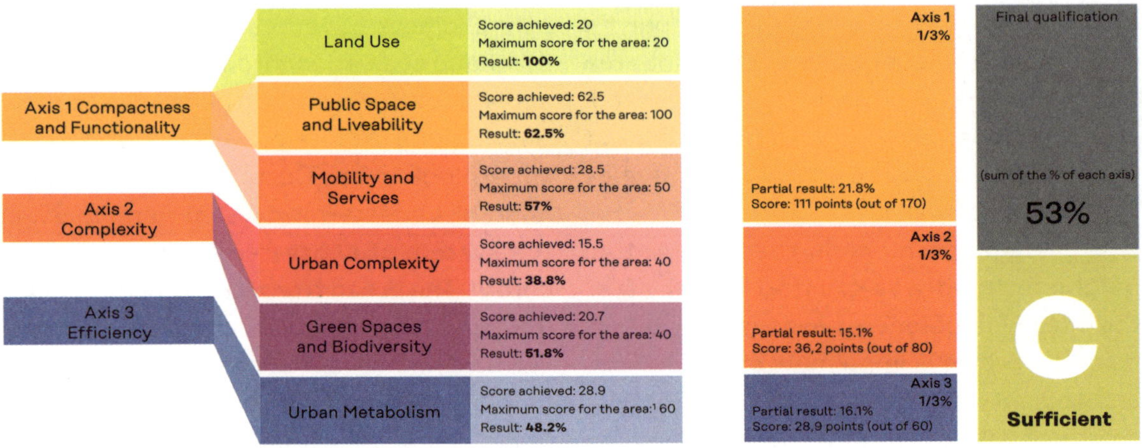

[1] Result on the total of indicators reported

EVALUATION OF THE FUTURE SITUATION WITH SUPERBLOCKS
Certification of the Urban Sustainability Level

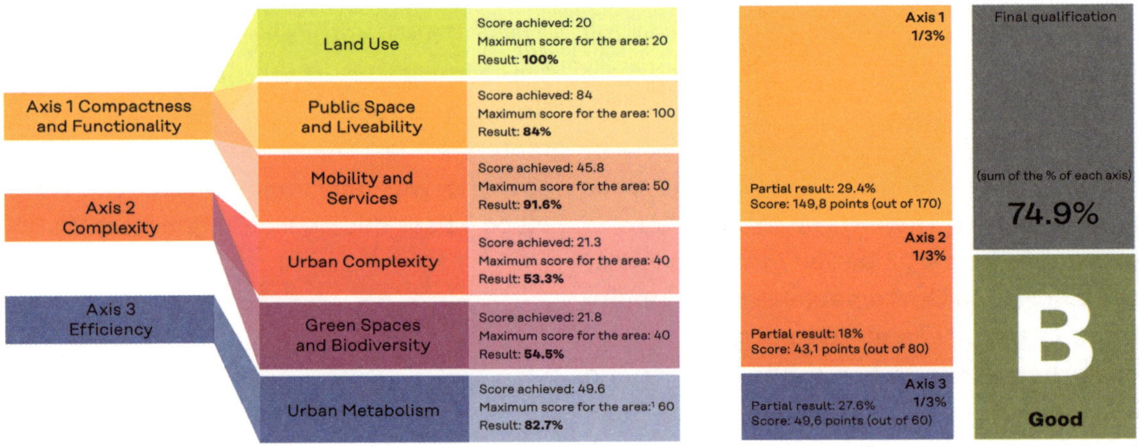

[1] Result on the total of indicators reported

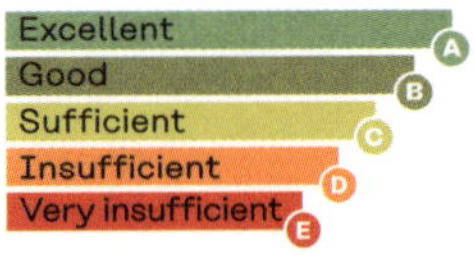

BARCELONA. LES CORTS. 2013. Pilot superblock in the neighbourhood of La Maternitat i Sant Ramon.
Benchmarking the assessment with sustainability indicators.
Source: BCNecologia

BARCELONA. LES CORTS. Pilot superblock in the neighbourhood of La Maternitat i Sant Ramon. Intervention in the Plaça de les Ceràmiques Vicens and in the Bacardi gardens.
Picture: Barcelona City Council

Some of the results from the El Poblenou and Sant Antoni superblocks were obtained by comparing the original situation and the changes detected one or two years after their creation. The implementation was a complex process. Previous interventions had not been free of controversy, but this time, the superblock project attracted significant media attention at a time of political polarisation; there were as many people for it as there were against it. Nonetheless, over time, the intervention came to be seen objectively, based on its real impact.

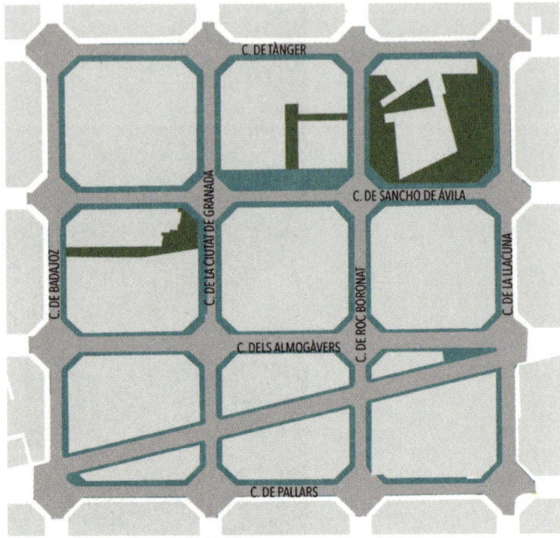

2016 – 31,575 m²

Pre-implementation of the superblock

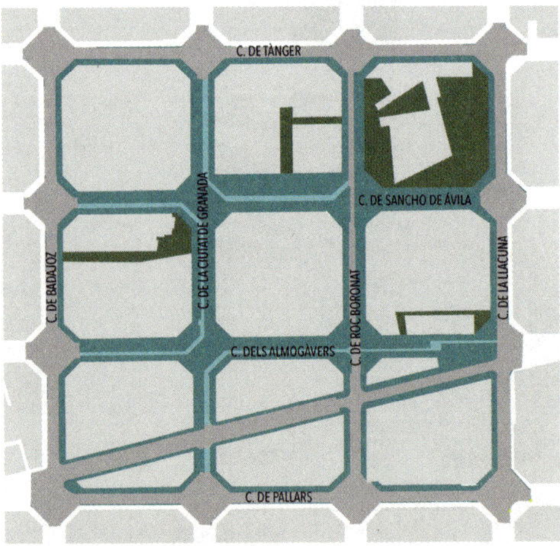

2017 – 47,707 m²

Post-implementation of the superblock

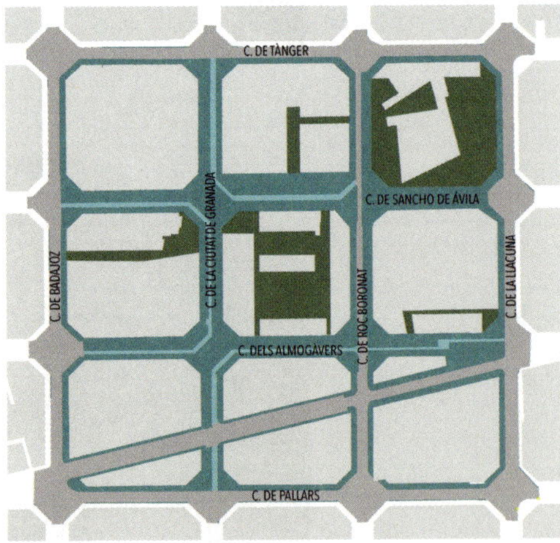

2018 – 54,276 m²

Post-implementation of the superblock

- Green space and/or public open spaces out of road space
- Motorised traffic space reclaimed for pedestrians + pavements
- Road space for pedestrian/vehicle coexistence

BARCELONA. 2016. 'Let's fill the streets with life' programme. Surface area of public spaces.
Source: BCNecologia

Conclusions

Barcelona's superblocks have been examples to follow in the implementation of this model and have led the way in the transformation of public space over the last twenty years. From the first superblocks in Gràcia to the El Poblenou and Sant Antoni superblocks, there has been a steady evolution in consultation and participation processes, public space design solutions and the public's degree of involvement.

One notable occurrence has been the incorporation of the superblock conceptual model into Barcelona City Council's strategic departments, with the city's Urban Mobility Plan of 2013 and its recent review in 2019. This has been the basis for transforming the mobility model, through a new orthogonal bus network. The Strategic Greenery and Biodiversity Plan for Barcelona also works in harmony with superblocks, as it involves urban green corridors and urban greenery strategies, both on street level and up high, with green roofs.

The Urban Planning and Mobility departments at Barcelona City Council have led the charge in creating pilot superblocks since 2013, with support from the Urban Strategy and Citizen Participation team and its Agenda 21 Action Plan and from the Citizen Commitment to Sustainability. The result of these efforts is the incorporation of superblocks into the Barcelona Urban Resilience Plan and the city's Climate Emergency Declaration, in the form of initiatives linked to green corridors. In the Social Rights Area, social superblocks are being developed, in collaboration with BCNecologia, as a tool for organising and for improving local social services.

The COVID-19 health crisis has highlighted cities' major weaknesses and inequalities. Today, the superblock model constitutes an opportunity to respond to needs deriving from the pandemic, by guaranteeing a safe distance between people in the public space, encouraging travel on foot, by bicycle or by personal mobility vehicle, and improving air quality.

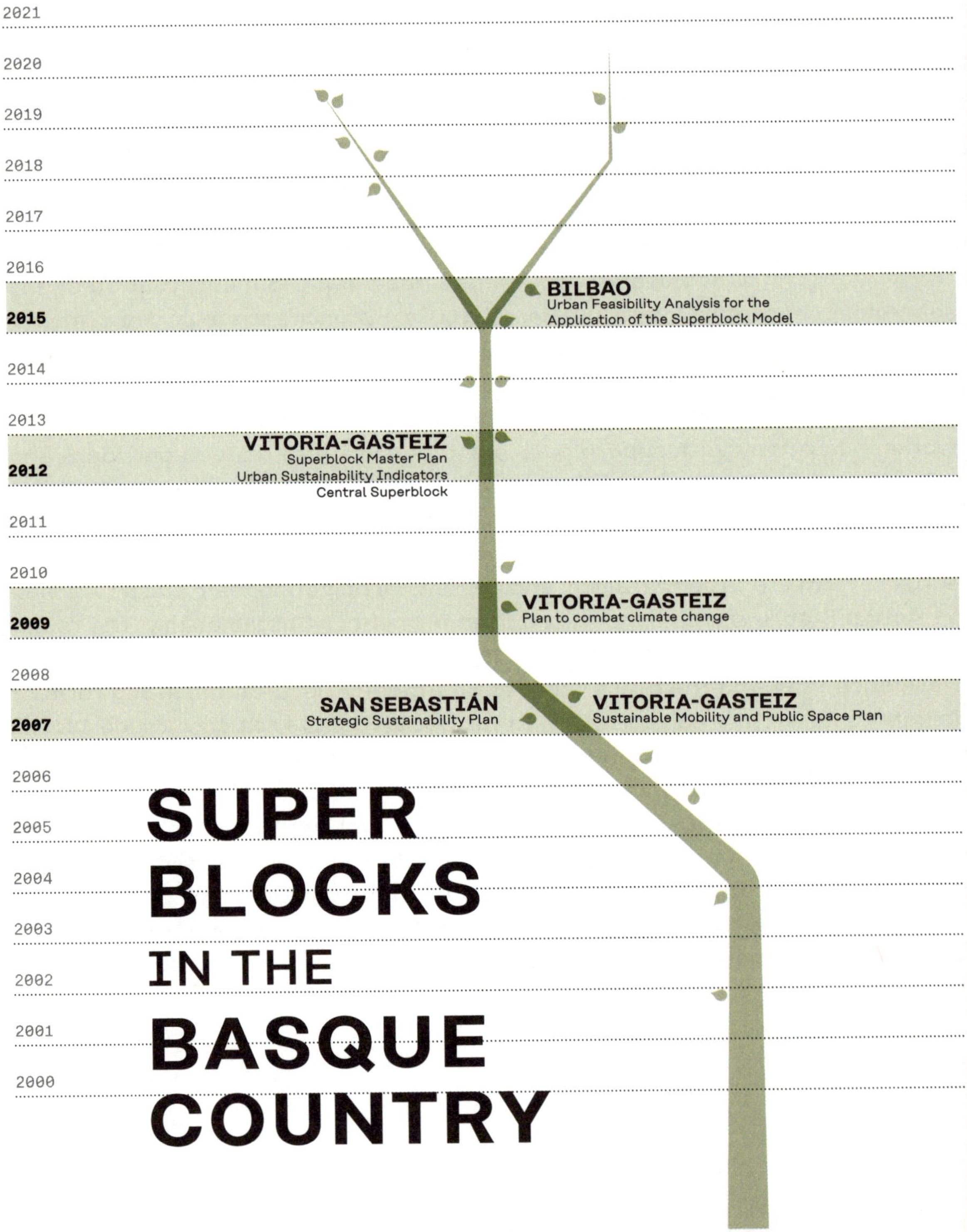

SUPER BLOCKS IN THE BASQUE COUNTRY

The Urban Ecology Agency of Barcelona has a special relationship with the Basque Country. The synergy between the two over the last twenty years has been rich and constant. The Agency's most relevant projects there to date took place in the provincial capitals: Vitoria-Gasteiz, San Sebastián and Bilbao. The experience of applying the superblock model in all of these projects has been highly rewarding, thanks to collaborations with municipal urban planning, mobility and environment departments.

The purpose of this chapter is to detail the projects and studies linked to superblocks the Agency helped to develop in these three cities. The projects examined here are as follows: the Superblock Master Plan and the Plan to Combat Climate Change in Vitoria-Gasteiz (2009); the Pilot Area Implementation Study – Urban Feasibility Analysis for the Application of the Superblock Model in Bilbao (2015); and the Strategic Sustainability Plan for San Sebastián (2007).

Vitoria-Gasteiz is one of the cities that best exemplifies the implementation of the superblock model. The starting point for this project was the creation of the Sustainable Mobility and Public Space Plan (PMSEP) in 2007, driven by the City Council through the Environmental Studies Centre (CEA) in collaboration with the Agency. Once the PMSEP was incorporated into the urban agenda, work started on various environmental areas and, in parallel, the process to reorganise the city's mobility networks began.

The Basque Country and, above all, the city of Vitoria-Gasteiz are highly significant for the Agency, due to their interest in and continued application of the superblock model and ecosystemic urbanism criteria.

From a methodological point of view, the projects carried out in the Basque Country contributed towards developing new tools, like the urban liveability index in Vitoria-Gasteiz or the proposed methodologies put forward in Bilbao to identify the potential of introducing superblocks to the city's neighbourhoods.

SUPERBLOCKS AND URBANISM IN VITORIA-GASTEIZ

PUBLIC SPACE DESIGN AND PLANNING

The evolution of the use of superblocks in the city's urban developments can also be categorised into different phases. The PMSEP lay the foundations for a long, fruitful collaboration between BCNecologia and Vitoria City Council. The CEA's participation was key in the development of various studies on the superblock-based urban model and the principles of ecosystemic urbanism.

Besides the mobility network plans stemming from the PMSEP, like the Cycling Mobility Plan or the School and Industrial Estate Mobility Plans, other plans emerged and impacted Vitoria-Gasteiz's urban space planning, as well as the definition of determining factors in the city's urban development. First, in 2010, BCNecologia was commissioned by Vitoria City Council to put together a proposal to create a 'Central Superblock', as a pilot project. This study provided the solutions needed to transform the public space on all the streets within the superblocks, by using the liveability index and incorporating urban furniture and design criteria considerations to reorganise mobility networks. Later, in 2011, a proposal for the urban path network was made: a project that involved identifying the main walking routes to encourage safe, comfortable mobility on foot. The Plan included public space planning and design criteria. The urban path network proposal also acted as a base on which the revitalisation strategies detailed in the Superblock Master Plan could be defined.

PROPOSALS FOR THE GENERAL PLAN FOR URBAN PLANNING

Before the municipality's General Plan for Urban Planning was reviewed, Vitoria-Gasteiz City Council commissioned BCNecologia to assess the city's future business-as-usual scenarios, and especially the one projected by the PGOU in effect at the time. The methodology used was based on the BCNecologia system of indicators: land use, public space and liveability, mobility and services, urban complexity, urban metabolism, green spaces and biodiversity, and social cohesion.

In this assessment, the Agency carefully examined all of the proposals and strategies included in the plans and studies carried out in the city. Fifty indicators revealed Vitoria-Gasteiz's situation in 2009 and analysed two business-as-usual scenarios, one in 2020 (Scenario 1) and the other in 2050 (Scenario 2). As well as taking any increase in population into account, the scenarios assumed that all housing planned in the PGOU would be built and all ongoing projects would be completed, such as the Sustainable Mobility and Public Space Plan and the Plan to

Combat Climate Change (2010–2020). The results obtained from the overall assessment revealed the opportunities and shortcomings presented by Vitoria-Gasteiz's urban fabric. In the analysis, the city scored well in the green spaces and biodiversity area, but poorly in others; the urban metabolism and land use indicators in particular revealed an urban reality that was far from compact. The existing scenario was rated 37.1 out of 100, while Scenario 1 showed a significant improvement, especially in the public space and urban metabolism areas, scoring 53.6. The indicators in the Vitoria plan later inspired those applied in Bilbao.

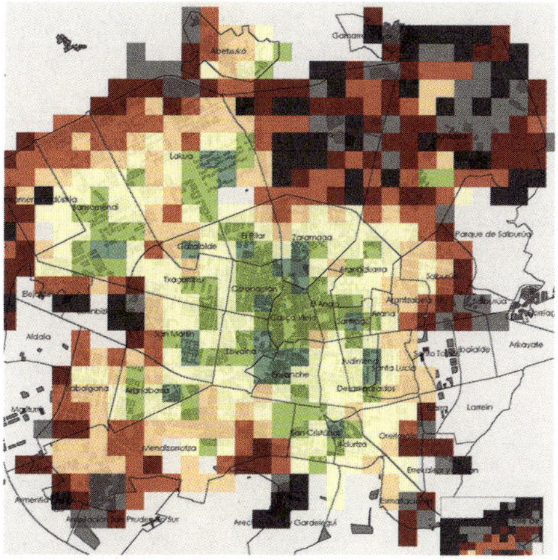

Initial situation **27%**

PGOU 2009 **65%**

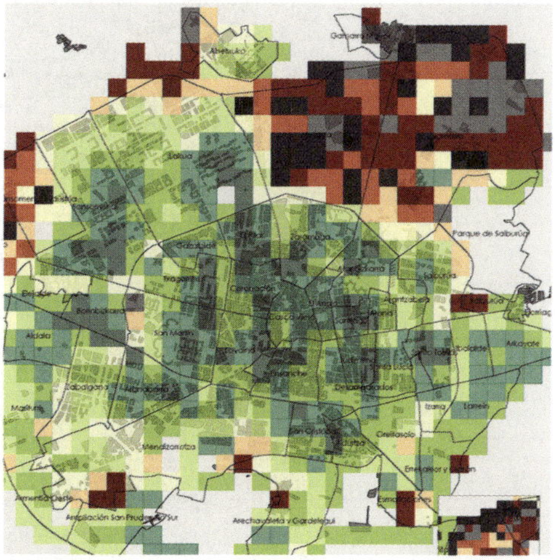

2050 **69%**

50 55 60 65 70 75 80 85

VITORIA-GASTEIZ. Comparison of the liveability index applied to forecast scenarios and to proposed planning scenarios with superblocks. Initial situation, PGOU in effect in 2009 and the horizon scenario 2050 with a superblock-based urban model implemented.
Source: BCNecologia

VITORIA-GASTEIZ. The analysis of the Vitoria-Gasteiz urban fabric revealed an urban reality that was far from compact.
Picture: CEA (Environmental Studies Centre). Vitoria-Gasteiz City Council

STRATEGIC CONNECTING ROUTES

- Consolidated routes
- Routes that could be improved

STRATEGIC FOCAL POINTS

- Existing focal point
- Proposal for public space that could be improved
- Proposal for use of equivalent land as a focal point

Urban Improvement Plans

- Renovation of squares and public open spaces
- Improvement of connectivity and permeability for pedestrians
- Green spaces in superblocks
- Public open spaces
- A Urban Unit Key

LIST OF EXISTING FOCAL POINTS

1. Txagorritxu-San Viator Sports Complex
2. Europa Conference and Exhibition Centre
3. El Pilar Civic Centre
4. Zaramaga Sports Complex
5. Iparralde Civic Centre
6. Aldabe Civic Centre
7. Museum
8. Arana Civic Centre
9. Performing arts school
10. Artium
11. Ariznavarra Civic Centre
12. Hegoalde Civic Centre
13. University buildings
14. Judimendi Civic Centre
15. Armoury Museum
16. Train station
17. Wholesale market
18. Market

VITORIA-GASTEIZ. 2012. Superblock Master Plan. Proposal for Strategic Connecting Routes.
Source: BCNecologia

Once the municipality's main needs were identified, the Superblock Master Plan was written up. This document was intended to act as a guide for the urban transformations that would need to be incorporated into the PGOU review for the superblock model to be made possible. The Plan detailed structural strategies relating to economic activity, urban greenery and energy efficiency.

SUPERBLOCKS IN STRATEGIC CITY INITIATIVES

STRATEGIC SUSTAINABILITY PLAN FOR SAN SEBASTIÁN

The Agency and San Sebastián City Council worked together to reflect strategically on the sustainable city model of the future, within the framework of the *Urban Environment Strategy (EMAU)*[10] approved by the Ministry of the Environment in 2006, and again as part of the San Sebastián Civic Declaration (2013).

In 2007, BCNecologia was commissioned by San Sebastián City Council to put together a sustainability strategy for the municipality. In the project, indicators relating to the different aspects of urban analysis (compactness, complexity, efficiency and social cohesion) were used to quantify to what extent the urban system complied with ecological urbanism principles, both in its original state and with the strategy proposals applied.

The strategy for San Sebastián proposed implementing the superblock model and studied the city's transport networks and the characteristics of its public spaces. At the same time, it defined the main road network and freed up the streets within the superblocks for pedestrian use, increasing the percentage of the space available for walking from 43% to 73%. Though population density varied greatly across the municipality, with a dense wider city fabric and a sparser old town, new public spaces were required all over. In the centre, they were needed because of density and large numbers of people on the street, leading to more demand, while in peripheral areas, more public space was needed to provide local services. Excessive space allocated to vehicles is a consistent issue across all of the cities analysed. Superblocks are the simplest, most effective tool for redistributing public space.

As well as proposing the superblock model, the strategy analysed how to increase the municipality's energy self-sufficiency and improve its water cycle and waste management. The project also included a relatively unexplored issue, namely the city's potential for food sovereignty. Finally, it offered a detailed analysis of themes relating to social cohesion, especially in reference to housing, at a time when ensuring access to this fundamental right was extremely difficult across Spain.

10 Ministry of the Environment; Network of Local Sustainable Development Networks. *Urban Environment Strategy (EMAU).* Madrid: Ministry of the Environment. General Technical Secretariat. Publications Centre, 2006.

FILTER I

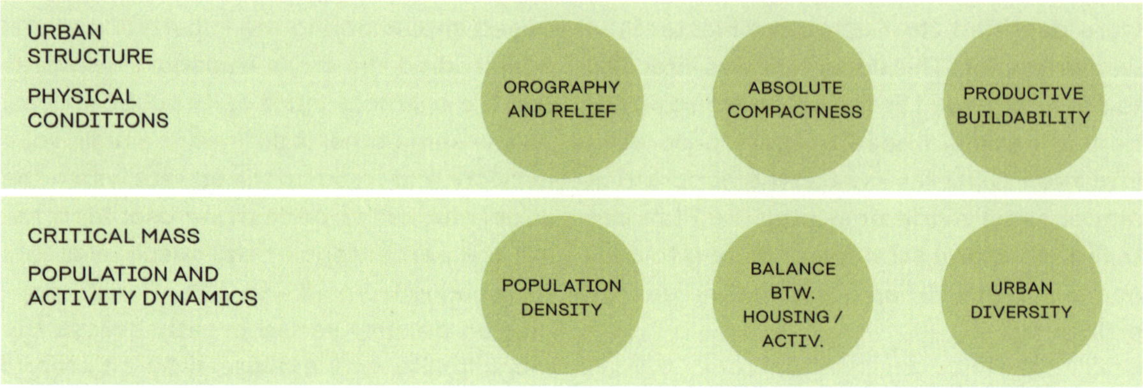

BILBAO. 2015. Multi-criteria analysis methodology to identify the urban feasibility of implementing superblocks in the city's neighbourhoods.
Source: BCNecologia

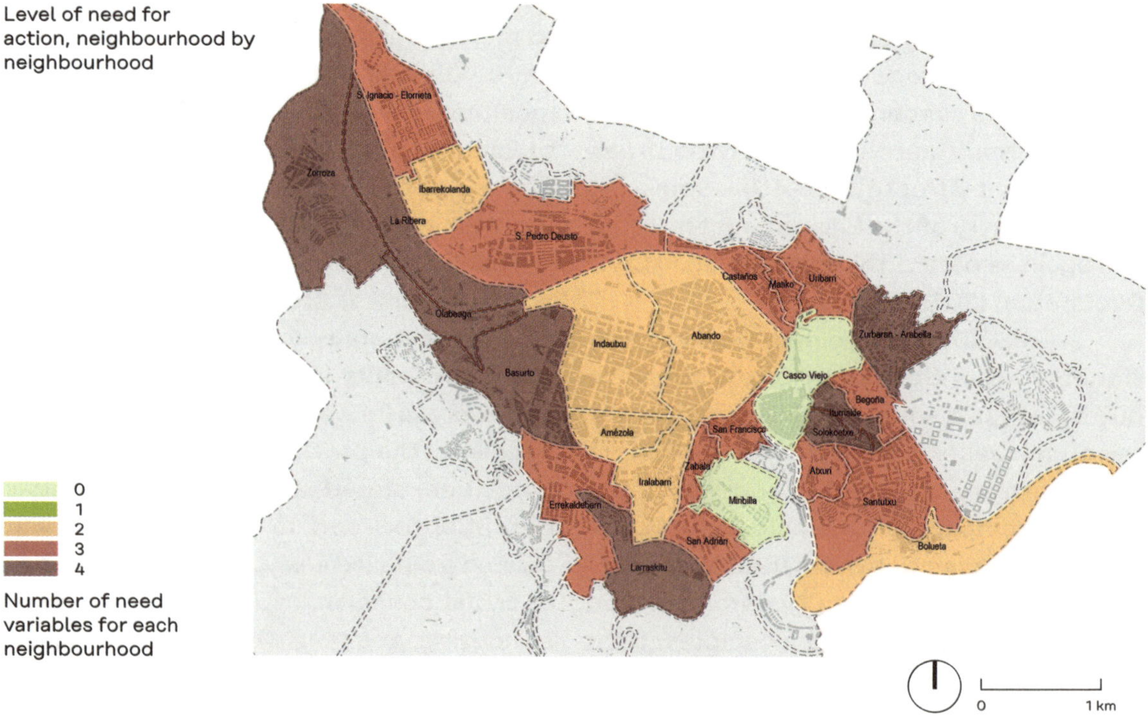

BILBAO. 2015. Level of need for action, neighbourhood by neighbourhood.
Source: BCNecologia

FILTER II

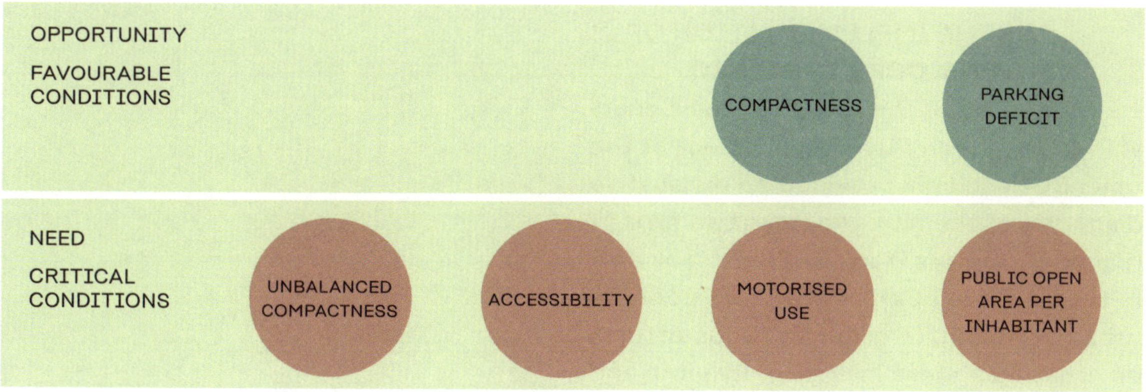

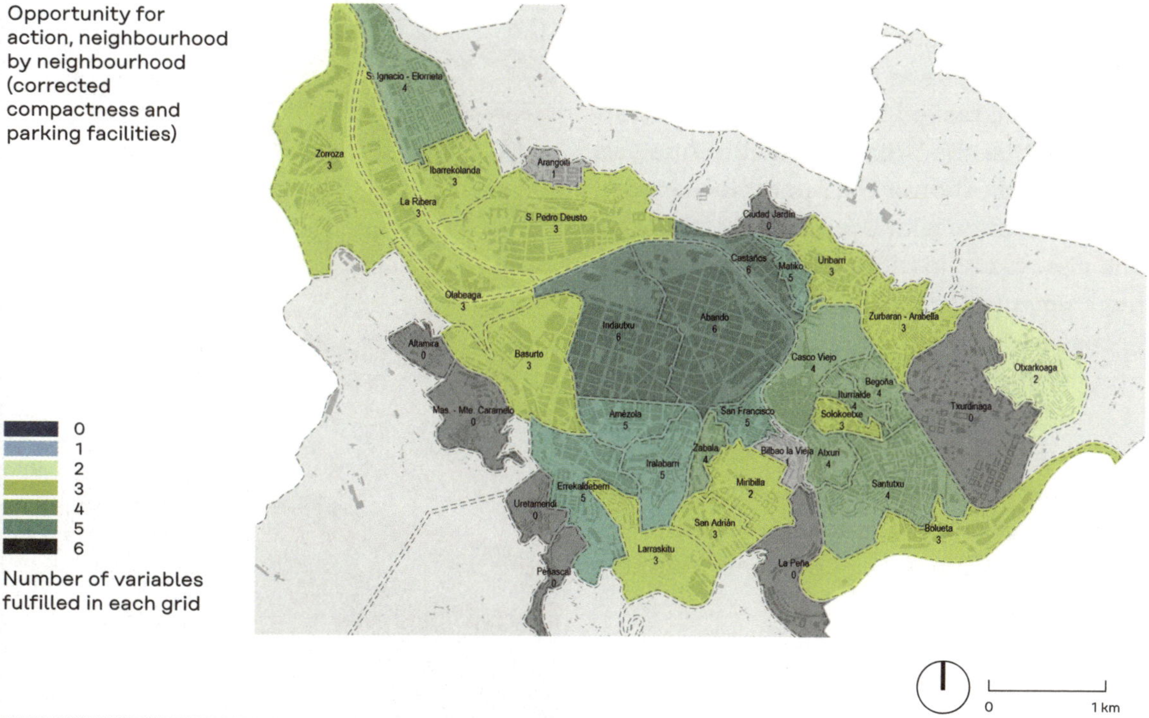

BILBAO. 2015. Feasibility of implementing superblocks according to the fulfilment of basic favourable conditions and opportunity for action in the short term.
Source: BCNecologia

URBAN PLANNING ANALYSIS FOR THE IMPLEMENTATION OF SUPERBLOCKS IN BILBAO

As part of the review of the General Plan for Urban Planning in effect at the time, BCNecologia provided an exhaustive diagnosis of the city and its urban fabrics (Bilbao Indicators Plan, 2012) and took part in the analysis of and reflection upon its urban planning, in order to focus efforts on creating a more inclusive, liveable and sustainable future. All the major challenges with repercussions on urban planning were on the table: demographic complexity (ageing, migrations), sustainability, territorial and social balance, governance, and more. With this first diagnosis as a starting point, Bilbao City Council tasked BCNecologia with putting together the Urban Feasibility Analysis for the Application of the Superblock Model, in collaboration with the city's Traffic Area. The aim was to identify the urban planning requirements and organisational instruments necessary to develop a superblock creation programme in the city.

The methodology used had to objectively justify each neighbourhood's potential for transformation. The analysis therefore revolved around the following aspects:

- Superblock-based urban planning criteria
- Urban planning requirements for implementing superblocks
- Potential for applying the superblock

BILBAO. 2012. When reviewing the PGOU, BCNecologia analysed the feasibility of applying the superblock model to the city.
Picture: Shutterstock (Jon Chica)

BILBAO. BCNecologia defined a methodology that could justify the neighbourhoods' potential for urban transformation.
Picture: BCNecologia

model to Bilbao's neighbourhoods, based on the existing situation and the possibility of adapting or transforming the urban fabrics

The methodology consisted of analysing the correlation of urban planning variables through two filters. The first focused on the urban structure (physical conditions) and critical mass (population and activity dynamics) of each neighbourhood, allowing the Agency to define the feasibility of creating the superblocks, based on existing opportunities.

The second involved examining the neighbourhoods that had successfully passed the first filter and analysing the opportunities (favourable conditions) and needs (critical conditions) of each unit studied, in order to prioritise the action to be taken.

The added value of this study was its unprecedented use of sustainability indicators without strictly following an axis-based assessment method. Instead, the assessment was based on the correlation of variables. This way, the information could be read and applied differently, opening up a new perspective that would help in the development of automation tools.

Conclusions

The city is an ecosystem that requires contact, regulation, exchange and communication to function. The structure and production of the city compose the framework in which citizens can interact through their urban activities.

One of the aims of implementing superblocks in the Basque Country was to establish guidelines to improve the liveability of the public space, with the addition of new services and activities. The tendency towards urban growth in cities like Vitoria-Gasteiz and Bilbao has led to less compactness in urban planning. In the case of Bilbao, this approach is largely justified by the city's complex orography. Nonetheless, over time, the aim is to renovate cities' functional structures in order to build a more sustainable model.

There is no doubt that the Basque Country has been an important region in the development of BCNecologia's theoretical framework and has played a leading role in promoting ecosystemic urbanism and the mobility and public space model based on superblocks. Vitoria-Gasteiz, in particular, has been one of the flagship cities throughout the Agency's twenty-year history, and a place where new methodologies have been developed to analyse various sectors: mobility, energy, water, waste, air pollution, etc. It is also the city where BCNecologia has been able to tackle the largest number of strategic areas.

Furthermore, the Basque Country has been a key territory for the Urban Ecology Agency of Barcelona because it has enabled the organisation to examine the characteristics of its cities in depth. The urban model represented by Vitoria-Gasteiz, San Sebastián and Bilbao differs greatly from that of Barcelona and has contributed towards furthering knowledge around reference values and evaluation of ecosystemic urbanism criteria.

SUPER BLOCKS AROUND THE WORLD

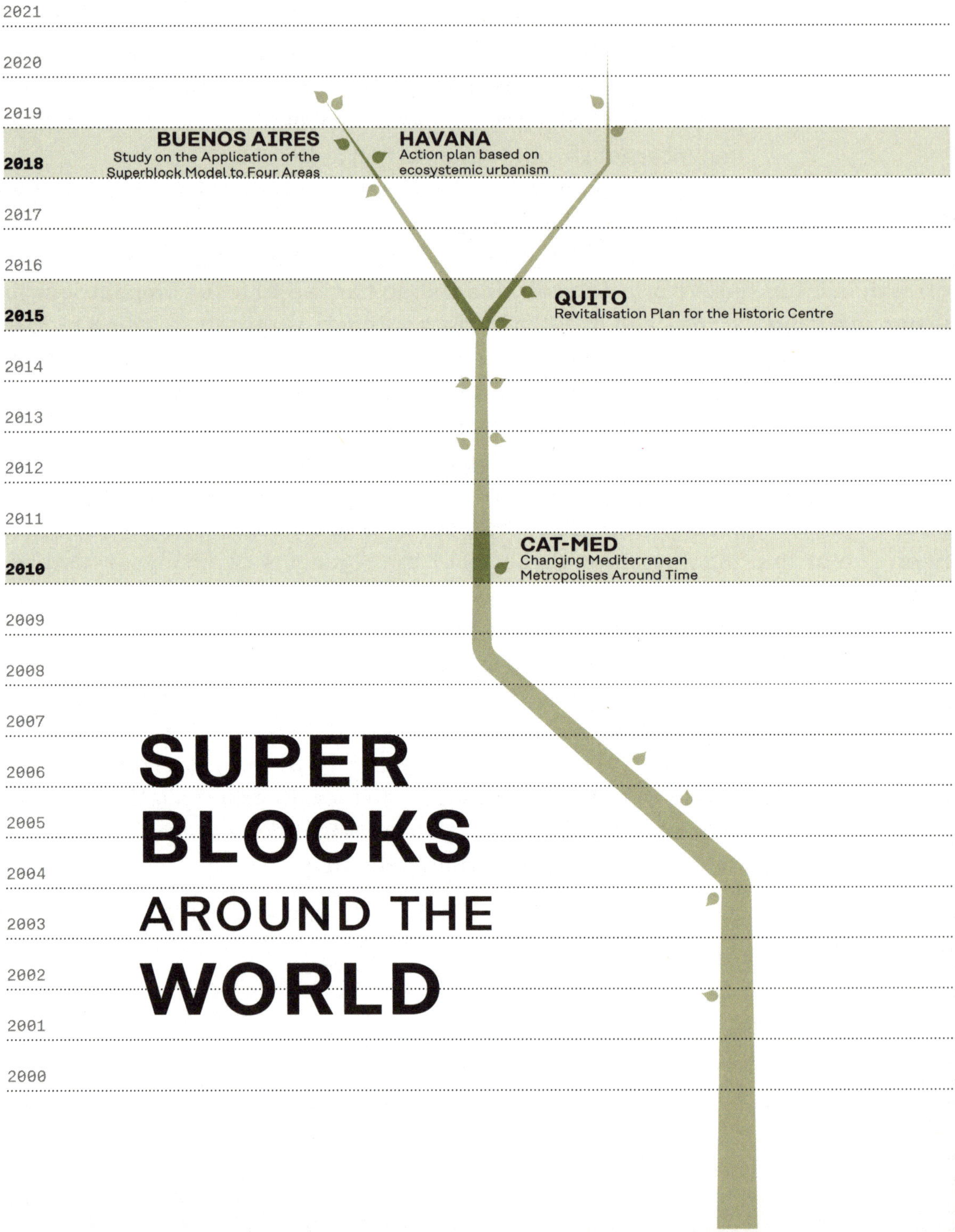

This chapter details how ecosystemic urbanism principles and the superblock model, applied to cities all over the world, have proven to be essential tools for territorial planning and organisation internationally.

The cities that have adopted the superblock model include Quito (Ecuador), Havana (Cuba) and Buenos Aires (Argentina), which shows that it is exportable to other spaces, cities and environments or, in short, to other urban realities. These were projects with huge repercussions and a significant social and urban impact.

The Revitalisation Plan for the Historic Centre of Quito, for example, took a comprehensive approach to the space and involved in-depth technical development of mobility, public space, social cohesion, economy, biodiversity and urban metabolism proposals. The Agency has also drawn up proposals for applying this urban model in France, Russia, Canada and India.

In the Action Plan for the Articulation of Planning and Management Instruments in Old Havana, the city's urban and functional model is reviewed to incorporate ecosystemic urbanism principles, in order to drive economic, social and environmental revitalisation. The Plan is composed of proposals to create a more inclusive, more productive, more self-sufficient, better organised city with more citizen participation and a better quality of life,

Finally, the Study on the Application of the Superblock Model to Four Areas of Buenos Aires analysed the implementation of the superblock-based model in the Argentinian capital and examined its potential benefits. The analysis also looked at its repercussions on social cohesion, mobility, urban morphology and structure, urban greenery and urban complexity.

REVITALISATION PLAN FOR THE HISTORIC CENTRE OF QUITO, ECUADOR

As a result of the interinstitutional cooperation agreement between the Quito Metropolitan District – Metropolitan Heritage Institute and the Urban Ecology Agency of Barcelona, work began on developing a public space and mobility system in the Historic Centre of Quito (HCQ), leading to the Revitalisation Plan for the Historic Centre.

This project was a challenge for BCNecologia because of the distance involved and the city's characteristics. The HCQ is a 376-hectare urban area with a population of approximately 40,000. It was named World Heritage by UNESCO in 1978 and constitutes one of the most important historic sites in Latin America. Despite the significant progress made in recent years, the HCQ continues to suffer from structural problems. High crime rates, widespread poverty among the population, the deterioration of some heritage buildings and the public space and a lack of basic services were determining factors in this project from the very beginning.

Urban regeneration and revitalisation processes are closely linked to the flow of people of varying ages, incomes, ethnicities and cultures that takes place in a certain space. A sufficient flow of people indicates that the public space is 'healthy' and represents an opportunity for economic development. A 'living' public space entails more interactions and urban functions, stronger organisation, and less insecurity. The Revitalisation Plan involved implementing the superblock-based urban model in the neighbourhoods of the historic centre.

One of the strategies proposed to this end was the González Suárez Superblock Densification Plan. Urban planning proposals were accompanied by a programme of incipient initiatives.

The key aspects for development in this area were mobility and security in the public space, as well as the adaptation of buildings for residential use.

The implementation proposal focused on the following:

- **Reorganising mobility**: traffic calming and mobility reorganisation measures were planned within the superblocks (speed limits and gradual conversion to prioritise pedestrians on the streets inside superblocks). Subsequently, the proposed solutions led to the creation of an Orthogonal Bus Network Plan for the whole city.
- **Public space**: the purpose of reorganising the city was to provide more housing, to offer basic local services in accordance with the desired population density, and to attract new, everyday activities that encouraged community life and extended the hours shops were open and public spaces were busy until at least 9 p.m.

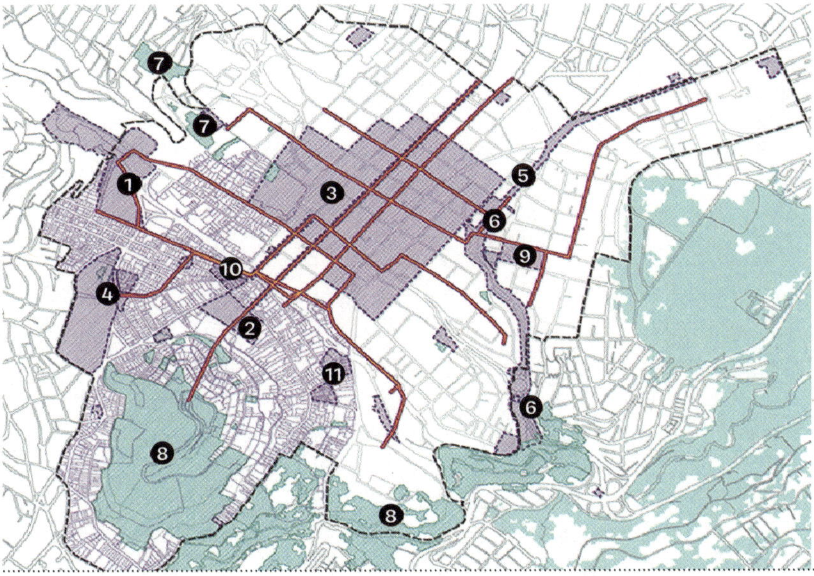

QUITO. 2015. Strategic connecting routes and urban regeneration areas.
Source: BCNecologia

- **Construction**: the strategy was to renovate buildings in poor condition or adapt suitable heritage buildings for residential use.

COMPREHENSIVE REVITALISATION OF OLD HAVANA, CUBA

This document was a product of the inter-institutional cooperation agreement between the Havana Master Plan Office, Barcelona City Council and the Urban Ecology Agency of Barcelona (2018).

The project aimed to promote the economic, social and environmental revitalisation of the historic centre and its area of influence, through a review of the city's urban planning and functional model. This work was carried out as part of the process to support the Special Comprehensive Development Plan, set out in Cuba's National Economic and Social Development Plan 2030.

The experience accumulated in Quito – a city that shares certain characteristics with Havana, including its monumental nature and shortcomings in its urban functionality – helped the Agency to present more effective, specific proposals and programmes. In addition, for three weeks, the Agency

HAVANA. 2018. Revitalisation Plan for the Historic Centre.
Source: BCNecologia

Buildings of interest (heritage/historical)
Public space of interest (squares, parks, street corners)

Connecting Axes

welcomed three experts visiting from the Havana Master Plan Office, including Dr. Patricia Rodríguez, director of the Master Plan for the Comprehensive Revitalisation of Old Havana. This exchange of experience and knowledge was highly enriching.

The project offered a holistic view of the city's issues and shortfalls through the application of indicators that systematically assessed the original state of each stretch of street. This revealed that 75% of buildings were in a mediocre or poor state of repair, that certain areas were geared towards tourism, and that the city lacked an adequate network of services and infrastructures.

The second part of the project offered a set of proposals and programmes that ensured the urban fabrics were balanced by applying ecosystemic urbanism principles. As a result, the historic centre was zoned according to superblocks. For each superblock, planning and management strategies, initiatives and instruments were defined to build a more liveable, sustainable city.

Today, city authorities are working to implement two superblocks in Old Havana.

APPLICATION OF THE SUPERBLOCK MODEL TO FOUR AREAS OF THE CITY OF BUENOS AIRES, ARGENTINA

This study came as part of the collaboration agreement between the Buenos Aires City Government's Ministry of the Environment and Public Space and the Urban Ecology Agency of Barcelona (2018).

The Agency had previously worked on the Guide to Public Space Design in Buenos Aires (2013), as a product of the policy to transform the public space with calming criteria and measures to improve the city's image.

As a result of the close relationship between BCNecologia and Buenos Aires, while studying the application of the superblock model in four areas of the city (Primera Junta, Constitución, Once and Tribunales), the Agency also advised the City Government during the creation of the new Urban Planning Code. With this new code, a city could be built at a human scale, with superblocks as the common instrument for proposals.

The study analysed the implementation of the superblock-based model in the city and provided technical justification for the feasibility of applying it in the future. To this end, four strategic areas that were especially relevant for the Buenos Aires City Government were chosen for revitalisation.

In the study, the implementation of the superblock model was analysed from the perspective of its impact on social cohesion, mobility, morphology, urban structure, urban greenery and urban complexity. Furthermore, at the same time, specific criteria and recommendations were established for each section, and a list of proposed action was drawn up.

In addition, the two phases required to implement the model were described: phase one would change mobility patterns, and phase two would focus on urban transformation.

SUPERBLOCKS IN THE EUROPEAN CONTEXT. CAT-MED

The Change Mediterranean Metropolises Around Time (CAT-MED) project, developed between 2010 and 2011, was a European MED initiative aimed at limiting greenhouse gas emissions through the identification of practical solutions within urban dynamics to reduce cities' environmental impact, with strategies shared between the eleven participant cities in Spain, France, Italy and Greece. Though it was a small-scale project, it is noteworthy because it was based on two of the Agency's main tools: sustainability indicators and superblocks. In fact, this was the first European project in which the Agency introduced the concept of superblocks.

First, common goals were identified and quantified through indicators, which were calculated with a transnational geographic information system (GIS) specifically de-

Density, type and diversity of activities in the Tribunales neighbourhoo

- Other services
- Leisure, cultural and sports services
- Associations
- Social and health services
- Education
- Public administration, defence and compulsory social security
- Business services
- IT services and related activities
- Machinery and equipment hire, personal goods hire
- Property services
- Insurance and pension fund administration services
- Financial intermediation and auxiliaries
- Postal and telecommunications services
- Ancillary transport services
- Transport service
- Hospitality and restaurants
- Store
- Wholesale
- Sale and repair of automobiles
- Facilities for buildings and civil engineering works
- Electricity, gas and water
- Furniture and mattress manufacturing Manufacturing industries
- Communication equipment manufacturing
- Machinery and electrical equipments
- Metal product manufacturing
- Non-metallic mineral product manufacturing
- Rubber and plastic product manufacturing
- Chemical substance and product manufacturing
- Publishing and printing
- Paper and paper product manufacturing
- Wooden products
- Leather goods and footwear manufacturing
- Clothes manufacturing
- Textile product manufacturing
- Food and drink product processing

Total typology of legal persons in the four study areas.

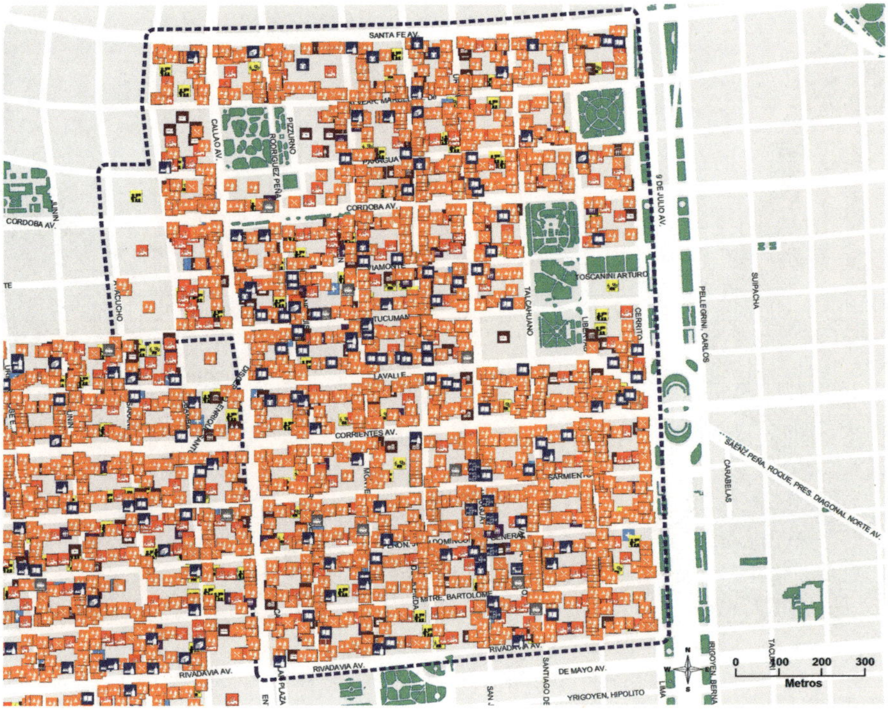

Complexity is conditioned by urban organisation and by how mixed the uses and functions of a certain territory are. Urban complexity is the reflection of the interactions established in the city between organised entities, or legal persons: businesses, associations, facilities and institutions.

It is linked to a combination of order and chaos: two intricately linked phenomena that can be analysed in urban systems to some extent, through the concept of diversity. Living organisms, especially humans, and their communities carry information and possess characteristics that, dynamically over time, indicate just how much information they have accumulated and their ability to exert a significant influence on the present and to control the future.

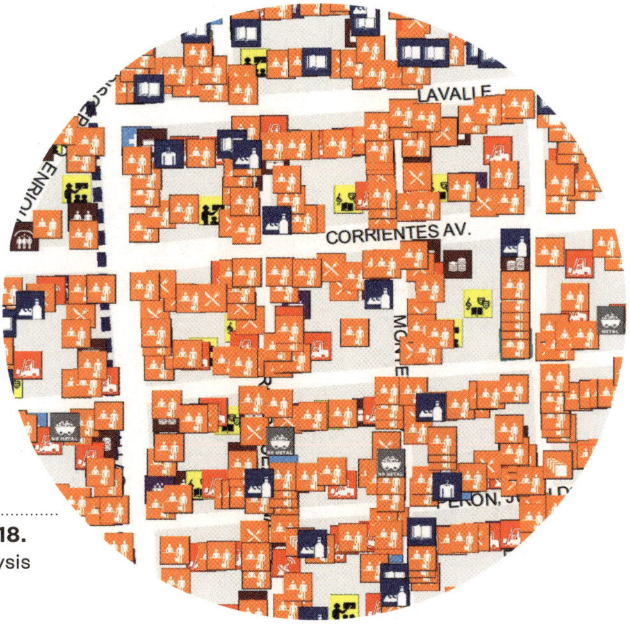

BUENOS AIRES. Tribunales neighbourhood. 2018. Superblock study. Original urban complexity analysis in base situation.
Source: BCNecologia and RUS (Residuos Urbanos Sólidos) project 2010

BUENOS AIRES. The Agency studied the application of the superblock model in four areas of the city. Picture: Shutterstock (Inspired By Maps)

signed for the project. Optimal values were set for the indicators and were deemed convergence objectives for the participating cities.

Next, each city worked on an eco-neighbourhood pilot project, inspired by the superblock concept, with criteria defined by the indicators.

On this occasion, BCNecologia helped to define the indicators and their optimal values. Many of them, such as compactness and complexity, had been developed and trialled previously by the Agency in other urban contexts. The Agency's superblock proposal was the Llevant Sector eco-neighbourhood in Figueres. The project dealt with sustainable mobility considerations and other issues linked to superblock development: energy efficiency and self-sufficiency, the material cycle, the water cycle and social cohesion.

Conclusions

This chapter has demonstrated that the superblock model, based on ecosystemic urbanism, can be applied to a diverse range of urban environments and realities and provide the same benefits every time, improving residents' quality of life considerably. Thanks to its adaptability and proven advantages, more and more cities are opting for the superblock model as an urban planning tool.

Urban environments are the sum of multiple factors, and it is important to take their proportionality into account. This is why the most crucial parts of analysis and work methodologies include constantly developing public space design solutions, honing consultation and participation processes, and perfecting indicator calculation formulas to make them more applicable. For this reason, the superblock model has become a universal planning tool.

For over a decade, the Urban Ecology Agency of Barcelona has carried out studies on implementing superblocks all over the world. It has proven the model's feasibility in any urban environment by designing scenarios and calculating sustainability indicators.

The COVID-19 crisis ravaging the planet has highlighted the key role urban planning plays in people's lives, especially when it comes to well-being and health. The superblock model provides a response to a host of current needs: it offers enough room to guarantee a safe distance between people in the public space, encourages travel by bicycle and by personal mobility vehicle, and reserves enough space on the road for these modes of transport.

Once again, superblocks have confirmed their status as an element of quality, sustainable urbanism and, above all, a universal tool.

SUPER BLOCKS AND URBAN LIVEA BILITY

2021

2020

2019
BARCELONA
Social superblocks

2018
CHARTER FOR THE ECOSYSTEMIC PLANNING OF CITIES AND METROPOLISES

2017

2016

2015
CÓRDOBA
Ciudad Jardín pilot superblock

2014

2013

2012

2011

2010
FIGUERES
Plan for Urban Planning in the Llevant Sector

2009
BARCELONA
Study of liveability in public space
Various districts

2008

2007

2006

2005
GRÀCIA
Implementation
of two superblocks

2004

2003
GRÀCIA
District Mobility and
Public Space Plan

2002

2001

2000

The superblock design process takes human and social considerations into account through liveability criteria. This chapter looks at how these two dimensions materialise in public space, housing and local social services.

Catering to the social facet involves identifying potential uses based on citizens' five basic rights: to safe movement, leisure, exchange, expression, and access to culture and knowledge.

Ecosystemic urbanism must ensure social cohesion through three types of space: public (streets, parks, squares, etc.), semi-public (businesses and facilities) and private (housing).

With this in mind, some key elements are required to prevent the exclusion of social groups in superblocks and, therefore, to make a more sustainable lifestyle possible. They include ensuring physical proximity between facilities, housing and businesses; providing affordable housing; offering a mixture of different types of housing that minimises the consumption of water, energy and materials; integrating vulnerable neighbourhoods; and prioritising pedestrian space.

As for housing liveability, superblocks incorporate accessibility criteria from an economic and physical point of view, remove architectural barriers, guarantee satisfactory sunlight and ventilation conditions, and provide biodiversity and energy through their roofs and terraces. This approach was included in the Plan for Urban Planning in the Llevant Sector of Figueres. Subsequently, in the superblock proposal for the Ciudad Jardín neighbourhood in Córdoba, the approach adopted also considered the population's degree of vulnerability, in order to define priority action in the implementation of the programme.

In Barcelona, social superblocks show how the form of urban space interacts with social policies to support the local economy and the care economy. The starting point for this planning activity is the Home Care Service (SAD), though the intention is to expand this to other care services later on.

LIVEABILITY AND PUBLIC SPACE

MORE USES AND RIGHTS IN THE PUBLIC SPACE

The main use of public space is determined by the physical and dynamic characteristics of the urban fabric. Design and planning criteria condition the public space's connectivity and relationship with the urban structure. Meanwhile, the distribution and type of activities that take place in the immediate surroundings condition how many people the public space attracts.

Most of the urban space, currently dedicated to mobility, must be reconverted and adapted for more uses and citizens' rights to make the streets a place for coexistence. The public space should be a home for everyone, a meeting place, an environment for exchange and for exercising all citizens' rights.

The superblock-based urban model clearly strengthens the civic nature of the public space and explores other ways in which it can be used in order to broaden its social and environmental spectrum. The model goes a step beyond pedestrian mobility in the strictest sense. It aims to ensure adequate accessibility parameters for mobility through alternative networks to the private motor vehicle and to guarantee citizens' rights fully in the public space (the right to exchange, to leisure and gathering, to movement, to expression and participation, and to culture and knowledge).

To achieve this, adequate liveability conditions must be guaranteed in the public space to make exchange and interaction between people possible. The surface area for civic use must be expanded through reorganisation of mobility networks and made more flexible to cater to a more diverse range of uses. The streets inside superblocks are designed to be spaces for harmonious coexistence, so they must be subject to traffic calming measures. Vehicle speed is therefore one of the key aspects of guaranteeing citizens' rights, and a limit should be set at 10 km/h on these interior streets, on kerbless streets, on boulevards and on avenues with calming measures.

Meanwhile, a variety of uses must be encouraged to attract and maintain activity throughout the day, among both residents and people who work in the area. Activity on ground floors of buildings and the distribution of legal persons (businesses, associations, institutions and facilities) affect how many people are attracted to the space, in accordance with the critical mass they generate and the streets' capacity for passers-by.

URBAN LIVEABILITY INDEX

The Agency has worked on a theoretical framework for the urban space based on the principle of urban liveability. This framework defines an analysis and assessment

Urban Liveability Index Variables.
Source: BCNecologia

methodology based on four dimensions of urban liveability:

1 Ergonomics in the public space (streets' accessibility and relationship between the width of the streets and the height of the buildings).

2 Attractiveness of the public space (density and diversity of legal persons and the presence of urban greenery on the streets).

3 Comfort in the public space (noise control, air quality and thermal comfort).

4 Walkability and proximity to basic services (public transport, essential businesses, basic facilities and green spaces).

This analysis is encapsulated in the urban liveability index: a multi-criteria assessment that summarises these four dimensions through thirteen indicators.

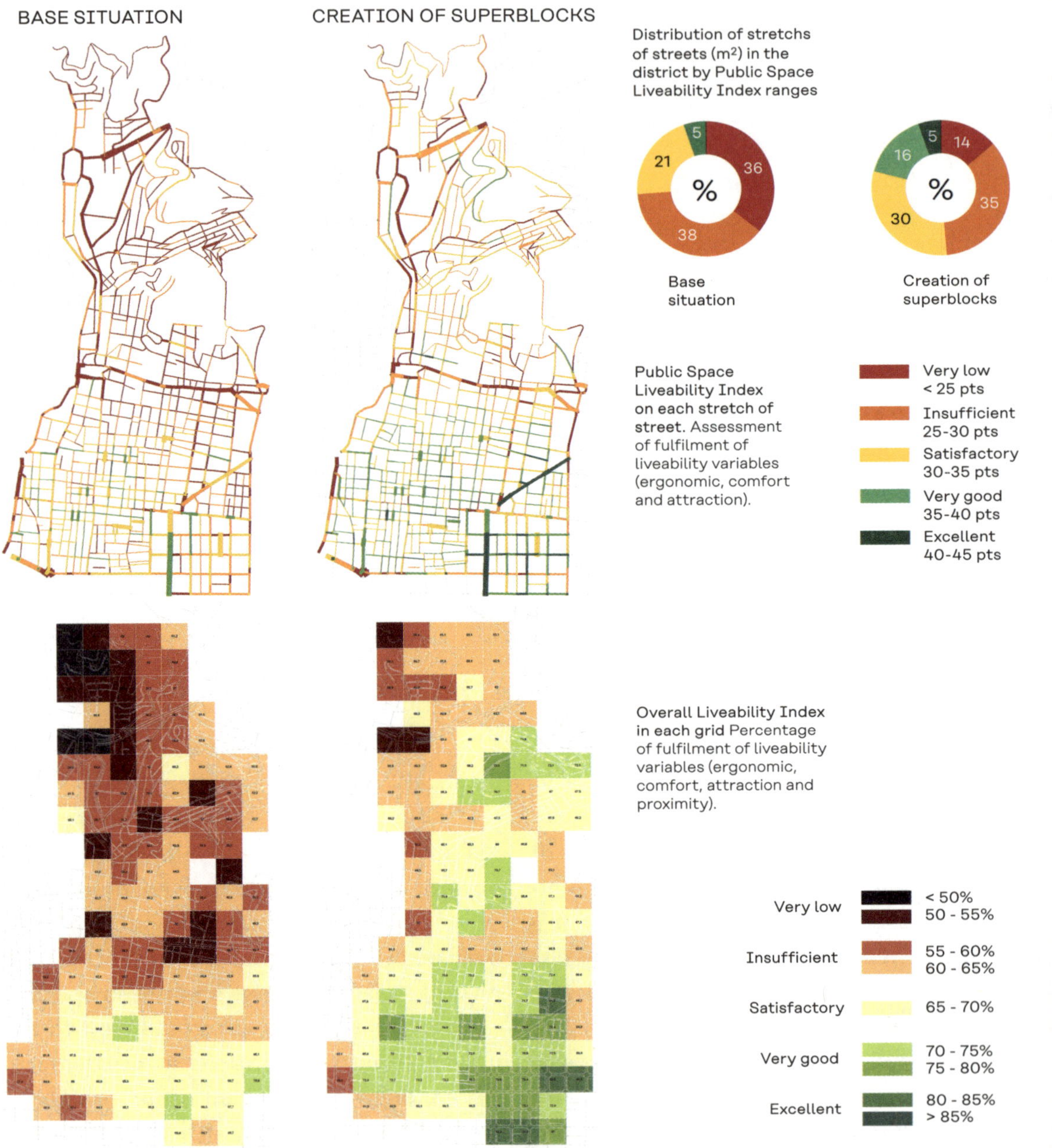

BARCELONA. GRÀCIA. 2008. Urban liveability index applied to the existing situation and to a scenario with superblocks implemented.
Source: BCNecologia

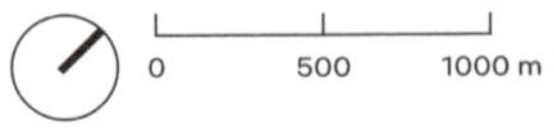

The urban liveability index developed by BCNecologia originates in the Vitoria-Gasteiz public space diagnosis of 2007. This was the first time every variable to be considered on each stretch of street was characterised in detail, through a combination of an overall representation and a 200x200 grid. Subsequently, in 2009, this index was proposed for a project commissioned by Barcelona City Council Environmental Services. BCNecologia applied the calculation methodology to four of the city's districts: Eixample, Sants-Montjuïc, Gràcia and Nou Barris. The analysis methodology was perfected and its reference values were adjusted to match the reality of the Barcelona area.

BCNecologia has since applied the liveability index to other cities and neighbourhoods it has analysed, during the process of implementing the superblock model and ecosystemic urbanism principles.

LIVEABILITY AND BUILDINGS

Buildings are the result of the need to establish adequate environmental and social conditions for human activities to take place in a certain space. In other words, buildings aim to achieve liveability.

The superblock – an urban cell and the basic unit for urban planning – also tackles liveability in housing and public facilities. Just as the ideal conditions for interaction between people are sought in the public space, classic liveability parameters are applied to buildings' interiors in the housing sphere.

One of the requirements of a superblock is good access to housing, which translates as a need for enough social housing provision. The environmental benefits entailed by a superblock-based planning model cannot be monopolised by the few. Administrations must guarantee the right to housing and make sure that as many people as possible are involved in sustainability strategies.

From a social cohesion point of view, the public facilities available to the population so that they can fulfil their needs in an accessible, local way are especially important. These facilities constitute the physical space dedicated to guaranteeing citizens' rights: to health, education, culture, etc.

In buildings and housing, liveability takes the form of a space that is flexible, multi-functional, sustainable and adaptable over time. Here, liveability is about adapting housing's use value to society's changing needs and maintaining this value for as long as possible. Nonetheless, housing liveability must also be considered within a whole – the urban space – to achieve a socially cohesive society designed with sustainability criteria in mind.

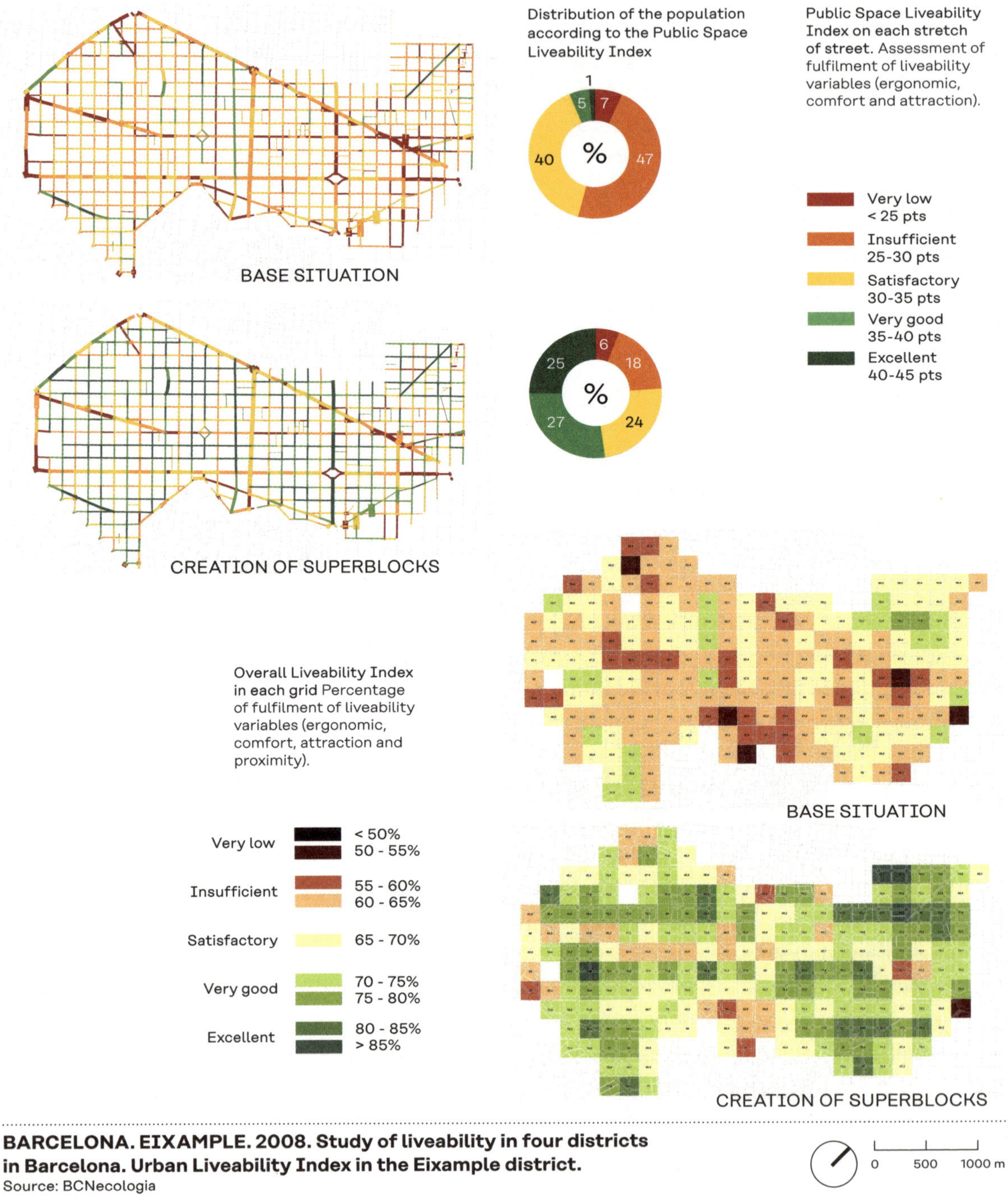

BARCELONA. EIXAMPLE. 2008. Study of liveability in four districts in Barcelona. Urban Liveability Index in the Eixample district.
Source: BCNecologia

LLEVANT SECTOR IN FIGUERES

This project was the product of a collaboration between four teams with complementary knowledge: the Rafael de Cáceres architecture and urbanism office, the Polytechnic University of Catalonia (UPC) research group led by Albert Cuchí, Lluís Brau's urbanism office and the BCN-ecologia team, led by Salvador Rueda.

The planning proposal led to the formulation of a series of considerations in terms of liveability parameters for housing, buildings and blocks. Planning allocation criteria were proposed block by block, with a view to optimising execution throughout the sector's different stages of development. The proposal also organised criteria and suitable land into three planning levels: surface, underground and roofs. The urban planning programme complemented a morphological analysis of the planned layout (the geometry of the blocks, the proportions and orientation of the streets) and provided housing and buildings that would adapt to weather variations, to changes in energy use and to evolving uses over time.

So that the project's environmental benefits would not be out of reach for anyone due to high prices, the proposal included 50% social housing, which was spread out equally across all the residential blocks to ensure the mixture of incomes needed to facilitate social cohesion.

As for weather variations and energy considerations, the proposed housing was well oriented, with enough hours of sunlight per day to guarantee enough solar energy in the winter. Furthermore, to make the housing flexible in terms of uses, buildings were designed with intermediate spaces to regulate the temperature (porches and terraces); with quality, long-lasting construction materials, especially for social groups with less purchasing power; and with an adaptability index of over 0.25 (modifiable usable floor area/total usable floor area).

On a building or block scale, a series of facilities were offered to encourage residents and users to adopt more sustainable habits. These included bicycle parking spaces, community composting areas and mechanical rooms with space for water storage equipment and solar panel heating systems.

CIUDAD JARDÍN SUPERBLOCK, CÓRDOBA

In 2015, VIMCORSA, the municipal housing company of Córdoba (Andalusia), commissioned the Agency to develop a revitalisation plan for the neighbourhood of Ciudad Jardín, including the corresponding pilot superblocks, as a continuation of the city's Mobility and Public Space Plan. This proposal focused on the following issues:

- **Public space**: planning of calming measures and reorganisation of mobility on the streets inside the superblocks.
- **Buildings**: strategy to carry out energy refurbishments on buildings and to determine which action to prioritise, according to buildings' and residents' level of vulnerability.
- **Public facilities**: strategy to produce renewable energy on site, through solar panels on educational institutions.

The study linked the proposals to subsidies and grants available in the Autonomous Community of Andalusia to predict the investment needed and the payback period.

Though neither of the plans detailed here materialised, they represent two approaches to action criteria in the building sphere, focusing on the opportunities created by superblock-based planning and on the application of liveability criteria to energy efficiency and social cohesion.

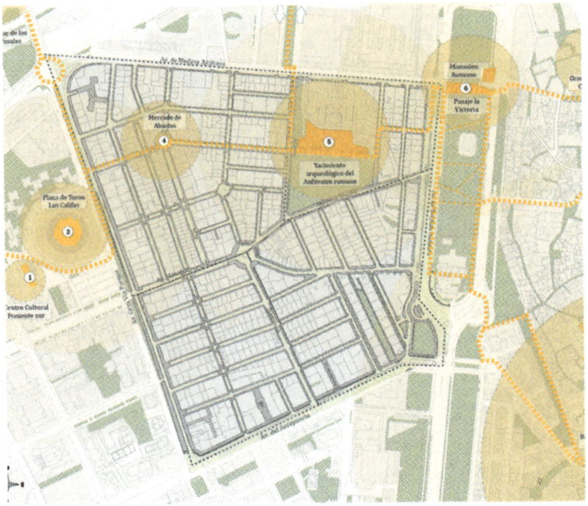

1. Renewable energy production in public facilities

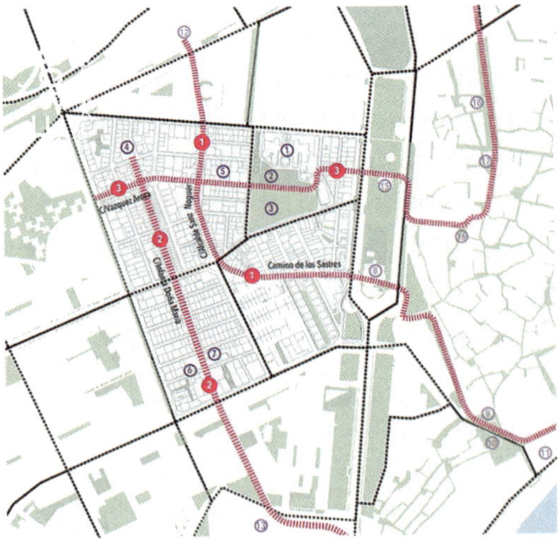

2. Work on the public space by axis

CÓRDOBA. CIUDAD JARDÍN. 2015. Urban Regeneration in the neighbourhood of Ciudad Jardín.
Priority for actions.
Source: BCNecologia

CÓRDOBA. NEIGHBOURHOOD OF CIUDAD JARDÍN.
Source: Córdoba City Council

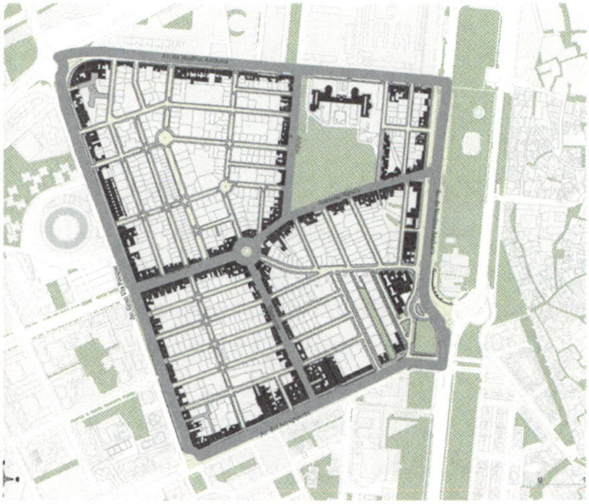

3. Energy refurbishments on building façades on the basic road network

LIVEABILITY AND SOCIAL COHESION

SOCIAL SUPERBLOCKS

Though social cohesion is a key aspect in the implementation of superblocks, the social superblocks project, led by the Home Care Service (SAD), is the first to deal with this issue exclusively.

The concept of sustainability goes beyond the strictly environmental sphere and incorporates economic and social aspects, such as social welfare and business. Superblocks take all of these elements into account and bring them to life in the public space. However, as the concept of the superblock has become more popular, issues linked to urban functionality, the local economy

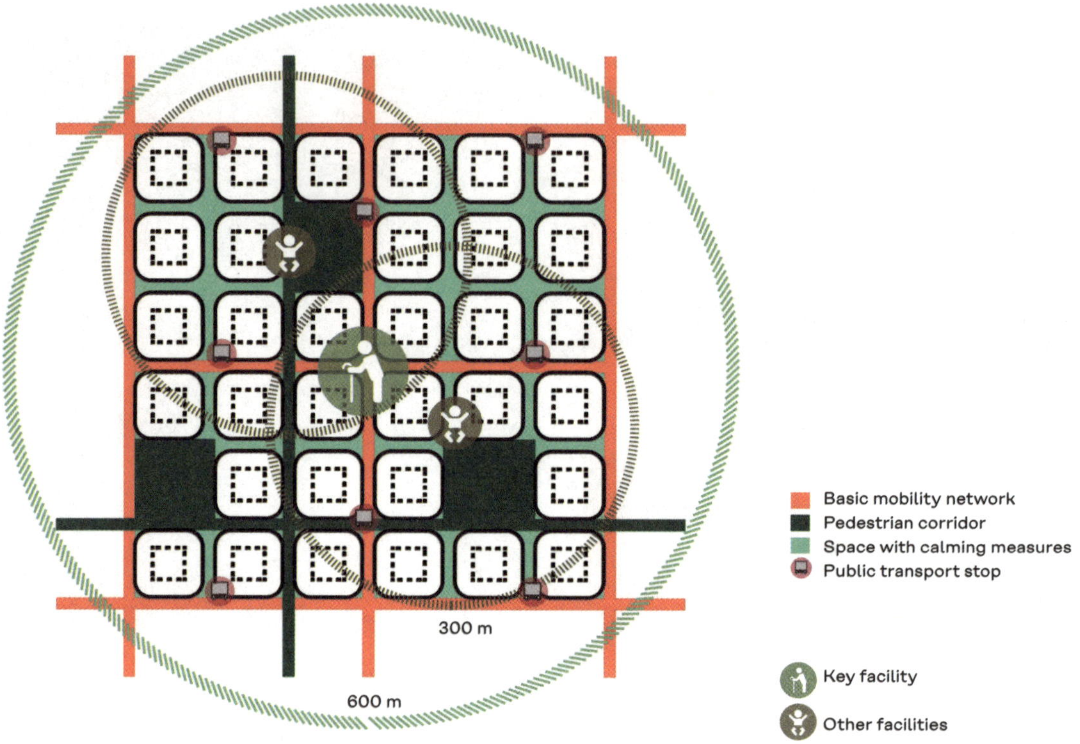

BARCELONA. 2019. The concept of social superblock.
Source: BCNecologia

and care have sometimes been forgotten, and the spotlight has shone exclusively on transforming mobility, although this is only the first step in addressing the other issues. It is important, then, to develop the social and care facet of superblocks and roll it out across the region. This new organisation model is based on the Home Care Service, though the aim is to extend it to other care services at a later date.

The current SAD service provision model has shown signs of reaching its limit, in terms of service quality and working conditions for professionals. Another challenge faced by the Service is the growing population. It puts a strain on both its funding and its organisation, as SAD must try not to leave anyone behind while finding the most efficient management methods possible. Planning social care on a scale where the services are both efficient and viable for the Administration and useful for users is a key part of this new regional and functional organisation of social services.

In 2019, the Social Rights Area of Barcelona City Council commissioned BCN-ecologia to design a resilient social super-block map, backed by urban elements with slow transformation times, that could adapt to variations in SAD services. Social super-blocks, which are smaller than the neighbourhoods of Barcelona, have thus become the minimum coverage area for many basic facilities and the unit considered the ideal environment: a space where residents belong, where everyone feels like part of a collective and can build a network of relationships and a sense of identity that satisfy them in their day-to-day lives.

The aim of the new Home Care Service is to trial a new kind of service provision, through pilot superblocks, based on local, community urbanism and professional teams that care for the users living in a certain superblock. This leads to more consistent, local, personalised care.

The social superblock land delimitation proposal organises the city into new urban cells of between 600x600 m and 900x900 m. In theory, the average population of each of these new superblocks is somewhere between 15,000 and 32,500. This new organisation model considers two basic criteria: resource allocation and the population's access to a network of basic services that is as complete as possible and at a walkable distance.

MAIN RESULTS

To configure these social superblocks, the Agency took heed of the limitations affecting social services, prioritised within an order of application, including adaptation to district limits, exclusion of green spaces of more than ten hectares, compatibility with mobility superblocks, consideration of orography and main roads, creation of functional areas offering between 1,400 and 1,800 hours of care monthly for SAD users, and interaction with other administrative divisions (neighbourhoods, social service centres and basic health areas).

BARCELONA. Social superblocks are intended to be a new, local care model.
Picture: Antonio Lajusticia

A set of 26 indicators were then formulated to characterise the social superblocks and categorised into two main groups: demographic/economic vulnerability and urban context. The first group of indicators characterises most people who could potentially use social services or may require special care due to age, financial means or a physical or mental disability. These groups represent the social service system's 'liabilities'. The urban context indicators, meanwhile, refer to a set of parameters that indicate places in the city where the urban fabric is denser and more complex, urban fabrics with more resources and proximity to urban services, and areas under the most pressure from urban development.

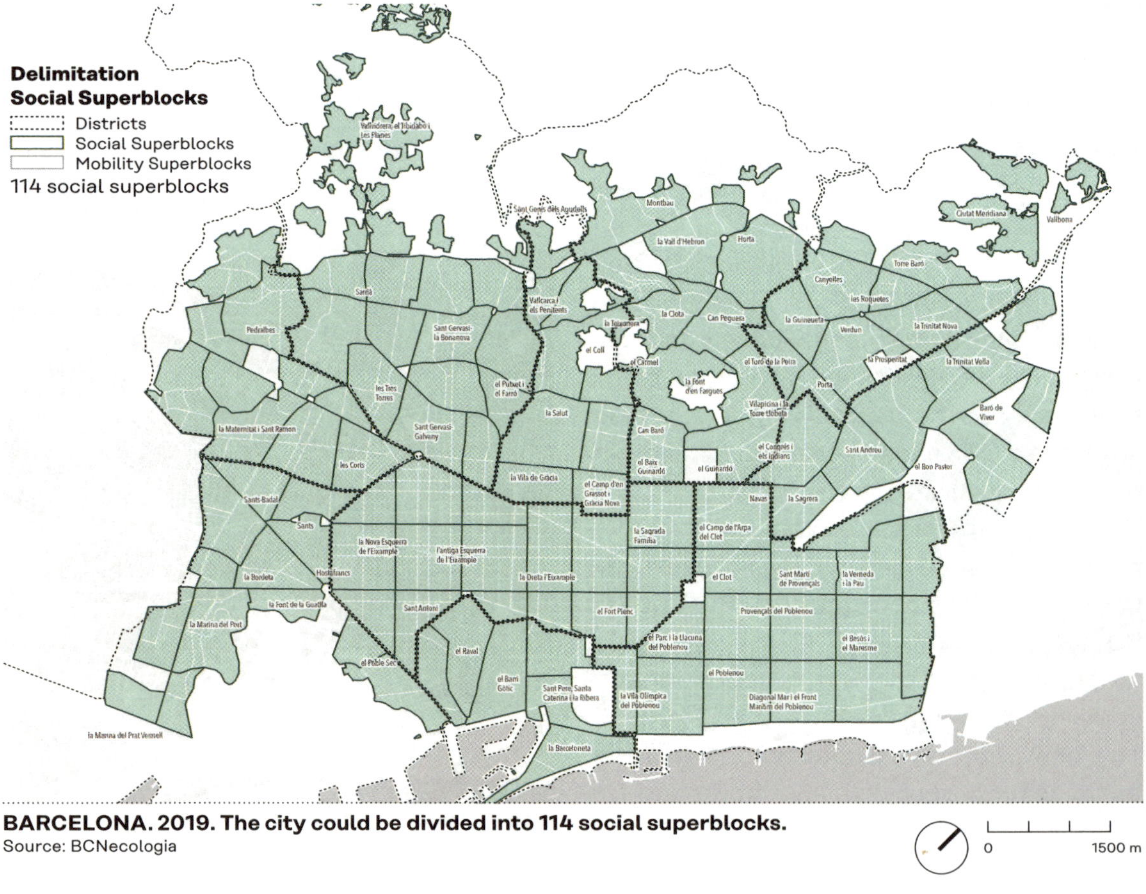

BARCELONA. 2019. The city could be divided into 114 social superblocks.
Source: BCNecologia

Conclusions

Analysing urban liveability and designing the liveability index are two tasks that have greatly enriched the Agency's expertise, as they have opened the window to new analysis perspectives that have impacted the design of strategies and methodologies in other areas, beyond the public space. This methodology has been applied to different cities and social fabrics, enabling BCNecologia to refine its definition of analysis and assessment variables and parameters through the liveability index.

Moreover, it is important to note that superblocks are an ideal instrument for making some of the main initiatives linked to social cohesion a reality, such as giving the streets back to the people and creating a local network of social services.

The social superblock proposal aims to go beyond the strictly environmental sphere and incorporate economic and social aspects, such as balanced relationships in the community, residents' social welfare and the businesses that operate there.

The Agency's main contribution to liveability projects and social superblocks has been ensuring that superblocks deal with social vulnerability from a standpoint of accessibility, health and social inclusion applied to housing, public space and local facilities.

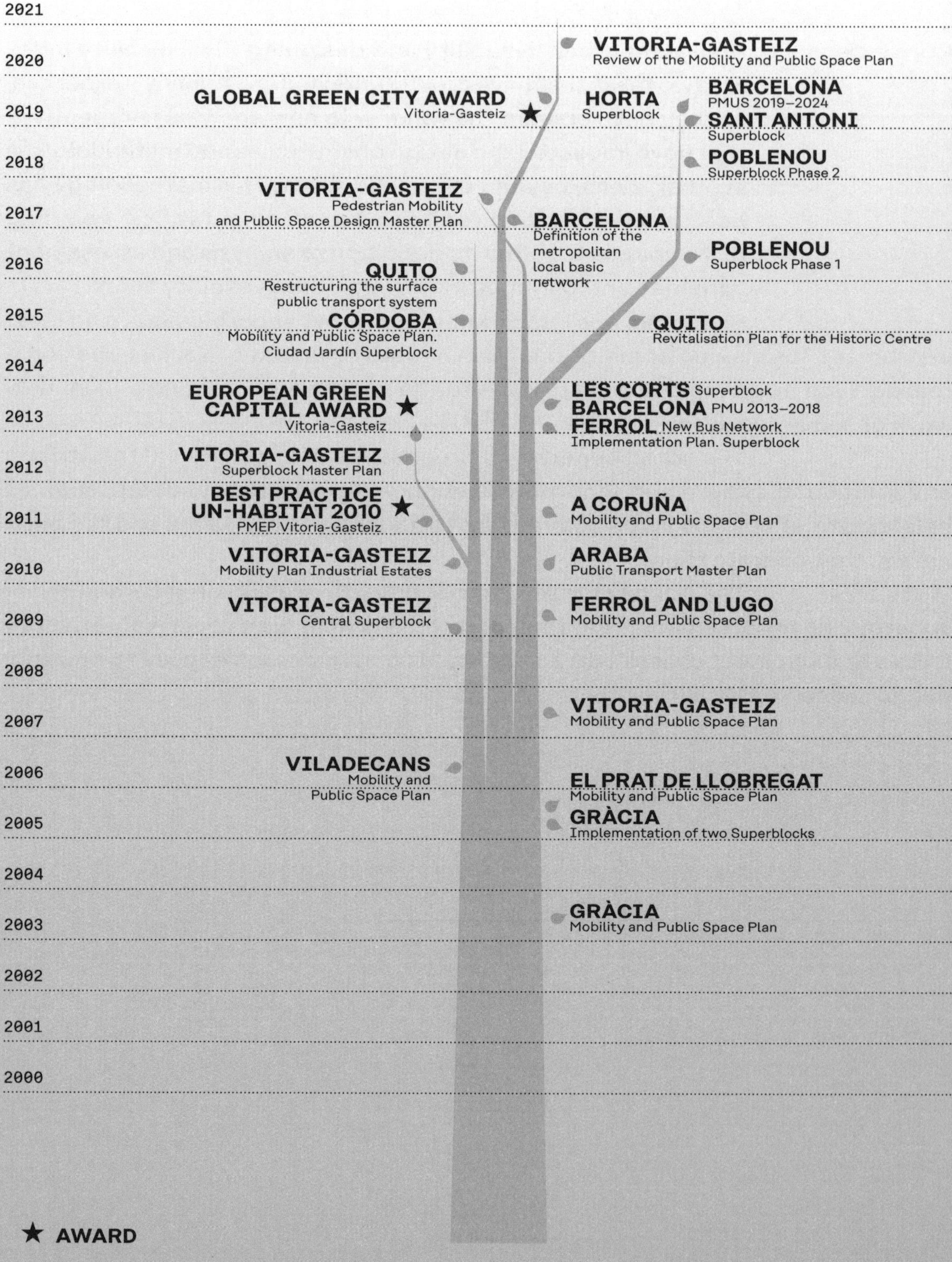
2021
2020
VITORIA-GASTEIZ
Review of the Mobility and Public Space Plan
2019
GLOBAL GREEN CITY AWARD
Vitoria-Gasteiz ★
HORTA
Superblock
BARCELONA
PMUS 2019–2024
SANT ANTONI
Superblock
2018
POBLENOU
Superblock Phase 2
2017
VITORIA-GASTEIZ
Pedestrian Mobility and Public Space Design Master Plan
BARCELONA
Definition of the metropolitan local basic network
2016
QUITO
Restructuring the surface public transport system
POBLENOU
Superblock Phase 1
2015
CÓRDOBA
Mobility and Public Space Plan. Ciudad Jardín Superblock
QUITO
Revitalisation Plan for the Historic Centre
2014
EUROPEAN GREEN CAPITAL AWARD ★
Vitoria-Gasteiz
LES CORTS Superblock
BARCELONA PMU 2013–2018
FERROL New Bus Network
Implementation Plan. Superblock
2013
2012
VITORIA-GASTEIZ
Superblock Master Plan
2011
BEST PRACTICE UN-HABITAT 2010 ★
PMEP Vitoria-Gasteiz
A CORUÑA
Mobility and Public Space Plan
2010
VITORIA-GASTEIZ
Mobility Plan Industrial Estates
ARABA
Public Transport Master Plan
2009
VITORIA-GASTEIZ
Central Superblock
FERROL AND LUGO
Mobility and Public Space Plan
2008
2007
VITORIA-GASTEIZ
Mobility and Public Space Plan
2006
VILADECANS
Mobility and Public Space Plan
EL PRAT DE LLOBREGAT
Mobility and Public Space Plan
2005
GRÀCIA
Implementation of two Superblocks
2004
2003
GRÀCIA
Mobility and Public Space Plan
2002
2001
2000
★ AWARD

MOBILITY AND PUBLIC SPACE

Today's cities fall short in many ways because of their obsolete mobility model based on mass use of private vehicles, which take up a high percentage of the public space and have serious health consequences. Motor vehicles are the biggest cause of air and noise pollution, which are two of the main environmental threats to the population's health.

From its very beginnings, the Urban Ecology Agency of Barcelona has fought to implement a , fairer, more sustainable, safer and more efficient mobility and public space model. This superblock-based model takes back much of the street space currently dedicated to mobility and adapts it for more uses and citizens' rights, thus making the streets a place for harmonious coexistence.

This change in model requires mobility plans that reorganise whole surface transport networks (walking and cycle routes, public transport, urban freight distribution and private transport) on a whole-city scale to free up as much space as possible for people, without detriment to urban functionality.

This section offers a review of the results achieved in the mobility and public space sphere, through various mobility plans drawn up in Barcelona and other cities in Spain.

The last chapter in this section focuses on the successful implementation of orthogonal bus networks in Barcelona and Vitoria-Gasteiz. This kind of network has emerged as the most efficient and competitive option for urban systems, as it has improved connectivity, service frequency, intermodality and accessibility for all users. The figures prove the effectiveness of the orthogonal network, which is an essential piece in the superblock model configuration. In Vitoria-Gasteiz, for example, in just two years, the number of bus users increased by 40%.

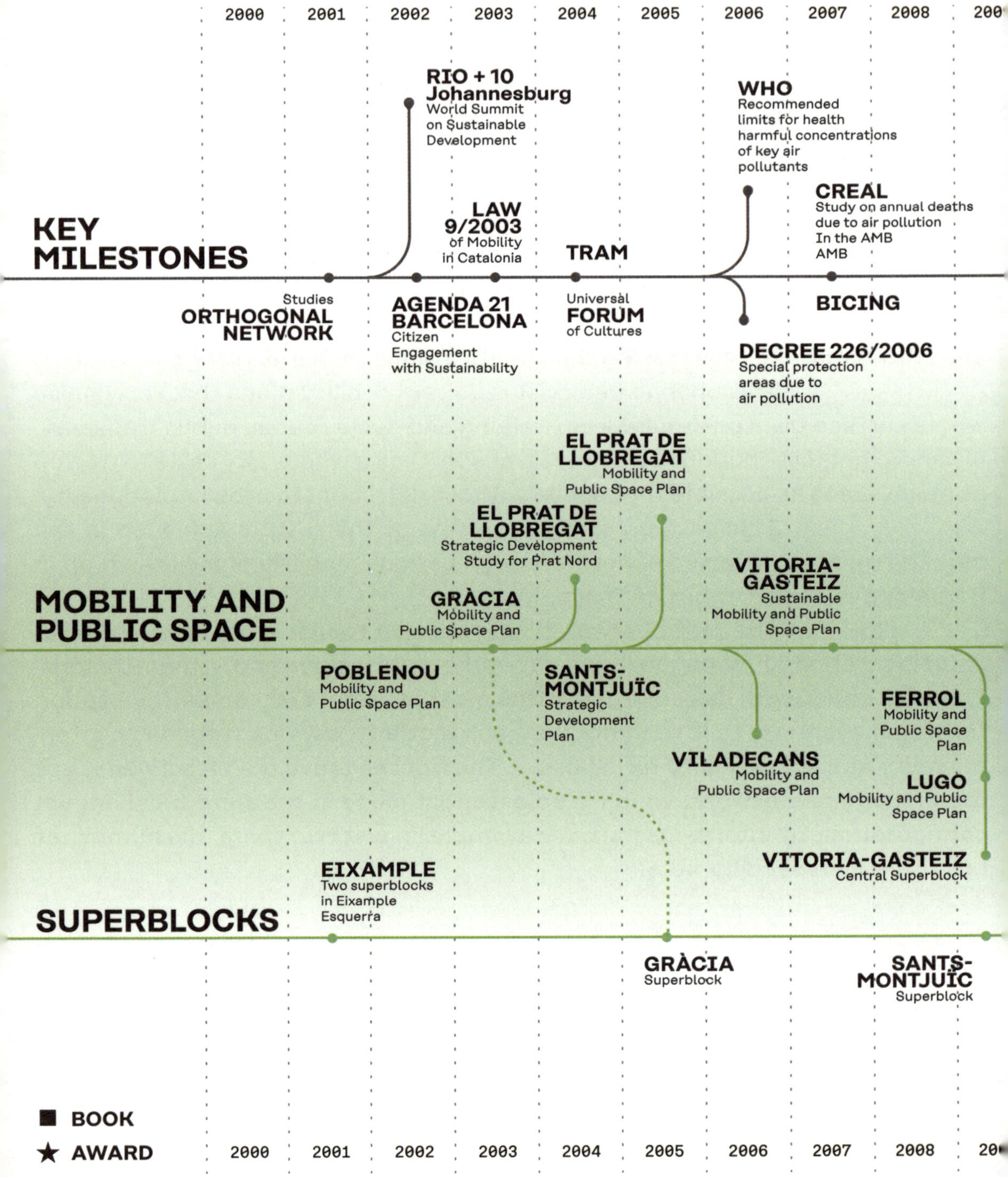
2000
2001
2002
2003
2004
2005
2006
2007
2008
KEY MILESTONES
RIO + 10 Johannesburg
World Summit on Sustainable Development
LAW 9/2003
of Mobility in Catalonia
TRAM
WHO
Recommended limits for health harmful concentrations of key air pollutants
CREAL
Study on annual deaths due to air pollution In the AMB AMB
Studies
ORTHOGONAL NETWORK
AGENDA 21 BARCELONA
Citizen Engagement with Sustainability
Universal
FORUM
of Cultures
BICING
DECREE 226/2006
Special protection areas due to air pollution
MOBILITY AND PUBLIC SPACE
EL PRAT DE LLOBREGAT
Mobility and Public Space Plan
EL PRAT DE LLOBREGAT
Strategic Development Study for Prat Nord
GRÀCIA
Mobility and Public Space Plan
VITORIA-GASTEIZ
Sustainable Mobility and Public Space Plan
POBLENOU
Mobility and Public Space Plan
SANTS-MONTJUÏC
Strategic Development Plan
VILADECANS
Mobility and Public Space Plan
FERROL
Mobility and Public Space Plan
LUGO
Mobility and Public Space Plan
VITORIA-GASTEIZ
Central Superblock
SUPERBLOCKS
EIXAMPLE
Two superblocks in Eixample Esquerra
GRÀCIA
Superblock
SANTS-MONTJUÏC
Superblock
BOOK
AWARD

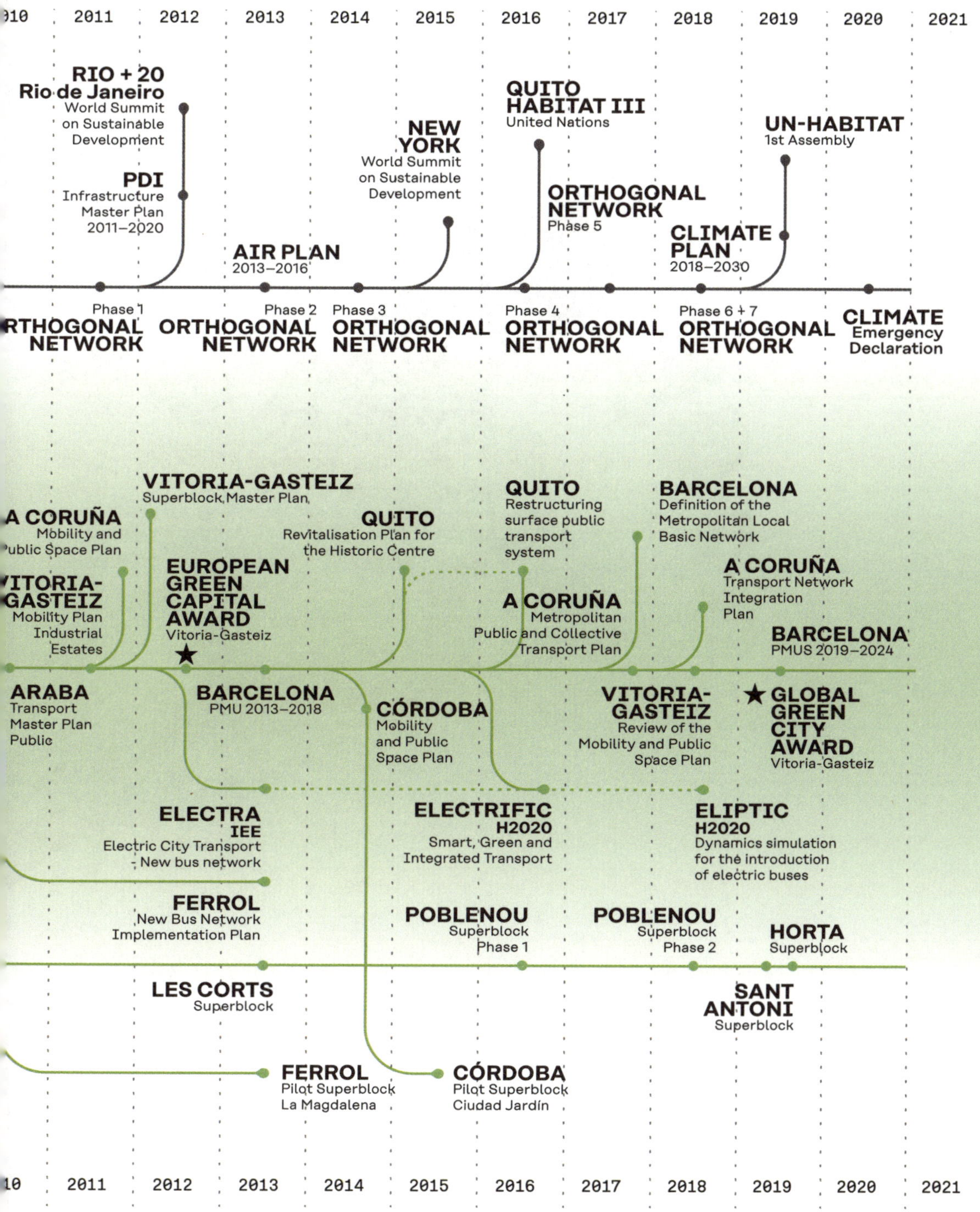

2010 2011 2012 2013 2014 2015 2016 2017 2018 2019 2020 2021
RIO + 20 Rio de Janeiro
World Summit on Sustainable Development
PDI
Infrastructure Master Plan 2011–2020
AIR PLAN
2013–2016
NEW YORK
World Summit on Sustainable Development
QUITO HABITAT III
United Nations
ORTHOGONAL NETWORK
Phase 5
CLIMATE PLAN
2018–2030
UN-HABITAT
1st Assembly
Phase 1
ORTHOGONAL NETWORK
Phase 2
ORTHOGONAL NETWORK
Phase 3
ORTHOGONAL NETWORK
Phase 4
ORTHOGONAL NETWORK
Phase 6 + 7
ORTHOGONAL NETWORK
CLIMATE
Emergency Declaration
A CORUÑA
Mobility and Public Space Plan
VITORIA-GASTEIZ
Mobility Plan Industrial Estates
VITORIA-GASTEIZ
Superblock Master Plan
EUROPEAN GREEN CAPITAL AWARD
Vitoria-Gasteiz
QUITO
Revitalisation Plan for the Historic Centre
QUITO
Restructuring surface public transport system
A CORUÑA
Metropolitan Public and Collective Transport Plan
BARCELONA
Definition of the Metropolitan Local Basic Network
A CORUÑA
Transport Network Integration Plan
BARCELONA
PMUS 2019–2024
ARABA
Transport Master Plan Public
BARCELONA
PMU 2013–2018
CÓRDOBA
Mobility and Public Space Plan
VITORIA-GASTEIZ
Review of the Mobility and Public Space Plan
GLOBAL GREEN CITY AWARD
Vitoria-Gasteiz
ELECTRA
IEE
Electric City Transport - New bus network
ELECTRIFIC
H2020
Smart, Green and Integrated Transport
ELIPTIC
H2020
Dynamics simulation for the introduction of electric buses
FERROL
New Bus Network Implementation Plan
POBLENOU
Superblock Phase 1
POBLENOU
Superblock Phase 2
HORTA
Superblock
LES CORTS
Superblock
SANT ANTONI
Superblock
FERROL
Pilot Superblock La Magdalena
CÓRDOBA
Pilot Superblock Ciudad Jardín
2010 2011 2012 2013 2014 2015 2016 2017 2018 2019 2020 2021

'At the head of the Councillor's Office for Mobility in the city of Barcelona, my experience at the Agency was key: from its urban planning philosophy and vision of a people-oriented city, to specific projects that develop this idea, which we explored in great depth, like the Urban Mobility Plan, the orthogonal bus network and superblocks. All of them involved a great deal of technical, participative and political work – and not without conflict, as is the case for all initiatives that significantly alter the road hierarchy and, at the cost of private motor vehicles, give space to those who have little'.

MERCEDES VIDAL
Environmentalist. Councillor for Mobility 2014-2019. Barcelona City Council.
Senior Technician 2006-2014. BCNecologia.

Picture: Marta Torrent

A MORE SUSTAINABLE MOBILITY AND PUBLIC SPACE MODEL FOR BARCELONA

- 2021
- 2020
- **2019** — **HORTA** Superblock; **BARCELONA** PMUS 2019–2024; **SANT ANTONI** Superblock
- **2018** — **POBLENOU** Superblock Phase 2
- 2017
- **2016** — **POBLENOU** Superblock Phase 1
- 2015
- 2014
- **2013** — **BARCELONA** PMU 2013–2018
- 2012
- 2011
- 2010
- **2009** — **SANTS-MONTJUÏC** Superblock
- 2008
- 2007
- 2006
- **2005** — **GRÀCIA** Implementation of two superblocks
- 2004
- **2003** — **GRÀCIA** Mobility and Public Space Plan
- 2002
- **2001** — **EIXAMPLE** Two superblocks in Eixample Esquerra
- 2000

This chapter reviews the history of the instrument that governs mobility in the city of Barcelona: the Urban Mobility Plan (PMU). Barcelona's urban mobility ecosystem covers a diverse range of journeys involving a number of parties, and from which a variety of initiatives emerge. All of these pieces and agents can be coordinated thanks to the urban mobility plans established by Law 9/2003 of 13 June, on mobility in Catalonia.

The city mobility model of recent decades, in which private vehicles take priority over all other modes of transport, has led to a series of problems that seriously affect Barcelona residents' quality of life. Time wasted due to traffic and pollution are just some of the problems to be solved when planning mobility.

BCNecologia has played a key role in the development of mobility plans for Barcelona. In 2003, the Agency put together the Gràcia District Mobility and Public Space Plan, in response to the main shortfalls in the district's mobility and public space. It later formulated the Urban Mobility Plan 2013–2018, which extended and standardised proposals and initiatives across the urban area, with a clear focus on sustainability. In 2019, BCNecologia was commissioned once again to draw up the Sustainable Urban Mobility Plan (PMUS) for the city for the six years following the original plan, to ensure continuity for the unprecedented urban mobility transformation process already under way.

The aim of the PMU is to promote safe, sustainable transport over more aggressive, polluting forms of mobility. At the same time, it seeks to minimise energy consumption and its negative effects on the environment and citizens' quality of life.

The Plan constitutes one of the Agency's most important achievements, as it is a key instrument that has helped to consolidate significant city projects, such as the orthogonal bus network and the roll-out of the superblock model across the area.

THE BARCELONA URBAN MOBILITY PLAN

Today, the Barcelona PMU is the leading instrument that promotes and articulates all the initiatives that shape the way the city's residents move around. Urban mobility covers all the journeys made by people and goods in the urban environment, in all possible ways, with the purpose of carrying out day-to-day activities. All the pieces and agents involved are coordinated through the implementation of urban mobility plans.

The Barcelona PMU, in particular, has played a key role in determining the ideal mobility model for the city and how to achieve it. For the Agency, the 2013–2018 PMU was an opportunity to reflect on the urban model approaching on the horizon. It was used to define future strategies to create a safe, healthy, sustainable, fair, smart mobility model for Barcelona. The aim of the plan was to promote safe, sustainable mobility; to reduce demand on more aggressive, polluting forms of transport; and to minimise energy consumption and its negative effects on the environment and people's quality of life.

The Urban Ecology Agency of Barcelona has played a key role in the development of Barcelona's PMU over the years, with innovative proposals like the orthogonal bus network and the superblock-based mobility model. These two ideas constitute a turning point in the city's urban model. The Agency has built every mobility plan following a detailed diagnosis of the existing situation at that specific time. Nonetheless, the common feature of all of its plans is the need to reverse the existing model, in which the motor vehicle takes precedence over all other modes of transport, and to minimise the externalities caused by this imbalance.

To understand the context from which these initiatives emerge, it is important to examine the mobility panorama at the end of the twentieth century. Over recent decades, in post-Olympic Barcelona, mobility has exploded and its model has evolved, tending to revolve around the private motor vehicle. This has undoubtedly had significant negative repercussions, worsened by Barcelona's status as a metropolitan city, where the urban centre must be considered a real city with four million inhabitants.

Among the main problems the Administration faces are pollution caused by gas and particle emissions from vehicles, noise pollution, a high accident rate, indiscriminate use of land and public spaces, unsustainable energy consumption, the collapse of infrastructures and services, and citizens' time wasted due to traffic.

That is why, in 1998, over thirty entities, supported by the City Council, signed the Barcelona Mobility Pact. This pact constitutes a space for participation and cooperation between Barcelona City Council and civil society, through various entities, associations and mobility experts. The subsequent

- Public open spaces
- Access within 200 m
- Access within 300 m
- Access within 400 m or more

0 400 m

GRÀCIA. BARCELONA. 2003. Access to public open spaces in the base scenario: gardens, squares and more than 1,000 m² of parks.
Source: BCNecologia

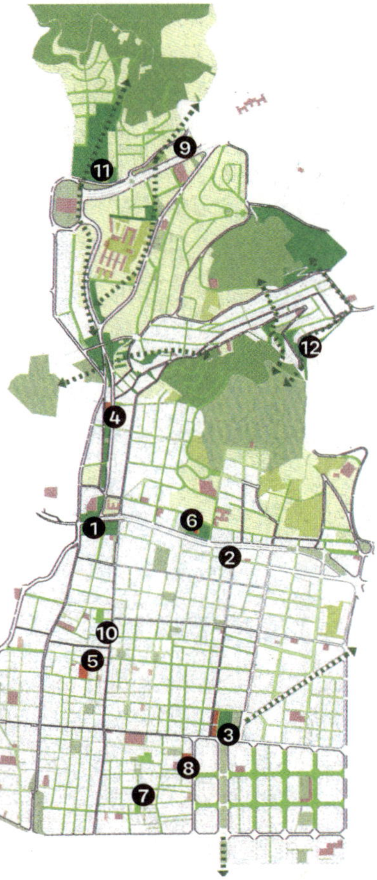

- Delimitation of superblocks
- Green corridor
- New green spaces
- New pedestrian areas
- Existing pedestrian streets
- Public open spaces
- Urban parks
- Woodland
- Private green spaces
- Light urban development with open spaces
- Public facilities
- Cultural facilities
- New facilities

1. Renovation of Pl. Lesseps
2. Renovation of Travessera de Dalt
3. Extension of Pl. Joanic and new facility
4. Renovation of Av. Hospital Militar
5. New cultural facility and pedestrian connection
6. New sports facility and pedestrian connection
7. Opening of Pl. Gato Pérez
8. New educational facility
9. Penitents Library
10. New square C. Santa Àgata
11. "Coixí" Garden
12. Redefinition of Coll del Portell

GRÀCIA. BARCELONA. 2003. Superblock proposal for the district, with improvements to the public space and intervention points.
Source: BCNecologia

PMUs incorporate the Pact's commitment to promoting consultation and participatory dynamics as a key working methodology and its goal to define the city's ideal mobility model for the following years, in collaboration with the Administration. The Pact monitors enforcement of the PMU and application of mobility policies to the city, though its constituent entities' level of involvement has varied over the years, according to the importance the city's governments have attached to participation policies. Even so, the Mobility Pact has always been the main space for debate around this issue in the City Council.

THE GRÀCIA DISTRICT MOBILITY AND PUBLIC SPACE PLAN

This year, the Gràcia District Mobility and Public Space Plan (PMEP, 2003) is celebrating its eighteenth anniversary. The idea behind the Plan was to improve mobility conditions, both for essential travel and

BARCELONA. PMU 2013–2018. Diagram of a typical superblock in the final phase of implementation with all constituent parts.
Source: BCNecologia

journeys for leisure purposes. For this reason, it was included in the Barcelona Agenda 21, Barcelona Mobility Pact and Gràcia Strategic Plan goals. The study contained a list of aims to give the public space back to the people and improve the quality of their journeys. These goals focused on reducing the space dedicated to vehicles and allocating more room in the public space to pedestrians, on improving liveability conditions and on maximising the accessibility of more sustainable modes of transport. To this end, a great deal of effort went into expanding the area's cycling infrastructure and bringing public transport closer to the residents of Gràcia.

With a view to achieving these goals, the Gràcia PMEP brought together the main mobility and public space initiatives proposed at that time. It also incorporated the concept of a new mobility and public space management unit: the superblock. The new model proposed implementing superblocks in every neighbourhood of Gràcia, by

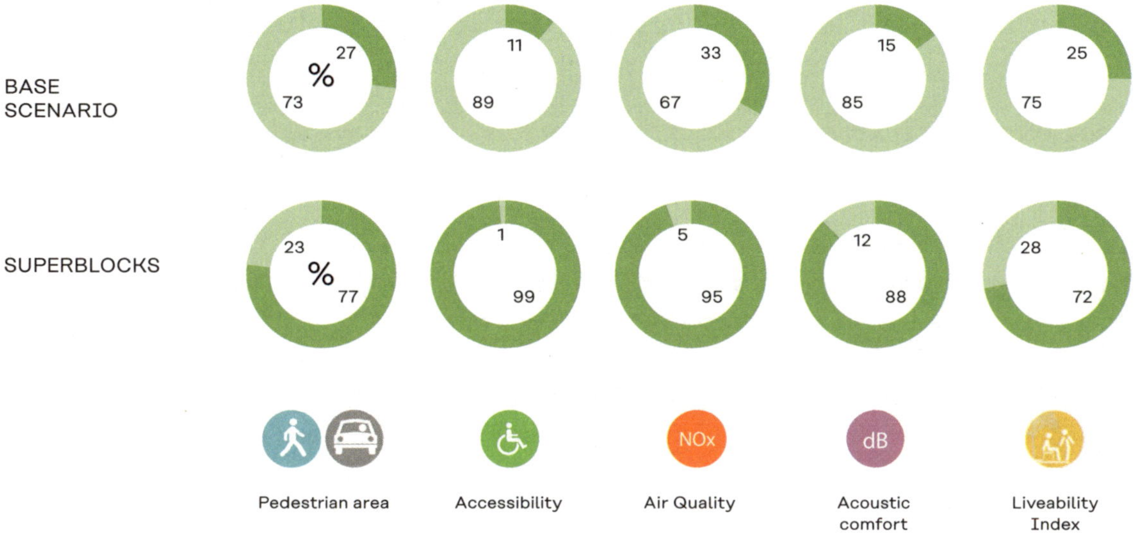

BARCELONA. PMU 2013–2018. Superblock in Les Corts neighbourhood. Simulation of the status of the variables that make up the liveability index for the pilot superblocks.
Source: BCNecologia

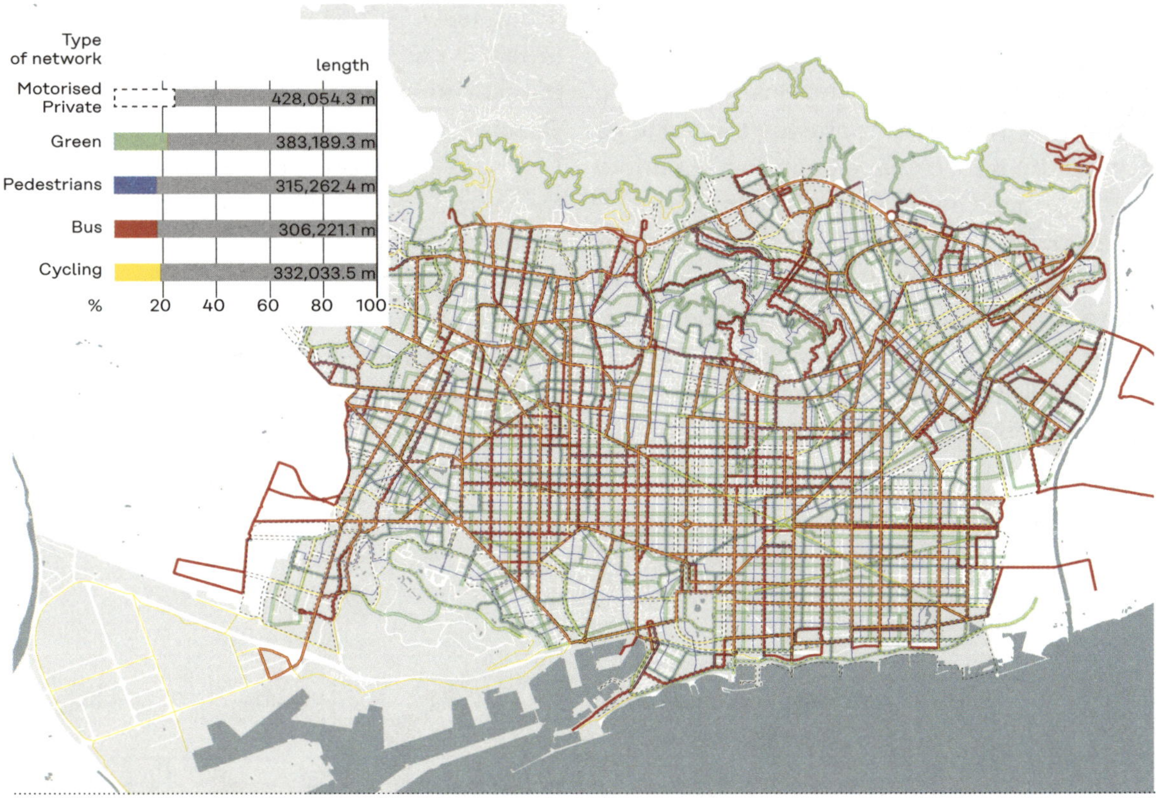

BARCELONA. SUSTAINABLE URBAN MOBILITY PLAN 2019–2014. Integrated network.
This network offers articulated connections between all the modes of transport that affect mobility in the city.
Source: BCNecologia

optimising the internal circuits in each area. These circuits improved internal accessibility for residents, as they guaranteed that all areas of the district were well connected. This had an effect on modal split, available parking and on the loading and unloading of goods.

The methodology used to put the plan together involved three execution phases: detailed analysis of the existing situation; definition of priorities through a participatory process (Mobility, Urban Planning and Environment Council, and meetings with representatives of the sectoral councils for citizens' participation in the district); and verification of results through simulation programmes. One of the unique features of this plan was its detailed proposal regarding how to take back the public space and improve public open spaces by transforming streets

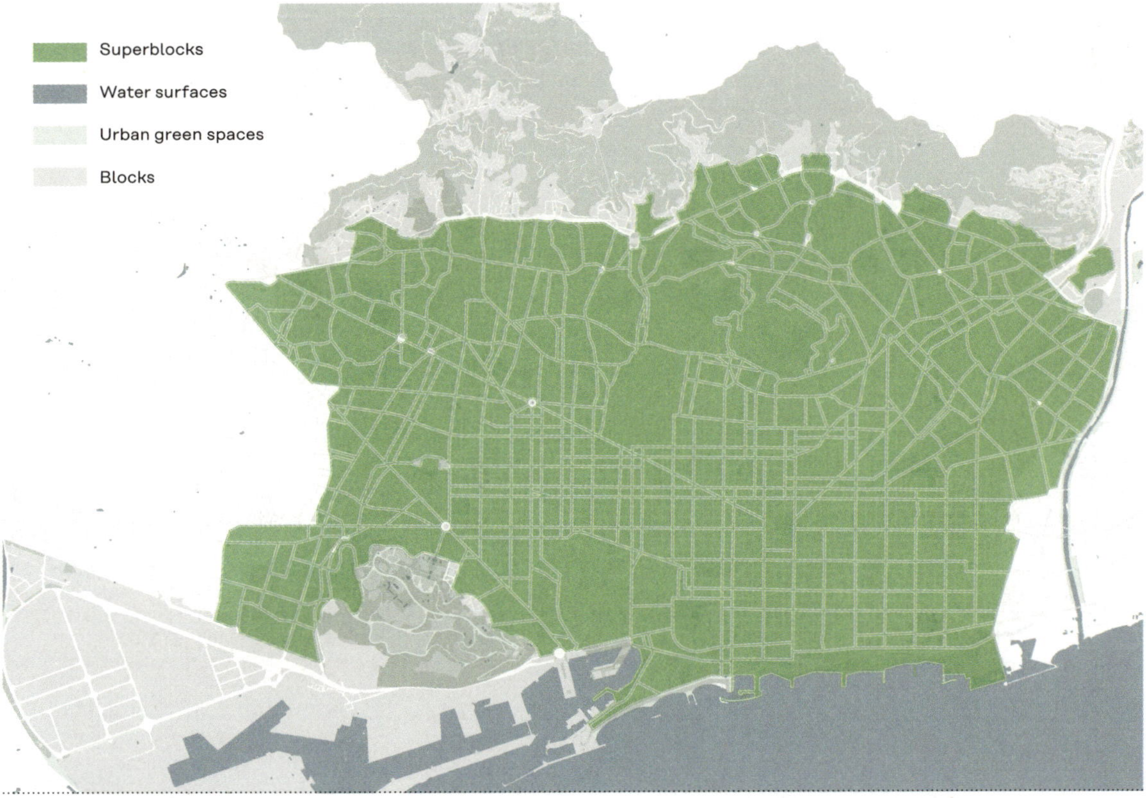

BARCELONA. Superblock plan. Plan containing 305 uniform superblocks across the city's built-up urban land, excluding Zona Franca.
Source: BCNecologia

with pedestrians in mind. This transformation was based on the definition of general sustainability criteria for the public space, which included aspects such as the materials to be used and set environmental quality standards for lighting and urban furniture.

The most significant results of the Plan materialised in two ways. The first was the reduced presence of vehicles on streets – in terms of both traffic and parked cars – and the second, a greater amount of public open spaces for local residents. Before the Plan was implemented, 40,192 vehicles per hour were driven in the district, while in the second phase of implementation, this number fell to 38,447. What is more, the Plan involved cutting the number of above-ground parking spaces and creating more underground parking, to make up for the parking deficit for residents. Finally, the cycle network

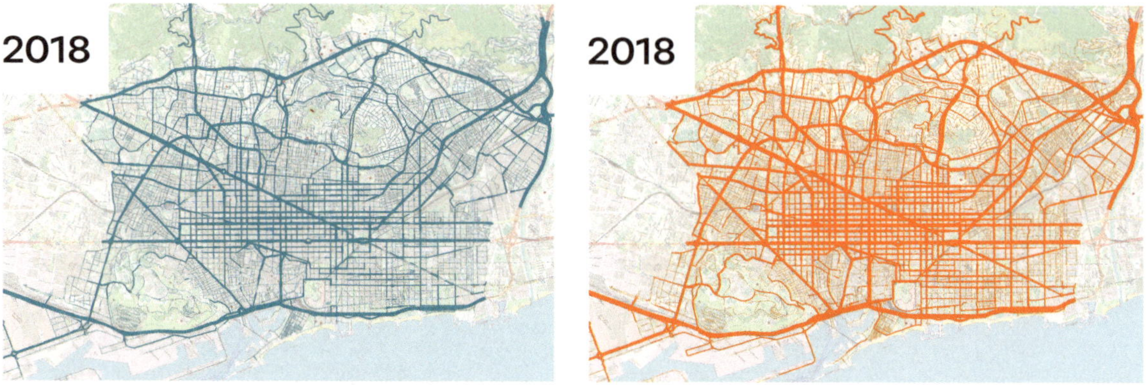

Base year 2018 (sub-scenario E1) in kg/km

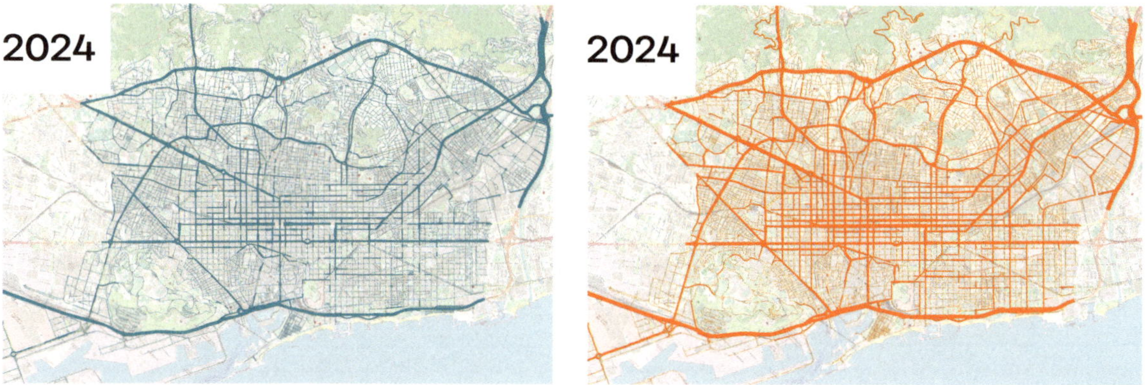

2024 scenario (-21%) and sub-scenario E3 in kg/km

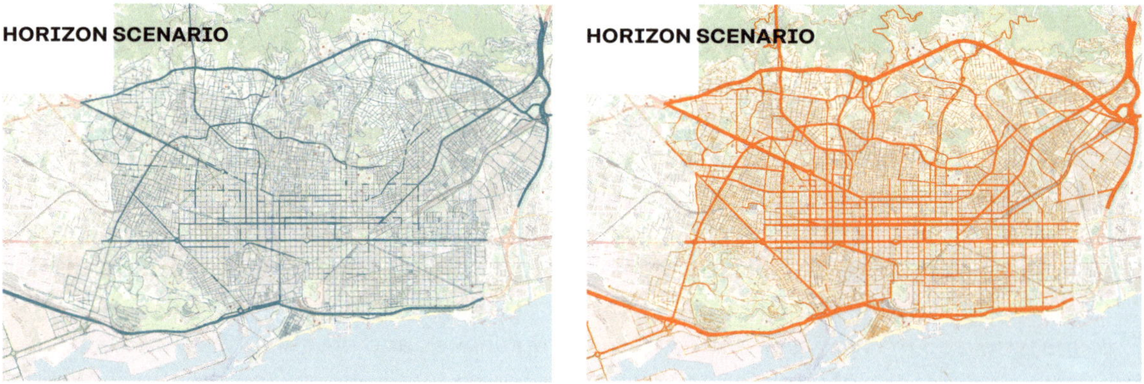

Horizon scenario (sub-scenario E3) in kg/km

BARCELONA. SUSTAINABLE URBAN MOBILITY PLAN 2019–2024. Map of NO_x and PM_{10} emissions from daily traffic.
Source: BCNecologia

NO_x (kg/km)	PM_{10} (kg/km)
< 2,000	< 200
2,000 - 5,000	200 - 500
5,000 - 10,000	500 - 1,000
10,000 - 15,000	1,000 - 2,000
>15,000	>2000

0 2 km

grew from 967 metres to over 15 kilometres, and more bicycle parking and the respective signage was provided.

URBAN MOBILITY PLAN 2013–2018

In 2012, Barcelona City Council commissioned the Agency to formulate the PMU for the 2013–2018 period. In this plan, the Agency incorporated the same principles applied to the PMEP for Gràcia. It also carried on from the process started by the PMU 2008–2012 and its aim to reflect on the urban model, while connecting different sectoral mobility policies and making them compatible. The new PMU consolidated the initiatives set out in the first Plan, by assessing their execution in depth, and established new measures that would make progress on the road to building a more liveable city.

The PMU 2013–2018 focused on four areas for action: safety, sustainability, fairness and efficiency in mobility, which would be achieved through 66 specific initiatives. For the first time, the Plan included the superblock as an essential part of the road hierarchy and a key element in leading the change to the city's mobility model, based on strengthening surface public transport and developing the cycle network.

Furthermore, it established new targets for reducing the use of private vehicles and for changing the modal split in an attempt to fulfil air quality standards – in terms of NO_x and PM_{10} – and greenhouse gas emissions parameters set by the European Union, while optimising traffic. Finally, the Plan regulated on-street and off-street parking, made urban freight distribution more efficient and therefore reduced pressure from loading and unloading (L/U) on the rest of the city's motor traffic.

The implementation of all the initiatives included in the Plan led to a reduction in mobility by private motor vehicle of 21%, which translated as increased use of more sustainable modes of transport. Public transport demand rose by 3.5%, and 10% more journeys were made on foot. However, the favoured mode of transport following the implementation of the plan was undoubtedly the bicycle: once the cycle lane network was expanded considerably, this kind of mobility grew by 67%. As well as complying with the environmental parameters defined by the European Union, the Plan aimed to reduce the number of deaths due to road accidents in the city by 30% and injuries by 20%.

It is worth noting that the economic and social situation in which the PMU 2013–2018 PMU was passed was not ideal, as the Administration could not afford to invest large sums. Administrations saw their budgets cut considerably. This affected the application of the measures proposed in the previous plan significantly, and especially

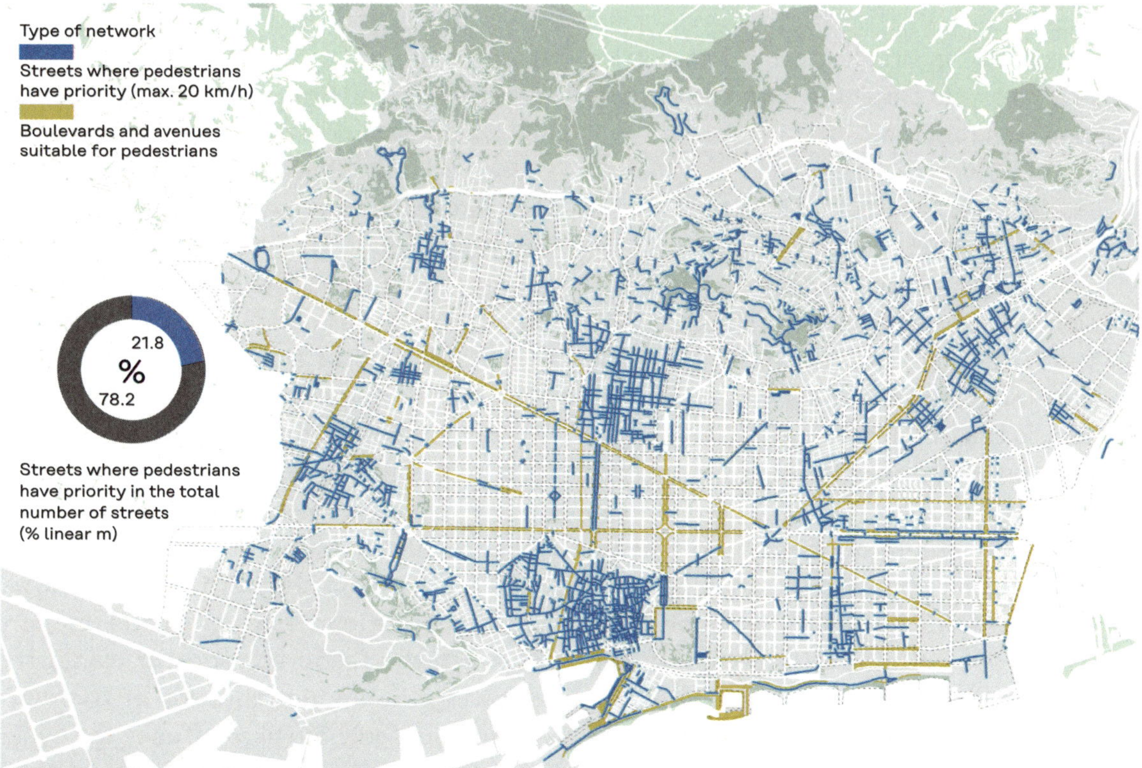

BARCELONA. SUSTAINABLE URBAN MOBILITY PLAN 2019–2024.
Base scenario of traffic-calmed streets in 2019. The current situation reveals a serious imbalance favouring vehicles, which occupy 78.2% of the road space.
Source: BCNecologia

those that required a great deal of investment into infrastructures or a cross-cutting management process involving various administrative entities. Nonetheless, during the time the previous Plan was in effect, the orthogonal bus network was consolidated and superblocks started to be rolled out in the city of Barcelona.

The Plan was approved during the last Full Council Meeting of the political term, and was therefore implemented in the next term (2015–2019). It became a real road map for the City Council's mobility initiatives, including the completion of the orthogonal network (carried out without any delay between terms) and the roll-out of superblocks, which, though tentative, constituted the most progress made since this model was included in the Agenda 21 in the year 2000. The Plan also proposed expanding the city's cycling infrastructure – in just one term, the length of the city's cycle lanes was doubled

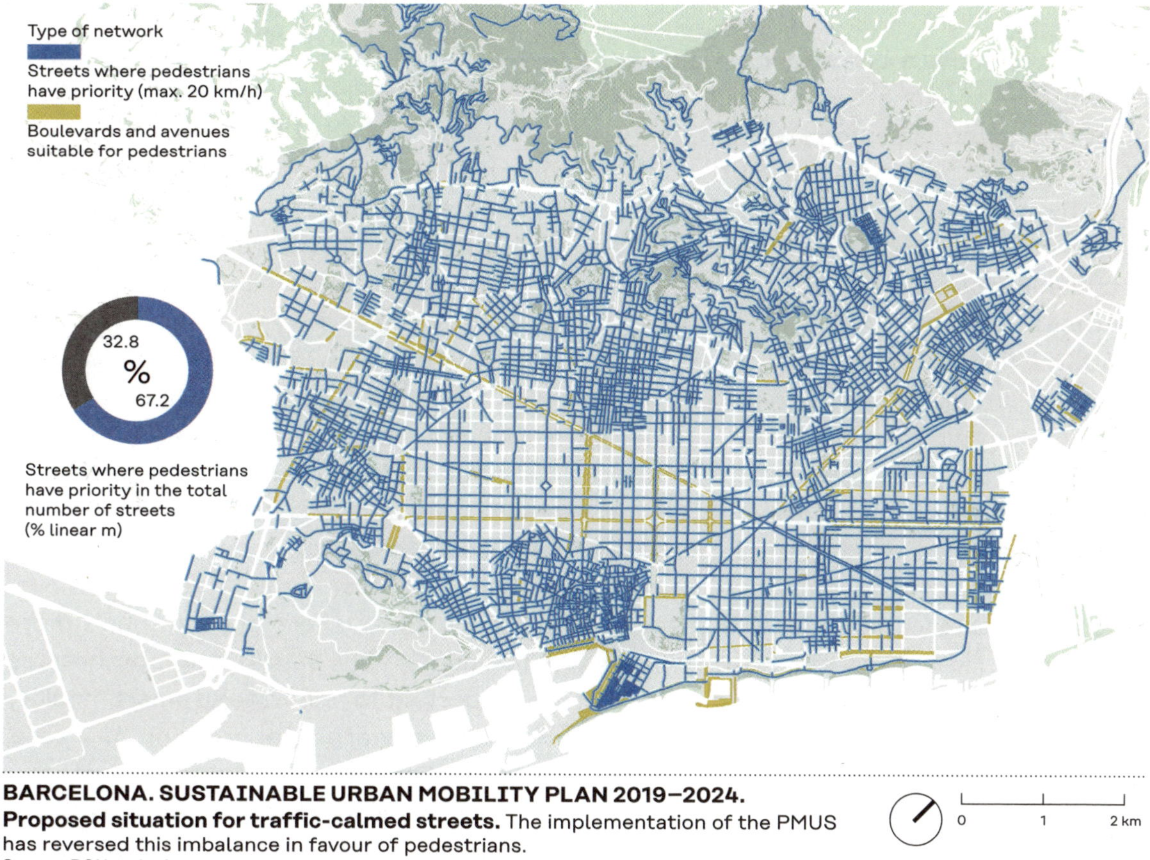

BARCELONA. SUSTAINABLE URBAN MOBILITY PLAN 2019–2024.
Proposed situation for traffic-calmed streets. The implementation of the PMUS has reversed this imbalance in favour of pedestrians.
Source: BCNecologia

– and tackled a particularly thorny issue in the city: the tram line connection. In the existing situation, however, a minimum target like complying with environmental legislation required an ambitious reduction in the use of private vehicles (21%). This could only be achieved by deploying all the tools in the PMU at the same time or by implementing new ones. In the end, the latter was chosen, and a measure to regulate motor traffic in urban areas was introduced. The new Plan has inherited the challenges examined here, and cannot avoid facing them.

SUSTAINABLE URBAN MOBILITY PLAN 2019–2024

In the Sustainable Urban Mobility Plan 2019–2024 (PMUS), BCNecologia reviewed the processes started in previous mobility plans, the 2008–2012 and 2013–2018 PMUs, and stepped up efforts to achieve a more integrated, sustainable mobility model.

The Plan contains a proposal to implement superblocks as a long-term mobility instrument and, at the same time, sets out a series of measures to be adopted to improve urban conditions in the short and medium term. Two future scenarios have therefore been established: one for the 2024 horizon, and another examining mobility in Barcelona in 2030. The PMUS 2019–2024 focuses on five areas for action. It seeks to ensure safe, sustainable, fair, efficient, smart mobility through 59 specific initiatives, measured using 62 follow-up indicators.

Among the aims of the 2019–2024 Plan are to improve the modal split – ensuring a larger share for more sustainable modes of transport, like active mobility (walking and cycling) and public transport – and, at the same time, to minimise energy consumption and its negative impact on the environment and residents' quality of life.

As well as consolidating some of the proposals put forward in the previous Plan, the current PMUS prioritises initiatives that limit the presence of motor vehicles in the public space. These measures include improving the liveability of the public space, creating more in-roadway cycling infrastructure, and reforming car and motorcycle parking regulations. It also introduces strict measures for reducing the number of the most polluting vehicles on the road, such as the implementation of urban tolls, low-emission zones (LEZ), and fleets of electric vehicles for public services.

As a result of the measures to discourage the use of private vehicles, public transport mobility has increased by 12.6%, while private vehicle demand has dropped by 21%. As for non-motorised modes of transport, 6% more journeys are expected to be made on foot, and 75% more by bicycle.

Another new feature in this Plan is the incorporation of smart mobility as a fundamental part of urban mobility. New technologies are permanently changing mobility habits, for both people and goods, and we are getting ever closer to total freedom of movement. However, there are more and more participants in the development process, so it is important to orientate all smart mobility initiatives towards the creation of a safe, flexible, efficient, sustainable ecosystem.

The previous PMU ended in 2018, and the Agency was tasked with putting together its successor during the 2015–2019 term. In this time, all of the technical formulation and participation phases were completed, but the final Plan was not approved. Due to the change in government, the Plan was reviewed again, and is currently at the final technical stages. The next step is the political negotiations needed for it to be approved by the Full Council Meeting.

Conclusions

The challenges presented by today's and tomorrow's mobility must be tackled by public administrations, alongside civil society and the businesses involved. To take on these challenges, the city of Barcelona has two key tools: the Mobility Pact and the Urban Mobility Plan.

The PMU offers an opportunity to reflect on the ideal urban model – in line with a safe, healthy, sustainable, fair, smart mobility system – and provides all the technical tools needed to fulfil any goals set. This makes it a guide that outlines and coordinates all city mobility model strategies in an integrated, consensual way, taking into account all modes of transport.

The Agency's influence on the formulation of the last two PMUS and on the Gràcia District Mobility and Public Space Plan has been reflected through increased space for pedestrians, an extended cycling infrastructure and a strengthened public transport network. These results have improved the city's modal split, increasing the share held by more sustainable modes of transport, and brought air quality and noise pollution levels closer to the limits set by the European Union.

Over the last decade, PMUS have proven able to lead the city towards a more sustainable model, even during serious economic crises. The Barcelona PMUS has been the vehicle for real transformation, both in the city's mobility and in its urban dimension, and has had a positive impact on the whole population.

SUSTAINABLE MOBILITY AND PUBLIC SPACE IN VITORIA-GASTEIZ

2021		
2020		
2019		★ **GLOBAL GREEN CITY AWARD** Vitoria-Gasteiz
2018		
2017		
2016		
2015		
2014		
2013		
2012	**VITORIA-GASTEIZ** Superblock Master Plan	★ **EUROPEAN GREEN CAPITAL AWARD** Vitoria-Gasteiz
2011		
2010	**VITORIA-GASTEIZ** Mobility Plan Industrial Estates	**ARABA** Public Transport Master Plan
2009	**VITORIA-GASTEIZ** Central Superblock	
2008		
2007		**VITORIA-GASTEIZ** Sustainable Mobility and Public Space Plan
2006		
2005		
2004		
2003		
2002		
2001		
2000		

★ **AWARD**

This chapter details the main results of the Vitoria-Gasteiz Sustainable Mobility and Public Space Plan (PMSEP 2007) and the review of this document, which has resulted in the PMSEP 2020–2030. It also presents the Intercity Transport Master Plan for the Historical Territory of Araba (2010), as it is highly relevant and closely linked to the Vitoria-Gasteiz PMSEP.

This PMSEP has played an important role in the Agency's history for several reasons. The development of this superblock-based plan constituted a real paradigm shift, in terms of both the new mobility model and the quality of the public space. It also attracted international recognition of the superblock model and prestigious prizes: Vitoria-Gasteiz was named the European Green Capital 2012 and won the Global Green City Award in 2019.

Another positive aspect of the PMSEP 2007 is that it marked the beginning of a fruitful relationship between the Agency and Vitoria-Gasteiz, resulting in a host of other projects. The most notable are the Territorial Sectoral Plan for Cycle Lanes and Green Routes and the Pedestrian Mobility and Public Space Design Criteria Master Plan.

The main feature of the PMSEP is its application of a superblock-based mobility and public space model. This model is governed by two main aims. The first is to slow down and reverse the private vehicle–oriented trend in the existing mobility model, and the second, to create a new type of public space that boosts urban liveability.

Another of the PMSEP's achievements was the implementation of a new bus network in 2009, following an intense citizens' participation and communication process. This new network caused the number of bus users in the city to rise by more than 50% and was a catalyst behind the creation of Barcelona's orthogonal bus network.

The PMSEP 2020–2030 has reviewed and updated the PMSEP 2007, with a systemic perspective of all mobility networks. The main goal is to apply the superblock model to the entire inner ring of the city in the near future.

VITORIA-GASTEIZ SUSTAINABLE AND PUBLIC SPACE PLAN 2007

The Vitoria-Gasteiz PMSEP 2007 was a comprehensive, internally consistent plan that dealt with the public space and mobility. It aimed to improve urban quality, quality of life for the city's residents, and the functionality and organisation of the urban system in Vitoria-Gasteiz.

The proposals it contained defined a new mobility model, as they intended to modify the percentage of journeys made by each kind of transport within the modal split. They aimed to reduce the number of journeys made by private transport in favour of more sustainable modes of transport. They also designed a new public space with a different distribution of uses and functions than the existing one at the time.

The result: 70% of the public space previously dedicated to cars was freed up. This shows that citizens – whose fundamental right is to occupy the public space without restrictions – took back power in a high-quality, quiet, unpolluted, safe, attractive public space that encouraged contact and peaceful coexistence between people of all ages and social groups. People were no longer simply pedestrians, and the street was no longer a place for passing through. It was a public open space where people could exist together and where most urban functions could be carried out.

Through the PMSEP, Vitoria-Gasteiz completed some unfinished business and set out its stall as a role model in the sphere of sustainable city development. There are many reasons behind its position in the international panorama of the most sustainable cities, including its biodiversity policy, its morphology and its compact and well-equipped structure. As the new Plan is rolled out, Vitoria-Gasteiz will undoubtedly become a world leader and enjoy all the economic, social and cultural benefits this status entails.

The PMSEP 2007 was based on a set of aims, established during a participatory process:

Sustainability

1 To take back the concept of sustainability for Vitoria-Gasteiz, beyond its environmental sense.

Sustainable mobility

2 To establish a new hierarchy in uses of the city, so that pedestrians are the protagonists, followed by non-motorised modes of transport and public transport, with private vehicles in last place.

3 To ensure all ways of moving around the city can exist together and guarantee intermodality, especially between non-motorised modes of transport.

4 To incentivise and promote the use of public transport, while discouraging the use of private vehicles.

5 To make non-motorised mobility a popular mode of transport.

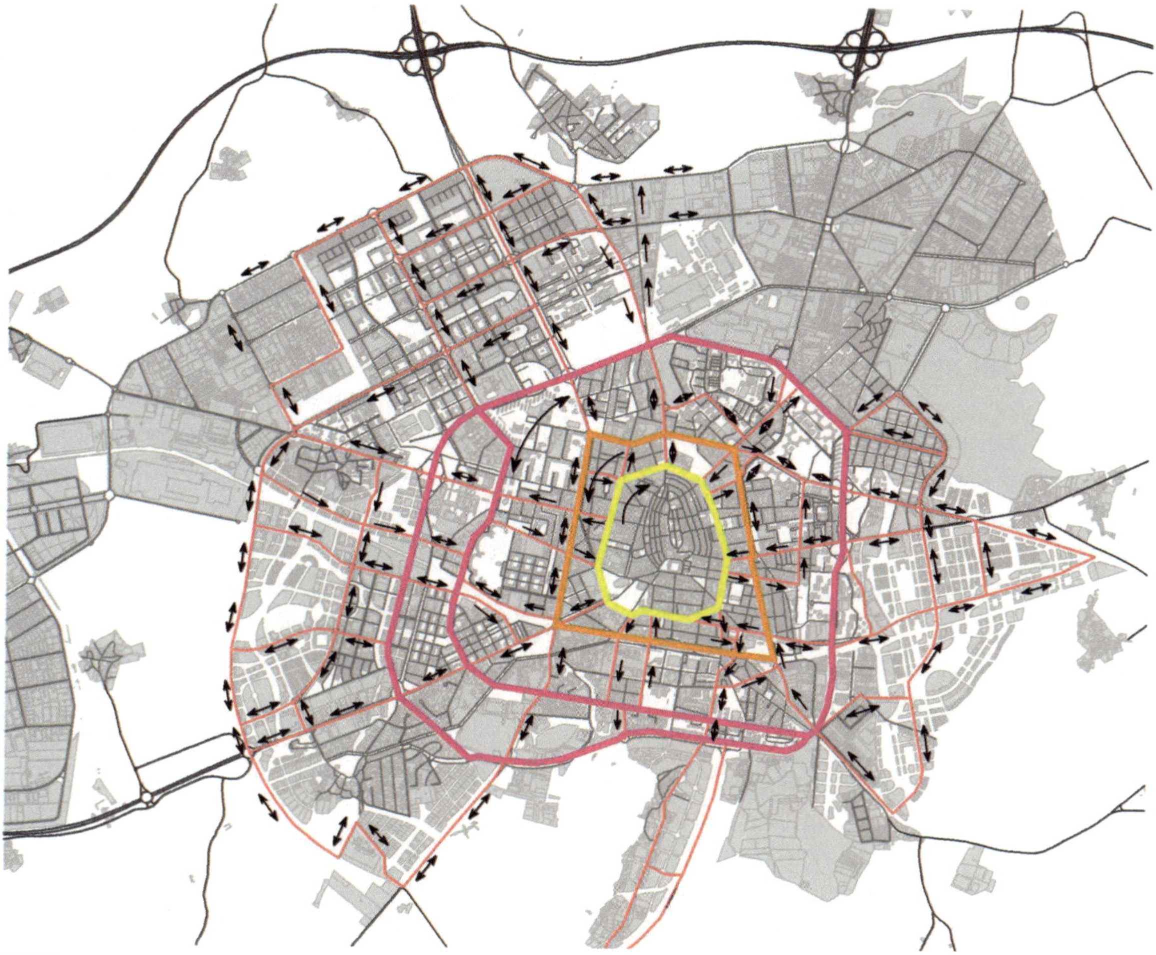

VITORIA-GASTEIZ. 2007. Superblock and basic traffic network proposal with directions indicated. Final scenario.
Source: BCNecologia

0 1000 m

Ring roads
1
2
3
Delimitation of superblocks
Private vehicle traffic direction

6 To guarantee effective, energy-efficient mobility.
7 To promote universal accessibility to different modes of transport.
8 To raise the public's awareness of the different modes of transport available.

City model

9 To build a safe, accessible city.
10 To create a quieter, less polluted city.
11 To seek mobility solutions that do not occupy land.
12 To include mobility in urban planning policies.
13 To expand the space available for people and restrict room for private motor vehicles, so that the public is prioritised over cars.
14 To construct a public space that fosters social and economic life and offers businesses, leisure facilities and services.

The final scenario is characterised by reorganised mobility networks, based on the superblock model, and a new perspective of liveability in the public space. It assumes that all the urban planning initiatives planned before this date will be completed. The new spot for the train station leaves room for an urban green corridor (Zabalgana—Salburua), which constitutes a strategic axis for connecting the city through more sustainable modes of transport.

RESULTS OF THE SUSTAINABLE MOBILITY AND PUBLIC SPACE PLAN 2007

The public transport transformation in Vitoria-Gasteiz was one of the most significant elements of the 2007 Sustainable Mobility and Public Space Plan (PMSEP). Once the Plan was in effect, the service frequency went from 20 to every 10 minutes, the average speed rose from 10.77 km/h to 12.73 km/h, and the percentage of the population who use public transport and have a bus stop within 300 m of their home, and/or a tram stop within 500 m, increased from 97% to 99.1%. The average journey time on public transport was cut by 10 minutes, even though more transfers were made. All of this led to a considerably improved accessibility index score.

This new public transport network was applied thus:

- December 2008: introduction of the T1 tram line.
- July 2009: introduction of the T2 tram line.
- 30 October 2009: introduction of the new bus network.
- October 2010: improvements to the new bus network.

SCENARIOS IN FIGURES		
	Scenario before PMSEP 2007	**Final scenario for the PMSEP 2007 proposal (Superblocks)**
MUNICIPAL AREA		
Population	229,080 inh.	249,697 inh.
Land area	277 km^2	277 km^2
Density	8.3 inh./ha	9.0 inh./ha
URBAN CENTRE AREA		
Population	225,317 inh.	245,596 inh.
Land area	35 km^2	35 km^2
Density	64.4 inh./ha	70.2 inh./ha
public space/inh. in m^2	52 m^2/inh.	53 m^2/inh.
open space/inh. in m^2	21 m^2/inh.	38 m^2/inh.
green space/inh. in m^2	12 m^2/inh. (without a ring road)	18 m^2/inh. (without a ring road)
	41 m^2/inh. (with a ring road)	47 m^2/inh. (with a ring road)

VITORIA-GASTEIZ. 2007. Scenario Analysis.
Source: BCNecologia

inh. = inhabitant, ha = hectare

SUSTAINABLE MOBILITY AND PUBLIC SPACE PLAN 2020–2030

The new PMSEP diagnosis shows that, in just a decade, the annual number of passengers on public transport went from 12.7 million (2008) to 23 million (2018). It is clear that the new tram system – a comfortable, fast, reliable option – has strengthened the city's public transport network. This, along with the improved bus network and new parking policy, directly contributed to the 35% reduction in the private vehicle's share of the modal split between 2006 and 2014. Indeed, the figure for the private car's share in the overall mobility distribution dropped from 37% in 2006 to 24% in 2014. Other trends observed include the significant growth of cycling mobility and a moderate increase in journeys made on foot.

Although these improvements have been made, Vitoria-Gasteiz still faces problems, especially in the climate change sphere: the city's current CO_2 values do not meet the targets set, so additional measures must be applied. The PMSEP 2020–2030 diagnosis shows that this could be achieved by implementing superblocks across the city centre. A considerable achievement made as part of this PMSEP is that consensus has been reached to create superblocks throughout the inner ring of the city.

As well as the superblock model, the PMSEP 2020–2030 considers all the changes to be made in the city in the next ten years, especially in terms of major public transport infrastructures and how they will affect the use of private vehicles and public transport (tram from the south of the city

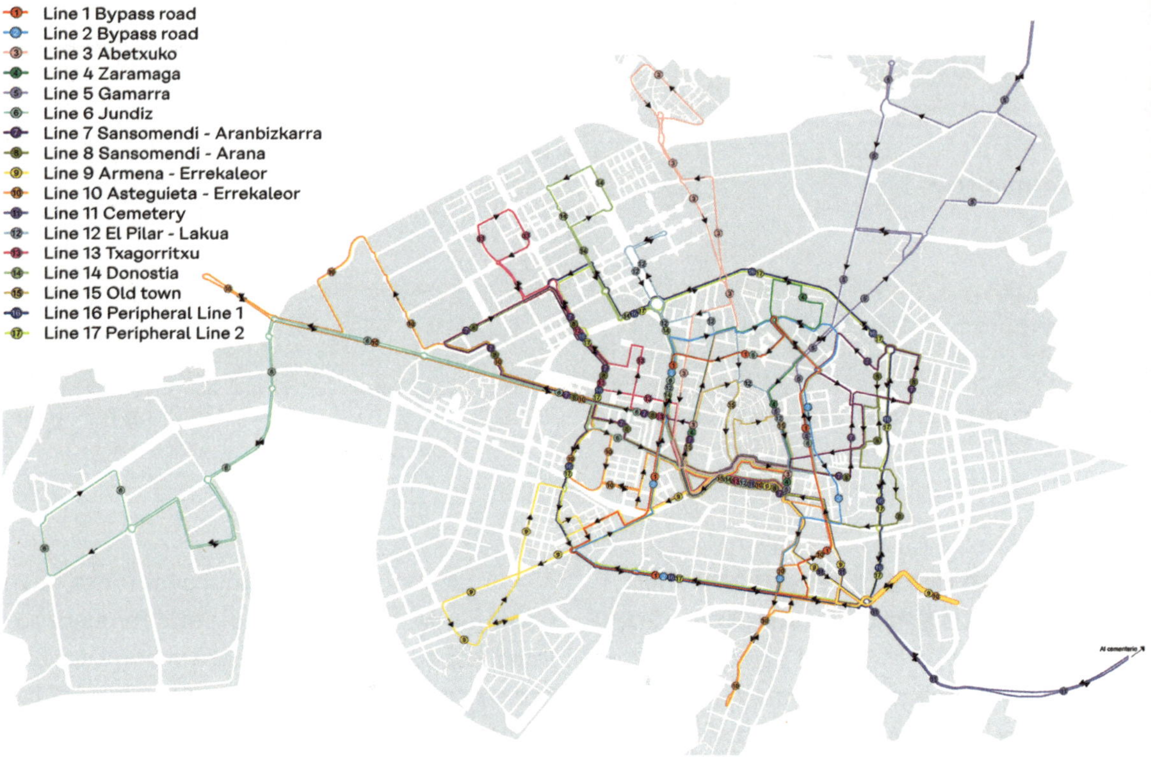

VITORIA-GASTEIZ. 2007. Bus network. Base scenario.
Source: BCNecologia

to the university, smart electric bus system (BEI), Salburua tram, Zabalgana tram, moving the railway underground, etc.). With this as a starting point, it then analyses and offers proposals for the public transport network (modification of the existing network), the private vehicle network (analysis of superblocks and hot spots), the pedestrian network and public space model, the cycling network, the parking network and the urban distribution network. In addition, it examines the process of electrifying mobility infrastructure, mobility in industrial estates, school mobility, the modal split (taking costs of private vehicles, public transport and parking into account) and the environmental consequences of the mobility model. The Plan has been made possible by an extensive citizen participation process.

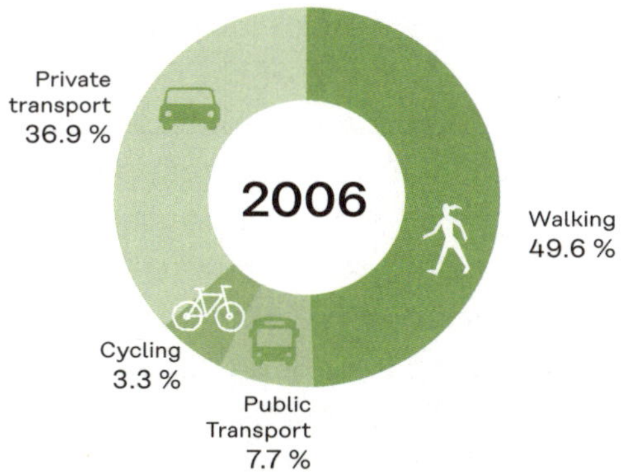

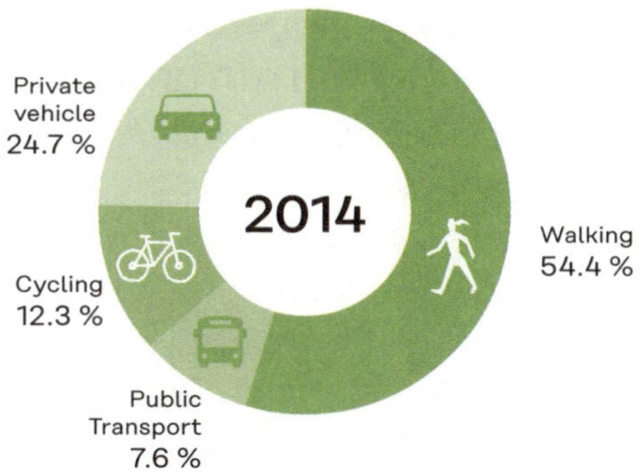

	2006 SURVEY		**2014** SURVEY		INCREASE **2006–2014**	
Population	228,187		242,924		6,5%	
Total journeys	581,336		911,307		56.8 %	
	Journeys	Modal split	Journeys	Modal split	Journeys	Modal split
Walking	288,343	49.6 %	495,751	54.4 %	71.9 %	9.7 %
Public transport	44,763	7.7 %	69,259	7.6 %	54.7 %	-1.3 %
Cycling	19,184	3.3 %	112,091	12.3 %	484.3 %	272.7 %
Private vehicle	214,513	36.9 %	225,093	24.7 %	4.9 %	-33.1 %

VITORIA-GASTEIZ. 2006–2014. Mobility Trends.
Source: Vitoria-Gasteiz City Council

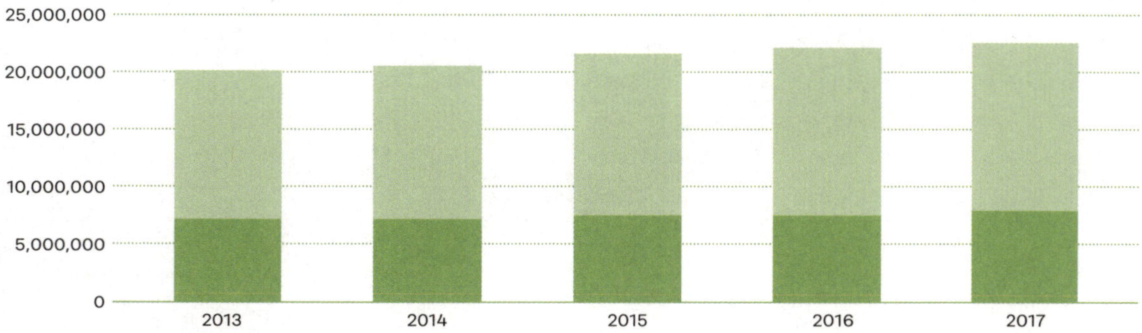

VITORIA-GASTEIZ. 2013–2017. Evolution of annual number of passengers on public transport.
Source: TUVISA/Euskotren

INTERCITY TRANSPORT MASTER PLAN FOR THE HISTORICAL TERRITORY OF ARABA

The motives behind this project were the end of the licence for the intercity bus lines, which is granted by Araba Provincial Council (DFA), and the outdated existing network.

The aims of the Plan were to increase the public intercity bus service's share of the modal split and reduce that of the car and to improve these bus lines' environmental and economic efficiency. But this project had to overcome a major intrinsic difficulty: the spread-out nature of the region.

The proposals that came out of this process included the creation of the Araba Regional Transport Authority, so that different modes of public could be integrated in terms of planning, management and pricing (involving zones and a single card for all tickets). They also provided for an overall improvement in service delivery, -a more frequent service at peak times (to cater to commuters) and reduced journey times (especially in urban centres with

VITORIA-GASTEIZ. 2018. New smart electric bus proposed in the revision of the PMSEP.
Picture: Quintas fotógrafos

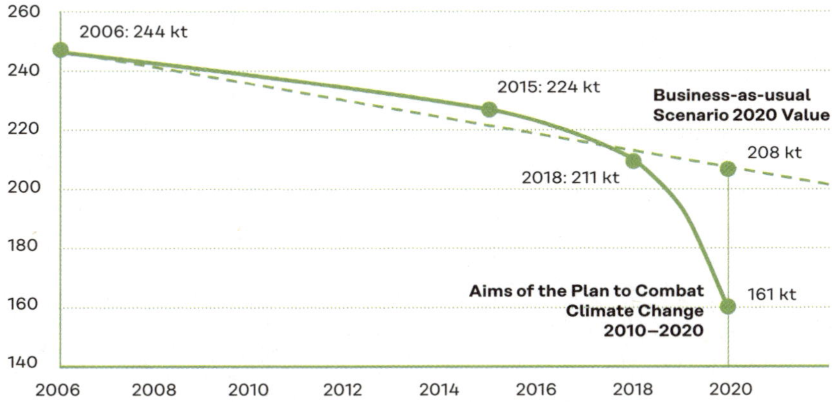

VITORIA-GASTEIZ. 2020. CO_2 emissions analysis between 2006 and 2020.
Source: BCNecologia

the most passengers). Better connections between intercity and urban transport in Vitoria-Gasteiz were also envisaged, with services to industrial estates, as well as a rationalised, hierarchised network where the type of route (direct or indirect, regular or demand-responsive), number of services and size of the vehicles match the potential demand. Finally, the proposals included the use of new technologies to improve the information available to the user and to those running the service.

The results of this project played a key role in the process to grant the new licences for the intercity bus lines, led by Araba Provincial Council. An expanded network structure allows for better structuring within each county, each with their own lines and hubs that facilitate access to Vitoria-Gasteiz.

One of the key requirements for any public transport network proposal for the historical territory of Araba (THA) to work is a fast, efficient connection with urban public transport in the city of Vitoria-Gasteiz, so that the use of a private vehicle is discouraged. For this reason, transfer points were defined. This aspect was examined both in the Master Plan for the Historical Territory of Araba and the PMSEP for Vitoria-Gasteiz (2007 and 2020–2030).

This Master Plan was followed by five additional projects, which ensured continuity and brought the public transport proposals for the region to life: 1. Detailed study on

VITORIA-GASTEIZ. The city is committed to more sustainable and efficient modes of transport such as cycling and the tram line, within the framework of the PMSEP strategic lines.
Picture: CEA. Vitoria-Gasteiz City Council

transport to industrial estates in the Historical Territory of Araba. 2. The Intra-County Mobility Plan for the Historical Territory of Araba, to study the connections between municipalities outside of Vitoria-Gasteiz. 3. Technical support in the process of implementing, promoting and disseminating the Intercity Transport Master Plan for the Historical Territory of Araba. 4. Study on the sizing and basic design of the demand-responsive transport management system in the Historical Territory of Araba, to provide a public transport mobility response to a large number of rural villages in Araba. 5. Extension of the previous study.

In addition, the Agency worked with Araba Provincial Council to carry out the Territorial Sectoral Plan for Cycle Lanes and Green Routes in Araba (2015) and the Comprehensive Electric Mobility Plan for the Basque Country (2018) projects.

Conclusions

The Vitoria-Gasteiz PMSEP is one of the Urban Ecology Agency of Barcelona's most transcendental projects for more than one reason. The first is its use of the superblock model in the city and the repercussions of this move, both nationally and internationally. The application of this model was a key factor in the city winning the prestigious European Green Capital prize in 2012. The second is the fact that it has generated more projects for the Agency in the region: up to fifteen in the city of Vitoria-Gasteiz itself and eight more in Araba region and the Basque Country generally.

As well as proposing the superblock model – and partially implementing it – the 2007 PMSEP implemented a new bus network, which was one of its main successes. This network is more efficient, using the same resources yet improving frequency and coverage. The result is constant growth in its number of passengers. Alongside this bus network, a tram system was implemented, which constituted another boost for public transport in the city.

The PMSEP 2020–2030 goes a step further. Though improvements were made with the PMSEP 2007, the city of Vitoria-Gasteiz is still facing the challenges associated with climate change. The new Plan offers a response: the implementation of superblocks across the urban centre. On another note, the new PMSEP has led to a significant achievement: political consensus has been reached to implement superblocks throughout the inner ring of the city.

The Intercity Transport Master Plan for the Historical Territory of Araba, meanwhile, was useful in the process to grant the new intercity bus line licences, as it increased the public intercity bus service's share of the modal split, reducing that of the private vehicle, and improved the network's environmental and economic efficiency.

OTHER SUPERBLOCK-BASED MOBILITY PLANS

2021

2020

2019

2018

2017

2016

2015

2014
CÓRDOBA Sustainable Mobility and Public Space Plan

2013

2012

2011
A CORUÑA Mobility and Public Space Plan

2010

2009
LUGO Mobility and Public Space Plan
FERROL Mobility and Public Space Plan

2008

2007

2006
VILADECANS Mobility and Public Space Plan

2005
EL PRAT DE LLOBREGAT Mobility and Public Space Plan

2004

2003

2002

2001

2000

In recent decades, the prevailing mobility model in cities, with the private motor vehicle as the protagonist, has caused a series of problems that seriously affect residents' quality of life. Pollution and time wasted because of traffic are the main issues faced by current mobility planning. But they are not the only challenges: public space must be totally rethought to improve liveability conditions and promote coexistence between different modes of transport.

Through Mobility and Public Space Plans (PMEP), the Agency has defined strategies and articulated initiatives to move towards a safe, healthy, sustainable, fair, smart mobility model. These plans take all modes of transport into account and favour active, non-motorised transport when organising mobility in the city.

This chapter looks at how the new superblock-based mobility model was rolled out beyond Barcelona and Vitoria-Gasteiz. It will detail how this new type of urban cell can be applied to any consolidated urban fabric that fulfils certain minimum levels of compactness and complexity.

It examines the Agency's projects in towns and cities with a diverse range of urban fabrics, including Córdoba, Lugo, A Coruña, Ferrol, El Prat de Llobregat and Viladecans. In all of these municipalities, the urban model is transformed to achieve better efficiency, more complexity, less pollution, more intermodality, and more public space for non-motorised transport.

Proof of this urban model's success can be found in the prizes awarded to studies carried out in Vitoria-Gasteiz, the European Green Capital 2012 – whose superblock-based Mobility and Public Space Plan was named Best Practice by UN-Habitat – and in the district of Gràcia, in Barcelona, which won the first BMW Initiative award in 2011 for its Pilot Superblocks Plan and was also recognised as Good Practice by UN-Habitat in 2010.

COMPREHENSIVE MOBILITY AND PUBLIC SPACE PLANS EL PRAT DE LLOBREGAT, VILADECANS AND FERROL

BCNecologia developed some of its first comprehensive mobility and public space plans on a municipal level in El Prat de Llobregat (2005) and Viladecans (2006). The El Prat Plan originated in the Strategic Development Study, carried out the year before for Prat Nord, which stabilised a new methodology based on advanced IT, statistics and information management tools. This prior study also strengthened a system of powerful simulators to analyse mobility and its environmental products: emissions and immissions, noise and energy consumption. The Agency gradually consolidated all of this expertise in subsequent projects.

These two initial plans, as well as their successors, sought to formulate an integrated proposal to solve a significant number of the problems generated by private transport networks, in terms of occupation and deterioration of the public space. Future scenarios were developed, based on the reorganisation of these networks to favour non-motorised mobility and the definition of a group of superblocks to directly influence uses of the public space. These plans managed to improve environmental conditions and residents' quality of life, as well as guaranteeing and extending citizens' rights.

In 2009, the Ferrol Mobility and Public Space Plan was formulated. This was a key project because, although it was only partially implemented (with the revitalisation and pedestrianisation of some streets in the historic centre), it had a knock-on effect on the subsequent plans for Lugo and A Coruña. Like its successors, this Plan responded to the aims and directives included in the *Urban Environment Strategy (EMAU)*[11] and the *Green Paper on Urban and Local Sustainability in the Information Age*,[12] both formulated by the Agency.

In Ferrol, the aim was to dedicate 63% of the public space to pedestrians: almost double the existing figure of 32%. This new model required all transport networks to be reorganised, based on a superblock model, to integrate the pedestrian network, cycling infrastructure, public transport (urban, rural and intercity) and private vehicles (including parking and urban freight distribution) more efficiently. This reorganisation created more public open spaces and greenery, thus reducing noise pollution and improving air quality.

The Plan also extended the cycle path network from 4.3 km to 26.9 km and suggested increasing the number of public bicycle sharing points from 4 to 30.

11 Ministry of the Environment; Network of Local Sustainable Development Networks. *Urban Environment Strategy (EMAU). Op. cit.*

12 Rueda, Salvador *[et al.]. Green Paper on Urban and Local Sustainability in the Information Age.* Madrid: Ministry of Agriculture, Food and Environment. General Technical Secretariat. Publications Centre, 2012.

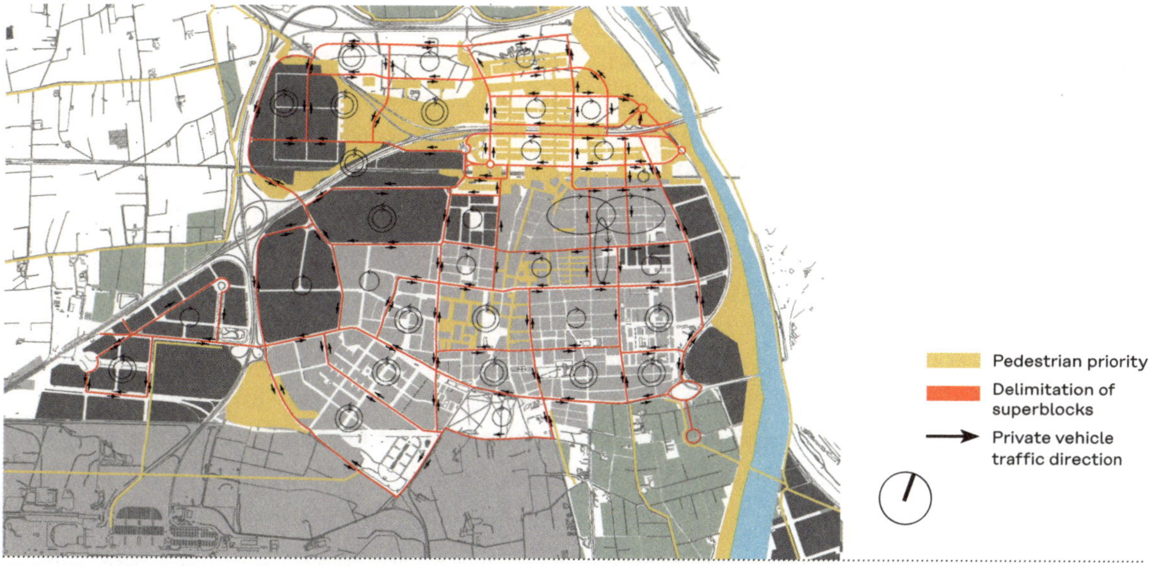

EL PRAT DE LLOBREGAT. 2005. Superblock Plan. Proposed scenarios of basic private vehicle network.
Source: BCNecologia

VILADECANS. 2006. Transport allocation. Superblocks scenario.
Source: BCNecologia

On public transport, meanwhile, travel time was significantly reduced; the percentage of the urban population who were less then 25 minutes from any other point of the city went from 28% to 67%, thanks to the new network structure, the expansion of the fleet into three units and the creation of a bus lane on the most congested stretches of road.

As a result of these and other measures, such as limitation and regulation of on-road parking, public transport demand rose by 75%, entailing a drop in journeys by private vehicle.

As the PMEP was welcomed widely, in 2013, the Agency was commissioned to put together the Pilot Superblock Implementation Plan for the La Magdalena Neighbourhood, which has gradually been consolidated, and the New Municipal Bus Network Implementation Plan.

In 2009, following the Ferrol project, a document was written up for Lugo (and updated in 2014). The new, superblock-based mobility model in the Plan reduced the proportion of public space rated poor or very poor in terms of liveability (from 77.5% to 54.7%) and increased the amount of good or excellent public space (4.8% to 19.7%).

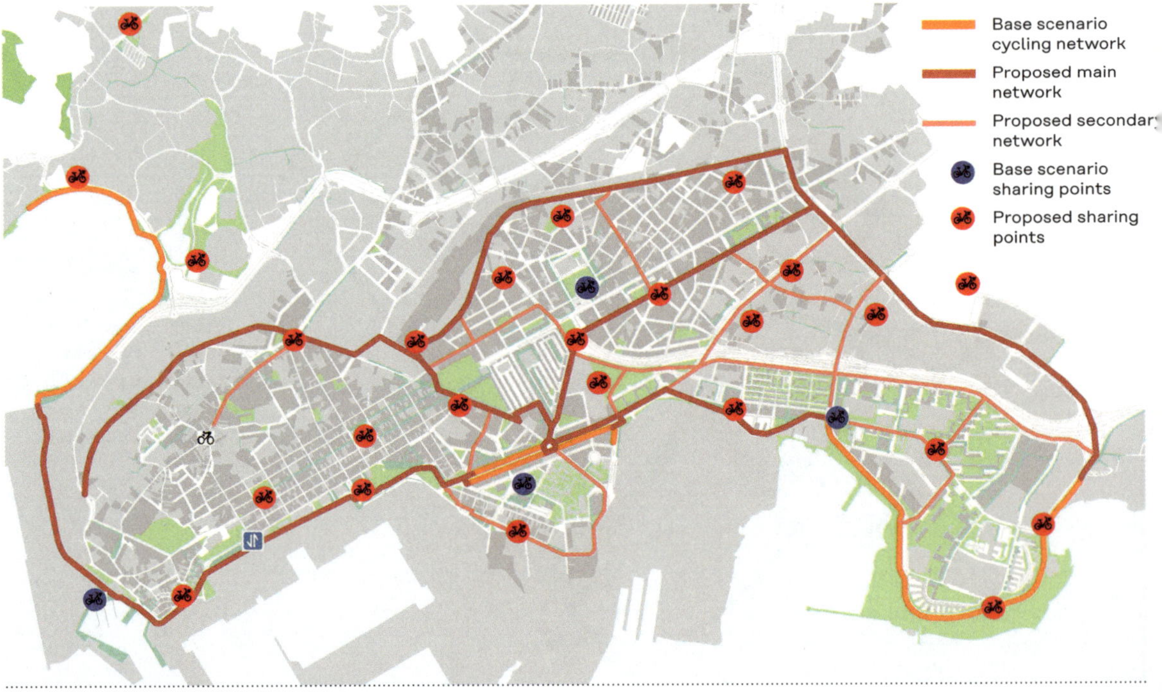

FERROL. 2009. Network proposal for cycling.
Source: BCNecologia

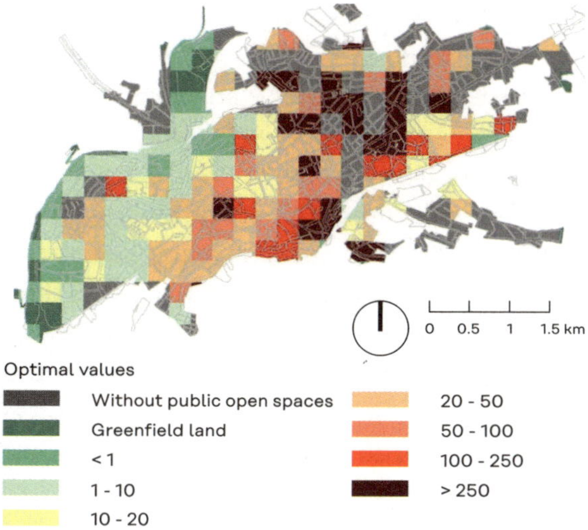

LUGO. 2009. Mobility and Public Space Plan.
Corrected compactness indicator.
Source: BCNecologia

To achieve these figures, the superblock proposal made more streets totally accessible (from 10.4% to 34.5%), reduced the shortage in public open space per inhabitant (areas with less than 10 m^2/inhabitant) from 72% to 30%, and redistributed the public street space, from 65% for the roadway to just 36%.

As for mobility, the average journey time on public transport was reduced by five minutes, cycling infrastructure was extended – the percentage of the population within 200 m of a cycle lane skyrocketed from 8% to 86% – and the number of public bicycle sharing points rose from 5 to 22. What is more, on-road parking was limited and regulated. In addition, a new logistics microplatform model was proposed for urban freight distribution. As a result, journeys by private vehicle were reduced by 7%, compared to the business-as-usual scenario, and noise levels and air quality were improved.

A CORUÑA

In 2011, the Agency formulated the A Coruña Mobility and Public Space Plan. However, the study of the city really began in 2008, with the commission to write the Environmental Sustainability Report for the review of the General Plan for Municipal Planning. The Mobility Plan for the UdC Campus in Elviña and Zapateira, attached to the city, was also created.

The A Coruña PMEP is a comprehensive, highly ambitious plan. Thanks to the superblock model and the many initiatives proposed to promote the use of alternative modes of transport (walking routes, extended cycling infrastructure, improved public transport, regulated on-street parking and microplatforms for urban freight distribution), the liveability of the public space improved considerably: the percentage of the population in areas rated good or excellent rose from 2% to 48.3%. This facilitated the creation of more urban greenery and public open spaces.

To bring about this improvement, general traffic needed to be reduced by

15% for the superblock model to work. This percentage was based on the modal distribution model generated specifically, and all of it (or at least the part corresponding to internal journeys) could definitely be covered by other modes of transport.

The private vehicle's share of the modal split for internal journeys thus dropped from 30.4% to 25.8%: a comparable figure to that seen in Vitoria-Gasteiz (24.7%), which is of a similar size.

There was still another problem to be solved, though: the issue of metropolitan mobility. The 15% reduction in private vehicle traffic resulted in a 69.9% share of the metropolitan modal split for this kind of mobility (down from 82.2%), but this was still too high for a city like A Coruña and revealed considerable shortfalls in the metropolitan public transport network.

For this reason, in 2017, this aspect was tackled directly in the A Coruña Metropolitan Public Transport Plan, which planned to implement Cambre–A Coruña suburban train lines (run by Renfe), restructure the whole metropolitan bus network (with express and semi-express services), and adapt the network to the proposed urban bus system.

These proposals aimed to reduce mobility by private motor vehicle by 25% in the metropolitan area, bringing it below 50% (49.3%): a percentage comparable to that of other metropolitan areas in Spain.

Subsequently, in 2018, this work was completed with the A Coruña Transport Network Integration Plan, designed to integrate all of the Agency's projects in the city and deal with the emergence of personal mobility vehicles (PMV) and the concept of mobility as a service: two new, powerful tools that could

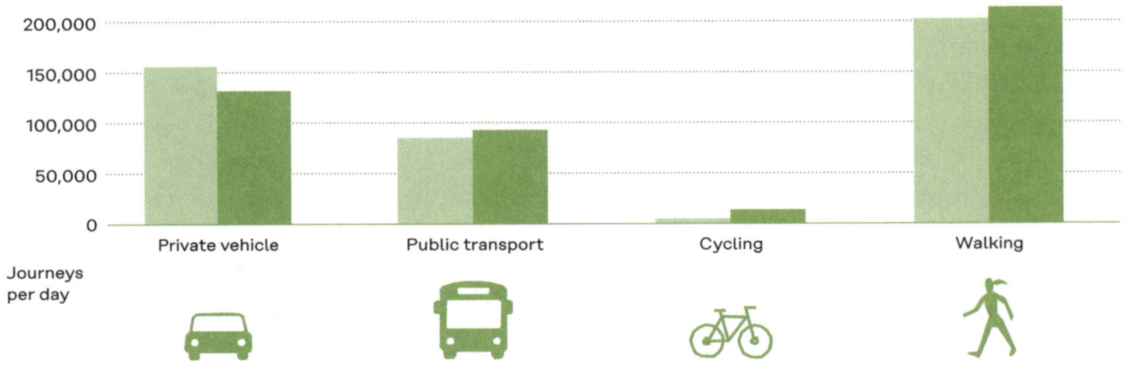

A CORUÑA. 2018. Modal split. Internal journeys.
Source: BCNecologia

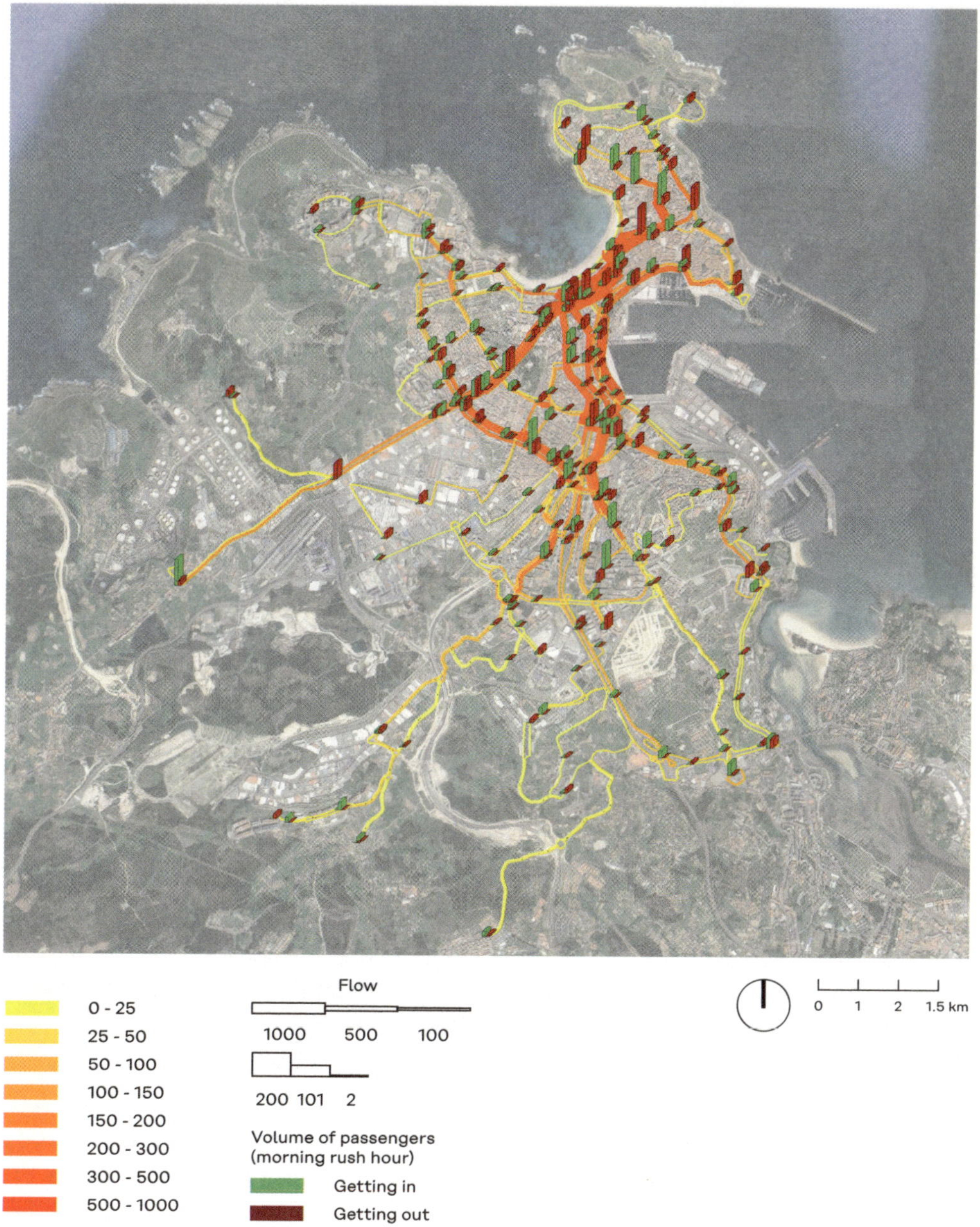

A CORUÑA. 2011. Passenger assignment on the urban bus network. Base scenario.
Source: BCNecologia

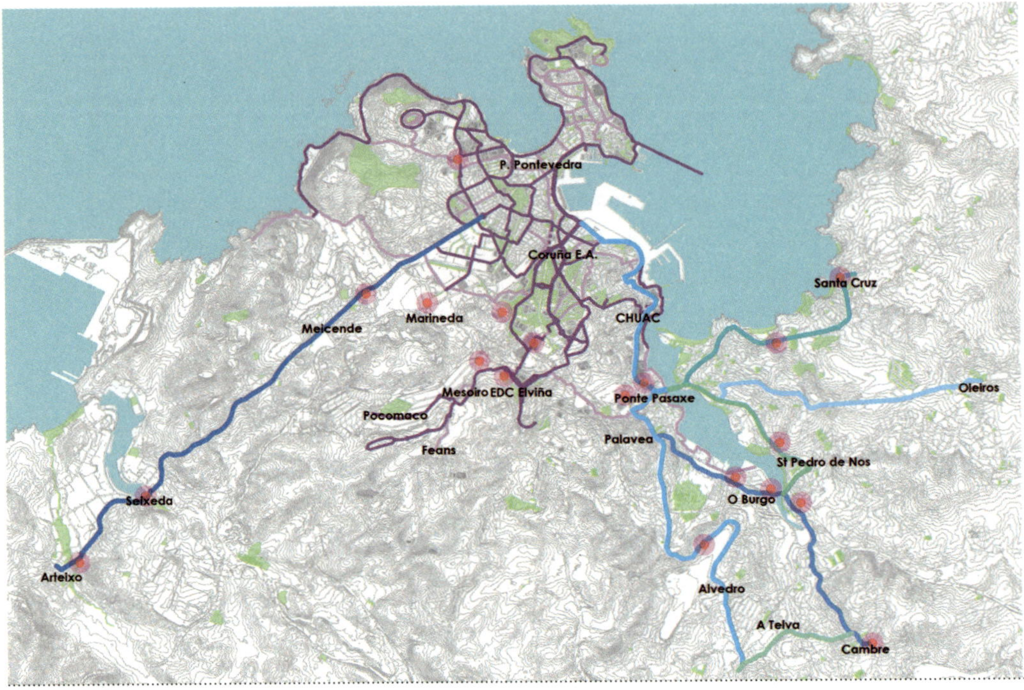

A CORUÑA. 2018. Metropolitan cycling network proposal.
Source: BCNecologia

Route	Length
A Coruña - Arteixo	10.04
A Coruña - Ponte Pasaxe	4.65
Ponte Pasaxe - Santa Cruz	4.93
Ponte Pasaxe - O Burgo (Riera)	3.81
Ponte Pasaxe - O Burgo - Cambre	7.07
Ponte Pasaxe - Oleiros	6.13
Ponte Pasaxe - Aiprt - A Pena	7.47
A Pena - Cambre	2.24
Total length (km)	**46.34**

0 3 km

Urban network
Contour lines (5 m)
Park and ride

accelerate the shift in the modal split away from conventional private motor vehicles.

As a result of this study, a proper municipal cycling network was designed, with over 70 km of new paths and 26 new public bicycle sharing stations, on top of the 23 existing ones. Furthermore, the Agency examined how this metropolitan network fitted within the Galicia Alternative Mobility Master Plan.

Though the Mobility and Public Space Plan was a tool established in the 2011–2015 political term, during the 2015–2019 term, the new government, which was in favour of the Plan, attempted in vain to generate a political consensus with the previous government (now on the opposition) to boost the implementation process. Expanding studies with metropolitan mobility plans was a way of moving forward, at least in the planning sphere.

CÓRDOBA

In 2014, work began on the Córdoba Mobility and Public Space Plan, which followed and extended the methodology used in previous plans. Córdoba, whose historic centre is one of the biggest in Europe and is a UNESCO World Heritage site, represented a significant challenge.

In this case, the new superblock-based mobility model entailed a reduction in energy consumption from mobility of 9%, and a similar drop in the number of inhabitants exposed to noise and air pollution. All of this was possible thanks to improvements to the municipal public transport network's efficiency, the expansion of the cycle lane network, the regulation and limitation of on-street parking, and the new urban distribution logistics system based on microplatforms. Among other benefits, these initiatives increased the amount of urban greenery and public open spaces and reduced mobility by private vehicle by 13%.

This drop in private mobility, needed for the overall superblock structure to work, was compensated by more sustainable modes of transport. Indeed, these measures increased the number of journeys made on foot by 3.9%, by bicycle by 110% – doubling its existing share of the modal split – and on public transport by 23%.

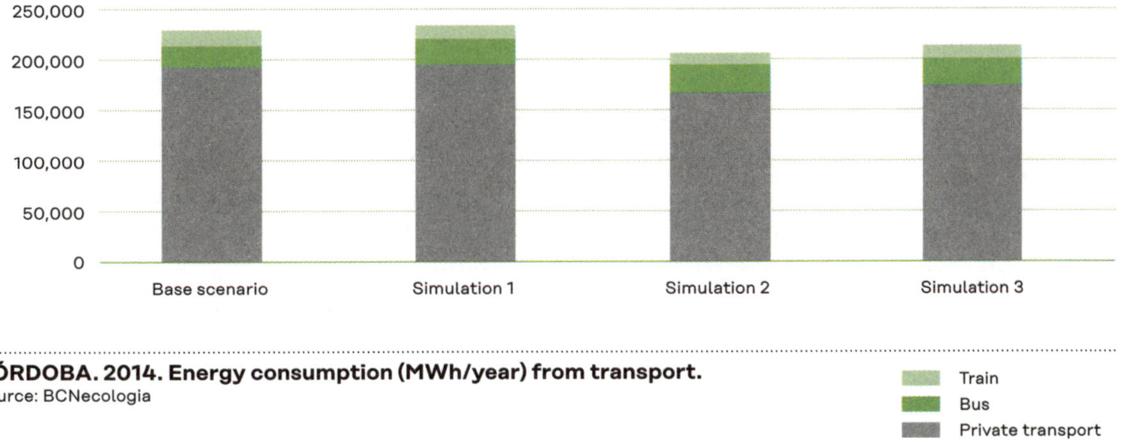

CÓRDOBA. 2014. Energy consumption (MWh/year) from transport.
Source: BCNecologia

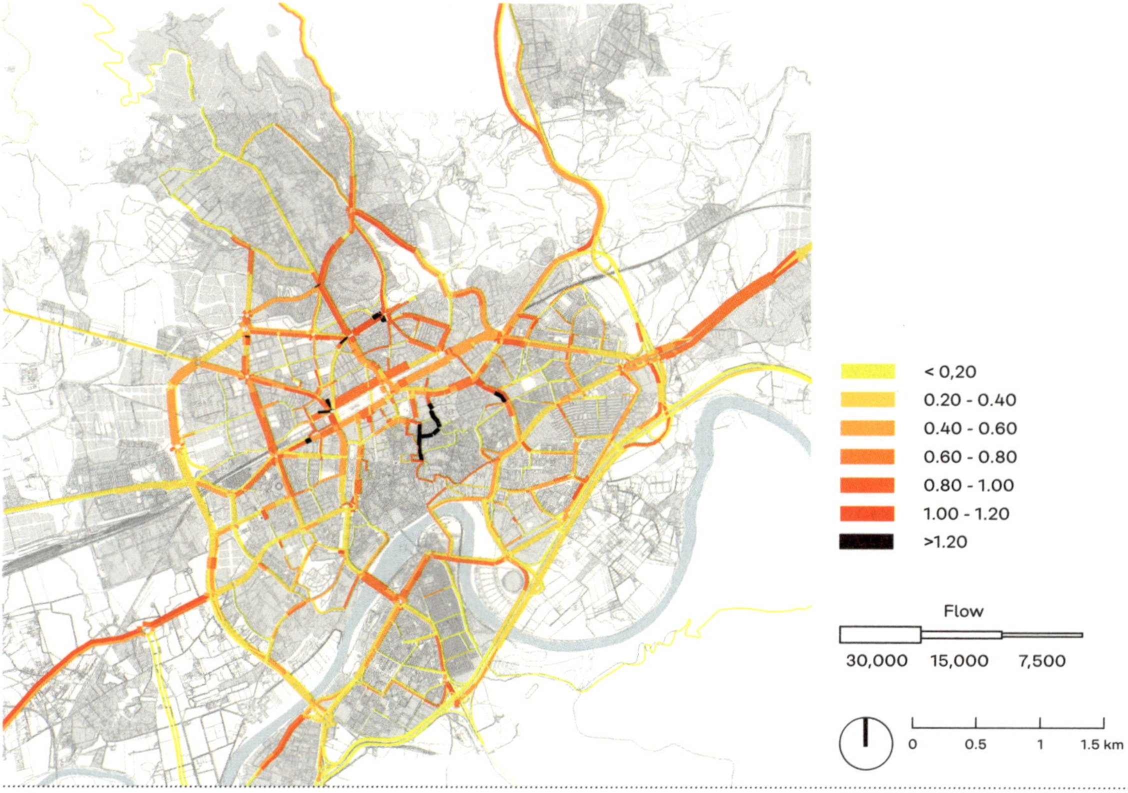

CÓRDOBA. 2014. Traffic congestion index. Base scenario.
Source: BCNecologia

With the same fleet and one fewer line, municipal public transport could ensure a service frequency of eight minutes or less in most cases. This way, both the population coverage and the percentage of the population with access to any other point of the city in less than thirty minutes were improved (by 7% and 9%, respectively), largely thanks to new longitudinal transport lines that crossed the city from north to south and allowed for easy connections. These lines also adapted their routes to the basic roads that make up the city's superblocks.

In parallel, the city's cycling infrastructure was extended considerably, from 51.8 km to almost 149 km. Furthermore, more bicycle parking was provided for citizens and public bicycle sharing stations were added (in 54 new locations).

CÓRDOBA. 2014. Average service frequency. Base scenario.
Source: BCNecologia

The result of all of this was a significant improvement in the public space's liveability: the percentage of its surface area considered good or excellent rose from 13.5% to 32.7% thanks to the proposal, and the percentage deemed poor or very poor dropped from 50.4% to 34.9%.

A year later, this Plan led to the creation of the neighbourhood of Ciudad Jardín Urban Regeneration Plan, which consisted of implementing a pilot superblock to revitalise the area. The Córdoba City Council promoted the Regeneration Plan on several occasions and in successive citizen participation meetings with the local entities and businesses involved.

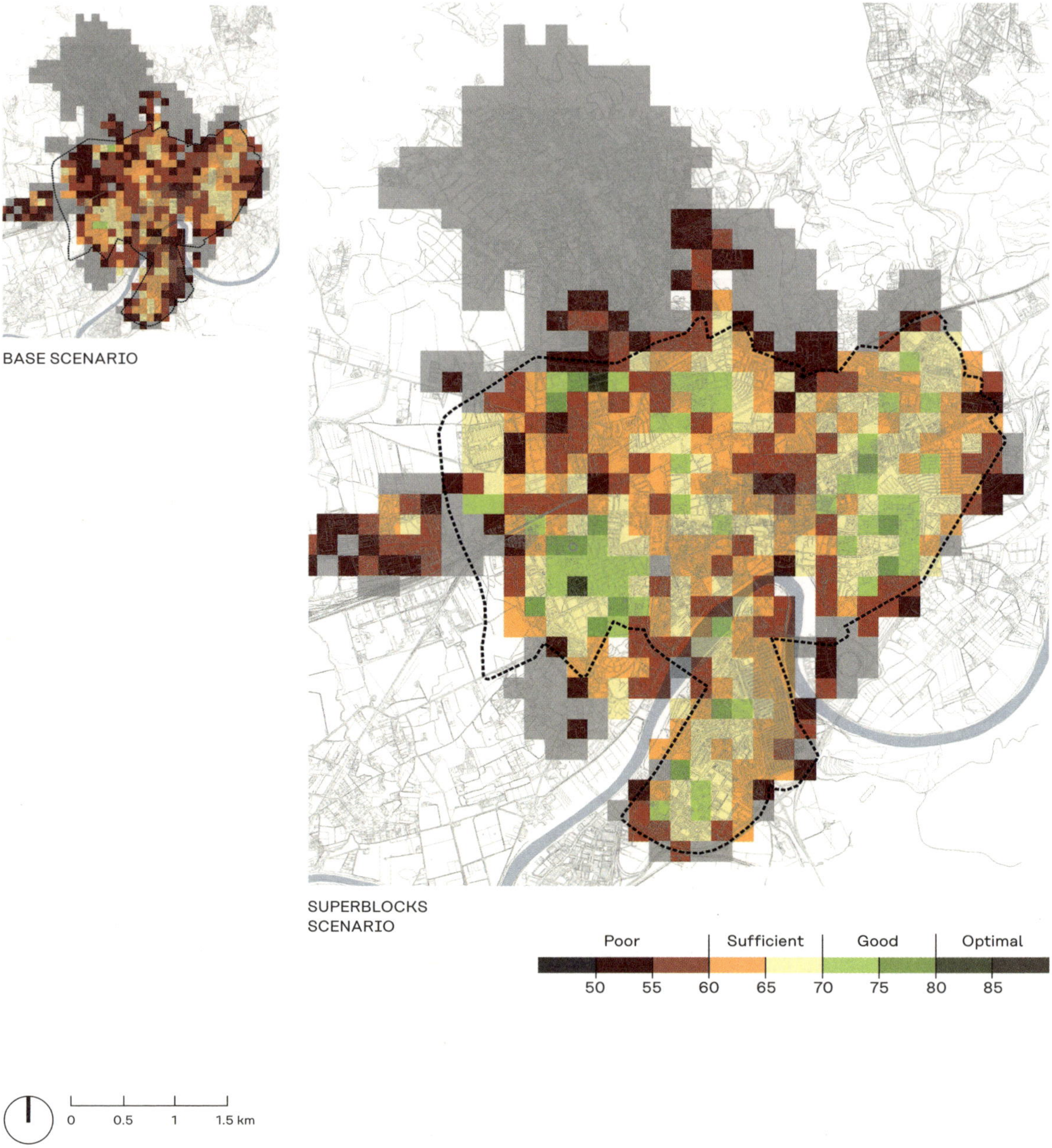

CÓRDOBA. 2014. Global liveability index in public space. Base scenario and superblocks scenario.
Source: BCNecologia

Conclusions

Motorised vehicles' dominance of streets is one of the main elements that distorts the public space's role as somewhere to be used and enjoyed by citizens. In fact, the physical characteristics of the public space condition the extent to which people can interact and coexist. They are a determining factor in the development of certain uses of each specific area.

By drawing up the aforementioned mobility and public space plans, the Agency has highlighted the urgent need to change our mobility model all over the world for the sake of the environment and people's health (the quality of the air we breathe and the noise to which we are exposed), social issues and citizens' rights. To this end, new public open spaces and urban greenery have been created in areas previously dedicated to cars.

The superblock model is a key part of a paradigm shift, and not just in Barcelona or other Mediterranean cities, as demonstrated by Vitoria-Gasteiz: a project awarded various recognitions by international bodies.

It is also important to note the essential role the public plays in the formulation of these strategic plans, as the aim is for residents to inhabit the city in the healthiest way possible while freely exercising their inherent rights as citizens (leisure, exchange, culture, expression and movement). Only this way can the city truly be democratised.

ORTHOGONAL PUBLIC TRANSPORT NETWORKS AND SUPERBLOCKS

2021

2020

2019

BARCELONA
Sustainable Urban Mobility Plan
2019-2024

2018

2017

BARCELONA
Definition of the metropolitan basic network

2016

QUITO
Restructuring the Public Transport System

2015

CÓRDOBA
Ciudad Jardín Superblock
Mobility and Public Space Plan

2014

2013

2012

2011

A CORUÑA
Mobility and Public Space Plan

2010

2009

FERROL AND LUGO
Mobility and Public Space Plan

2008

2007

VITORIA-GASTEIZ
Mobility and Public Space Plan

2006

VILADECANS
Mobility and Public Space Plan

2005

EL PRAT DE LLOBREGAT
Mobility and Public Space Plan

2004

2003

2002

2001

2000

The surface public transport network has a crucial role to play in paving the way for the future mobility model: it must absorb the journeys no longer made by conventional private vehicles. The structure of this network will be shaped by the new hierarchisation of basic circulation roads. These routes and the design of superblocks, among other elements, will be determining factors in this urban reorganisation.

One of the main instruments developed by the Urban Ecology Agency of Barcelona is the orthogonal bus network: a grid of horizontal and vertical axes, in alternating directions, that cross over at internal transfer points. This kind of network is easy to understand because it *isotropises* the city, structuring it in a similar way to metro networks so that it becomes much clearer and more readable for users. Furthermore, most destinations can be reached with just one transfer, which simplifies use of the network and eliminates the need to be familiar with each line individually.

The concept of the orthogonal network emerged in the early 2000s within the Agency as a new methodology to transform urban mobility on the basis of efficiency, sustainability and accessibility criteria. When it is implemented, waiting and travel times are reduced and connectivity between different modes of transport are improved, resulting in a more attractive public transport network. This way, transport flows on the road network are reorganised and the superblock model is easier to implement.

This chapter will examine the orthogonal networks in Barcelona and Vitoria-Gasteiz (applied directly) and the restructuring of the surface public transport network in the Metropolitan District of Quito, which is currently awaiting the final implementation of its first metro line. It will also deal with municipal and metropolitan networks designed in the Agency's other mobility plans (Córdoba, Lugo, A Coruña, Ferrol, Viladecans and El Prat de Llobregat).

THE ORTHOGONAL BUS NETWORK

This network is the basic structure for the development of the superblock model on built-up urban land. In each area, the system of bus lines is optimised to move towards a network system, based on the criteria below.

MORPHOLOGY AND ISOTROPY

The network's topology – in the form of a grid – increases the city's isotropy in terms of access time, strengthens the most peripheral areas, helps to decentralise the public transport system and prevents excessive overlapping.

COVERAGE AND ACCESSIBILITY

The network must be accessible for the whole population, so that everyone is less than 300 metres (or 5 minutes) from a bus stop. The network's fractal design ensures optimal coverage across the city and competitive journey times compared to those offered by conventional private vehicles.

CONNECTEDNESS AND CONNECTIVITY

The system is simplified, with bus stops distributed evenly every 400–500 metres, especially at transfer points between axes and different modes of transport. This way, citizens have access to as many routes as possible within the public transport network and intermodality is boosted.

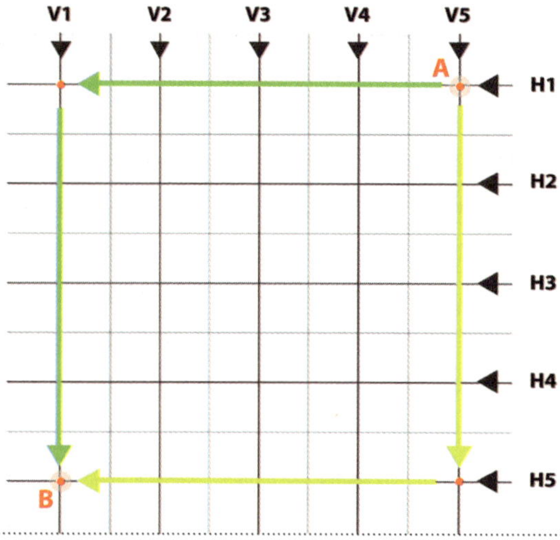

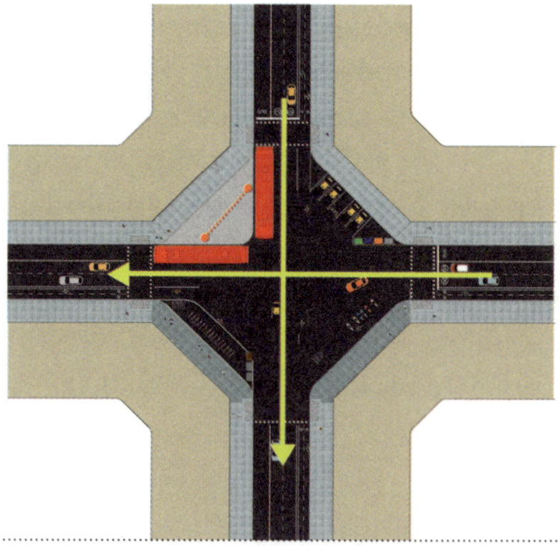

BARCELONA. 2004. Bus-bus transfer point at corner of two roads. A network emerges when the structure is rationalised and becomes orthogonal, and as a result, to go from one point of the map to another in the urban area, only one transfer is required.
Source: BCNecologia

BARCELONA. PMUS 2019-2024.
Basic road network proposed for superblocks.
Source: BCNecologia

PREFERENCE AND PRIORITY

The surface public transport network must flow along the city's basic roads, and separately from other vehicles, provided the service frequency is high enough. This way, friction with private vehicles is reduced and bus priority signals at traffic lights improve public transport operating speed (the average speed on each journey).

The functionality and purpose of orthogonal networks goes far beyond a mere increase in the number of public transport users. These networks help to create the ideal context for facilitating a modal shift towards sustainable mobility. This reduces the number of journeys made by private motor vehicle and the health impact caused by the air pollution, noise and traffic associated with the current mobility model.

BARCELONA. 2012–2018. New Orthogonal Bus Network.
Source: BCNecologia

THE ORTHOGONAL NETWORK IN BARCELONA

The Agency began the study for the orthogonal network project in Barcelona in 2001. The project was presented in 2004 and consisted of a network with 28 axes: 17 vertical, 7 horizontal and 4 diagonal.

Between 2004 and 2013, 18 more studies were carried out for Barcelona Metropolitan Transport (TMB) on the new orthogonal network, analysing predicted demand, operational speed, the extension of the bus lane network and priority measures, connections with the metropolitan area, types of stop and user information, fleet renovation, energy consumption and emissions, the psychosocial impact of a new network, and the communication and participation process.

All of these preliminary studies culminated in the formulation of the Barcelona PMU 2013–2018: the document that consolidated the orthogonal network. This document highlighted that, with the same number of vehicles in the fleet (903), the number of lines could be reduced from 98 to 77, the average service frequency on the orthogonal lines could be set under 5 minutes, and the percentage of the population within 40 minutes of all other points in the rest of the municipality of Barcelona could be increased from 37.6% to 47.8%. Overall, these measures cut journey times by an average of 0.52 minutes.

As the implementation phases of the Barcelona orthogonal urban bus network advanced (in the 2012–2018 period, over two consecutive political terms with different governments in charge), the percentage of journeys made on these lines increased significantly, until reaching almost 60% in the final stage. The completion of this system was the most important change for surface public transport in the city since the tram network was dismantled in the 1960s.

Finally, the topology of the orthogonal network largely adapts to the structure of basic roads in the Barcelona superblock model; therefore, both of the city's motorised transport networks are efficiently integrated.

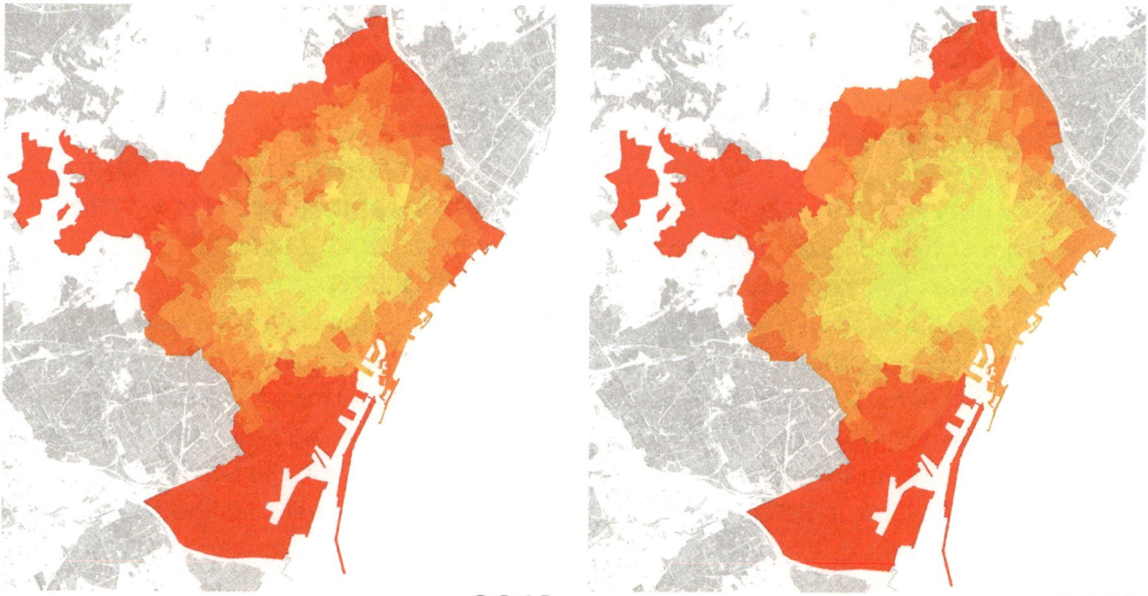

RADIAL MODEL **2013**

ORTHOGONAL MODEL **2019**

35 40 45 50 55 60

Overall Accessibility Index (min)

BARCELONA. Evolution of the number of passengers on the orthogonal routes following the different implantation stages (2012–2018).
Source: BCNecologia

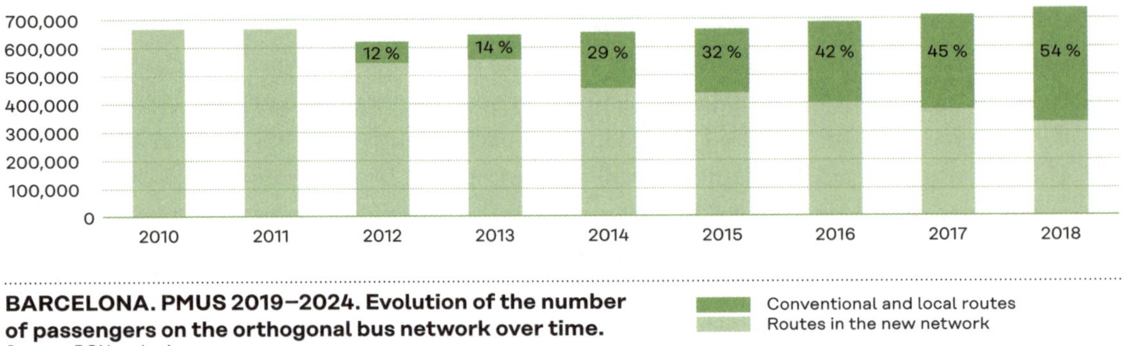

BARCELONA. PMUS 2019–2024. Evolution of the number of passengers on the orthogonal bus network over time.
Source: BCNecologia

THE ORTHOGONAL NETWORK IN VITORIA-GASTEIZ

In parallel, in 2007, the Vitoria-Gasteiz Sustainable Mobility and Public Space Plan was formulated. Two years later, in October 2009, after completion of the first phase, the new orthogonal urban bus network was implemented, among other measures.

This network reduced the number of lines from 17 to 7 (plus 2 new tram lines) and improved service frequency from 15–30 minutes to 10 minutes on all routes. Furthermore, 12 vehicles were added to the fleet.

Since it was launched, the new transport network in Vitoria-Gasteiz has not stopped growing, in terms of number of users: in 2018 alone, it welcomed almost 23 million passengers.

In addition, its network-based topology is a perfect fit for the system of basic roads inherent in the superblock model designed for the city. The next step, after integrating all transport networks and configuring new low-emission zones, is to free up public space on the street for civic functions and uses other than private motor vehicle traffic.

RESTRUCTURING THE PUBLIC TRANSPORT SYSTEM IN THE METROPOLITAN DISTRICT OF QUITO

Subsequently, in 2016, work began on restructuring the surface public transport system in the Metropolitan District of Quito (DMQ): a far-reaching project with considerable repercussions in the Ecuadorian capital. The district, with over two and a half million inhabitants spread out over 4,000 km^2, had a fragmentary transport system with poor service quality that catered to demand seg-

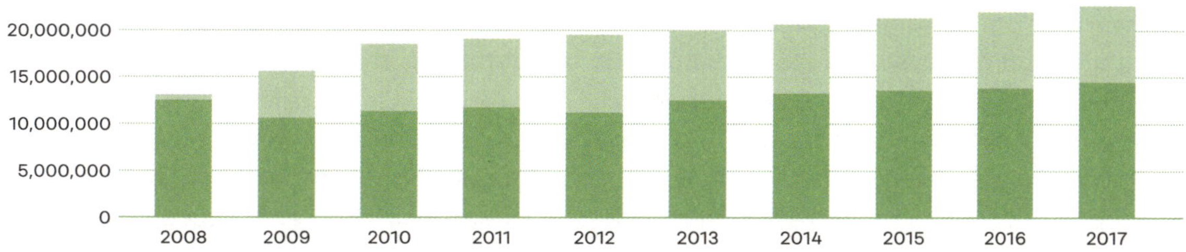

VITORIA-GASTEIZ. 2018. Evolution of annual number of passengers on public transport.
Source: TUVISA/EUSKOTREN

VITORIA-GASTEIZ. The implementation of the orthogonal bus network was a success thanks to awareness-raising campaigns that informed the population of the new routes.
Picture: Eltis.org. The Urban Mobility Observatory (Harry Schiffer)

ments using traditional, inefficient logics. The various conventional urban bus routes were not well organised or well connected with the MetrobusQ system. Management of the system was fragmented, with 68 different operators serving 258 routes – including MetrobusQ lines (bus rapid transit, BRT) and feeder, urban and parish buses – across the metropolitan region, with a heterogeneous fleet of 3,524 vehicles.

One of the study's main aims revolved around the operational integration of the surface public transport network with the city's first metro line, which would cross the urban area from north to south, and with the cable cars known as the Quito-Cables. Another focus was the rationalisation and reorganisation of the existing tangle of bus lines to avoid overlapping and improve service frequency, quality and comfort across the system.

In Quito, more than 2,600,000 journeys are made by public transport every day, representing 61.3% of the modal split. The proposal designed to tackle this challenge was based on an orthogonal grid and ensured that, to go from one point of the map to another in the urban area, only one transfer was required (or two if one of the points was in the parish areas in the surrounding valleys).

In the urban area, the resulting network topology extended and reinforced the longitudinal, north–south movement of the MetrobusQ system with horizontal and diagonal routes and complemented it with a feeder subsystem with vertical perpendicular routes. On a parish level, meanwhile, the proposal was to create new, more powerful metropolitan corridors into the city (with express and semi-express services), backed up by a local network strengthened by vehicles transferred from the urban fleet.

Though the same fleet was maintained, the new network configuration brought about a host of benefits for the system: it reduced the number of routes from 241 to 191 (excluding the BRT system); it significantly boosted operational speed, doubling service frequency; it increased the percentage of the population less than an hour away from any other point in the metropolitan district from 39.3% to 73.5%; and it cut one-part journeys by six minutes, two-part journeys by fourteen and three-part journeys by twenty.

This improved connections across the urban area, between the mountainsides, and with the surrounding valleys, balancing the urban and parish fleets out to be almost equal, when previously, the parish buses made up only 27% of the total fleet.

The idea was for this restructuring to play a key role in the new mobility and city model being promoted and to help to ease congestion in the Historic Centre of Quito – a UNESCO World Heritage Site – in accord-

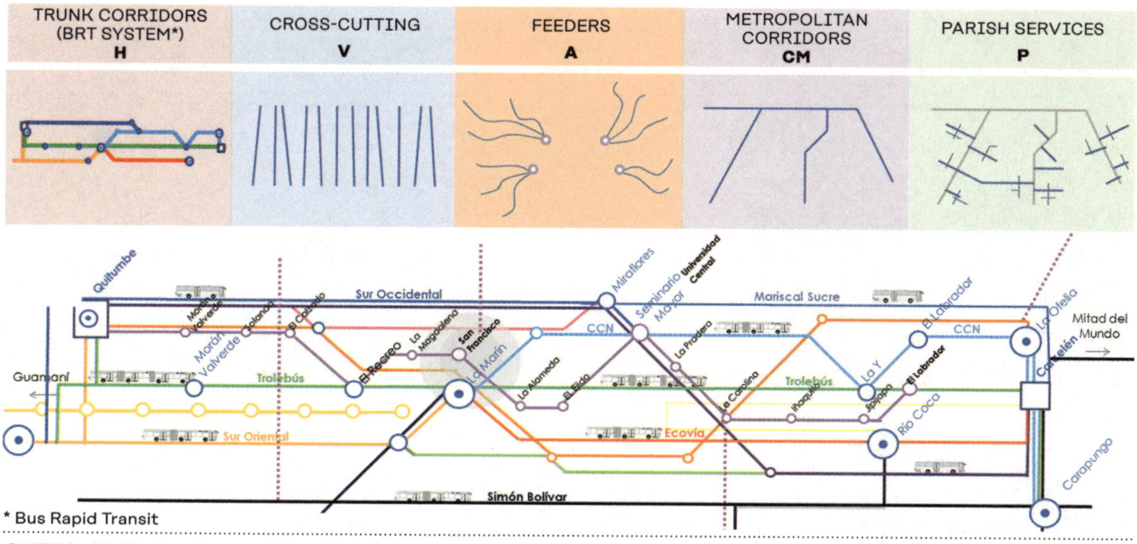

QUITO. 2016. Surface public transport restructuring plan in the Metropolitan District of Quito.
Source: BCNecologia

The morphology and topography of Quito lend themselves to a network with a north–south longitudinal movement hierarchy (H), accompanied by a perpendicular feeder subsystem. The key to achieving a homogeneous network lies in an efficient, convenient articulation between the different subsystems (V, A, CM, P) that make up the integrated system.

BASE SC. E0 round trip	Operational speed (km/h)	Journey time (min)	Lenght (km)	E0 Frequency (min)	Vehicle Capacity	Numb. of routes
FEEDER	17.5	37.3	10.6	11.4	85.5	74
URBAN	17.7	57.2	16.1	8.4	86.7	109
PARISH	24.1	58	23.7	10	56.7	58
						241

SC. E1-E2 Round trip	Operational speed (km/h)	Journey time (min)	Lenght (km)	E1 Frequency (min)	E2 Frequency (min)	Vehicle Capacity	Numb. of routes
VERTICALS (East - West)	18.9	24.7	7.7	5.8	4.7	90	61
HORITZONTALS (North - South)	19.6	42.1	13.6	4.6	4.8	90	13
DIAGONALS	18.7	97.2	30.2	3	4.6	90	4
TERMINAL FEEDERS	21.8	23.3	8.5	7.3	7.3	90	37
METROPOLITAN CORRIDORS	31.8	55.2	28.9	4.7	4.7	45.4	44
PARISH	24	39.7		13	12.1	90	32
							191

ANALYSIS OF AVERAGE JOURNEY TIME BY NUMBER OF PARTS			
NUMB. PARTS	1	2	3
AVERAGE JOURNEY TIME (min)			
BASE scenario	32.9	63	91.1
Scenario 1	29.7	52.5	77.4
Scenario 2	26.7	48.9	71.1

QUITO. 2016. Surface public transport restructuring plan in the Metropolitan District of Quito. Scenario improvement analysis.
Source: BCNecologia

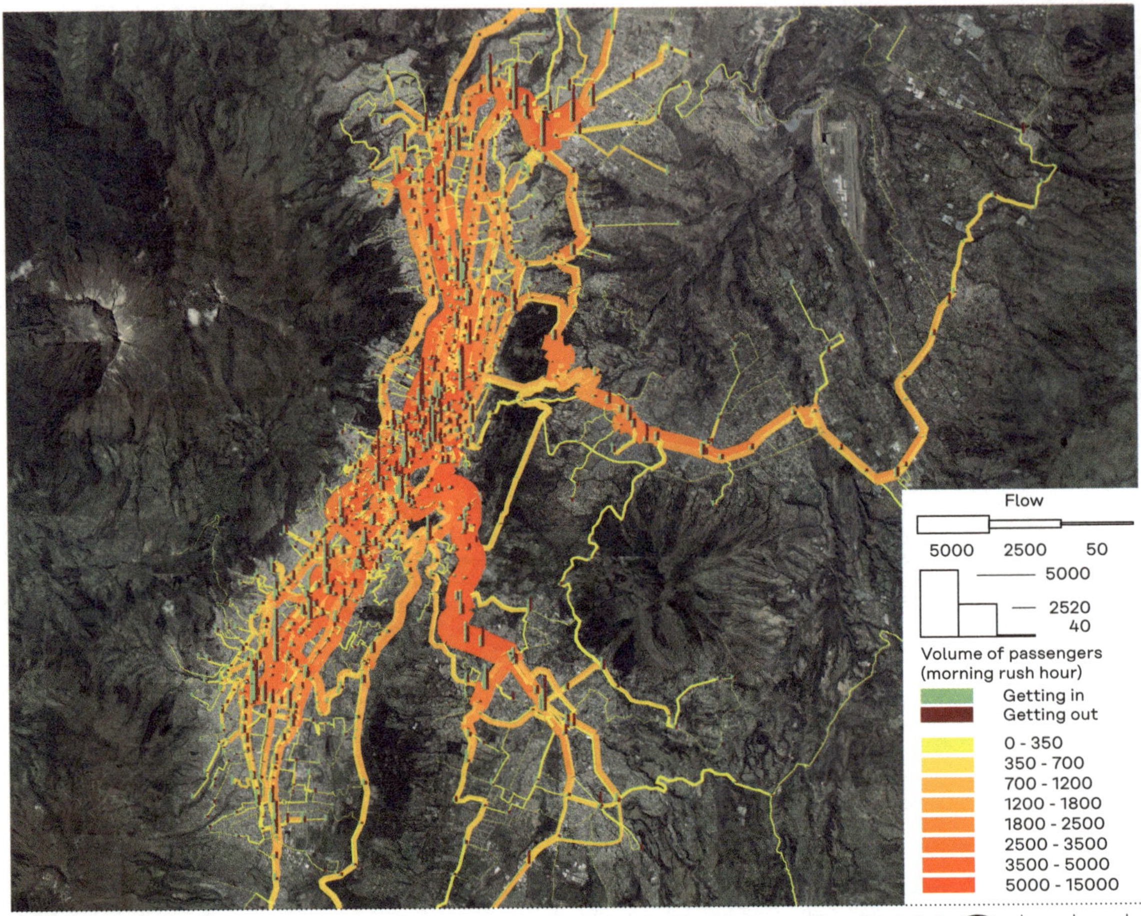

QUITO. 2016. Surface public transport restructuring plan in the Metropolitan District of Quito. Passenger assignment on public transport. Proposed or future scenario.
Source: BCNecologia

ance with the Revitalisation Plan, which the Agency also wrote up in 2013. For this reason, a superblock model has been integrated into this orthogonal network system, in order to encourage a paradigm shift in mobility and uses of the public space.

OTHER ORTHOGONAL NETWORKS

The other orthogonal networks studied in various mobility and public space plans formulated by the Agency have been met with various degrees of acceptance. Some have come close to implementation, as detailed below, but have not been brought to life due to various factors (usually related to political circumstances or an economic crisis).

Some notable cases are Ferrol (2009), A Coruña (2011) and Córdoba (2014): three networks studied in depth through mobility plans and put to the test through passenger assignation in a transport simulator. A demand evolution analysis and forecast were also carried out for these cities. The Ferrol and A Coruña networks were reviewed subsequently, in specific implementation (2013) and metropolitan connection plans (2017) respectively, with approval from municipal technical teams and councillors for mobility, and involvement from the public companies that held the licences to the networks (Tranvías de Ferrol and Tranvías de La Coruña).

In the case of Ferrol all the bus networks operating in the municipality were redesigned and integrated. The new urban network, with the same fleet and more population coverage, would improve service frequency by almost five minutes, and would almost double the percentage of the population less than 25 minutes away from any other point in the city. The rural network, with its fleet maintained, would offer five more services every day and a fixed timetable on the hour or at half past. As for the intercity bus network, entry flows into the city would be reorganised and the terminus would be moved to the bus station.

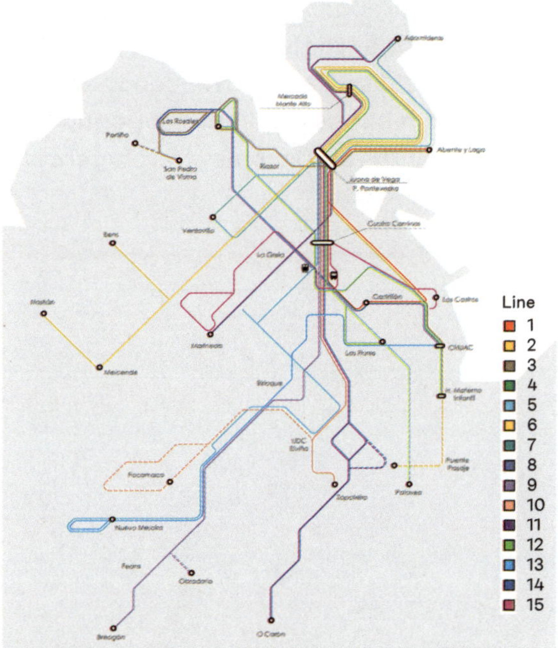

A CORUÑA. 2018. Plan for the implementation of the new bus network. Urban bus plan. Proposed scenario.
Source: BCNecologia

In A Coruña, the fleet would be preserved and three fewer lines would be offered. In addition, bus stop coverage would be improved by 8% and the percentage of the population less than 25 minutes away from any other point in the city would be increased by 10%. A bus lane would also be created on some main roads and the metropolitan bus network would be reformulated, incorporating express and semi-express services and adapting hubs for the urban network.

In Córdoba, with the same fleet and one fewer line, the proposed orthogonal network could set service frequency at eight minutes in most cases, improve population coverage by 7%, and increase the percentage of the population within 30 minutes of any other point in the city by 9%, largely thanks to new, longitudinal routes that crossed the city from north to south and made transfers easier.

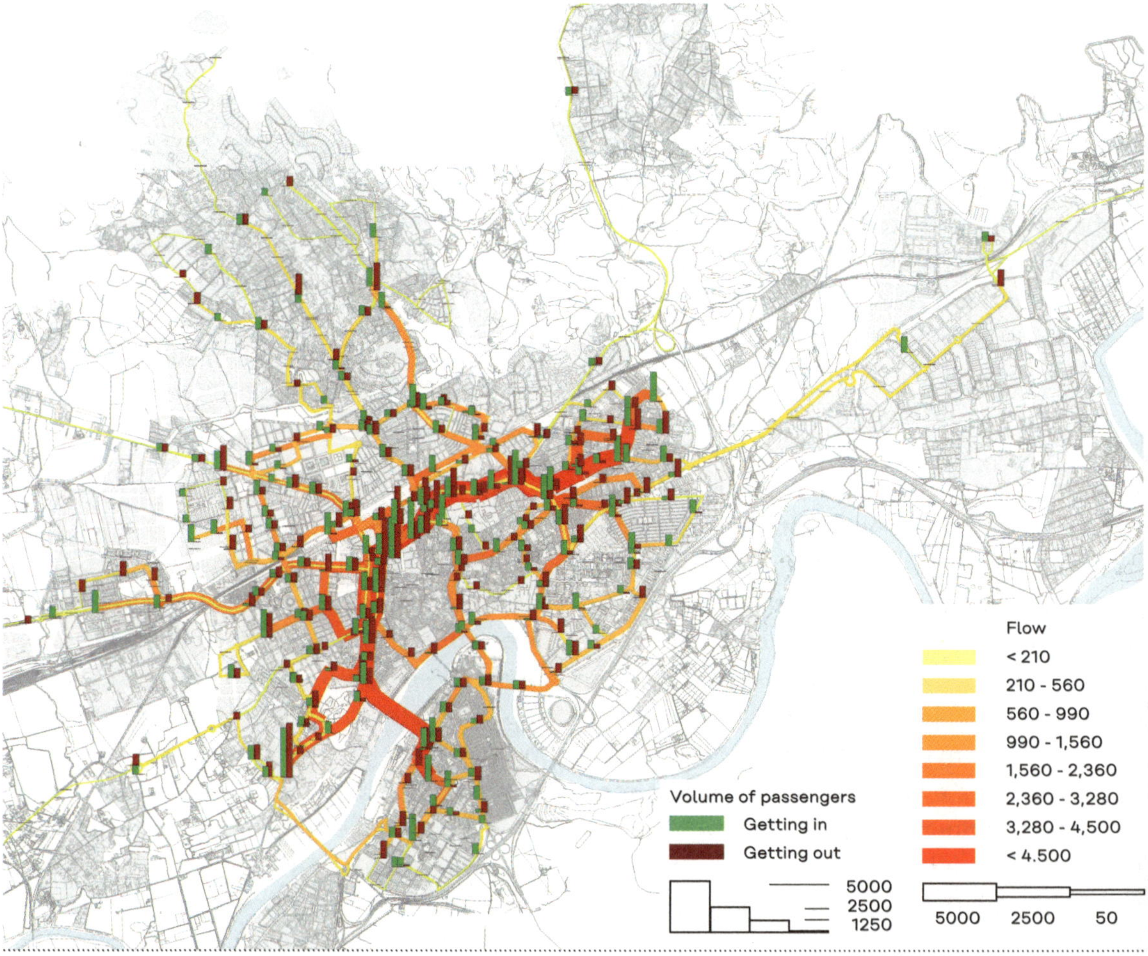

CÓRDOBA. 2014. Proposed scenario.
Source: BCNecologia

Conclusions

Orthogonal surface public transport networks are a key part in the configuration of the superblock model. As seen in the paragraphs above, they determine the structure of a city's basic roads. The application of this kind of network is therefore the first step towards implementing this urban model and is necessary for a modal shift towards more sustainable forms of transport to take place.

Our expertise is backed up by experience from the Vitoria-Gasteiz and Barcelona projects. In the former, the implementation of the orthogonal bus network in 2009 marked the beginning of a paradigm shift in the urban model and a turning point for the city's modal split, in which the private vehicle's share has since shrunk considerably. This was followed by successive superblock implementation plans, like the Central Superblock Plan (2010) and the Superblock Master Plan (2012), which were consolidated with the Review of the Vitoria-Gasteiz Sustainable Mobility and Public Space Plan in 2018.

The development process was similar in Barcelona. From the initial phases of implementing the orthogonal bus network in 2012, interest and municipal initiatives surrounding superblocks grew steadily, with the implementation of a superblock in Les Corts in 2013, then in El Poblenou (2016 and 2018), Sant Antoni (2019) and Horta (2019). The new Barcelona Sustainable Urban Mobility Plan 2019–2024 proposes rolling out superblocks all over the city.

It is safe to say, then, that the orthogonal public transport network is an essential instrument for implementing superblocks. Indeed, a superblock structure would make no sense without an orthogonal bus network, and vice versa.

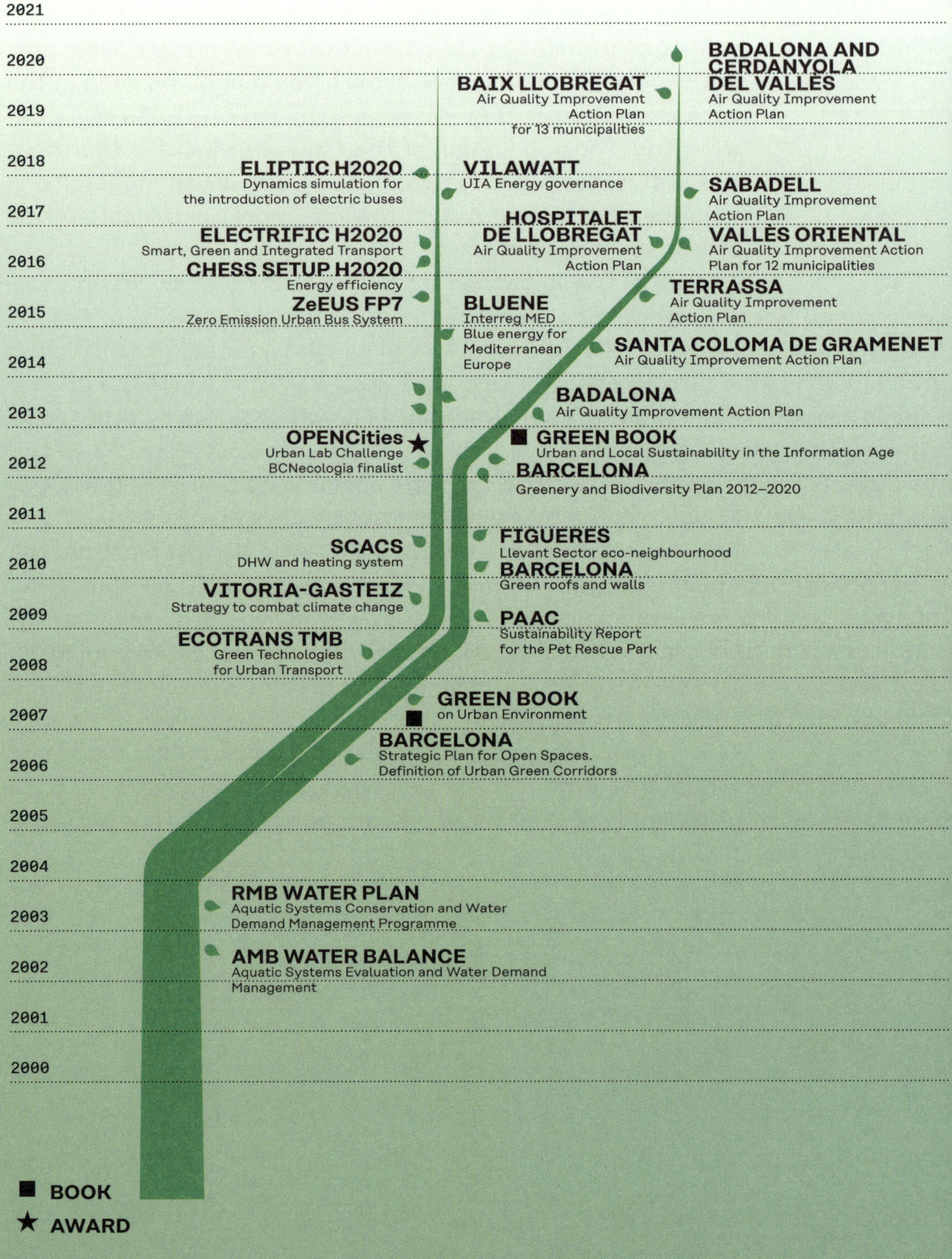
2021
2020
2019
2018
2017
2016
2015
2014
2013
2012
2011
2010
2009
2008
2007
2006
2005
2004
2003
2002
2001
2000
BADALONA AND CERDANYOLA DEL VALLÈS
Air Quality Improvement Action Plan
BAIX LLOBREGAT
Air Quality Improvement Action Plan for 13 municipalities
ELIPTIC H2020
Dynamics simulation for the introduction of electric buses
VILAWATT
UIA Energy governance
SABADELL
Air Quality Improvement Action Plan
HOSPITALET DE LLOBREGAT
Air Quality Improvement Action Plan
ELECTRIFIC H2020
Smart, Green and Integrated Transport
VALLÈS ORIENTAL
Air Quality Improvement Action Plan for 12 municipalities
CHESS SETUP H2020
Energy efficiency
TERRASSA
Air Quality Improvement Action Plan
ZeEUS FP7
Zero Emission Urban Bus System
BLUENE
Interreg MED
Blue energy for Mediterranean Europe
SANTA COLOMA DE GRAMENET
Air Quality Improvement Action Plan
BADALONA
Air Quality Improvement Action Plan
OPENCities
Urban Lab Challenge
BCNecologia finalist
GREEN BOOK
Urban and Local Sustainability in the Information Age
BARCELONA
Greenery and Biodiversity Plan 2012–2020
SCACS
DHW and heating system
FIGUERES
Llevant Sector eco-neighbourhood
BARCELONA
Green roofs and walls
VITORIA-GASTEIZ
Strategy to combat climate change
PAAC
Sustainability Report for the Pet Rescue Park
ECOTRANS TMB
Green Technologies for Urban Transport
GREEN BOOK
on Urban Environment
BARCELONA
Strategic Plan for Open Spaces. Definition of Urban Green Corridors
RMB WATER PLAN
Aquatic Systems Conservation and Water Demand Management Programme
AMB WATER BALANCE
Aquatic Systems Evaluation and Water Demand Management
BOOK
AWARD

ENVIRONMENT

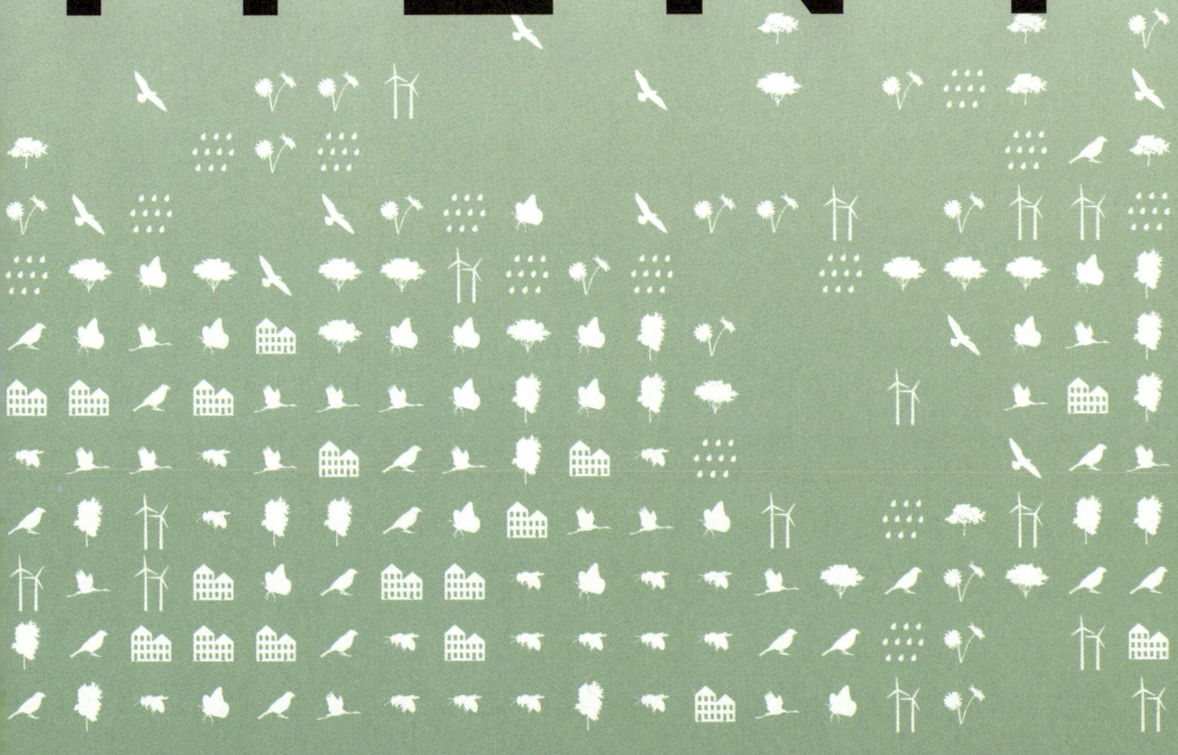

People tend to associate the concept of the environment with nature, but it takes on a specific dimension in the urban space. Problems related to water consumption, energy and climate change, for example, mainly originate in how we inhabit the urban space. In other words, the way cities are organised has wide-reaching consequences on our planet's ecosystems, as well as specific effects on the urban areas themselves and their populations. The flows of materials and energy in and out of cities shape our world, so it is vital that we manage them as efficiently as possible. The Agency has examined all these flows closely, through both projects with a single focus (like energy) and urban regeneration projects that incorporate all aspects of ecosystemic urbanism, as seen in previous chapters.

The first chapter in this area deals with water treatment, mainly in reference to the project that set the tone for this subject within the Agency: the Aquatic Systems Conservation and Water Demand Management Programme in the Barcelona Metropolitan Region (RMB).

The following chapters talk about energy, including projects relating to climate change. As well as being the focus of some of the Agency's own work, energy has been the subject of careful consideration in urban regeneration projects, as it affects buildings, public space and mobility.

Meanwhile, air quality is a key factor in urban health and is dictated by the city's mobility model, as motor traffic is the leading source of air pollution in urban spaces. One of the chapters in this area examines the projects that have built strategies to control this aspect of our cities: the Air Quality Improvement Action Plans.

Finally, this area concludes with urban biodiversity and the green network in Barcelona, as the flow of genetic material tends to be forgotten in examinations of material flows, even though it brings life to cities' much-appreciated green spaces.

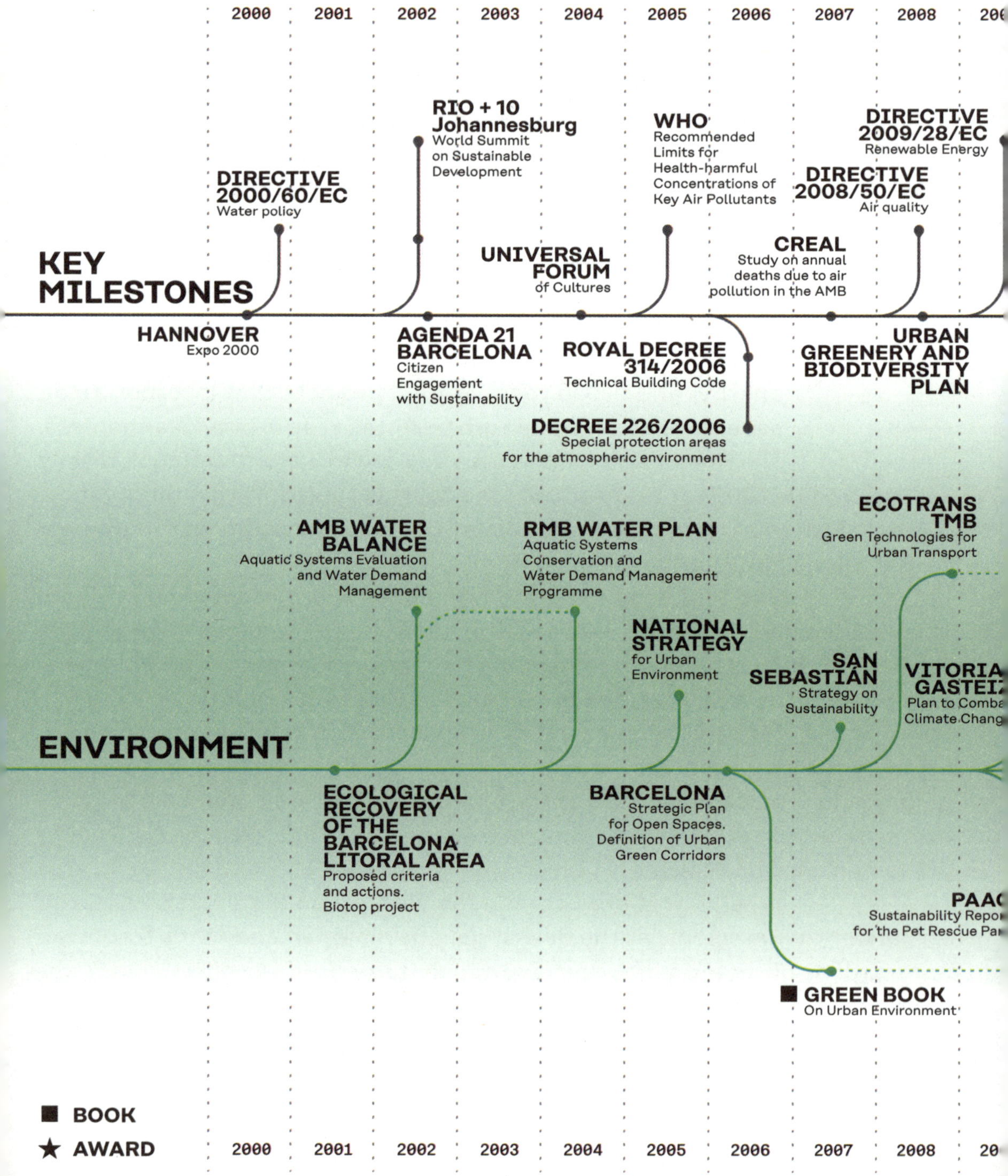
2000 2001 2002 2003 2004 2005 2006 2007 2008 20
KEY MILESTONES
DIRECTIVE 2000/60/EC
Water policy
RIO + 10 Johannesburg
World Summit on Sustainable Development
UNIVERSAL FORUM
of Cultures
WHO
Recommended Limits for Health-harmful Concentrations of Key Air Pollutants
CREAL
Study on annual deaths due to air pollution in the AMB
DIRECTIVE 2008/50/EC
Air quality
DIRECTIVE 2009/28/EC
Renewable Energy
HANNOVER
Expo 2000
AGENDA 21 BARCELONA
Citizen Engagement with Sustainability
ROYAL DECREE 314/2006
Technical Building Code
DECREE 226/2006
Special protection areas for the atmospheric environment
URBAN GREENERY AND BIODIVERSITY PLAN
ENVIRONMENT
AMB WATER BALANCE
Aquatic Systems Evaluation and Water Demand Management
RMB WATER PLAN
Aquatic Systems Conservation and Water Demand Management Programme
NATIONAL STRATEGY
for Urban Environment
SAN SEBASTIÁN
Strategy on Sustainability
ECOTRANS TMB
Green Technologies for Urban Transport
VITORIA GASTEI
Plan to Comba Climate Chang
ECOLOGICAL RECOVERY OF THE BARCELONA LITORAL AREA
Proposed criteria and actions. Biotop project
BARCELONA
Strategic Plan for Open Spaces. Definition of Urban Green Corridors
PAA
Sustainability Repo for the Pet Rescue Pa
■ GREEN BOOK
On Urban Environment
■ BOOK
★ AWARD
2000 2001 2002 2003 2004 2005 2006 2007 2008 20

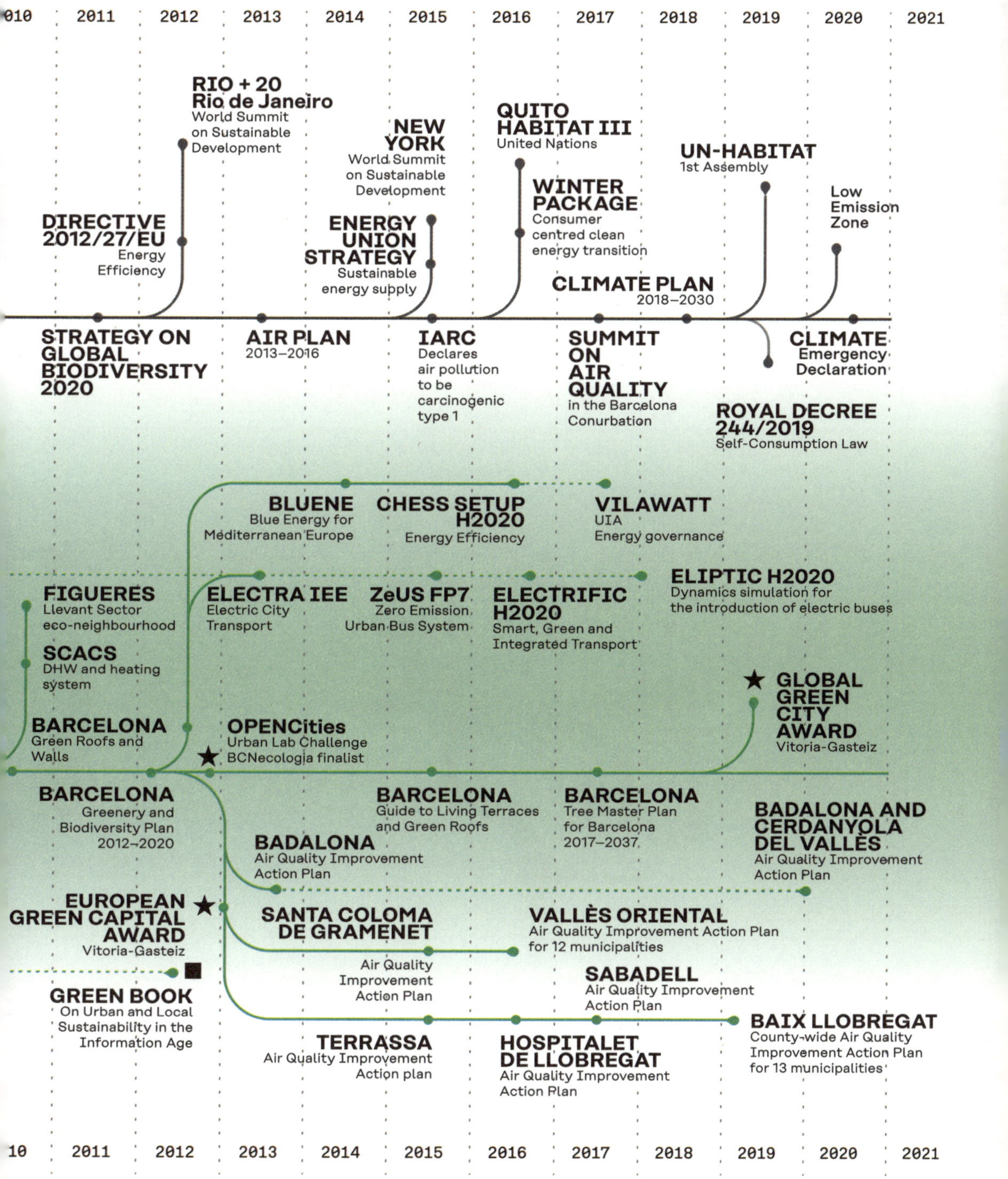
2010 2011 2012 2013 2014 2015 2016 2017 2018 2019 2020 2021
RIO + 20 Rio de Janeiro
World Summit on Sustainable Development
NEW YORK
World Summit on Sustainable Development
QUITO HABITAT III
United Nations
UN-HABITAT
1st Assembly
DIRECTIVE 2012/27/EU
Energy Efficiency
ENERGY UNION STRATEGY
Sustainable energy supply
WINTER PACKAGE
Consumer centred clean energy transition
Low Emission Zone
CLIMATE PLAN
2018–2030
STRATEGY ON GLOBAL BIODIVERSITY 2020
AIR PLAN
2013–2016
IARC
Declares air pollution to be carcinogenic type 1
SUMMIT ON AIR QUALITY
in the Barcelona Conurbation
CLIMATE
Emergency Declaration
ROYAL DECREE 244/2019
Self-Consumption Law
BLUENE
Blue Energy for Mediterranean Europe
CHESS SETUP H2020
Energy Efficiency
VILAWATT
UIA
Energy governance
FIGUERES
Llevant Sector eco-neighbourhood
SCACS
DHW and heating system
ELECTRA IEE
Electric City Transport
ZeUS FP7
Zero Emission Urban Bus System
ELECTRIFIC H2020
Smart, Green and Integrated Transport
ELIPTIC H2020
Dynamics simulation for the introduction of electric buses
GLOBAL GREEN CITY AWARD
Vitoria-Gasteiz
BARCELONA
Green Roofs and Walls
OPENCities
Urban Lab Challenge
BCNecologia finalist
BARCELONA
Greenery and Biodiversity Plan 2012–2020
BARCELONA
Guide to Living Terraces and Green Roofs
BARCELONA
Tree Master Plan for Barcelona 2017–2037
BADALONA
Air Quality Improvement Action Plan
BADALONA AND CERDANYOLA DEL VALLÈS
Air Quality Improvement Action Plan
EUROPEAN GREEN CAPITAL AWARD
Vitoria-Gasteiz
SANTA COLOMA DE GRAMENET
Air Quality Improvement Action Plan
VALLÈS ORIENTAL
Air Quality Improvement Action Plan for 12 municipalities
GREEN BOOK
On Urban and Local Sustainability in the Information Age
SABADELL
Air Quality Improvement Action Plan
TERRASSA
Air Quality Improvement Action plan
HOSPITALET DE LLOBREGAT
Air Quality Improvement Action Plan
BAIX LLOBREGAT
County-wide Air Quality Improvement Action Plan for 13 municipalities
10 2011 2012 2013 2014 2015 2016 2017 2018 2019 2020 2021

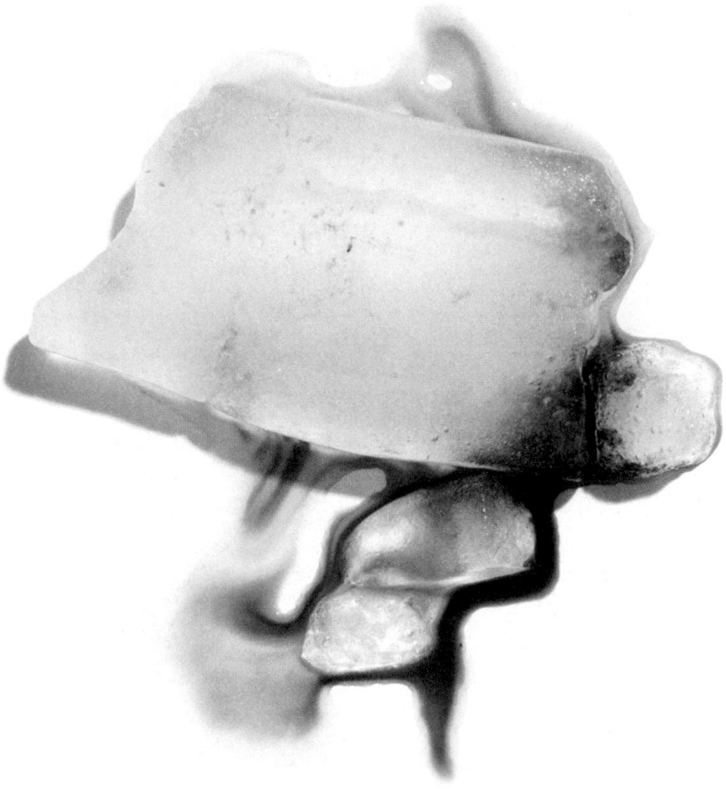

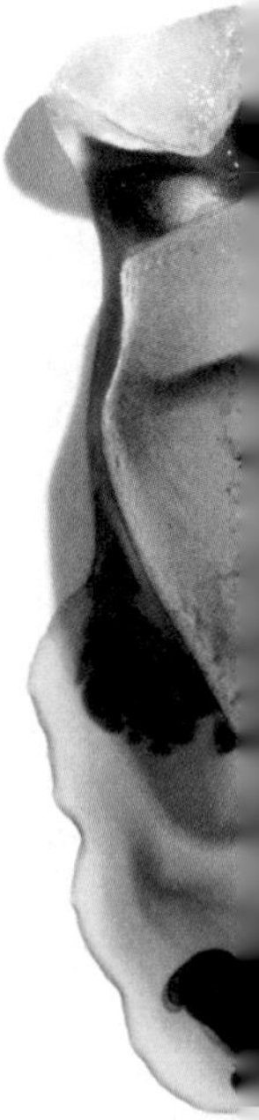

"Our motto was: 'Don't aim low. Create for a city where no rules are set in stone'. This opens up a world of opportunities for creation and generation".

MOISÈS MORATÓ
Engineer. Responsible for the Energy Area 2002–2019. BCNecologia.

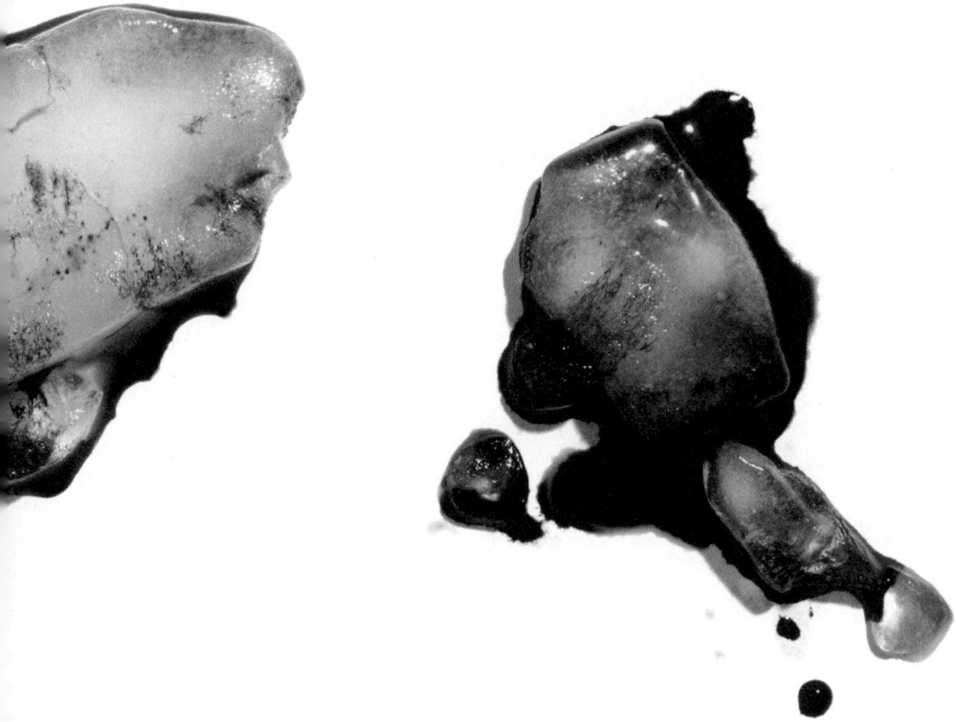

Picture: Marta Torrent

WATER CYCLE MANAGEMENT

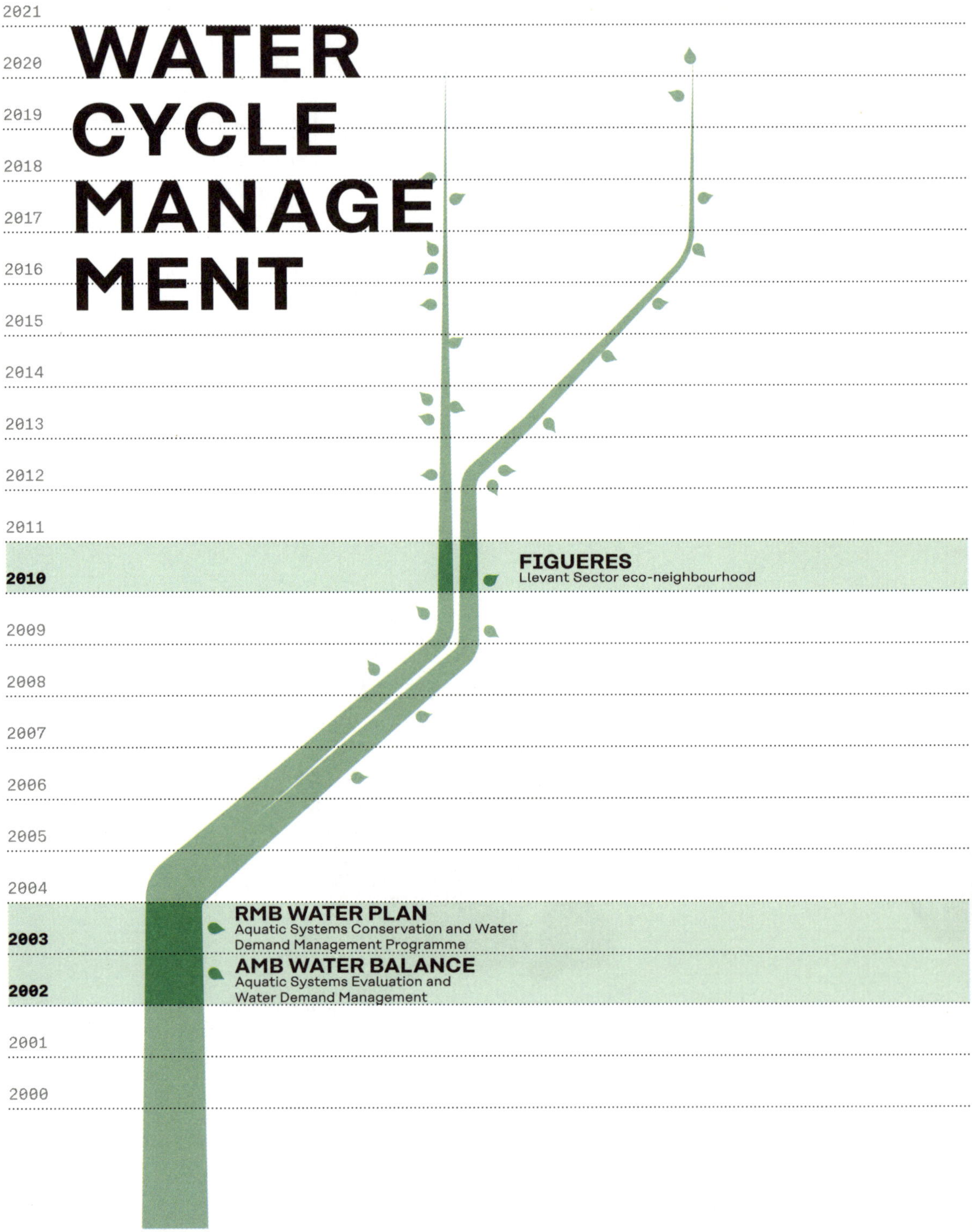

In 2002, BCNecologia carried out a study on the Water Balance of the Barcelona Metropolitan Area (AMB). The project dealt with the total water demand in the AMB and combined an innovative methodology with a study of alternative water sources.

With this analysis as a starting point, the Agency has kept sustainable water management at the heart of its projects, which propose diverse sustainable management models deriving from a wide variety of scenarios created by local conditions and the characteristics of the urban model. The most noteworthy cases are those of Viladecans-Gavà-Castelldefels, Cortijo de Cuarto (Seville), A Coruña, San Sebastián and the Llevant Sector eco-neighbourhood in Figueres.

In Viladecans-Gavà-Castelldefels, an integrated, intermunicipal solution was applied. It involved the recovery of the south-east part of the Llobregat River Delta Aquifer, the reclamation of 75% of the effluent from the Viladecans Waste Water Treatment Plant (EDAR), optimised management of irrigation areas, and a self-sufficient water supply.

In Cortijo de Cuarto (Seville), a small endorheic basin, formed by the left dike of the Guadalquivir River, acts as a lagoon that uses rainwater and wastewater, thus creating a large park where the flora and fauna affected by the urbanisation process can recover. The A Coruña project, meanwhile, focuses on the substitution of raw water in the lower course of the Mero River with reclaimed water, in order to increase the potential amount of resources available without affecting the estuary's biodiversity. In San Sebastián, the topographical conditions of new urban development areas were used to transfer reclaimed marginal water from higher-altitude urban areas to lower altitudes, without any energy being consumed. In the Llevant Sector eco-neighbourhood in Figueres, greywater and rainwater undergo pretreatment before being discharged into an artificial lagoon through a bioregeneration system.

This chapter also mentions the Aquatic Systems Conservation and Water Demand Management Programme in the Barcelona Metropolitan Region.

WATER MANAGEMENT IN THE BARCELONA METROPOLITAN REGION

The Aquatic Systems Conservation and Water Demand Management Programme in the Barcelona Metropolitan Region (RMB), commissioned by the Ecology Section of the Barcelona Metropolitan Area, constitutes the logical development of Directive 2000/60/EC of the European Parliament and of the Council of 23 October 2000 establishing a framework for Community action in the field of water policy (Water Framework Directive, WFD). The Programme bases its approach on this directive. For the Agency, it is also a consequence and an evolution of a previous, smaller project: the Water Balance of the Barcelona Metropolitan Area.

The WFD establishes the water resources policy to be applied in the EU and, therefore, in Barcelona and Catalonia as a whole. The starting point for this directive is a simple yet undeniable truth: we depend on aquatic ecosystems for our water supply. As a result, we will only have a safe, healthy water supply if our aquatic ecosystems are also safe and healthy.

The Water Plan's contribution to sustainability, inasmuch as it uses the WFD as a reference, is founded on a series of proposals that conform perfectly to the principles of sustainable development. For the Agency, it becomes a paradigm of the sustainable planning of a resource largely consumed in urban areas, but with an impact (the impact of this consumption) on all of Catalonia, beyond the Metropolitan Region.

GOALS OF THE PROGRAMME

The Aquatic Systems Conservation and Water Demand Management Programme in the Barcelona Metropolitan Region was structured around three essential goals. The first was based on restoring river basins and improving their ecological condition and, therefore, their water quality. The second focused on supplying water of sufficient quantity and quality for all uses required in the Metropolitan Region. Finally, the third consisted of establishing emergency water sources for periods when quality water is scarce (extreme drought).

In order to deal with the restoration of the river basins (first goal), the basic concepts in the new water policy, deriving from the WFD, were placed at the centre of the project. The aim was to reach a proposal to reconcile the RMB and its rivers, aquifers and, ultimately, the river basins of the Llobregat, the Besòs and the Ter.

GOAL ONE. RESTORE RIVER BASINS

To help to restore the river basins, the project involved retaining water in the basins of the RMB by repairing riparian woodland and riverside areas. These communities of species have been greatly damaged by anthropogenic influence and activities such as agriculture, which have traditionally taken control over this biodiversity to gain more space for crops and avoid any potential competition. To regenerate the riparian woodland, a series of actions were planned, starting with the treatment of existing vegetation to boost its development and growth.

The most effort was made to recover the Besòs basin, as it was the most damaged site of the three and played an essential ecological role, as a green corridor between different habitats. The Besòs basin connects the Coastal and Pre-Coastal mountain ranges, as well as various valleys in the Pre-Coastal Range. Within these areas, there are many protected spaces, areas included in the Plan for Spaces of Natural Interest (PEIN), and other zones of interest.

To examine water retention in the basins, the programme also analysed the growth of woodland in the Llobregat, Ter and Besòs basins; the evolution of soil cover in the RMB between 1993 and 2000; and the influence of soil cover on the area of study. Regarding the latter issue, an analysis of land use in the three drainage basins showed that the total surface that could be regenerated or managed better constituted 28% of the total region: an area large enough to necessitate an in-depth study.

As well as water retention – mainly determined by the state of the riparian ecosystem and land uses in the basin – restoring the basins required improved water quality.

MEASURES TO REDUCE POLLUTION

To achieve this goal, the project analysed the measures needed to reduce pollution of urban origins, through the Urban Wastewater Treatment Plan (PSARU, 2002), and to reduce pollution from industrial sites while quantifying discharge and establishing reduction criteria, as well as making proposals to monitor this discharge.

Furthermore, the issue of organic waste in the county of Osona – from pig farming, specifically – was confronted: a diagnosis was made and alternatives and other action were considered, on a local, county-wide and national level. Finally, the impact of mines and salt deposits in Bages on water quality in the Llobregat River was analysed, and various solutions to this problem were proposed.

GOAL TWO. PROVIDE ENOUGH QUALITY WATER FOR DIFFERENT CONSUMPTION USES

First, the project analysed current water demand in the RMB, the evolution of demand in the Region's municipalities, and how much water is consumed by the urban, industry and agriculture sectors.

SALLENT FROM LLOBREGAT RIVER. Cogulló salt deposits. One of the salt deposits in Bages, which can have a negative impact on the water quality of the Llobregat river.
Picture: Arxiu Salvador Redó. *Regió7*. 28 January 2018.

Nonetheless, as the programme was designed to become a tool for current and subsequent management, a prediction of future water demand in the RMB was required. This prediction, needed to estimate population growth in the Region and increases in urban and industrial demand for water according to current consumption trends, was based on approved plans.

In this estimation of future water demand, it was also deemed necessary to consider situations other than the business-as-usual scenario. Therefore, three scenarios were considered: growth in urban and industrial demand for water in a new regional planning model, growth in demand with water-saving measures applied to existing urban fabrics, and a scenario with water-saving measures applied to industry and agriculture. Finally, the possibility of reusing reclaimed wastewater was analysed in the following contexts: industrial reuse, urban reuse, agricultural reuse, environmental reuse and reuse for golf course irrigation.

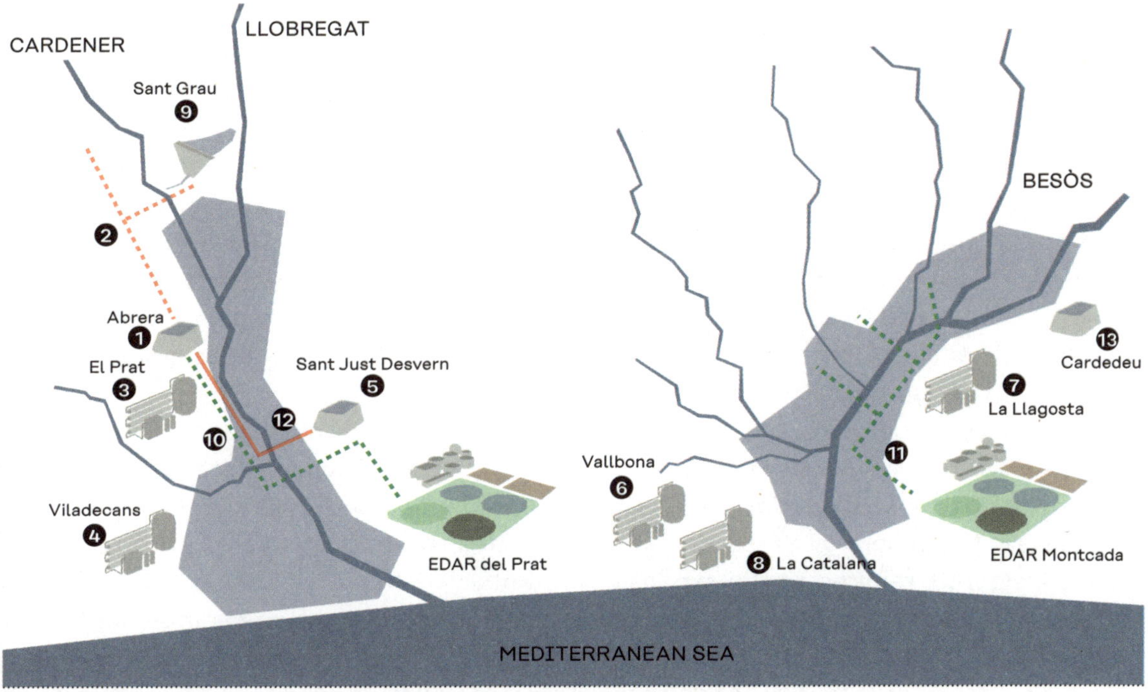

Aquatic Systems Conservation and Water Demand Management Programme in the RMB. Goal Two. Provide Enough Quality Water for Different Consumption Uses.
Source: BCNecologia

1. Abrera Extension (8 m^3/s)
2. Ponç-Abrera pipe (4 m^3/s)
3. * El Prat de Llobregat RO plant (15 hm^3/year)
4. * Viladecans RO plant (5 hm^3/year)
5. Reconversion SJD** Plant, groundwater treatment (30 hm^3/year)
6. * Vallbona RO plant (15 hm^3/year)
7. * Cubeta de la Llagosta RO plant (10 + 10 hm^3/year)
8. * La Catalana RO plant (10 hm^3/year)
9. Sant Grau's off-stream reservoir (storage: 12 ha/m^3)
10. Reuse of generated water
11. EDAR*** from Prat-Abrera (2 m^3/s) Reuse of generated water
12. EDAR*** Montcada-middle basin (20 ha/m^3 per year) Transfer between Abrera and SJD** ETAP (existing tube)
13. Cardedeu Water Treatment Plant

* RO Plant: Reverse Osmosis Plant
** SJD: Sant Just Desvern
*** EDAR: Waste Water Treatment Plant

To determine the region's water supply capacity in terms of quantity and quality, aside from current and predicted demand, it was important to examine the resources available and the viability of using them in a sustainable way.

WATER RESOURCES FROM THE LLOBREGAT, BESÒS AND TER RIVERS

The water sources analysed included groundwater resources in the Baix Llobregat and Baix Besòs areas and surface water resources from the Llobregat, Besòs and Ter rivers. This examination of groundwater in the Llobregat and Besòs Delta systems, including the plain of Barcelona, led to conclusions regarding its capacity to fulfil some of the RMB's water demand. As for surface water, the hydrological characteristics of the three rivers' basins were defined and other proposals in the sphere of hydroeconomics were considered, relating to the expansion of reservoirs and the creation of detention reservoirs.

The conclusion was that the reservoirs in the Llobregat and Ter basins had a near-optimal degree of regulation, thus ruling out the option of expanding existing reservoirs. Finally, based on the analysis of the supply and demand of water in the RMB, the Programme proposed various scenarios for ensuring a sufficient, quality water supply, and included energy and emissions assessments in two of those scenarios.

GOAL THREE. ESTABLISH EMERGENCY WATER SOURCES OF SUFFICIENT QUANTITY AND QUALITY IN PERIODS OF SCARCITY

These water sources needed to be identified and designed in accordance with a series of premises in each scenario. Initially, without using water from basins other than the ones studied, the necessary measures were as follows:

- exhausting all water-saving potential
- reducing less important public consumption and/or fulfilling demand with reclaimed water from wastewater treatment plants

Should Catalonia's internal basins (basically, the aforementioned basins) be unable to provide the quantity or quality of water necessary in extreme circumstances, the Programme proposed bringing water from other basins, under a series of conditions.

The Programme put forward a scenario for fulfilling water demand in the RMB in periods of extreme drought: transferring water from the Oliana reservoir, in the Segre basin, to the Cardener basin.

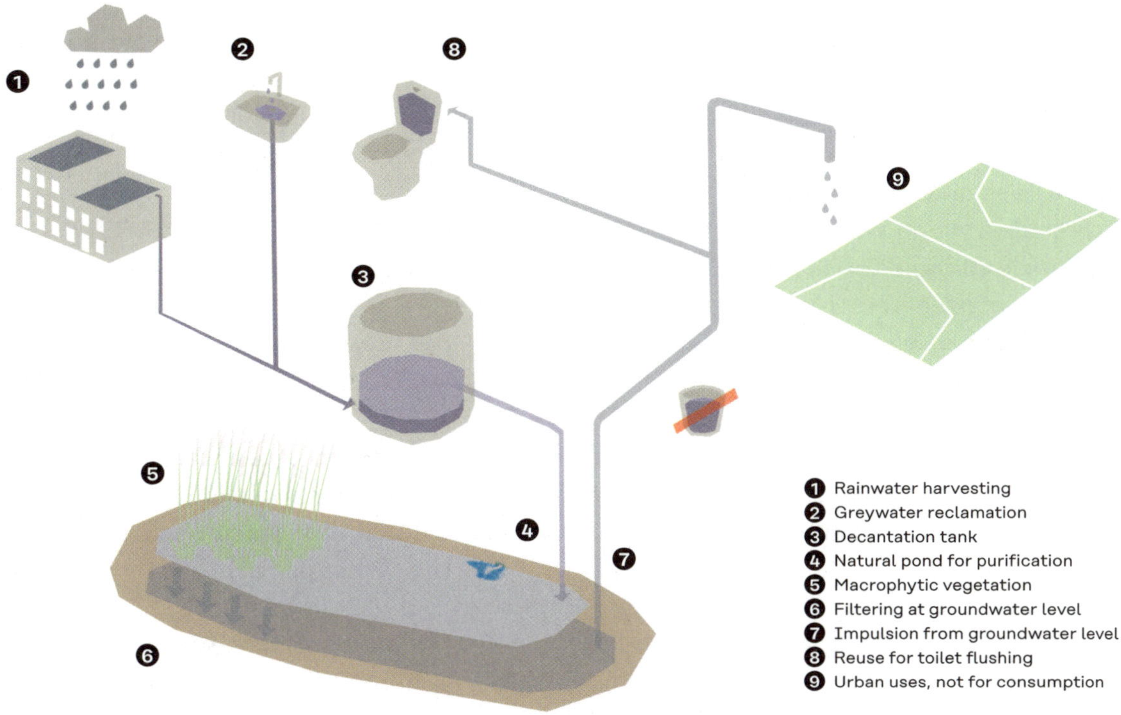

FIGUERES. Llevant Sector eco-neighbourhood. Reuse of water resources as an alternative to drinking water.
Source: BCNecologia

WATER MANAGEMENT AND FIGUERES'S ECO-NEIGHBOURHOOD

In 2010, Figueres City Council commissioned the Agency and various architectural offices (Rafael de Cáceres, Albert Cuchí and Lluís Brau) to design an eco-neighbourhood in the Llevant Sector of Figueres, with a population of around 4,000 inhabitants. It would be located in the Muga River basin (a sub-basin of the Manol River, a tributary of the Muga) along the lower course of the Mal Pas brook, which tends to flood and reach a relatively high crest during long, intense episodes of rain.

The water management strategy focused on three key axes (quality, guarantee and efficiency) and two main goals, namely:

- to make the most of usable marginal water (rainwater harvested on roofs and in public spaces, domestic greywater, groundwater)

• to achieve the highest possible degree of water self-sufficiency

The quest for sustainability requires a broadening of the scope of resources that can be used and a shift from the traditional view that drinking water from the general network is suitable for all uses. The project aimed to optimise water management by promoting a new culture of water that allowed for the treatment of wastewater without contaminating the receiving environment and the reclamation of urban marginal water, through the application of suitable management criteria and technology.

Within the context of hydroclimatology, the study also included a more specific focus on the behaviour of local supply sources, including both current and future, unconventional sources. They were examined in two concrete scenarios: one of abundant water, and one of scarcity, even precarity, under the predicted impact of climate change in the medium to long term.

USE OF MARGINAL WATER

The marginal water management model included:

- the reclamation of greywater (from showers and sinks) through separate sewer systems
- centralised treatment of greywater in mechanical rooms in each block, until the required quality for reuse was achieved
- the incorporation of rainwater into overall reclaimed water
- the use of reclaimed water for groundwater recharge

Type	Multi-family intensive			Multi-family semi-intensive			Single family		
Use	Potable	Non-potable	Total consumption	Potable	Non-potable	Total consumption	Potable	Non-potable	Total consumption
Domestic	64	18	82	68	28	96	70	90	160
Public		14	14		14	14		14	14
Commercial	4	4	8	4	4	8	4	4	8
Total	**68**	**36**	**104**	**72**	**46**	**118**	**74**	**108**	**182**

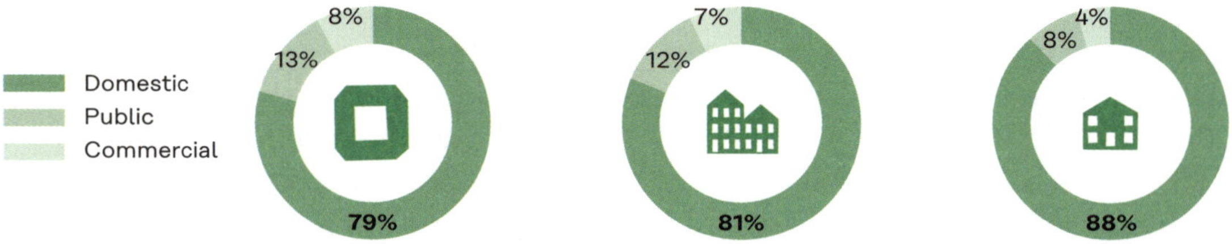

FIGUERES. Llevant Sector eco-neighbourhood. Maximum degree of water self-sufficiency. Optimised water consumption and according to quality (litres per day and per person).
Source: BCNecologia

- the harvesting of partially untreated groundwater to be used as non-potable water in the urban environment (toilets, irrigation, street cleaning, etc.)
- the incorporation of a purification system that meant the necessary component of potable water could be obtained separately when the effects of climate change so required

WATER MANAGEMENT STRATEGY

The short-term strategy proposed continuing with the municipal supply of potable water (105,00 m^3/year) and fulfilling demand for non-potable water (47,000 m^3/year) with aquifer water, using an existing well. Returning reclaimed water to the aquifer through artificial groundwater recharge (130,700 m^3/year) would result in a positive recharge balance (83,000 m^3/year).

The management strategy in times of water scarcity, meanwhile, was to separate the neighbourhood from the municipal network and to provide potable water from the aquifer below it.

WATER SUFFICIENCY FOR NON-POTABLE AND TOTAL WATER DEMAND

The potential water demand was estimated based on the threshold demand indicators established by BCNecologia as a result of the statistical processing of data from a survey of over one hundred cities, complemented by water-saving measures (state-of-the-art technology and a high degree of public awareness). The total optimised consumption for the eco-neighbourhood was 104 litres per person per day (82 litres per day for domestic use).

The result of the proposed management model was that 100% of demand for non-potable water and of the total water demand could be fulfilled by using marginal water and applying saving and efficiency measures.

IMPACT OF THE SUPERBLOCK ON WATER MANAGEMENT

The Llevant Sector eco-neighbourhood is a single superblock, measuring approximately 20 hectares. The possibility of increasing permeable surfaces and more easily implementing sustainable urban drainage and water filtration systems into the soil and subsoil leads to an expanded rainwater receiving environment, which allows for more effective use of separate sewer systems for rainwater collected on roofs. The result is a more circular approach to water in urban environments, whereby the use of phreatic water can be increased for applications where it does not make sense to use the potable water network, such as flushing toilets.

NEW WETLAND HABITAT

The project also planned to regenerate the Mal Pas canal. To make the most of this system, from both an urban and a biological standpoint, it proposed the creation of a pond from the area's regenerated greywater and rainwater, once treated by decantation and phytofiltration. This would serve two purposes: increasing the diversity of bird habitats and creating a habitat for native amphibians and fish, and regulating the flow of the waterway when the water rises.

The recovery of this space completes the area's water system, as the Figueres stream flows into the canal, as well as increasing the amount of wetlands and riverbank vegetation and improving the scenery.

Big-sized crown trees
- *Magnolia grandiflora*
- *Quercus ilex, Quercus suber, Juglans regla*
- *Aesculus hippocastanum*
- *Robinia pseudoacacia*
- *Tilia sp*
- *Castanea sativa*
- *Ginkgo biloba*
- *Jacaranda mimosifolia*
- *Liriodedron tulipifera, Quercus rubra*
- *Ficus carica, Olea europaea*
- *Sophara japonica*
- *Pinus pinea*

Medium-sized crown trees
- *Cercis siliquastrum*
- *Prunus serrulata*
- *Catalpa bignonioides*
- *Melia azedarach, Paulownia tomentosa*
- *Acer palmatum, Liquidambar styraciflua*
- *Acer campestre, Acer monspessulanum, Albizina julibrissin, Tipuana tipu*
- *Betula pendula, Koelreuteria paniculata*

Small-sized crown trees
- *Magnolia x soulangiana*
- *Hibiscus syriacus*
- *Laburnum anagyroides*
- *Acer campestre, Acer cappadocicum*
- *Arbustus unedo*
- *Lagerstroemia indica, Prunus dulcis*

Bushes
- *Lonicera sp*
- *Cotoneaster sp, Crataegus monogyna, Prunus laurocerasus, Prunus spinosa, Sorbus aucuparia, Viburnum sp*
- *Mahonia sp*
- *Ribes sp, Ruscus aculeatus*

Mal Pas irrigation canal

FIGUERES. Llevant Sector eco-neighbourhood. This is the possible look of the neighbourhood in spring. The water system has been recovered, the number of humid areas has increased, as well as the amount of riverbank vegetation and the landscape has improved.
Source: BCNecologia

Conclusions

The Aquatic Systems Conservation and Water Demand Management Programme in the Barcelona Metropolitan Region (RMB) was the product of a very specific historical moment. In just a few years, the north of the country experienced periods of extreme drought and the central government put forward the Spanish National Water Plan (PHN, Law 10/2001 of 5 July, later modified by Law 11/2005 of 22 June). As a result, the public became acutely aware of the importance of preserving and managing aquatic systems in a sustainable way.

With these factors as a starting point and the Water Framework Directive (WFD 2000/60/EC) as a reference and guide for water management, the Programme identified the main threats to the quality of the water in the drainage basins that supply the Barcelona Metropolitan Region and developed proposals to protect these ecosystems and, therefore, this resource itself.

The Agency has always tried to stay one step ahead of future challenges, such as the impact of climate change, in order to find both short- and long-term solutions. To anticipate future episodes of extreme drought, the Programme aimed and managed to find a solution for the RMB that would not require significant economic investment or have the environmental impact of the solution proposed by the PHN. The Segre–Cardener interbasin transfer emerged as an emergency supply system for the RMB in periods of scarcity that was much more suitable than any initiative put forward in the PHN.

A self-sufficient water supply for urban environments, with local, renewable resources, is crucial in the water cycle, both for the overall water balance and to reduce the use of resources and the negative impact on the environment. These premises have guided all of the Agency's projects in which water has been a key consideration.

EFFICIENCY AND ENERGY TRANSITION

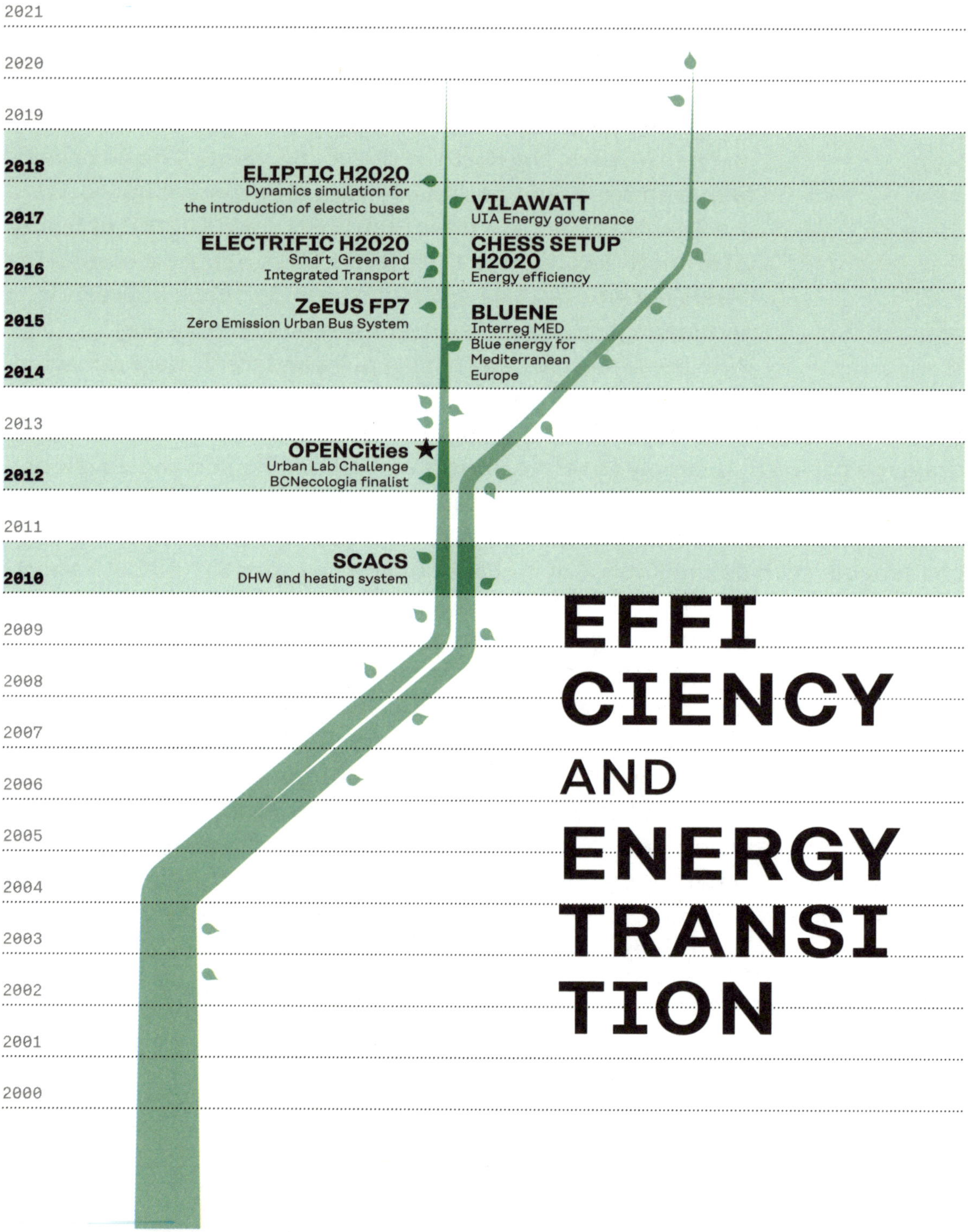

★ **AWARD**

Energy is an essential resource for our society to function properly. It is the key to all sustainable development. In practice, energy generation processes and the sources used are factors that have a huge impact on the environment.

As traditional energy consumption is both essential and unsustainable, one of the Agency's battlegrounds from the very beginning has been energy efficiency and the energy transition.

Cities are responsible for a large proportion of the world's overall energy consumption. In an urban environment – the backdrop to BCNecologia's projects – the biggest energy consumers are buildings (mainly residential) and transport. In the former, the general strategy taken is based on architectural and construction solutions that are adapted to the area's climate, to ensure comfort all year round without consuming too much energy. In the latter, modes of transport, strategies tend to be oriented towards the energy transition.

This chapter deals with these issues by presenting a set of studies, tools and methodologies prepared internally – such as the new energy model proposal for Barcelona – that constituted the germ of some of the Agency's most significant studies and initiatives, and the origin of its subsequent participation in the European projects BLUENE, Chess Setup, Vilawatt, Eliptic, ZeEUS and Electrific.

The three latter projects' main goal is the transition to clean energy in public and private transport, though they also have an impact on mobility more generally. BCNecologia's Energy Area has worked on these projects, as they have a bearing on Barcelona's electricity infrastructures. This is why energy efficiency has been a recurring theme in most of the Agency's most cross-cutting work, namely urban mobility plans and strategic plans in various cities all over the world.

THE GERM OF MAJOR PROJECTS

The path taken by the Agency in the sphere of energy before arriving at major projects has been a long one. In 2003, progress was made from a preliminary stage in which tools and studies were developed internally. These would be used as a base for dealing with challenges of greater magnitude. Within this context, the Agency created software to assess energy phenomena, such as:

- Potenclima. Program for calculating a household's energy consumption based on climate factors and housing's structural characteristics.
- Cercasol. Software for calculating solar radiation in urban environments and extracting the solar potential of buildings and public spaces.

From this moment onwards, the Agency's first energy-based studies were carried out, including the Nou Barris Environmental Audit (2003), the Cervera Energy Analysis (2005), the Energy Strategy for San Sebastián (2008), the Energy Proposals for the Historic Centre of Quito (2013), and the Analysis of the TMB Bus Fleet's Consumption and Emissions (2011, 2014 and 2017), among others.

Furthermore, internally, the Agency developed a host of different ideas and studies regarding energy possibilities: theoretical analyses of energy phenomena (thermal stratification in large seasonal storage reservoirs), ideas for new urban energy generation and distribution models (testbed for the future Vilawatt project), proposals for regulations to improve the city's energy self-sufficiency and for planning regulations regarding new buildings' roofs, innovative technological formulas relating to heat and cold flows (the origin of the SCACS and Chess Setup European projects), and much more. All of these studies and analyses were later used as tools to design projects or as a basis for BCNecologia's future major European projects.

AN INNOVATIVE METHODOLOGY

In parallel, a new methodology was being created to understand and confront the energy phenomenon. From this methodology emerged innovative concepts like the 'basic energy regimen' or key consumption, human, physical and technical, and technological factors.

AN ALTERNATIVE ENERGY MODEL FOR BARCELONA

This document was drawn up internally at the Agency over the 2015–2017 period. It carried out a comprehensive examination of the requirements for Barcelona to become a self-sufficient city. Though the document was never published, it was a useful exercise as it became the basis for various urban efficiency projects.

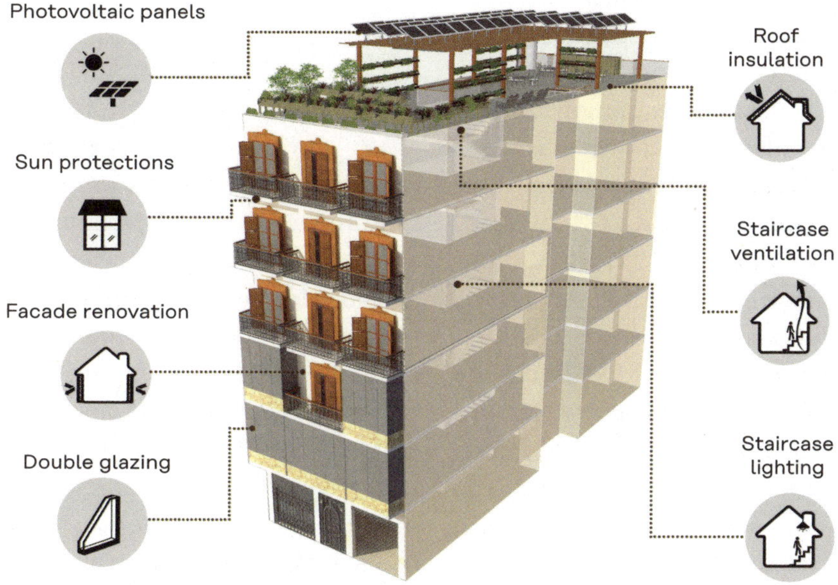

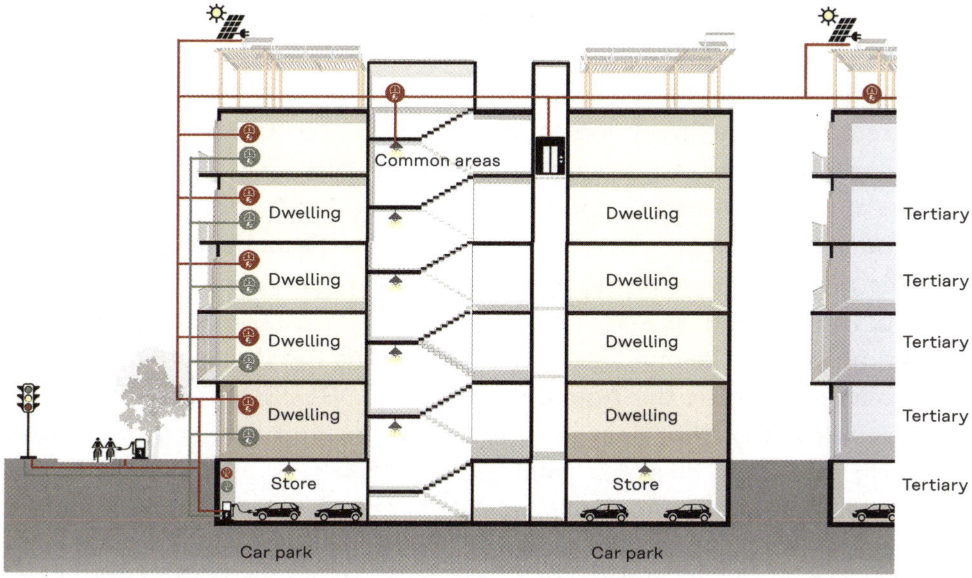

BARCELONA. 2015–2017. Proposal for energy efficiency and local energy production for community self-consumption in buildings.
Source: BCNecologia

NEW CONCEPTS, ANALYSES AND MODELS

Concepts like the 'basic energy regimen' were created, meaning the minimum amount of energy needed per person without superfluous consumption and with maximum efficiency. For an average family in Barcelona, this consumption figure in a totally electric household sat at around 2,000 kWh per year. This was much lower than the expected number, but still possible.

Among other issues, the analyses dealt with how much surface area would be needed to cover domestic energy consumption. According to this analysis, 100% of buildings' roofs should be covered with solar panels. This challenging requirement is not viable currently, due to the poor planning and different heights of roofs within the same block. From this analysis emerged the need to establish regulations with roof planning requirements, including at least the pre-installation of photovoltaic pergola structures and grid-tie cables compatible with the roof's other uses.

This new model also highlighted energy harvesting and/or rejection systems through passive techniques. One of the systems designed by the Agency was a double window that lets heat in or out while letting light in: an idea that emerged from glare problems in the Agency's office in La Barceloneta. This proposal was a finalist in the Urban Lab Challenge 2012, in the framework of the European OPENCities project.

A DISTRIBUTED ENERGY GENERATION SYSTEM

On a broader scale, the model put forward a distributed energy generation system, in which any citizen could produce energy and contribute to reducing the strain on the grid, thus moving away from a highly centralised model. However, there were constant obstacles to applying these systems, as state regulations at the time prohibited collective self-consumption, despite multi-family residential being the most common housing format in large cities. Still, this gave rise to ingenious ideas regarding how to overcome these difficulties.

THE AGENCY'S EUROPEAN PROJECTS

BLUENE: MARINE ENERGY FROM THE MEDITERRANEAN

The European project BLUENE Interreg Med was developed in 2014 and 2015, with collaboration from the regional governments of Lazzio (Italy) and Attiki (Greece), and the Croatian government.

BLUENE focused on 'blue energy' in Mediterranean Europe. As well as offshore wind power, which was growing in popularity rapidly in Europe, it involved renewable marine energy technologies, such as tidal power, tidal barrage, harvesting sys-

CAP DE CREUS. GIRONA. A place in the Mediterranean with potential for generating energy.
Picture: Shutterstock (Oleg_P)

tems, wave power and ocean thermal energy conversion, which were (and still are, in some cases) in their initial development stages.

The programme gathered comprehensive information on the state of marine energy in the overall MED programme and in the participating regions and defined specific pathways for building marine energy initiatives through sustainable cooperation in the following years.

The results of BLUENE led to the conclusion that, apart from three specific points – the Strait of Gibraltar, Cap de Creus and the area between Corsica and Sardinia – the Mediterranean had very little potential for generating energy. However, the study was useful as a testbed for preliminary testing, with prototypes of the machines that would later be used in seas with more potential.

ELIPTIC AND ZEEUS: STUDIES FOR NEW TMB ELECTRIC BUS ROUTES

The Agency participated as an external partner in the ZeEUS (Zero Emission Urban Bus System, 2015–2018) and Eliptic (Electrification of Public Transport in Cities, 2017–2018) projects, carrying out the detailed and simulation studies TMB (Barcelona Metropolitan Transport) would use to size its electric bus charging stations. The study was later applied on the V13 and H16 bus routes.

BUS ROUTE MANAGEMENT

There are many ways to manage electric bus routes: overnight charging, fast inductive charging at various stops during service, etc. TMB opted for the *'opportunity charging'* system, where buses recharge their batteries for a few minutes at high power (between 500 and 600 kW) at the end of their route, which gives them enough battery life for their next journey.

This strategy consists of setting off every morning with 100% battery power, then carrying out partial charging throughout the day, keeping the battery above 20% at all times. The main problem with this kind of system occurs at the charging station as, if the services are irregular, several buses may need to recharge at the same time.

SIMULATION ANALYSIS

For this study, the Agency carried out a detailed analysis based on the simulation of the fleet's dynamic behaviour with different bus distribution possibilities on along the route. These ranged from perfect distributions, where the buses reached the end of the route at the planned times, to highly irregular distributions, where the buses all arrived at the same time.

These cases pointed to different possibilities in terms of the number of charging stations needed to guarantee a service of optimal quality. A good-quality service could be offered with a minimal number of charging stations, but to ensure service continuity when buses arrived at random, a greater number of stations was required. As well as more space, this would require a lot more financial investment (around €500,000 per station).

The simulations carried out by BCNecologia allowed for analysis of the different scenarios TMB could face in the deployment of its electric bus network and enabled the organisation to anticipate what would be required of its routes.

ELECTRIFIC: THE ELECTROMOBILITY OF TOMORROW

The Electrific project (2016–2019) comes as part of an EU research and innovation programme (Horizon 2020). Its main aim is to improve electric vehicles' performance and integration into the transport system and the power grid, while maintaining the system's overall sustainability. Electrific has developed new technologies and theoretical knowledge to guarantee seamless, attractive and sustainable electromobility, through smart vehicle–user–grid integration and maximised use of renewable energy sources. These technologies aim to increase electric vehicles' battery life, prevent instability in the power grid and promote the use of renewable energy.

In particular, Electrific promotes the consumption of renewable energy via

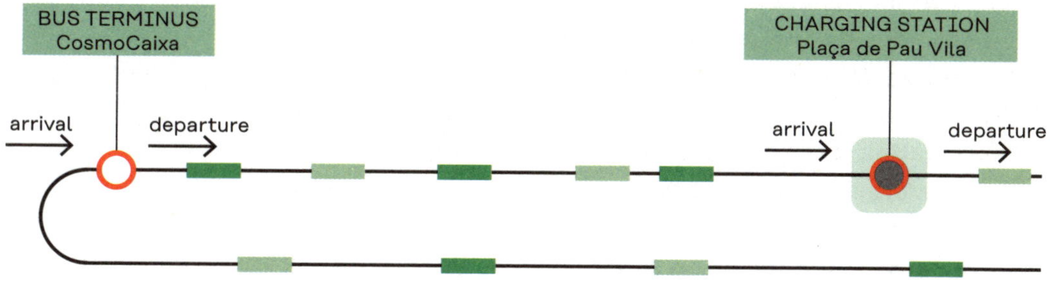

ZONES AND STATES

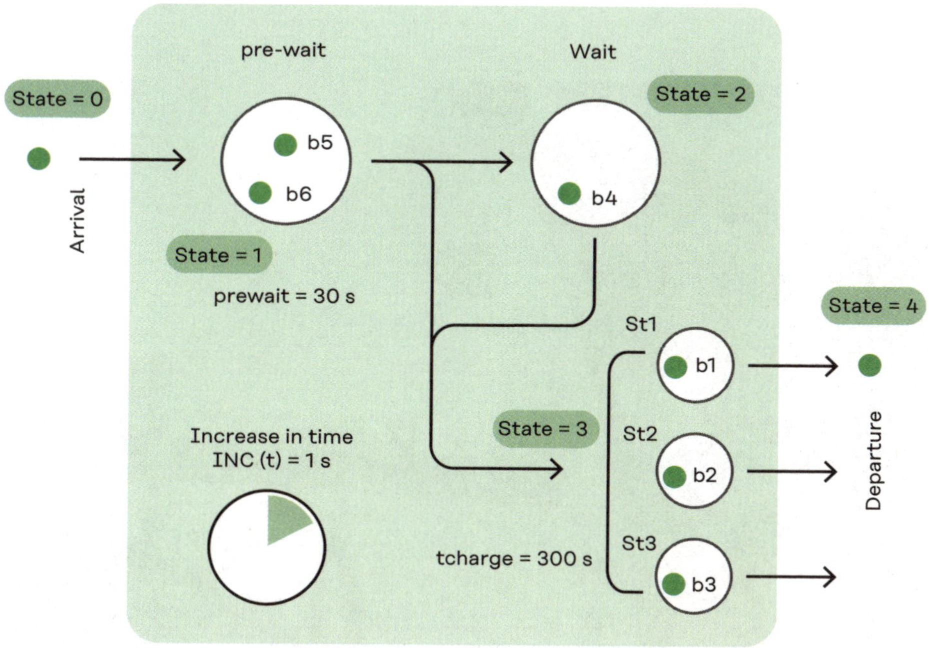

BARCELONA. 2017. Trials for the V13 bus routes (TMB). Simulation of opportunity charging management for the future electric bus network in Barcelona.
Source: BCNecologia

smart charging point operators, which invite drivers to recharge when there is ample renewable energy available at their charging points. Furthermore, during project development, an application has been created, through which users can select the quickest, cheapest and most environmentally friendly journey. Various experiments have taken place to analyse behavioural patterns and acceptance of the tool.

The project was applied by eleven partners in five European countries. The main contribution made by the Urban Ecology Agency of Barcelona was its collaboration with TMB to promote its bus fleet's green transition. As the company's current priority is to electrify its buses through opportunity charging on its routes and overnight charging at depots, Electrific has carried out initial trials for a charging planning programme designed specially for the fleet operator, which can help to organise the charging of Barcelona's electric buses based on energy efficiency criteria.

BARCELONA. 2018. TMB electric bus. This is the first 100% electric articulated bus model by the Basque company IRIZAR, which covers the city's H-16 line, integrated into the orthogonal bus network.
Picture: TMB

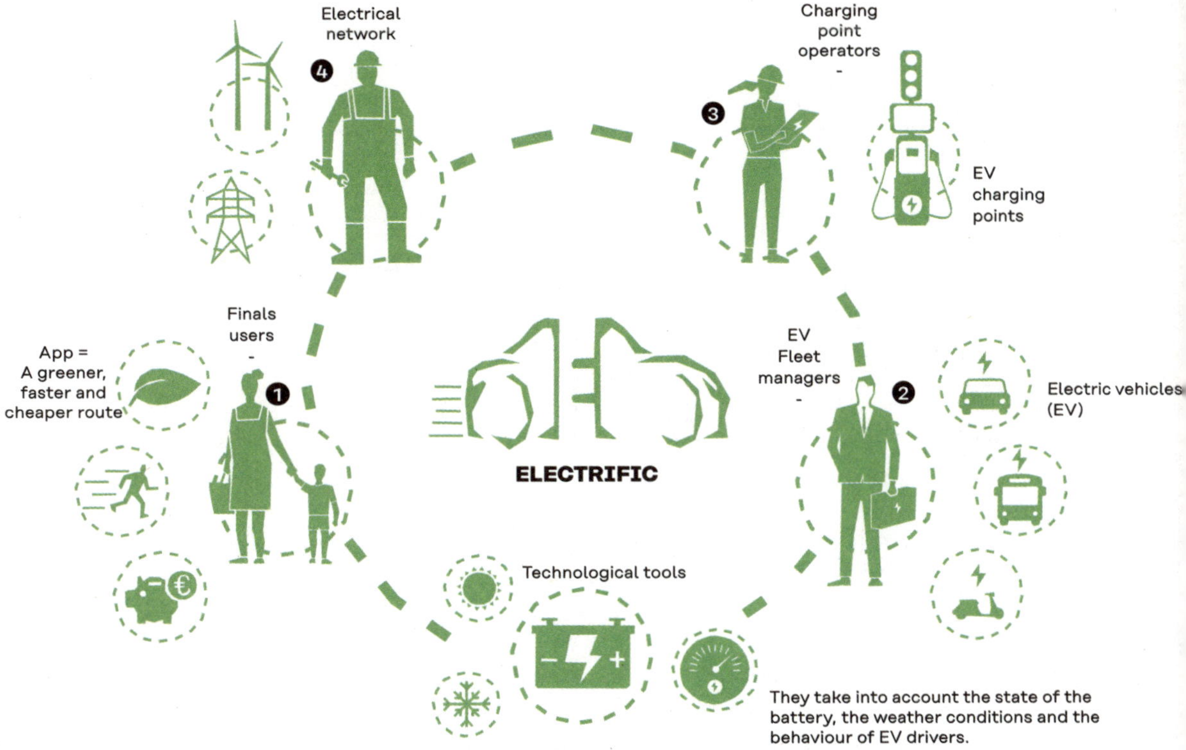

ELECTRIFIC PROJECT. 2016–2019. Diagram illustrating the Electrific Ecosystem. This diagram shows the integration between the various actors and the technological tools developed within the framework of the project.
Source: BCNecologia

SCACS HEAT SUPPLY SYSTEM

SCACS transfers solar thermal energy from summer to winter.
It offers an innovative and efficient solution for meeting heating demands. The system is based on two principles: the transfer of summer radiation to winter periods using a Large Seasonal Accumulator (LSA) and the use of heat pumps to transfer this heat under optimal conditions.

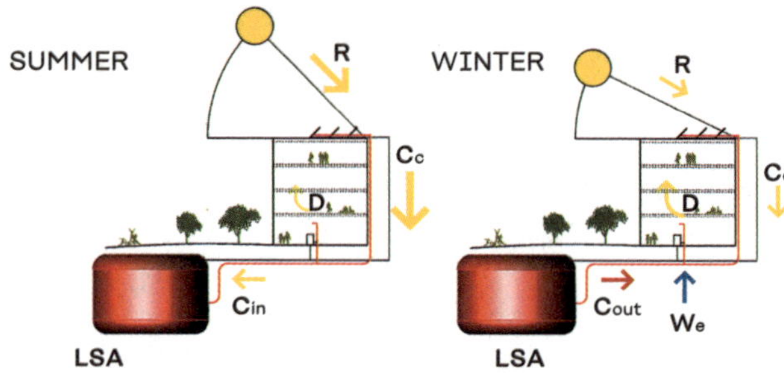

LSA: Large Seasonal Accumulator
R: radiation
Cin: heat sent to the accumulator
Cc: heat from the collector

D: heating demand (DHW and heating)
Cout: heat provided by the **LSA**
We: power consumption

During the summer, solar radiation is abundant (R), and the heating demand is low (D); therefore, a large amount of the heat absorbed by the collectors (Cc) is diverted to the LSA (Cin).

In the winter, demand (D) increases, while solar radiation can only supply a fraction of that demand. Under these conditions, the heat pump begins to work, absorbing heat from the LSA (Cout) while consuming only a small fraction of electricity relative to the amount of heat supplied.

SCACS ENERGY BALANCE

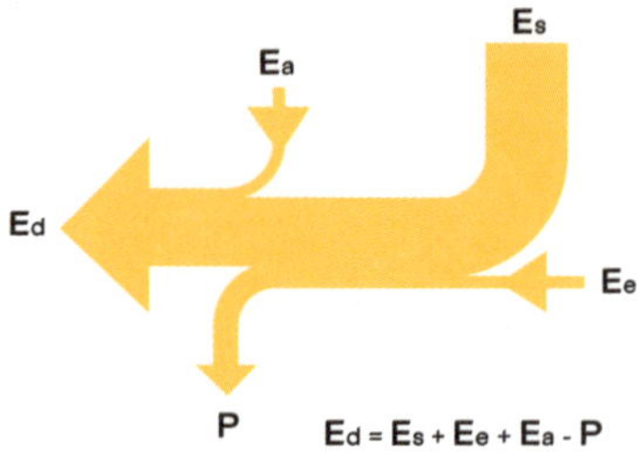

$E_d = E_s + E_e + E_a - P$

$E_d + P = E_s + E_e + E_a$

E_d = demanded energy
E_s = solar energy
E_e = electrical energy
E_a = auxiliary energy
P = loss

SCACS PROJECT. 2010. Diagram of the energy flows of the system developed by the engineer Moisès Morató.
Source: BCNecologia

CHESS SETUP: HOW TO IMPROVE BUILDINGS' ENERGY EFFICIENCY AND REDUCE THEIR EMISSIONS

SCACS: THE PREDECESSOR TO CHESS SETUP

The European project Chess Setup (2016–2020), which revolves around creating solutions to improve buildings' efficiency and energy self-sufficiency, is a stand-out example among the Agency's energy-based projects. It comes as a follow-up to another project, which is key to understanding its design and subsequent development: SCACS (DHW and Heating System through Seasonal Thermal Storage).

The SCACS system, created by the Agency in 2010, has become the germ of Chess Setup – an acronym for Combined HEat Supply System by using Solar Energy and heaT pUmPs. SCACS is rooted in the need for a solution to cover buildings' thermal energy needs, based on solar radiation and efficient thermal energy transfer in optimal conditions.

Though production of solar heat for domestic hot water (DHW) is a viable alternative in terms of both actual coverage and finances, there is one major disadvantage associated with heating through solar radiation: the peak heating demand period coincides with the period with the lowest solar radiation index (winter). The winter months require solar energy harvesting surfaces that are much too big for the rest of the year, thus generating extra costs. The SCACS system goes beyond the conventional solar energy system: it stores solar energy when it is in surplus and provides thermal energy through a heat pump that takes heat from the storage system's 'cold' source.

APPLICATION OF SCACS

The Chess Setup project consists of applying SCACS in a practical way. In other words, it involves the study and implementation of a system to satisfy heating and domestic hot water demand using thermal solar energy, heat storage in large reservoirs and heat pumps. In parallel, research has been carried out into the possibility of integrating the system with other heat sources (geothermal, biomass, residual heat) and technologies (cogeneration, solar cooling, hybrid solar panels).

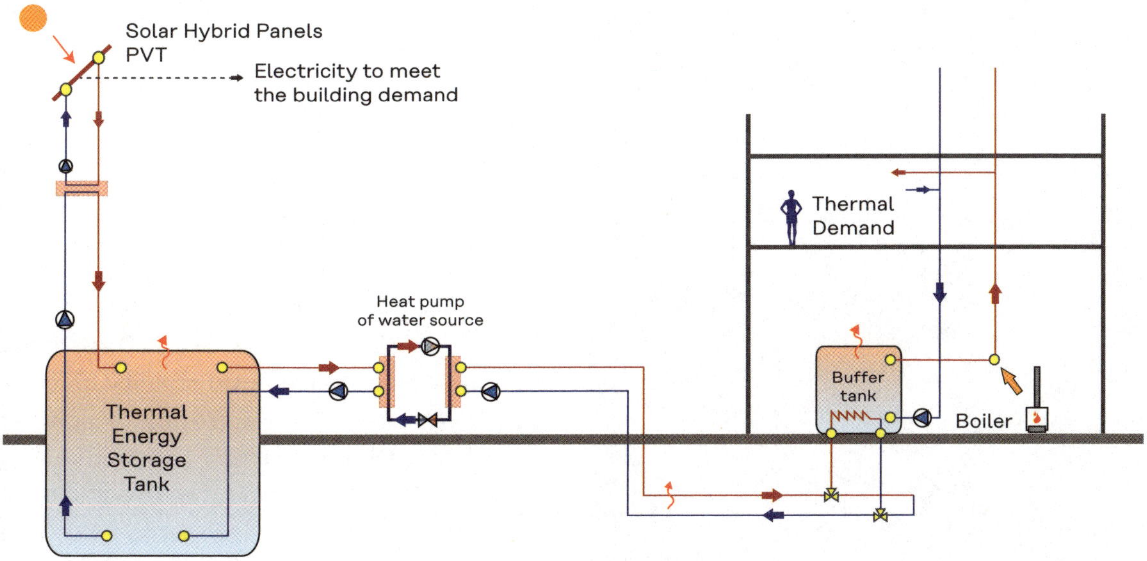

CHESS SETUP PROJECT. 2016–2020. Diagram illustrating the system operation.
Source: BCNecologia

ENERGY AND ECONOMIC OPTIMISATION

In addition, the project has been finished off with a monitoring and management device that optimises the system economically and in terms of energy, according to the price of electricity, users' habits, the integration of renewable energies into the power grid and weather forecasts, among other factors.

CHESS SETUP PILOT PROJECTS: SUCCESS STORIES

Ten members from six European countries took part in the project: Ulster University and Electric Corby (UK); Wansdronk Architektuur (Netherlands); Eurogrant GmbH (Germany); Edenway SAS (France), and Lavola, Wattia Innova, Veolia, Sant Cugat del Vallès Council and the Urban Ecology Agency of Barcelona, the project leader (Spain).

Three pilot experiences were developed as part of the Chess Setup project: a prototype at the Lavola head office (Manlleu, Spain), a system for 29 new-build dwellings in Corby (United Kingdom), and a third for a new sports centre in Sant Cugat del Vallès (Barcelona, Spain). The latter involves a swimming pool heated by solar heat stored in tanks: the first in the world with this kind of heating system.

In short, Chess Setup is an innovative project that has taken a step beyond theory and brought an idea to life, thanks to teamwork and collaboration between the various institutions affiliated with the project. As a result, three different proposals have been put forward that demonstrate the SCACS system's ability to produce DHW and heating with solar radiation as the energy source.

SANT CUGAT DEL VALLÈS. BARCELONA. Visit with the partners of the Chess Setup project to the new Eurofitness municipal sports centre in Sant Cugat.
Picture: Sant Cugat del Vallès Council

VILAWATT: THE MUNICIPAL ENERGY TRANSITION

The Vilawatt (2017–2020) project was carried out in the municipality of Viladecans, as part of the European Regional Development Fund's Urban Innovative Actions (ERDF-UIA) programme. It was aimed at towns and cities of more than 50,000 inhabitants with innovative responses to

CORBY. UNITED KINGDOM. 2020. Aerial view of the first four homes of the pilot of the Chess Setup project, executed by Electric Corby.
Picture: Electric Corby

MANLLEU. BARCELONA. View of the photovoltaic solar installation in the pilot eco-building and headquarters of Lavola, one of the project partners.
Picture: BCNecologia

global challenges, such as sustainable urban development.

Vilawatt supported Viladecans in its energy transition process towards a single model of energy production, distribution, management and consumption. To achieve this, a local energy governance body was created for the programme: the Vilawatt Consortium. This partnership was made up of public-sector entities (Viladecans Municipal Council and the Barcelona Metropolitan Area); private-sector organisations, represented by the Viladecans Association of Businesspeople for the Energy Transition; and the Viladecans Citizens' Association for the Energy Transition, on behalf of the town's residents. This new governance body proposed the creation of a single energy operator, the Vilawatt Energy Company, to ensure efficient energy management and to monitor the energy transition on a municipal level.

MAIN INITIATIVES

As part of the project, energy was supplied to the municipality through the Vilawatt Energy Company, a local digital currency was introduced (the Vilawatt), 60 dwellings were renovated to make them more energy efficient – initially in the neighbourhood of La Montserratina – and citizens' advice services relating to energy culture were provided at the offices of the new local energy company.

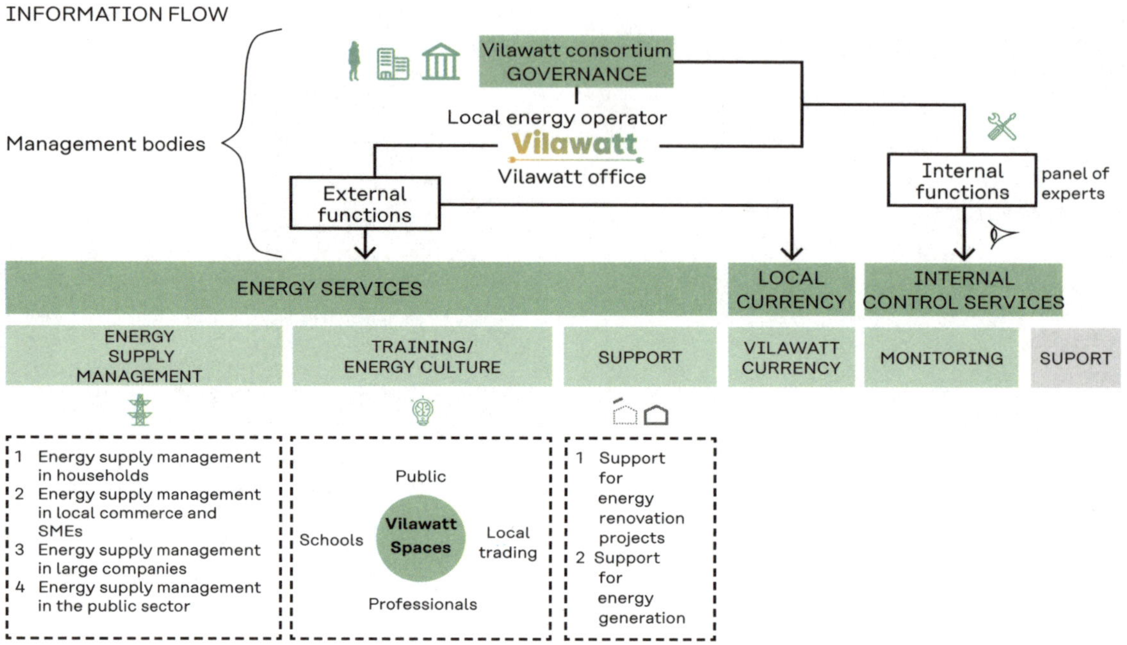

VILADECANS. VILAWATT PROJECT. 2016–2020. Monitoring the energy transition in the municipality.
Source: BCNecologia

THE AGENCY'S PARTICIPATION

The Urban Ecology Agency of Barcelona was one of the institutions involved most heavily in the Vilawatt project. It played a key role in designing and launching the local energy operator, in defining the services to be provided, and in creating a set of indicators as an essential tool for assessing and monitoring the implementation process, the project's impact and the ongoing energy transition in Viladecans.

The Agency was tasked with establishing a conceptual model that could facilitate a real energy transition. The model was to have three main branches: energy culture, supply management (through the energy operator) and support for projects (renovations and installation of photovoltaic panels). Initially, most members decided to forgo any production through photovoltaic panels. Nonetheless, BCNecologia argued that this technology was crucial: without production, there could be no transition.

Conclusions

Energy consumption in urban areas has expanded beyond the boundaries of sustainability and has been placed in the cross hairs as a key factor in the climate emergency. It is unquestionable that cities must take a leading role in the quest to achieve energy efficiency and in the transition to clean energies.

Cities are where the battle for sustainability will be won or lost. This is largely because urban areas are where almost all resources, including energy, are consumed, both actively (direct energy consumption) and passively (energy incorporated in products or services).

European projects have acted as a platform for putting the Agency's energy efficiency research into practice, especially through the development of technological solutions. Projects like BLUENE, Chess Setup, Vilawatt and Electrific, among others, have led to the dissemination and exchange of experiences and best practice among various European countries, and have strengthened and promoted knowledge through common methodologies and tools. These kinds of project are a great opportunity to bring theory to life, through trials and scalability on a European level. None of these programmes would have been possible without the studies, analyses and methodologies developed internally in the Energy Area of BCNecologia over the years.

Within these outstanding European projects, the Agency has developed a series of important systems and technologies, including the use of solar energy and heat pumps to provide thermal energy for multi-purpose buildings all year round in the most energy-efficient and economically optimal way, through storage and monitoring systems. Furthermore, it has played a part in local energy governance through participatory management and has developed software to improve smart vehicle–user–grid integration. These technological models deal with everything from the most technical aspects of design and implementation to management, governance and communication regarding energy efficiency.

CLIMATE CHANGE ADAPTATION AND MITIGATION

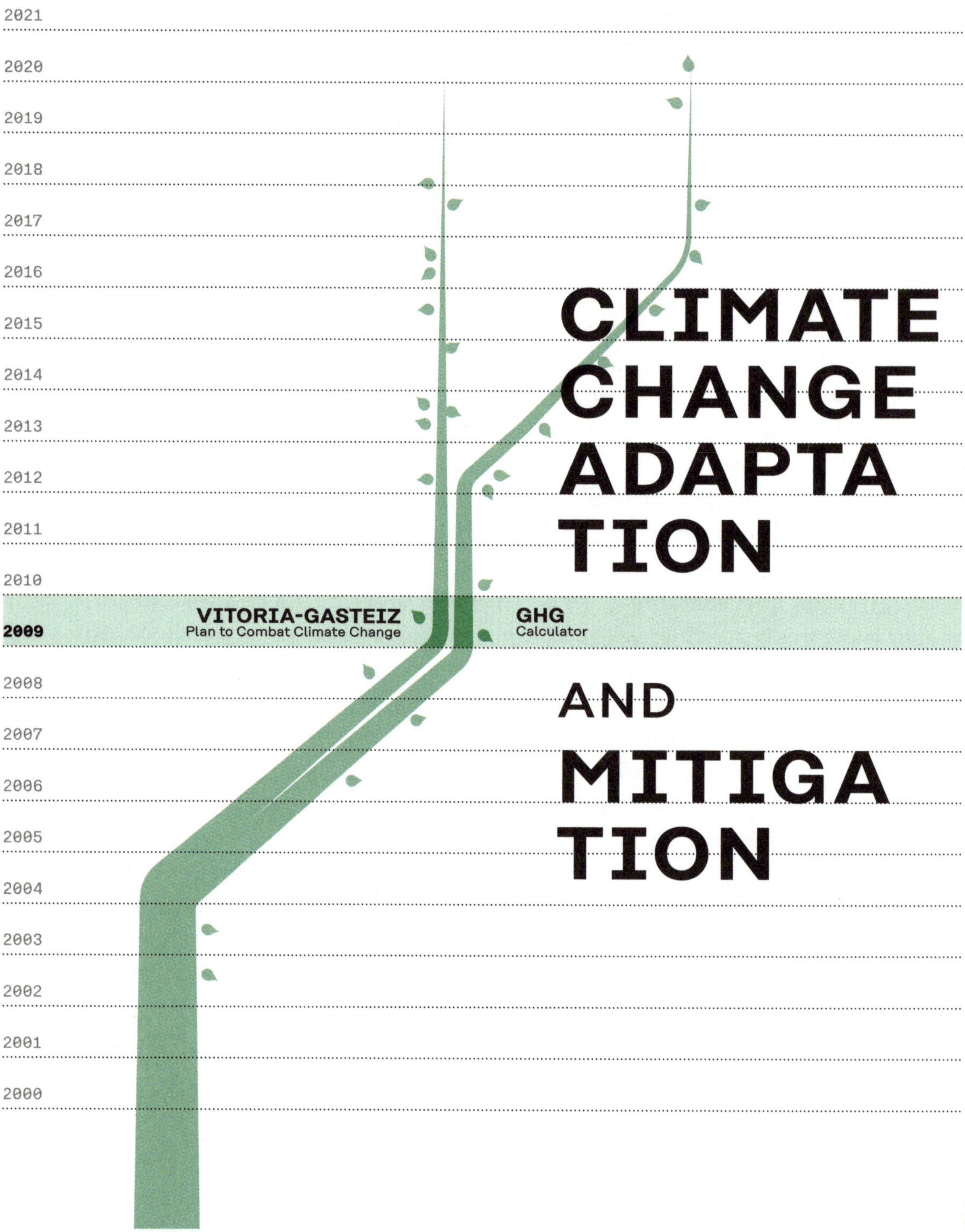

Climate change has come to the forefront of most environmental agendas, generating different levels of powers, strategies, plans, initiatives and policies on a local, national and international scale, all with a view to reversing the current trend towards the destruction of our natural environment. This paradigm shift has once again been ratified internationally, through the UN's passing of the 2030 Agenda (in 2015), which highlights 17 Sustainable Development Goals (SDGs).

But another, national-level plan had already been made back in 2007: the *Spanish Strategy for Climate Change and Clean Energy, Horizon 2007–2012–2020.*[13] This strategy defined different measures to contribute towards sustainable development and the use of clean energy and proposed action to comply with the Kyoto Protocol[14] (signed in 2002 by the European Union). It was inspired by the *Spanish Sustainable Development Strategy (EEDS).*[15]

Within this context, BCNecologia is taking on sustainability challenges in order to revitalise cities and reactivate the economy, and helping to overcome various economic, social and environmental crises. In some cases, its local climate change action responds to legislative obligations; in others, it is a result of voluntary initiatives driven by municipal governments.

In 2009, BCNecologia worked alongside the Fundación Biodiversidad to create a computer application: a calculator to take stock of greenhouse gas emissions (GHGs). This tool facilitates the development of methodological and instrumental resources and the creation of Local Climate Change Strategies. The aim of the project was to examine the complexity of urban systems and how they work, in order to formulate proposals that help to reduce GHG emissions.

In the same year, Vitoria-Gasteiz City Council tasked the Agency with putting together a Plan to Combat Climate Change. This chapter will take a closer look at these two projects.

13 Ministry of Environment. *Spanish Strategy for Climate Change and Clean Energy, Horizon 2007–2012–2020.* Madrid: Ministry of Environment, 2007.

14 UN. Kyoto Protocol - United Nations Framework Convention on Climate Change (United Nations, 1998).

15 Ministry of Environment. *Spanish Sustainable Development Strategy (EEDS).* Madrid, Ministry of Environment, 2007.

TOWARDS A LOCAL CLIMATE CHANGE STRATEGY: METHODOLOGICAL AND INSTRUMENTAL RESOURCES

BCNecologia and the Fundación Biodiversidad worked together in 2009 to create a computer application, consisting of a calculator that helps users to develop methodological and instrumental resources and, thus, prepare a Local Climate Change Plan. The main aim of the project was to examine the complexity of urban systems and how they work, in order to develop proposals that aimed to reduce greenhouse gas emissions.

The purpose of this tool – a calculator that takes stock of GHG emissions – is to diagnose current emission levels and generate a business-as-usual scenario. This way, the scenario can be analysed, reduction measures can be applied to various sectors – residential, mobility, water cycle, waste management, urban cleaning, services, primary sector, and municipal facilities and services – and common criteria can be adopted to put together strategies to combat climate change.

To this end, the aim was to create a broad IT tool that would cover the spectrum of emissions from most sectors, other than industry, in order to establish reduction goals, assess the impact of certain policies and, above all, generate results upon which policies to combat climate change could be constructed.

In the case of Barcelona City Council, the tool had to be an instrument for taking stock of GHG emissions attributable to the Council specifically, and to the municipality in general. This instrument was to create scenarios based on concrete action taken to reduce emissions.

FUTURE SCENARIOS

Using this calculator and the results of the diagnosis, municipal technicians can generate future scenarios. They can then apply various initiatives to these scenarios and calculate how much they reduce GHG emissions, thus finding out whether they are enough to meet the targets set by the Council. At this point, these professionals have all the information they need to draw up a local strategic plan and quantify the reduction in GHG emissions entailed by applying these initiatives, both by sector and overall.

The calculator can generate future scenarios, on the basis of which action to reduce energy consumption and emissions can be chosen. Therefore, a business-as-usual scenario and another scenario are generated, and reduction initiatives are applied to the latter in accordance with the targets set by each municipality.

PLAN TO COMBAT CLIMATE CHANGE IN VITORIA-GASTEIZ

At the Third Local Meeting of Villages, Towns and Cities for Sustainability, organised by CONAMA in 2009, a team of Spanish experts presented the report *Global Change Spain 2020/50: Cities Programme. Towards a Pact between Spanish Cities Faced with Global Change*,[16] inspiring the city of Vitoria-Gasteiz to move towards an environmental revolution and take on the challenge of climate change.

This was how BCNecologia came to prepare the Plan to Combat Climate Change in Vitoria-Gasteiz (2010–2020), based on the outline put forward by the *Spanish Urban and Local Sustainability Strategy (EESUL)*.[17]

This plan examined six scenarios:

- 2006: base scenario for subsequent comparisons.
- 2008: current scenario.
- 2020 T: business-as-usual scenario, without any consumption reduction action.
- 2020 R: future scenario with consumption reduction action.
- 2020 R+P: future scenario with consumption reduction and energy production action.
- 2020 R+P+S: future scenario with consumption reduction and energy production action and calculation of the effect of carbon sinks.

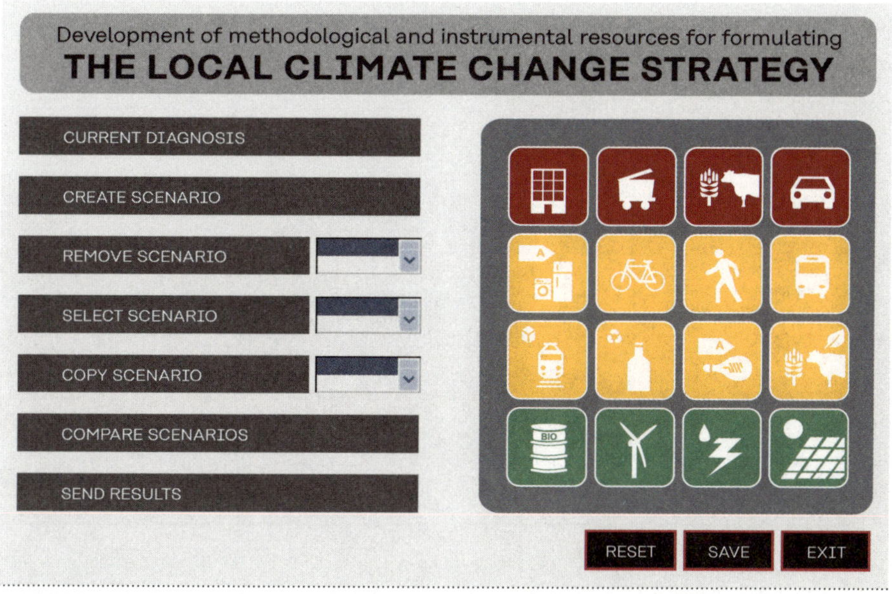

BARCELONA. The calculator. Tool to carry out a GHG emissions inventory.
Source: BCNecologia

16 CONAMA. *Global Change Spain 2020/50 Cities Programme. Towards a Pact between Spanish Cities Faced with Global Change*. Madrid: CONAMA, 2009.

17 Ministry of the Environment, Rural and Marine Affairs. General Directorate of Quality and Environmental Assessment; Ministry of Public Works and Transport. Secretariat of State's Housing and Urban Actions. *Spanish Urban and Local Sustainability Strategy (EESUL)*. Madrid: Government of Spain: Ministry of the Environment, Rural and Marine Affairs, Ministry of Public Works and Transport, 2011.

PHASES IN THE PREPARATION OF THE PLAN

The study to prepare the plan was divided into three phases:

Phase 1 Diagnosis of the city's energy consumption and greenhouse gas emissions 2006–2008. The base year used to set goals for mitigating GHG emissions was 2006.

Phase 2 Presentation of a catalogue of measures for reducing emissions and producing energy, with a horizon of 2020. The aim was to reduce GHG emissions by 20% compared to 2006.

Phase 3 Public participation and monitoring and management of the plan.

phase 1

- Information gathering and filtering
- Diagnosis of energy consumption and GHG emissions

phase 2

- Business-as-usual scenario 2020
- Catalogue of measures for reducing GHG emissions and producing renewable energy
- Carbon sinks

phase 3

- Public participation
- Monitoring and management plans
- Plan for communication with the public

VITORIA-GASTEIZ. According to the Plan's diagnosis, building renovations to make them more energy-efficient could reduce energy consumption by over 40%.
Picture: Quintas fotógrafos

AIMS OF THE PLAN

The main aim of the plan was to assess the city's CO_2 emissions (2008) and to generate a scenario (2020) in which, through the implementation of a series of initiatives, these emissions were reduced by 20%.

The plan was based on the following:

- Renovation of all housing and its use of energy to reduce its consumption by over 40%.
- Transformation of the city's structure and mobility to reduce journeys by private vehicle (10% of journeys in the city centre).
- Waste reduction and recycling to close material and energy cycles.
- Improvement of urban greenery's capacity for capturing CO_2.
- Promotion of the production and local consumption of foods with a low carbon footprint to get closer to the biocapacity of the municipality of Vitoria-Gasteiz.

Year	Consumption (GWh)	Emissions (tCO_2eq)
2006	965.33	269,927
2008	1,081.54	281,373
2020	1,161.2	302,229

VITORIA-GASTEIZ. Evolution of consumption and of CO_2 emissions in 2006 and 2008, and an estimate for 2020.
Source: BCNecologia

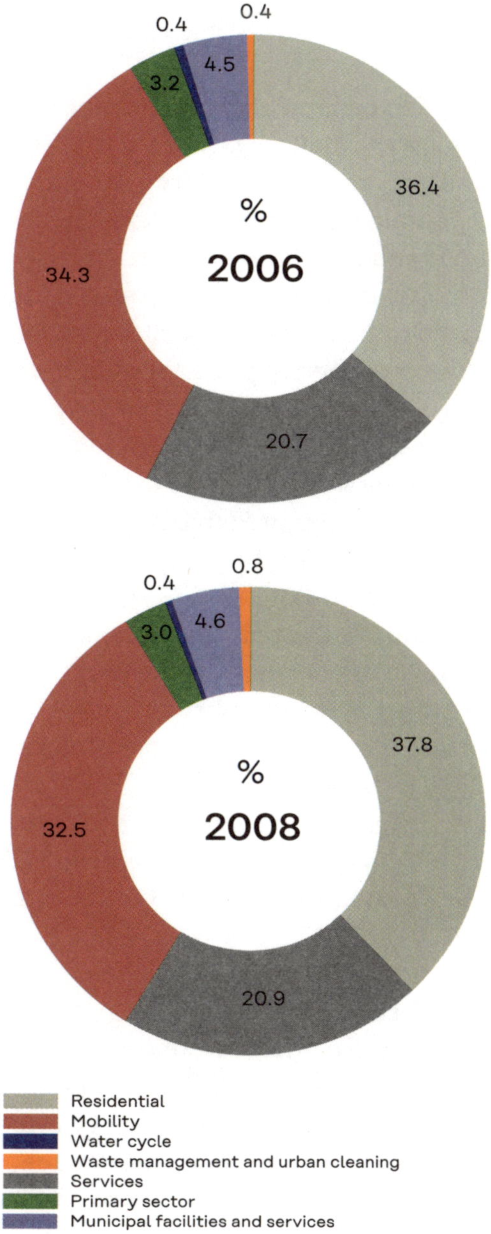

VITORIA-GASTEIZ. Percentage of energy consumption by sector during 2006 and 2008.
Source: BCNecologia

ENERGY CONSUMPTION DIAGNOSIS

The general energy consumption diagnosis of the municipality of Vitoria-Gasteiz took all production sectors into account, except industry, and distinguished between Council and municipal sectors.

The data to carry out the diagnosis, generate a business-as-usual scenario and decide on the action to be taken in the plan was provided by Vitoria-Gasteiz City Council and based on the following documents, among others:

- Local Energy Plan 2007–2012
- Vitoria-Gasteiz Climate Change Strategy 2009–2010
- Vitoria-Gasteiz Sustainable Mobility and Public Space Plan 2006–2007
- Partial Review of the General Urban Planning Plan for Salburua and Zabalgana 2009
- Mugarri Plan. Promotion and Development of Renewable Energies in Araba 2009
- Strategy and Action Plan 2010–2020

30% REDUCTION IN EMISSIONS

Based on the local diagnosis of GHG emissions and the initiatives proposed by BCNecologia, Vitoria-Gasteiz City Council set a target of reducing greenhouse gas emissions by at least 30% in the water sector, in municipal facilities and services, and in waste management.

The proposed action consisted of reducing emissions and producing renewable energy.

RESULTS ANALYSIS

Once analysed, the results revealed that the energy source that emitted the most GHGs in Vitoria-Gasteiz was petroleum and its products (37.3%), followed by electricity (33.6%) and natural gas (20%). The City Council's emissions made up 5.7% of the municipality's total.

The residential sector emitted the most GHGs, with 32.8%, followed by transport (29.2%) and commerce (22.5%).

TOWARDS RENEWABLE ENERGIES

Catering for 100% of demand with renewable energy was a difficult task. The only sources suitable for cities are solar thermal systems, solar panels, small wind turbines and municipal solid waste. At that time, the first three of these renewable energy sources involved very expensive technology and came with space restrictions.

Because of these limitations, BCNecologia suggested using the whole Araba region to supply Vitoria-Gasteiz with energy through other technologies (wind, community solar farms, hydropower and biomass). However, these systems also have limitations, such as their visual and environmental impact, the space they take up and, in the

VITORIA-GASTEIZ. The capital of the Araba region has set itself the target of becoming a carbon-neutral city for the 2020–2050 horizon.
Picture: Quintas fotógrafos

case of biomass, the limited nature of the resource.

It was decided that only a portion of the energy produced all over the Araba region would be used in Vitoria-Gasteiz. The percentage of energy needed is calculated based on population. Therefore, as 75% of the region's population lived in Vitoria-Gasteiz, fair distribution dictated that the same percentage of the overall energy produced would go to the city.

VITORIA-GASTEIZ: A CARBON-NEUTRAL CITY

The capital of the Araba region set itself the target of becoming a carbon-neutral city for the 2020–2050 horizon. Carbon neutrality is achieved when the energy a city uses is produced or offset with renewable sources, resulting in zero net GHG emissions. BCNecologia worked with the City Council to make this ambitious goal viable, through a programme of initiatives. The main lines of action were as follows:

VITORIA-GASTEIZ. The Plan proposes to reduce the use of private transportation and promote the use of alternative transport, such as cycling.
Picture: CEA. Vitoria-Gasteiz Council

- Rethinking the city's mobility system, by reducing journeys by private vehicle drastically (by over 70%) and creating more efficient, environmentally-friendly transport systems (more public transport, promotion of cycling, transition to electric and hybrid vehicles, etc.). These initiatives can reduce consumption by 82%.
- Reducing energy demand from buildings by renovating their envelope and reducing consumption by replacing appliances, lighting and boilers with more efficient systems. These measures can bring the average consumption per household below 7,000 kWh per year (a reduction of over 40% compared to the existing value).
- Designing and constructing new buildings with maximum efficiency criteria (the best orientation, natural lighting, passive solar systems, underfloor heating, efficient

appliances, etc.). With these elements, a household's power consumption can be reduced to under 5,000 kWh yearly.

- Reducing energy consumption in the public space, mainly by replacing streetlights and traffic lights with more efficient systems. This can reduce energy consumption by over 40%.
- Minimising waste generation and implementing a waste management model that recovers materials, firstly, and energy, secondly, from waste. This measure does not save energy, but it generates around 88.4 GWh per year.
- Reducing drinking water consumption through network efficiency improvements, changes in consumption habits, the installation of water-saving systems and the promotion of unconventional water sources (rainwater, grey water, etc.). This action represents an energy saving of 17%, compared to previous values.
- Reducing primary sector emissions and achieving food self-sufficiency. This challenge can be met through sustainable production of local products and promotion of their consumption in the municipality.
- Realising renewable energy production potential in the municipality. Estimates place this production ceiling at around 460 GWh per year, and most of it comes from solar energy (thermal and photovoltaic). The contribution of small wind turbines and municipal solid waste (MSW) is also notable.
- Maximising renewable energy production in the region of Araba (biomass, hydropower, wind power, community solar farms) to supply the municipality of Vitoria-Gasteiz. The energy produced is mainly electric and comes from hydroelectric plants and wind farms. Biomass also makes a significant contribution, especially by generating biofuels.
- Developing a power system able to guarantee an electrical supply at all times

Sector	(GWh)	(MWh/inh.)	(t CO_2eq/cap)	(t CO_2eq/cap)
Residential sector	1,161.2	4.53	302.229	1.18
Service sector	706.58	2.75	229.934	0.89
Mobility sector	1,037.62	4.05	274.215	1.07
Primary sector	85.15	0.33	79.421	0.31
Water cycle	12.24	0.05	5,449	0.02
Municipal facilities and services	152.12	0.59	44,239	0.17
Waste management and urban cleaning	-47.01	-0.18	-2,503	-0.01
Total	3,081.96	12.02	925,421	3.61

VITORIA-GASTEIZ. 2010. Estimation of energy consumption and GHG emissions by sector for the 2020 business-as-usual scenario. Consumption and emission indicators per capita.
Source: BCNecologia

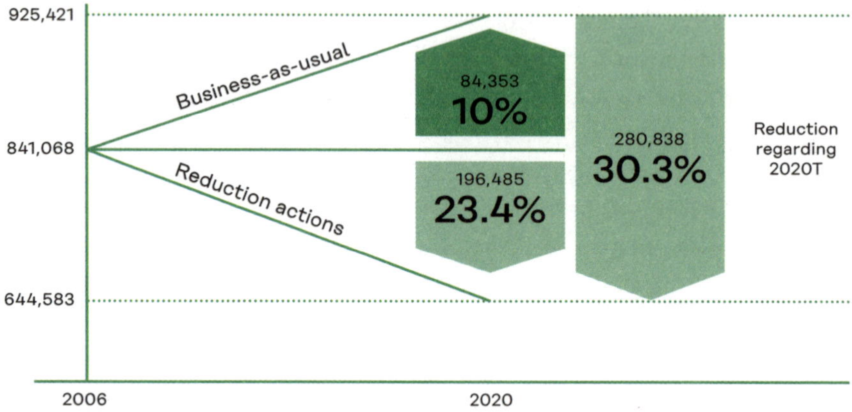

VITORIA-GASTEIZ. 2010. Diagram to illustrate the reduction of GHG emissions thanks to the application of the action plan.
Source: BCNecologia

across the municipality (with smart networks, pumped-storage hydropower, electricity mix with contributions from all renewable sources, etc.).

- Increasing CO_2 capture through urban greenery, in the form of green roofs (40,000 m^2 more) and wooded land (2,500 ha more). Overall, a total of 209,186 tonnes of CO_2 could be fixed.

PROPOSED ACTION

The strategy proposed by BCN-ecologia was based on 79 initiatives, mainly relating to management, technology, education (awareness-raising), regulations and taxation.

Once applied, they resulted in a reduction of 41.3% in the emissions generated by sectors related to the City Council (water cycle, waste management, municipal facilities and services) and of 30.3% in the total municipal emissions, compared to the 2020 business-as-usual scenario. In the base scenario (2006), the estimated reductions were 43.8% and 23.4%, respectively.

Conclusions

Climate change is the great failure of our time. Evidence of its impact shows that human activity has accelerated changes in the Earth's climate. If we fail to drastically reduce our dependence on fossil fuels and greenhouse gas emissions, the consequences will be catastrophic, and we are already starting to see them. In the fight against these environmentally devastating changes, local administrations must play their part.

To combat climate change on a local level, municipalities must assess their greenhouse gas emissions. This is why our collaboration with Fundación Biodiversidad in 2009 to create an IT tool was crucial. This tool could diagnose and take stock of emissions, quantify the base situation, detect especially sensitive sectors, predict future scenarios and quantify measures to reduce emissions in these municipalities.

To establish a new strategy to combat climate change on a local scale, a conceptual framework must be defined, with new methodologies and instruments. Vitoria-Gasteiz City Council saw that the city needed a Plan to Combat Climate Change and decided that BCNecologia was the right organisation to prepare it.

This plan, which aimed to reduce GHG emissions through the application of around sixty proposals, was the seed to help Vitoria-Gasteiz to grow and, one day, become a carbon-neutral, self-sufficient city, in terms of energy and food.

With these two projects as a starting point, the Agency was able to identify municipalities' main sources of greenhouse gas emissions, establish key goals and initiatives, and fulfil the needs and requests of local organisations.

AIR QUALITY IMPROVEMENT PLANS

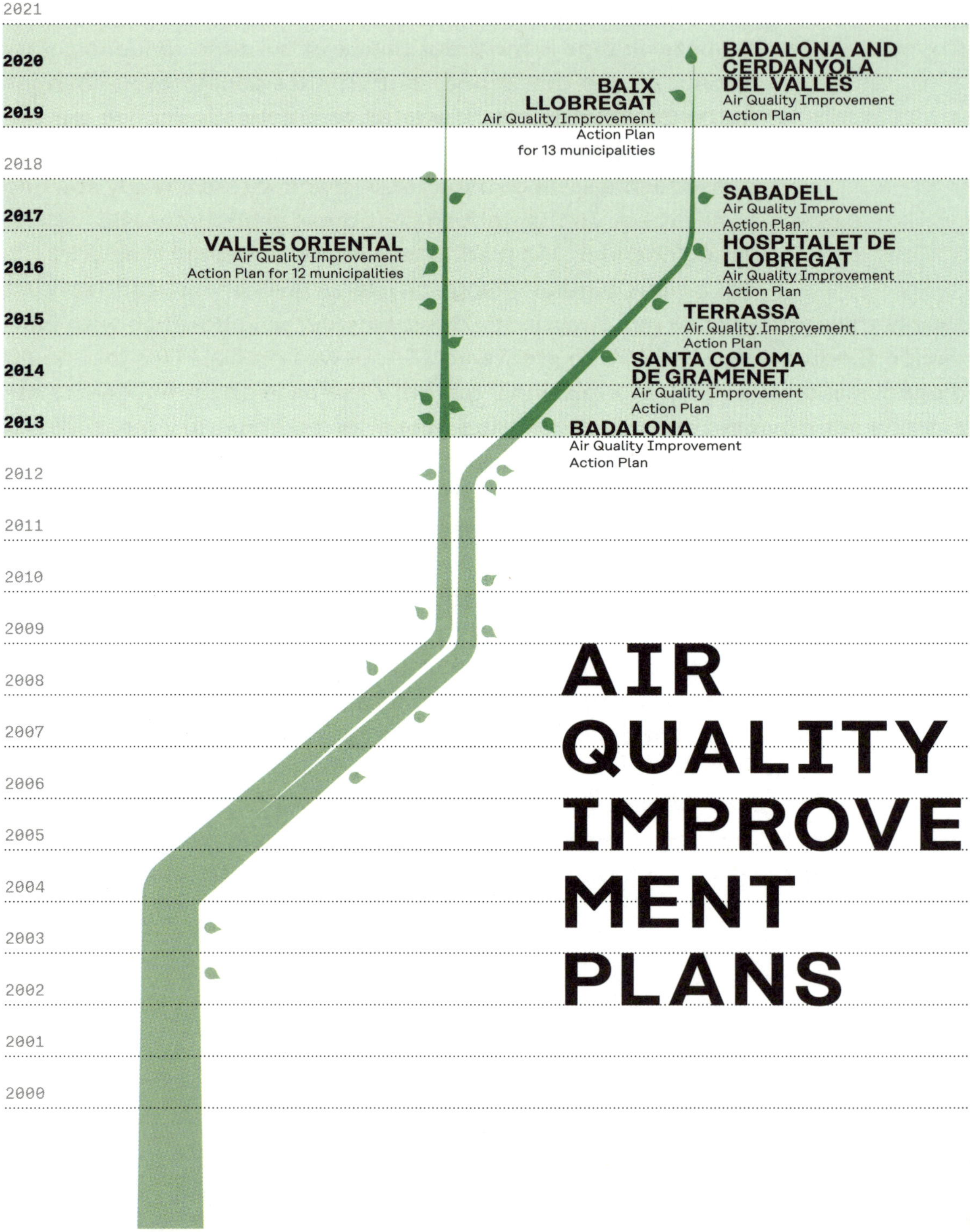

Air pollution is a serious public health problem. The World Health Organisation (WHO) and a growing number of scientific studies point to a direct correlation between poor air quality and a high incidence of respiratory, cardiovascular, neurological and autoimmune diseases, cancers and learning disabilities in children.

Since European institutions created a legislative framework to reduce the limit values for pollution present in urban agglomerations, Member States, regions and municipalities have drawn up air quality improvement plans, in order to take accountability for complying with the maximum concentration values set.

Within this context, the Urban Ecology Agency of Barcelona has put together new Air Quality Improvement Action Plans (PAMQA) for Barcelona Provincial Council. These plans have analysed a total of 31 municipalities in the province of Barcelona, while two of them are county-wide (Vallès Oriental and Baix Llobregat).

To prepare these plans, a methodology was created to draw up an inventory of a municipality's emissions according to different variables, such as motor traffic (flows, vehicle fleet composition, speed, etc.) and energy consumption. Air pollution mainly comes from specific sources of industrial emissions in known locations and from thousands of scattered points: the exhaust pipes on internal-combustion-engine vehicles, which form linear concentrations of emissions, made up of roads and motorways.

Through the action plan, the Agency has put forward proposals linked to ecosystemic urbanism, such as the hierarchisation of roads according to the superblock model, which significantly reduces mobility by private motor vehicle and promotes public and active transport (walking and cycling). The initiatives proposed have been classified into groups related to their aims, and according to their intrinsic characteristics.

THE CHALLENGE OF IMPROVING AIR QUALITY IN THE METROPOLITAN REGION OF BARCELONA

Directive 2008/50/EC of the European Parliament and of the Council of 21 May 2008 on ambient air quality and cleaner air for Europe is the regulatory framework for preparing air quality improvement plans and aims to reduce the concentration of pollutants present in the air in urban agglomerations. It was transposed into Spanish law through the Royal Decree 102/2011 of 28 January on improving air quality, which declares that municipalities with over 100,000 inhabitants that exceed the pollution limit value established by the Directive must draw up a plan to meet this target and improve their air quality. The Catalan government, meanwhile, has its Decree 226/2006 of 23 May, determining the forty municipalities in the Barcelona Metropolitan Region belonging to air quality zones 1 and 2, which are special protection areas due to air pollution from nitrogen dioxide (NO_2) and particulate matter smaller than 10 microns (PM_{10}). Within the special protection zone, there are six municipalities with more than 100,000 inhabitants: Badalona, Barcelona, L'Hospitalet de Llobregat, Sabadell, Terrassa and Santa Coloma de Gramenet.

On 6 March 2017, the Air Quality Summit took place, constituting the first institutional agreement to improve air quality in the conurbation of Barcelona. The Government of Catalonia, Barcelona City Council, Barcelona Metropolitan Area, Barcelona Provincial Council and local representatives committed to reducing emissions linked to traffic by 10% by 2022 and 30% by 2032 to gradually move towards the levels recommended by the World Health Organisation.

Urban air pollution has been an obvious problem for years. The first and most important issue it poses is its impact on public health, especially among groups considered vulnerable. These children, older adults and people with respiratory and cardiovascular diseases make up a significant part of urban populations.

There are a host of recent studies that provide scientific evidence of the impact of air pollution on public health. In *Air Quality in Europe – 2018 Report*,[18] the European Environment Agency highlights the impact of NO_2 and PM_{10} pollutants on the Spanish population's health. An estimated 9,000–28,000 premature deaths are caused per year and between 92,000 and 290,000 years of life are lost because of air pollution, depending on the pollutant and the reference concentration.

The main aim of air quality improvement initiatives is to produce action plans with targets, measures and indicators to encourage the improvement and restoration of air quality in municipalities, in terms of NO_2 and PM_{10} pollutants.

18 European Environment Agency. *Air quality in Europe – 2018 report.* Copenhagen: European Environment Agency, 2018.

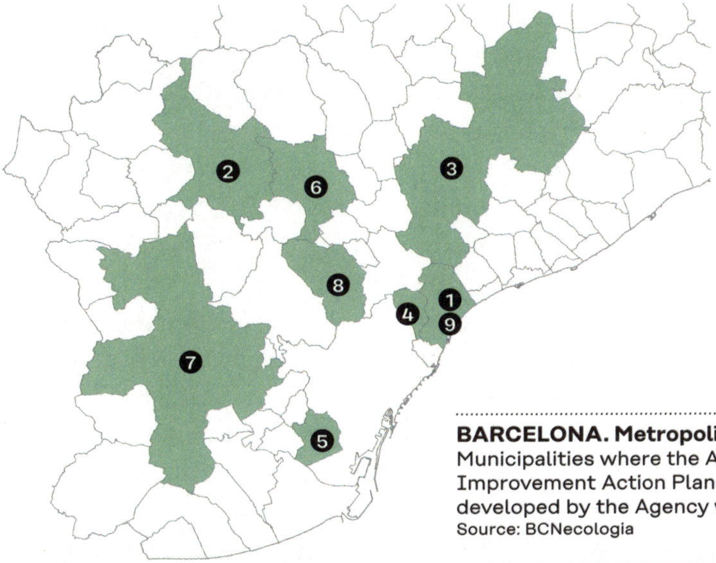

BARCELONA. Metropolitan Region. Municipalities where the Air Quality Improvement Action Plans (PAMQA) developed by the Agency were drawn up.
Source: BCNecologia

	Development year	Period of validity	Plan	Municipalities
1	2013	2015	Air Quality Improvement Action Plan in Badalona (2008–2015)	Badalona
2	2014	2020	Air Quality Improvement Action Plan in Terrassa (2015–2020)	Terrassa
3	2016		County-wide Air Quality Improvement Action Plan in Vallès Oriental	Canovelles, Les Franqueses del Vallès, Granollers, La Llagosta, Lliçà de Vall, Martorelles, Mollet del Vallès, Montmeló, Montornès del Vallès, Parets del Vallès, La Roca del Vallès and Sant Fost de Campsentelles
4	2016	2020	Air Quality Improvement Action Plan in Santa Coloma de Gramenet (2008–2020)	Santa Coloma de Gramenet
5	2016	2020	Air Quality Improvement Action Plan in the municipality of l'Hospitalet de Llobregat (2008–2015–2020)	L'Hospitalet de Llobregat
6	2017	2022	Sabadell 2022 - Air Quality Improvement Action Plan	Sabadell
7	2019	2025	County-wide Air Quality Improvement Action Plan in 13 municipalities from Baix Llobregat (2019–2025)	Castellbisbal, Cervelló, Corbera de Llobregat, el Papiol, la Palma de Cervelló, Martorell, Molins de Rei, Pallejà, Sant Andreu de la Barca, Sant Climent de Llobregat, Sant Feliu de Llobregat, Sant Vicenç dels Horts and Torrelles de Llobregat
8	2020	2025	Badalona's Air Quality Improvement Action Plan Update	Badalona
9	2020	2025	Air Quality Improvement Action Plan in the municipality of Cerdanyola del Vallès	Cerdanyola del Vallès

BARCELONA. Metropolitan Region. Air Quality Improvement Plans drawn up by the Agency.
Source: BCNecologia

METHODOLOGY FOR PREPARING AIR QUALITY IMPROVEMENT PLANS

The first phase of each plan introduces the background and regulatory framework. It also includes an examination of the municipality's socio-economic characteristics and air quality situation. The most relevant part of the diagnosis is the emission inventory, which identifies the main sources of emissions and outlines their contribution to the municipality's total pollution, in order to make concrete proposals to reduce their effect.

To diagnose the municipality's air quality, data is taken from the measurement points at the stations that make up the Catalan government's Air Pollution Monitoring and Prevention Network (XVPCA in Catalan) and from one-off pollution analyses carried out in the area.

The anthropogenic sources of air pollutants – specifically, nitrogen oxides (NO_x) and PM_{10} particles – that affect air quality in the area being studied are also examined. The sectors evaluated are intercity transport, urban transport, industry and the domestic and commercial sector.

In the second phase, the measures to be developed within the action plan are detailed, structured through lines of action and strategies. Each initiative is developed through a sheet that includes information on aims; planned deadlines; predicted costs; degree of priority and monitoring indicators; the estimated reduction in emissions; stakeholders; services and organisations involved; and interrelation with other plans established by councils, the Government of Catalonia or the Spanish State, among other aspects.

CO_2	Carbon Dioxide
GWh/year	Gigawatt hours per year
kWh/year	Kilowatt hours per year
NO_2	Nitrogen Dioxide
NO_x	Nitrogen Oxides
PM_{10}	Particulate Matter smaller than 10 microns

Measurement unit and chemical element abbreviations.

As Air Quality Improvement Action Plans (PAMQA) have significant and varying implications for municipal services, a cross-cutting approach is taken, and the process of writing and reviewing the plan is carried out jointly and agreed upon by the municipal services involved.

It is worth noting that the PAMQA is just one of four plans regularly developed in cities with a cross-cutting approach, common strategy and focus on aspects relating to mobility, with a view to meeting targets set to combat climate change and improve environmental quality. The graphic shown below illustrates this crossover between the Sustainable Energy Action Plan (PAES), the Urban Mobility Plan (PMU), the Air Quality Improvement Action Plan (PAMQA) and the Strategic Noise Plan (PRS).

The scenario analysis part includes estimates and assessments of the emissions and immissions associated with various future scenarios: a business-as-usual scenario, depicting how the situation will develop without the plan's measures, and a scenario where the PAMQA measures are implemented. This way, the potential reduction in emissions achieved by the proposed measures can be calculated.

THE ACTION PLAN

The initiatives proposed in the plans can be classified into eight groups related to their aims.

- **Streamline the use of private vehicles and reduce their emissions.** The high density of motorised traffic in cities and the amount of diesel engines in the vehicle fleet are key factors in the high levels of emissions from the mobility sector. The main measures in this set of actions aim to reduce the number of motorised vehicles in the city, through the planning, organisation, monitoring and promotion of the modal shift to other, less polluting modes of transport.

- **Promote urban and intercity public transport and reduce its emissions.** Public transport networks, especially buses, play a key role in mobility, both within municipalities and in connections between them. They must absorb increases in demand, either due to a changing modal split or planned new urban developments. The proposal is to optimise bus networks and renew the bus fleet, with hybrid and electric vehicles.

- **Encourage a transition to active mobility (walking and cycling).** As well as not polluting, active mobility entails a host of

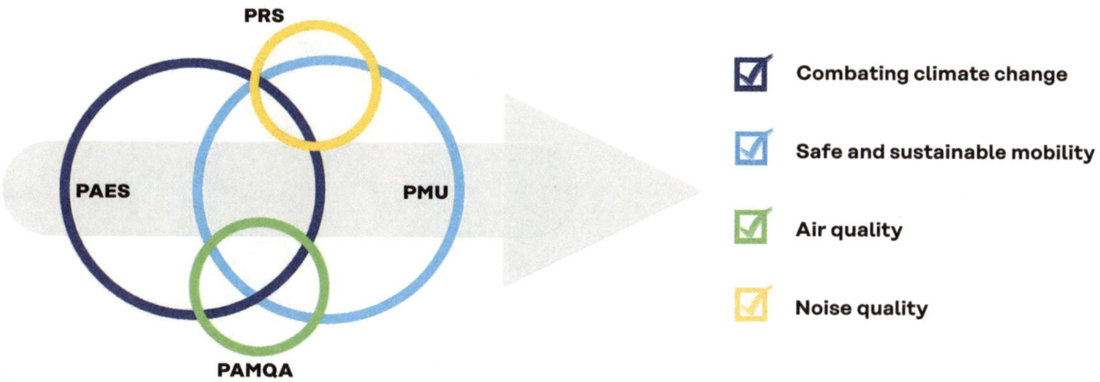

TERRASSA. Crossover between the different plans relating to mobility (PMU), energy (PAES), air quality (PAMQA) and noise (PRS).
Source: PMU from Terrassa 2016–2021

social and health benefits. This is why public authorities must promote it over other modes of transport. What is more, most journeys within municipalities are made by foot: a little-known reality that does not receive the attention it deserves. To improve the quality of journeys on foot and encourage them, the creation of high-quality pedestrian routes connecting neighbourhoods has been proposed. Another proposal is the hierarchisation of the pedestrian network, based on the superblock model and the implementation of school route projects.

As for cycling, the appropriate infrastructure should be provided, made up of a network of safe, connected cycle routes with safe parking. Alongside, complementary initiatives should facilitate and promote cycling among the public, such as traffic calming measures or education and awareness-raising activities.

- **Reduce emissions deriving from urban goods distribution.** Goods loading and unloading activity should be optimised and rationalised, through an organisation

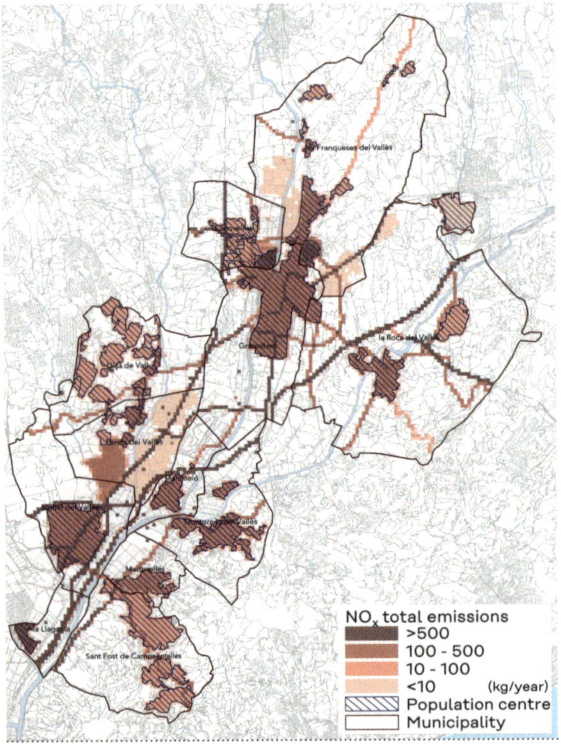

VALLÈS ORIENTAL. 2011. NO_x emissions map from PAMQA.
Source: BCNecologia

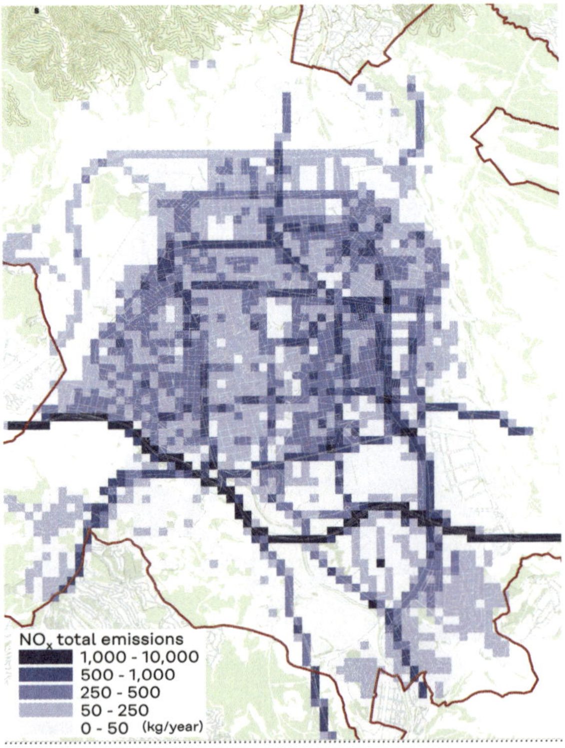

TERRASSA. 2011. NO_x emissions map from PAMQA.
Source: BCNecologia

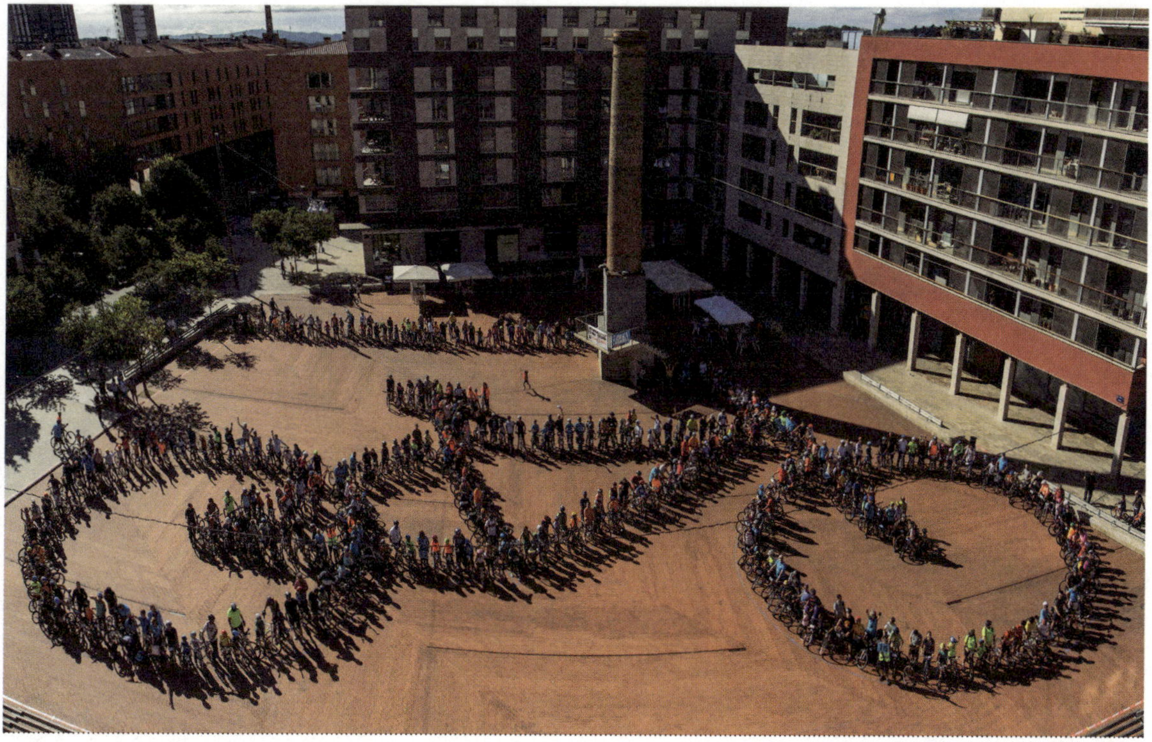

TERRASSA. 2016. Human bicycle mosaic in Plaça Nova in Terrassa. Sustainable Mobility Week.
Picture: Terrassa City Council

proposal that takes into account shops' and services' supply and demand, opening hours, loading and unloading bays, new ICT, smart management and the viability of an urban goods distribution logistics centre. Benefits for the cleanest vehicles (electric vehicles and cargo bicycles) may also be considered, with special time slots for loading and unloading activity and special bays for them.

- **Reduce emissions from municipal services.** The local administration is responsible for the air pollution generated during the provision of municipal services. Though this figure is much lower than the emissions generated by private motor vehicles, it is important for the administration to lead by example in the municipality, demonstrating the proposed initiatives and technologies and bringing them closer to the population.

The proposed measures are renewing the fleet of municipal vehicles with environmental criteria in mind; establishing environmental requirements for the fleet of vehicles used by outsourced municipal services; and creating a single management system for the fleet of municipal vehicles, with a *car sharing* application.

- **Reduce combustion emissions from households, construction work and other sources.** This group includes the creation and approval of a catalogue of basic measures to reduce emissions from construction and building demolition work. In the domestic sphere, the installation of efficient heat production systems should be encouraged, while the installation of biomass boilers should be monitored. In municipalities where agricultural activity means that it is common to burn green waste, alternatives to burning must be offered, like an *on-site* agricultural waste shredding service or collection for composting.

- **Promote education, awareness-raising and public participation.** The initiatives proposed mainly consist of campaigns, exhibitions and courses; internal dissemination of information among all the municipal teams involved; and communication through the media and councils' social networks.

SABADELL. Pedestrian area.
Picture: BCNecologia

- **Monitor air quality and its impact on health.** It is important to establish procedures for monitoring the implementation of the Plan, to improve the accuracy of the emission inventory, to create a protocol for monitoring industrial emissions, and to gather data on the population's exposure to air pollutants.

Conclusions

Even though these plans had been established, in mid-2019, the European Commission took the Spanish State to the Court of Justice of the European Union for infringing European air quality legislation, because of NO_x emissions in Madrid, Barcelona and the Baix Llobregat-Vallès area. In 2020, Barcelona City Council permanently implemented the Low Emission Zone (LEZ). Many other municipalities in the vicinity plan to do the same in the coming years, and by 2025, it is to be expanded to the entire Barcelona Metropolitan Area.

The industrial hubs in the metropolitan region generally use the best techniques available and are carefully monitored, so the main area in which air quality can be improved is motor traffic on express roads. Administrations above the municipal level have the power to turn the situation around, primarily with heavy investment in public transport, cycle networks between municipalities, and a toll policy that regulates demand, among other measures.

During the COVID-19 pandemic, lockdown measures led to an unprecedented fall in nitrogen dioxide (NO_2) pollution – one of the main pollutants linked to traffic in cities – of between 70% and 80% in Barcelona. This showed that changes that seemed impossible could be made in just a few days and that, furthermore, interventions could be made in cities for health reasons. Looking beyond the pandemic, this could lead to a different city model with new priorities and clean air as one of the cornerstones of this new age.

URBAN BIODIVERSITY AND GREEN NETWORK IN BARCELONA

2021

2020

2019

2018

2017

2016

2015

2014

2013

2012 — **BARCELONA**
Greenery and Biodiversity Plan 2012–2020

2011 — **STUDY MODEL**
Economic and energy costs of maintaining and conserving urban green areas

2010 — **BARCELONA**
Green Roofs and Walls

2009 — **PAAC**
Sustainability Report for the Pet Rescue Park

2008

2007

2006 — **BARCELONA**
Strategic plan for open spaces
Definition of urban green corridors

2005

2004

2003

2002

2001

2000

Barcelona's green network and its biodiversity have played a key role in developing a more sustainable city model. Over the years, the city has created a network of quality, increasingly green public spaces: an essential feature in one of the densest metropolises in Europe, in terms of population.

Any urban centre's green network must be viewed as a coherent, cohesive whole. There is no use in a town having excellent parks and gardens if its streets have no trees, as these green areas will remain isolated and disconnected from the rest of the network. Improving the ecological condition of Barcelona and its environs requires a stronger connection between green spaces all the way from the coast to the mountains, and from the Besòs to the Llobregat river.

BCNecologia's contribution to the promotion of green areas has focused on defining strategies and a system of indicators. Its main project in this area has been the Strategic Plan for Open Spaces in Barcelona. Definition of the Urban Green Corridors (2006). Other key initiatives in this sphere were the Study on the Potential of Green Roofs and Walls (2010–2014) and, to a lesser extent – though they also provided specific, unique contributions – the Model for the Study of the Economic and Energy Costs of Maintaining and Conserving Urban Green Areas (2011) and the Sustainability Report for the Pet Rescue Park (PAAC 2009).

Although the Agency has carried out very few studies dealing exclusively with urban greenery, planning of green spaces and care for them have been present in all of its projects, as a distinctive feature of ecosystemic urbanism.

Strategies for greening the public space involve environmental services – to improve soil permeability and planting potential – and access to nature for all, while minimising the impact on biodiversity.

THE ECOLOGICAL CONNECTIVITY

Ecological connectivity refers to the quality of the natural environment and of the semi-developed spaces that, as well as allowing organisms to move and spread around, perpetuate ecological processes and the flows that characterise them (water, matter and, most importantly for biodiversity, DNA).

An ecological connector is a relatively large sector of land defined by certain morphological features and a structure of habitats that encourage continuity.

A green corridor is a strip of land that, thanks to its environmental charac-

BARCELONA. 2006. Urban green corridors proposal.
Source: BCNecologia

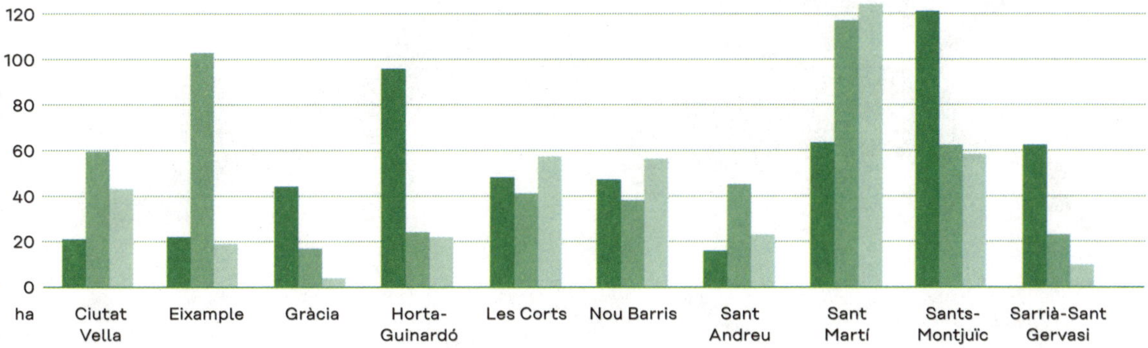

BARCELONA. 2006. Pedestrianised surface area by district.
Source: BCNecologia

teristics, can link two natural areas that would otherwise be isolated from each other. This connection between different areas increases ecosystems' viability, as they tend to deteriorate when separate from one another. In an urban context – another kind of ecosystem – green corridors constitute a link between different types of green areas, and between these areas and the ecosystems outside the city.

The urban ecosystem is extraordinarily complex, with layers of different functions and multiple activities. The main functions of a network of green corridors include:

- Increasing biodiversity.
- Improving soil permeability.
- Mitigating the 'urban heat island' effect.
- Improving the accessibility of public spaces.
- Promoting alternative mobility networks.

GREEN CORRIDORS IN BARCELONA

BCNecologia has always participated in the strategic definition of Barcelona's green network with a systemic approach that emphasises the ecological factor of vegetation and how it fits in with the management of green spaces.

Barcelona City Council tasked BCNecologia with putting together the Strategic Plan for Open Spaces in Barcelona. Definition of Urban Green Corridors (2006). The main aim of this plan was to identify

BARCELONA. 2006. Public space typology.
Source: BCNecologia

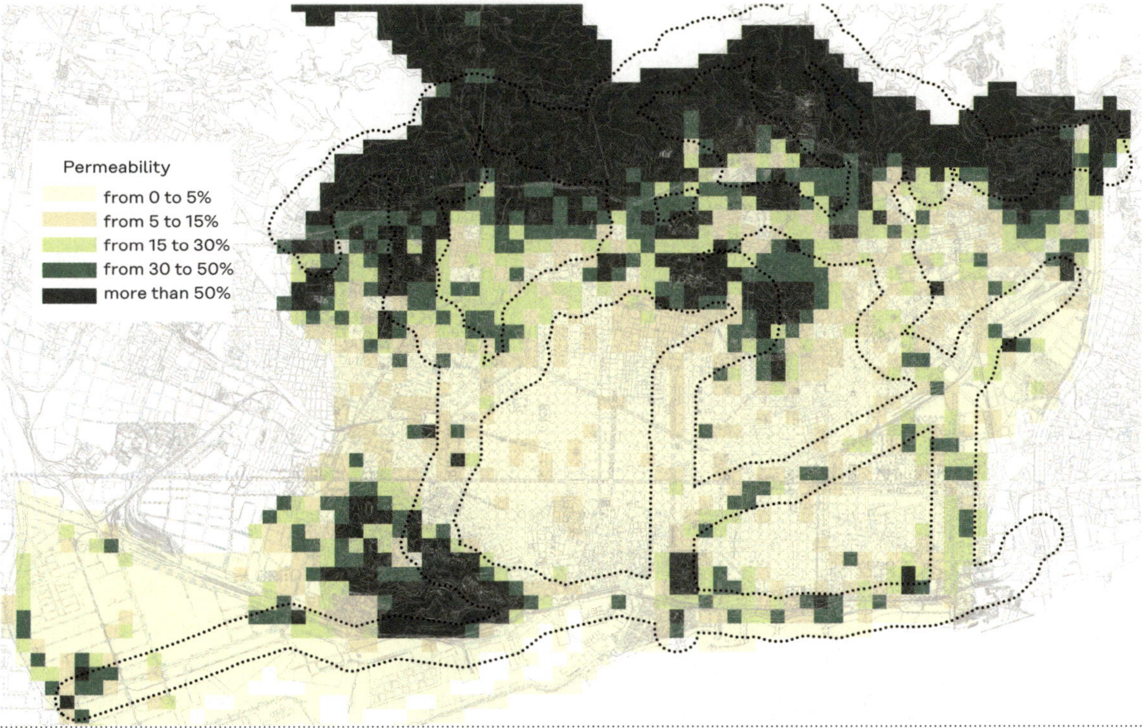

BARCELONA. 2006. Percentage of permeable surface per a 200x200 m grid.
Source: BCNecologia

the main green routes to connect the mountains and the sea and the Besòs and Llobregat rivers, as part of Barcelona's Agenda 21 Action Plan.

This document defined and calculated a series of indicators to analyse the structure of urban fabrics and their compactness. Based on the estimation of the city's corrected compactness, the plan identified the opportunities posed by the existing urban fabric and the need to free up and calm public spaces.

Corrected compactness is an estimation of the balance between the full and the empty, between urban compression and decompression. The indicator is calculated from the volume of buildings divided by the surface area of public spaces. This proposal aimed to free up the most suitable spaces in order to connect potential corridors.

Once potential corridors were identified from the corrected compactness, a series of other aspects were analysed, relating to degree of permeability, accessibility through alternative transport networks, and degree of complexity and urban diversity.

GREEN ROOFS AND WALLS

Around 2010, Barcelona City Council commissioned another study from the Agency, with a view to highlighting the need to create mechanisms and strategies that encourage the growth of vegetation in the urban context. The aim of this study was to analyse and evaluate the potential surfaces in public spaces and on public buildings in Barcelona that could be turned into green roofs and walls.

LES CORTS. BARCELONA. Green wall in the Tarradellas garden: a green lung measuring space of 250 m².
Picture: BCNecologia

The study included private roofs on hotels, museums and cinemas, which could also potentially be considered for urban regreening programmes.

The goal was to define which locations could be utilised strategically by the local administration and the considerations to keep in mind when implementing these green roofs and walls in the city's districts, so that they could be used as a model.

In parallel, as well as defining future urban green spaces, BCNecologia also pointed out the sustainability criteria established by current and future conditions to maintain the environmental benefits brought to the city by urban greenery.

THE IMPACT ON BIODIVERSITY. THE PET RESCUE PARK CASE

The Sustainability Report for the Pet Rescue Park (PAAC) analysed the possible environmental impact of this facility and emphasised its potential effect on urban green corridors and ecological connectivity.

The report was a prime example of environmental sustainability applied to an urban context, with a focus on biodiversity. It offered a detailed examination of the possible impacts on the surroundings,

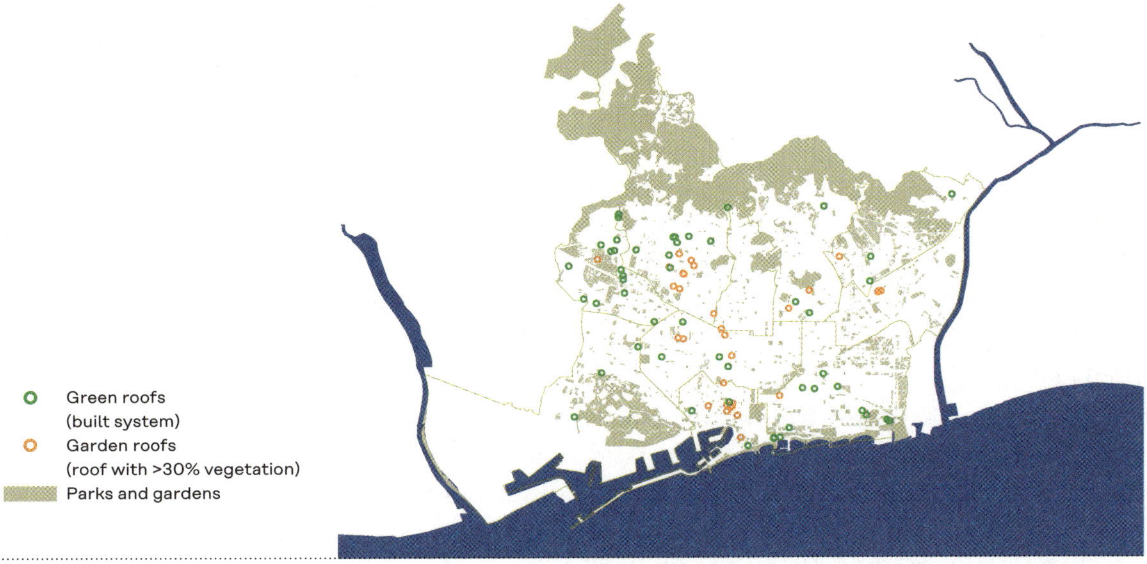

BARCELONA. 2010. Classification of existing roofs by height. Greenery on roofs added 3.88 ha (a total of 85 points) to the city's greenery, where green roofs made up 3.5 ha and roofs with complete gardens constituted 0.38 ha.
Source: BCNecologia

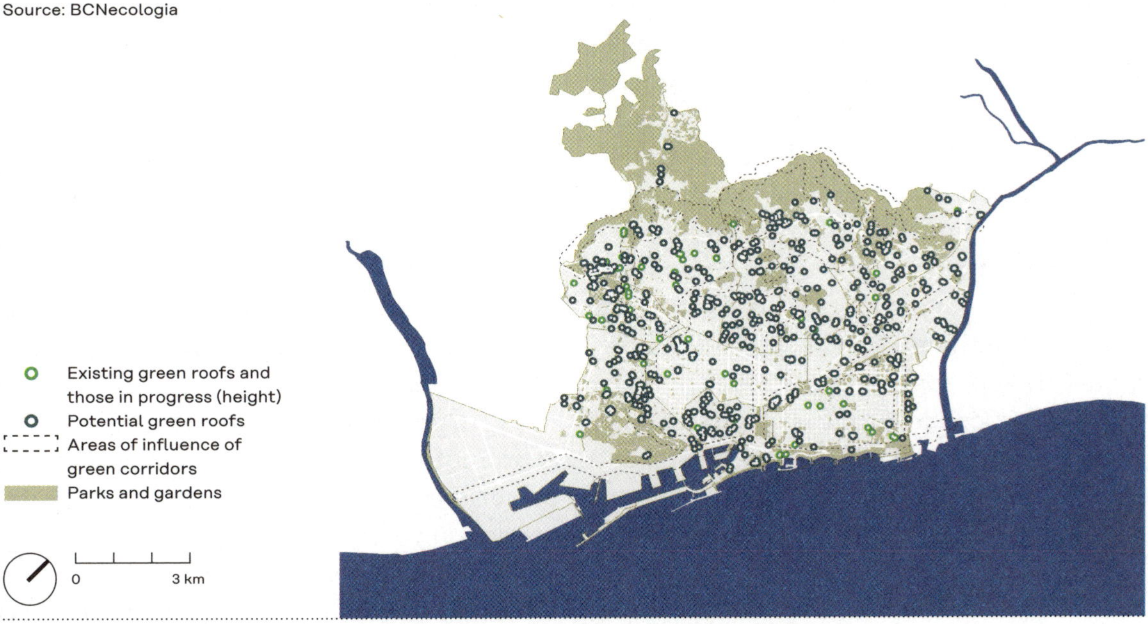

BARCELONA. 2010. Surface area of potential green roofs on public facilities.
Source: BCNecologia

especially the effects on ecological connectivity caused by its unique location, in the Collserola mountains, next to the L'Oreneta Park, in an important green corridor leading into the city and one of the main entrance routes for biodiversity. The report indicated that the connection between the Collserola Nature Park and the L'Oreneta Park was maintained through the implementation of green roofs and walls and through this project.

It also assessed the facility's impact in terms of noise and smells, and concluded that the corrective measures planned in the rescue centre project were enough to minimise them. In addition, it analysed issues like energy efficiency, water management and mobility. As well as evaluating the project's impact, the report also developed proposals for improving and achieving goals from an environmental point of view. To make sure the centre ran smoothly and these goals were met, the report recommended putting together a management plan.

In the end, the rescue centre was built in Montcada i Reixac. Barcelona Regional (BR) prepared the project and the planning procedures for the Modification of the General Metropolitan Plan (MPGM) and the Special Urbanistic Plan.

GREENERY AND CLIMATE CHANGE

As part of a project for the Fundación Biodiversidad in 2011, the Agency created the Model for the Study of the Economic and Energy Costs of Maintaining and Conserving Parks, Gardens and Urban Trees. The study analysed the different aspects of greenery management by gathering and examining different management models used in various Spanish municipalities. The final result detailed the economic and energy costs associated with this management. This analysis was linked to the climate change situation and proposed green area management criteria based on sustainability (recycling of waste, no herbicides or insecticides, biodiversity of flora and fauna, water-saving techniques, etc.) and eco-friendly maintenance.

The proposed tool indicated the costs of maintaining urban greenery in cities. This information could be used to draw up management plans for sustainable, economically viable maintenance. It could also be utilised for the assessment of new greening projects, as it included sustainability factors, which were objectifiable because they could be quantified.

Currently, the municipal government is promoting a new greenery maintenance culture in the city, in its commitment to conserving and improving our natural heritage so that everyone can enjoy and benefit from it. Barcelona is thus making progress

BIODIVERSITY

1 Preserving and promoting plant diversity
2 Preserving and promoting wildlife biodiversity
3 Connecting green areas

WATER

1 Adapting species management and selection to xeriscaping criteria
2 Minimising water losses in irrigated areas and improving the drainage system
3 Using of irrigation efficiently
4 Using alternative water sources
5 Ensuring ornamental use of water is efficient and environmentally friendly

WASTE AND MATERIALS

1 Minimising waste production
2 Avoiding the production of toxic and hazardous waste
3 Sorting the generated wastes at the source and managing it correctly
4 Optimising the consumption of materials and resources
5 Choosing techniques, materials and production processes with a low environmental impact

ENERGY

1 Using more efficient lighting for reduced light pollution
2 Using renewable energies
3 Reducing machinery's energy consumption

VISITORS

1 Promoting public participation in greenery maintenance and management
2 Developing educational and informative activities in green areas
3 Guaranteeing and facilitating the public use of green areas

2011. Greenery sustainability criteria according to environment vectors.
Source: BCNecologia

towards the ecological transition of its green public spaces and greenery management in a context of climate change. There are three plans in effect to achieve this goal. The first is the Urban Greenery and Biodiversity Plan for Barcelona 2012–2020. This is a general instrument for planning the long-term action needed to build an ecological infrastructure able to offer environmental and social services, to insert nature and all the life it contains into the city, to connect the city to the surrounding region and, finally, to make the city more fertile and resilient (i.e. able to withstand pressure and overcome the challenges generated by climate change and the city itself). The second is the *Guide to Living Terraces and Roofs (2015)*.[19] With this guide, the City Council aims to encourage the

19 Barcelona City Council. *Guide to Living Terraces and Roofs.* Barcelona: Urban Ecology Area. Barcelona City Council, 2015.

greening of these spaces, where residents can enjoy views of the city while improving the city's environmental quality. The guide explains the social and environmental benefits of green roofs and offers technical advice for choosing the right kind of terrace and information on how to proceed to use it. The third of these plans is the Tree Master Plan for Barcelona 2017–2037, which seeks to plan, manage and conserve the city's public and private trees. This will guarantee the trees' contribution to a healthier city for the current population and future generations in a context of climate change, in which nature and greenery are a key factor in creating a living and liveable public space for residents.

BARCELONA. 2014. Green roof from the Sant Gervasi-Joan Maragall Library.
Picture: Sebastià Rambla

Conclusions

The Urban Ecology Agency of Barcelona carries out studies for urban systems all over the world, through which it promotes the city's transition to a more sustainable model. Though biodiversity is not usually a popular aspect of these analyses, it plays a fundamental role in the Agency's ecosystemic urbanism approach, whether through specific proposals or through a presence in projects that involve the whole urban system.

As reflected in the studies presented in this chapter, BCNecologia shines a light on regions' potential for re-naturalisation through a network of green corridors, when mobility networks are reorganised and vehicles are given less space. This process expands the public space and fills it with greenery.

As well as proposing strategies and solutions, the Agency creates tools to calculate the costs involved in regreening cities to improve biodiversity, linked to maintenance, the water cycle, waste generated and lighting.

It is important to remember the main benefit of urban biodiversity, beyond its aesthetic, sensory or symbolic value: its essential role within the ecosystem. The urban green network generates a complex structure between different natural habitats, connecting them, protecting them and helping them to develop.

The strategies that improve species diversity index in cities are those that seek a balance between urban uses and functions, based on the definition of determining urbanistic factors. Regreening these spaces has a significant impact on the urban landscape. But the main justification for this process is ecological connectivity: creating a green network connects the city to its natural surroundings, which tend to be forgotten in urban-centric perspectives.

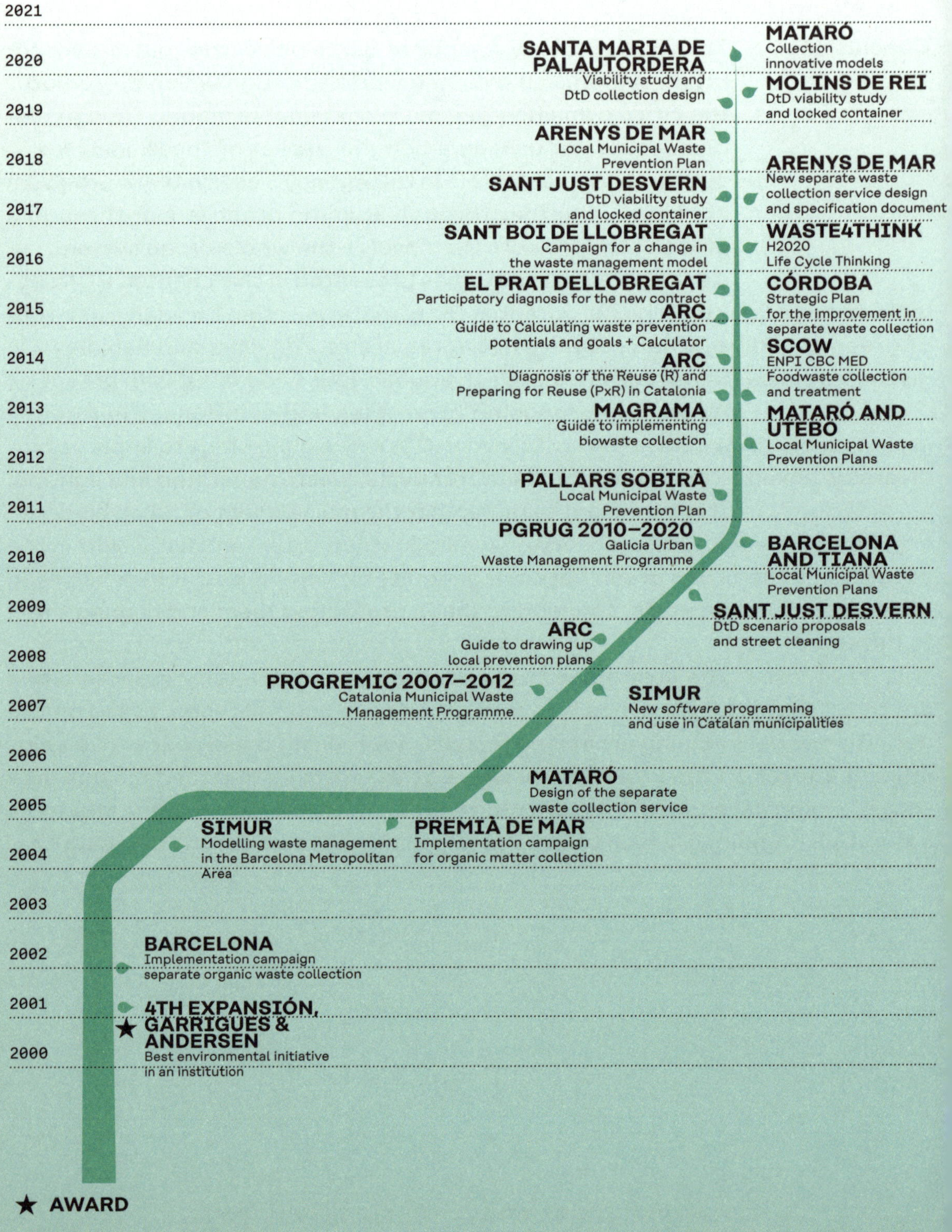
2021
2020
2019
2018
2017
2016
2015
2014
2013
2012
2011
2010
2009
2008
2007
2006
2005
2004
2003
2002
2001
2000
MATARÓ
Collection innovative models
SANTA MARIA DE PALAUTORDERA
Viability study and DtD collection design
MOLINS DE REI
DtD viability study and locked container
ARENYS DE MAR
Local Municipal Waste Prevention Plan
ARENYS DE MAR
New separate waste collection service design and specification document
SANT JUST DESVERN
DtD viability study and locked container
SANT BOI DE LLOBREGAT
Campaign for a change in the waste management model
WASTE4THINK
H2020
Life Cycle Thinking
EL PRAT DELLOBREGAT
Participatory diagnosis for the new contract
CÓRDOBA
Strategic Plan for the improvement in separate waste collection
ARC
Guide to Calculating waste prevention potentials and goals + Calculator
ARC
Diagnosis of the Reuse (R) and Preparing for Reuse (PxR) in Catalonia
SCOW
ENPI CBC MED
Foodwaste collection and treatment
MAGRAMA
Guide to implementing biowaste collection
MATARÓ AND UTEBO
Local Municipal Waste Prevention Plans
PALLARS SOBIRÀ
Local Municipal Waste Prevention Plan
PGRUG 2010–2020
Galicia Urban Waste Management Programme
BARCELONA AND TIANA
Local Municipal Waste Prevention Plans
SANT JUST DESVERN
DtD scenario proposals and street cleaning
ARC
Guide to drawing up local prevention plans
PROGREMIC 2007–2012
Catalonia Municipal Waste Management Programme
SIMUR
New *software* programming and use in Catalan municipalities
MATARÓ
Design of the separate waste collection service
SIMUR
Modelling waste management in the Barcelona Metropolitan Area
PREMIÀ DE MAR
Implementation campaign for organic matter collection
BARCELONA
Implementation campaign separate organic waste collection
4TH EXPANSIÓN, GARRIGUES & ANDERSEN
Best environmental initiative in an institution
★ AWARD

CIR CULAR ECON OMY

Waste generation (municipal waste, industrial waste, livestock excrement, etc.) is one of the most obvious, enlightening indicators of just how unsustainable our societies are. In a finite world, wasting resources is clearly not a winning strategy.

For a long time, we have ignored the waste (whether solid, liquid or gas) that our activities as a society have generated and accumulated. Unfortunately, only as a reaction to pollution problems, health issues and lack of space where we can 'hide' our rubbish in recent decades have we started to talk about using waste as resources. This has led to the introduction of waste sorting and recycling of some waste streams. But that is not enough. We must change our perspective and prevent resources from becoming waste. Starting from this idea, we have gradually added various terms until arriving at the concept of the circular economy.

This vision has permeated the Agency's projects, as evidenced by the volume and type of work done by the Waste and Materials Cycle Area. All studies have been carried out from a practical, applied standpoint. This perspective has also been present throughout all other projects, constituting part of an overall view of ecosystemic urbanism, into which urban metabolism is introduced as a key branch for proposing new solutions for our cities.

This area also includes work to promote innovative separate waste collection models. BCNecologia has played a part in the introduction of organic waste collection in Barcelona and in the implementation of individualisation through door-to-door systems or smart containers in other municipalities. In addition, it has helped to create waste prevention strategies, describing planning tools, plans and management programmes, and practical instruments for waste management, developed by the Agency itself.

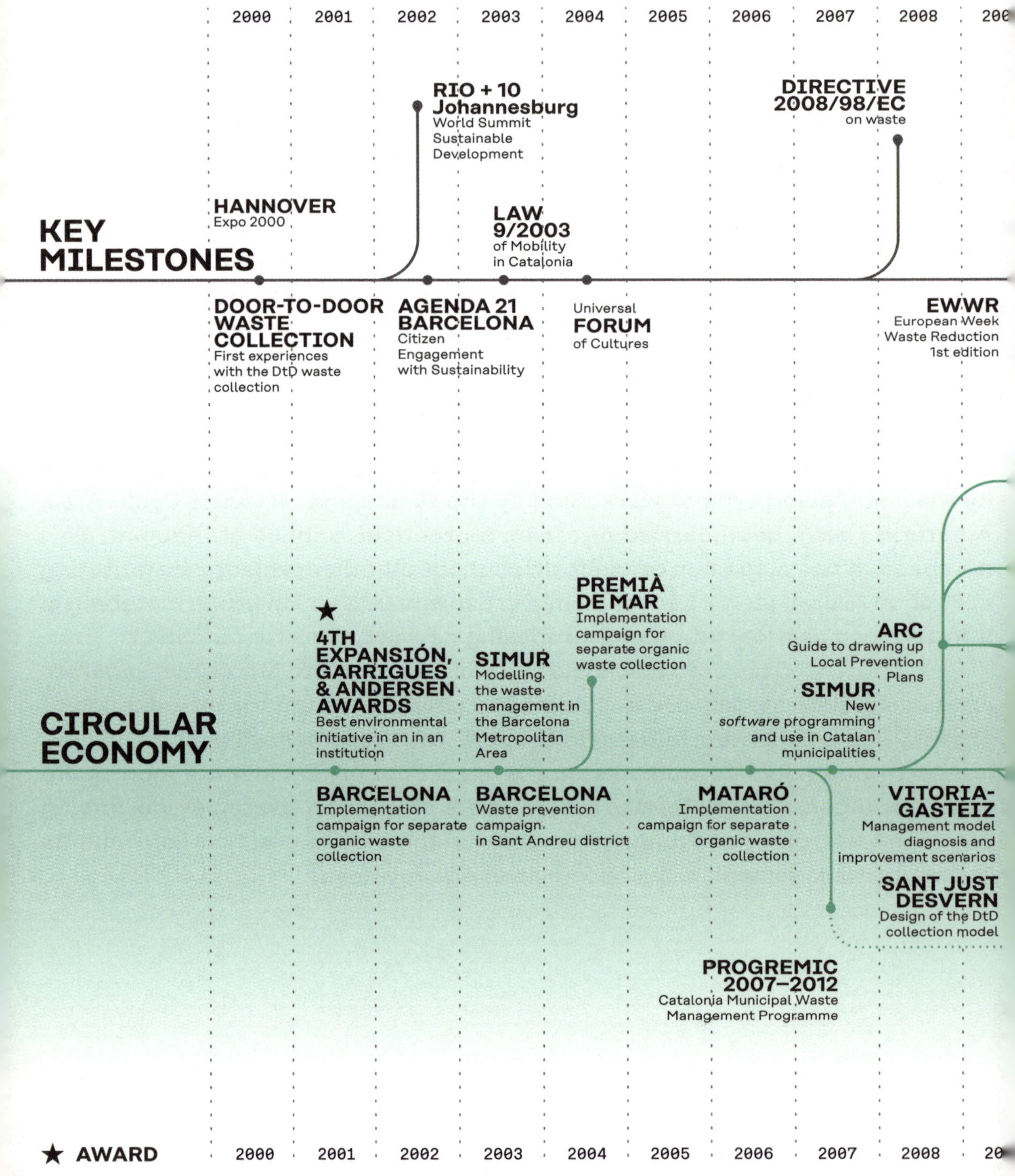
2000
2001
2002
2003
2004
2005
2006
2007
2008
KEY MILESTONES
HANNOVER
Expo 2000
RIO + 10 Johannesburg
World Summit Sustainable Development
LAW 9/2003
of Mobility in Catalonia
DIRECTIVE 2008/98/EC
on waste
DOOR-TO-DOOR WASTE COLLECTION
First experiences with the DtD waste collection
AGENDA 21 BARCELONA
Citizen Engagement with Sustainability
Universal FORUM of Cultures
EWWR
European Week Waste Reduction 1st edition
CIRCULAR ECONOMY
★
4TH EXPANSIÓN, GARRIGUES & ANDERSEN AWARDS
Best environmental initiative in an in an institution
SIMUR
Modelling the waste management in the Barcelona Metropolitan Area
PREMIÀ DE MAR
Implementation campaign for separate organic waste collection
ARC
Guide to drawing up Local Prevention Plans
SIMUR
New software programming and use in Catalan municipalities
BARCELONA
Implementation campaign for separate organic waste collection
BARCELONA
Waste prevention campaign in Sant Andreu district
MATARÓ
Implementation campaign for separate organic waste collection
VITORIA-GASTEIZ
Management model diagnosis and improvement scenarios
SANT JUST DESVERN
Design of the DtD collection model
PROGREMIC 2007–2012
Catalonia Municipal Waste Management Programme
★ AWARD
2000
2001
2002
2003
2004
2005
2006
2007
2008

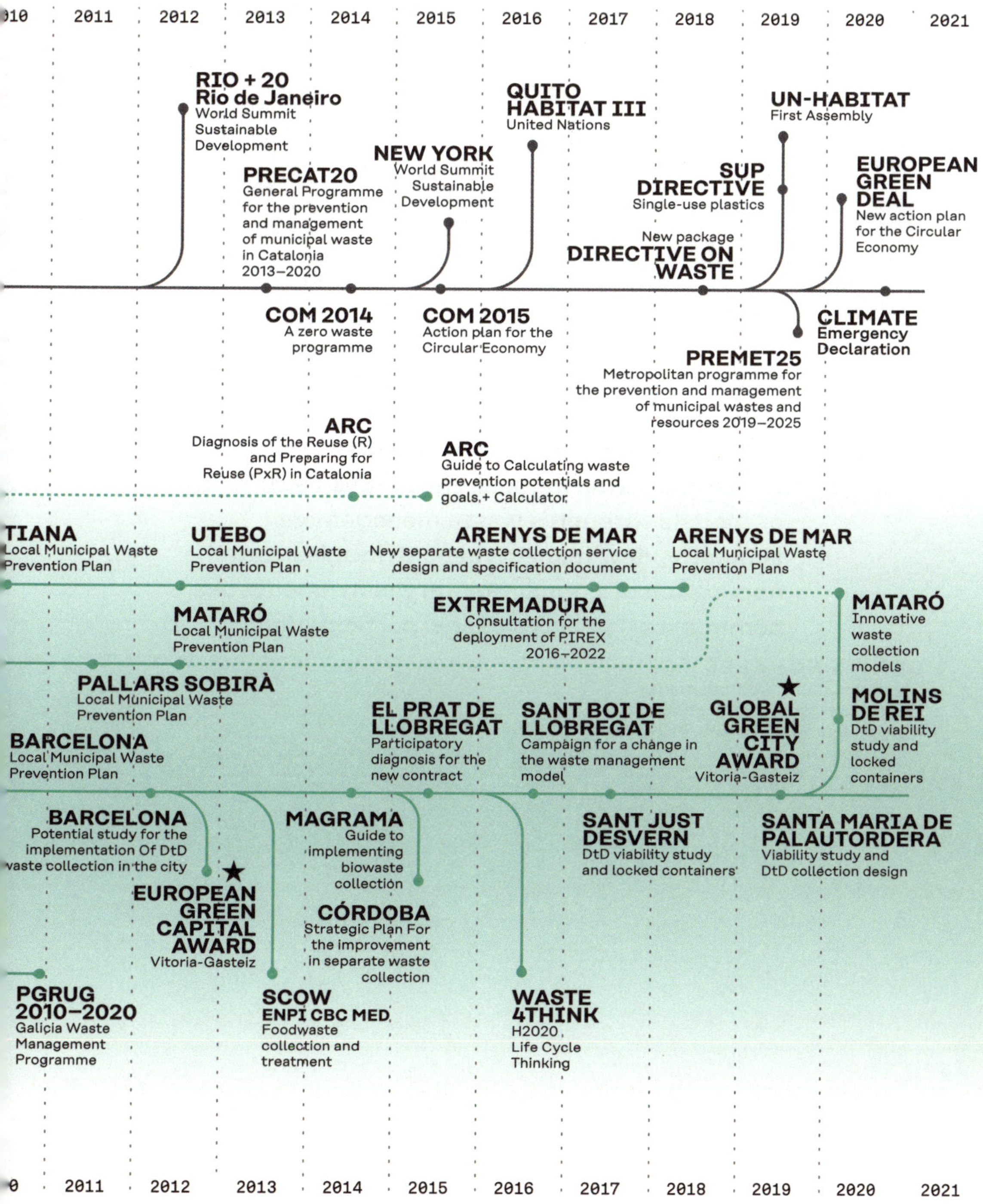

2010 2011 2012 2013 2014 2015 2016 2017 2018 2019 2020 2021
RIO + 20 Rio de Janeiro
World Summit Sustainable Development
PRECAT20
General Programme for the prevention and management of municipal waste in Catalonia 2013–2020
NEW YORK
World Summit Sustainable Development
QUITO HABITAT III
United Nations
SUP DIRECTIVE
Single-use plastics
New package
DIRECTIVE ON WASTE
UN-HABITAT
First Assembly
EUROPEAN GREEN DEAL
New action plan for the Circular Economy
COM 2014
A zero waste programme
COM 2015
Action plan for the Circular Economy
CLIMATE
Emergency Declaration
PREMET25
Metropolitan programme for the prevention and management of municipal wastes and resources 2019–2025
ARC
Diagnosis of the Reuse (R) and Preparing for Reuse (PxR) in Catalonia
ARC
Guide to Calculating waste prevention potentials and goals + Calculator
TIANA
Local Municipal Waste Prevention Plan
UTEBO
Local Municipal Waste Prevention Plan
ARENYS DE MAR
New separate waste collection service design and specification document
ARENYS DE MAR
Local Municipal Waste Prevention Plans
MATARÓ
Local Municipal Waste Prevention Plan
EXTREMADURA
Consultation for the deployment of PIREX 2016–2022
MATARÓ
Innovative waste collection models
PALLARS SOBIRÀ
Local Municipal Waste Prevention Plan
EL PRAT DE LLOBREGAT
Participatory diagnosis for the new contract
SANT BOI DE LLOBREGAT
Campaign for a change in the waste management model
★ GLOBAL GREEN CITY AWARD
Vitoria-Gasteiz
MOLINS DE REI
DtD viability study and locked containers
BARCELONA
Local Municipal Waste Prevention Plan
BARCELONA
Potential study for the implementation Of DtD waste collection in the city
★ EUROPEAN GREEN CAPITAL AWARD
Vitoria-Gasteiz
MAGRAMA
Guide to implementing biowaste collection
CÓRDOBA
Strategic Plan For the improvement in separate waste collection
SANT JUST DESVERN
DtD viability study and locked containers
SANTA MARIA DE PALAUTORDERA
Viability study and DtD collection design
PGRUG 2010–2020
Galicia Waste Management Programme
SCOW
ENPI CBC MED
Foodwaste collection and treatment
WASTE 4THINK
H2020
Life Cycle Thinking
2010 2011 2012 2013 2014 2015 2016 2017 2018 2019 2020 2021

'The Agency's waste management and prevention projects have always been novel and innovative, dealing with areas like new separate waste collection models, the assessment of models through a waste management simulator, new management strategies, and the application of complementary instruments like communication and citizens' participation'.

GEMMA NOHALES
Environmentalist. Coordinator for
Waste Management Projects and
Material Cycle 2003–2019. BCNecologia.

Picture: Marta Torrent

INNOVATIVE SEPARATE WASTE COLLECTION MODELS

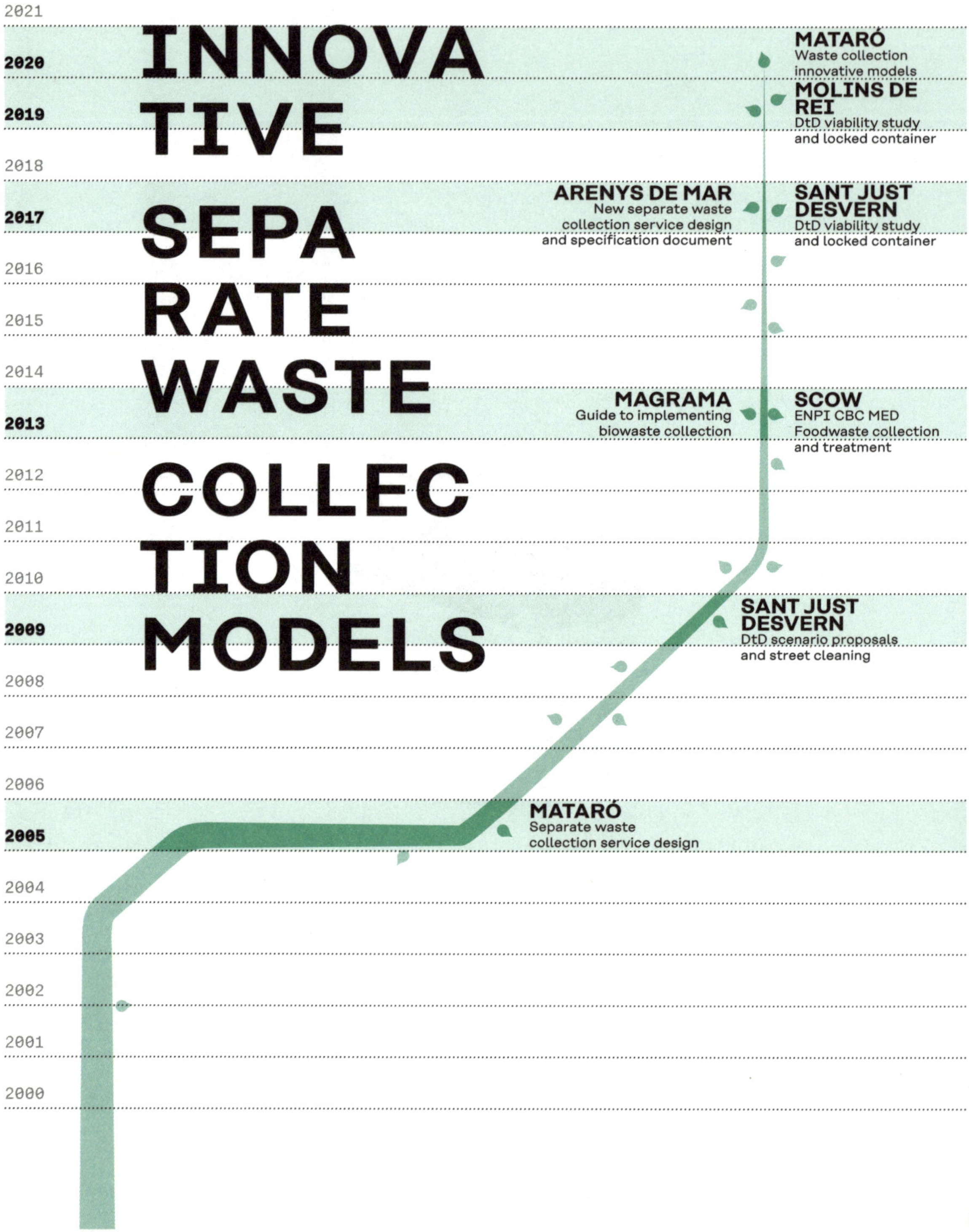

This chapter details the most relevant work BCNecologia has done over its twenty-year history in developing and promoting new municipal separate waste collection models.

In this time, waste management and collection models have changed significantly, from the expansion of new separate waste collection systems – especially organic waste collection in Catalonia – to new, individualised models, like door-to-door (DtD) or smart containers, which encourage co-responsibility from waste generators and the implementation of a fairer waste tax system.

This evolution is reflected in the work carried out by the Agency during this period. On many occasions, BCNecologia has anticipated change, and even driven it. Other times, it has helped local organisations to implement and design new separate collection models, tailoring them to each area's needs and context.

The demands of the recycling targets to be met (set by regulations) and the introduction of other instruments, such as the waste tax in Catalonia, have required municipal bodies to adapt, sometimes rapidly. To this end, by way of example, the Agency was a driving force behind the development of efficient models that incorporated separate organic waste collection – which would become a cornerstone of the management model – while ensuring maximum separation quality and, therefore, generating compost that could be reintroduced into the soil to fertilise it and prevent erosion. It has also promoted individualised collection models, like the door-to-door system (DtD) and locked containers with user identification. These models encourage co-responsibility and better waste separation at the source, in terms of both quantity and quality, thus producing quality resources that make a truly circular economy possible.

This chapter offers a sample of the viability studies and designs of new separate waste collection models that have helped municipalities to improve their results and to control or correct spending in this area.

CITIZENS' CENTRE FOR WASTE PREVENTION AND RECYCLING

Initially, the current Waste and Material Cycle Area – originally called the Citizens' Centre for Waste Prevention and Recycling (CCMRR) – focused its efforts on helping municipalities to implement separate organic waste collection. This support consisted of developing specific tools, such as communication campaigns (see the 'Waste Management Instruments' chapter), and adding organic waste collection to all existing collection models.

Separating organic waste is the pillar of all waste separation systems. For this reason, in Catalonia, Law 6/1993 (of 15 July, regulating waste) made it compulsory, ahead of European regulations, which only recommended it at this time. It was not until the Circular Economy Package, passed in 2018, that the separation of organic waste was deemed essential. Indeed, without effective separation of this waste fraction, in terms of both quality and quantity, it is impossible to achieve the goals set. And without effective, quality separation, a resource desperately needed for our soil – compost – cannot be made. It is especially in demand in the Mediterranean basin, where there are serious soil erosion and fertility problems.

The Agency's most significant projects in this field include the creation of the *Guide to Implementing Separate Organic Waste Collection and Treatment. Municipal Management of Biodegradable Waste* (MAGRAMA, 2010–2013),[20] the design and preparation of specification documents, and the subsequent implementation of this collection system in the city of Mataró (Technical Consultation and Preparation of the Waste Management and Street Cleaning Programme for Mataró, with development of the technical specification for the new contract, 2005). In this study, municipal technicians were accompanied throughout the process of designing new collection

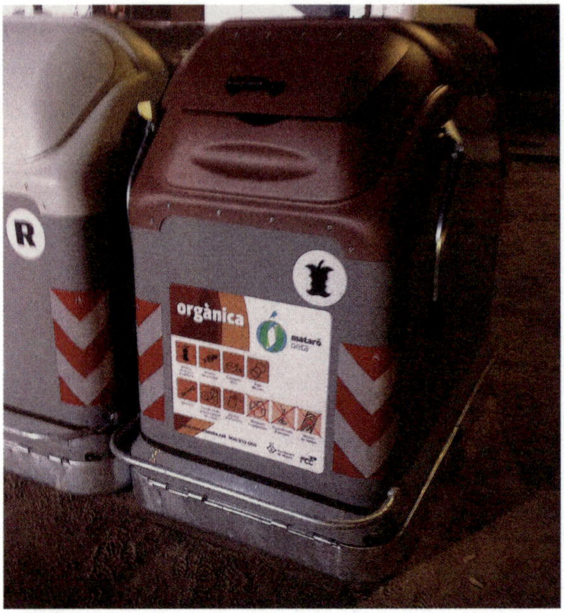

MATARÓ. 2015–2016. Two-way organic waste container. Designed through a participatory process for the new waste collection contract in the city.
Picture: Marta Vila

20 Ministry of Agriculture, Food and Environment. *Guide to Implementing Separate Organic Waste Collection and Treatment. Municipal Management of Biodegradable Waste.* Madrid. Ministry of Agriculture, Food and Environment (MAGRAMA), 2013.

systems, signing the new contract and subsequently implementing the new service.

SUPPORT FOR THE EXPANSION OF INDIVIDUALISATION MODELS IN CATALONIA

Meanwhile, when it comes to type of collection, recent years in Catalonia have been characterised by a significant shift towards models that encourage greater individualisation and better efficiency in separate waste collection. Precisely when BCNecologia was created, the first door-to-door experiences were launched in three Catalan municipalities. In the year 2000, the municipalities of Tiana, Tona and Riudecanyes became the first to implement this model in Catalonia. Few municipalities incorporated this kind of collection in the following years. It was likely the introduction of the landfill and incineration tax and the extensive educational work done by the Waste Agency of Catalonia and the Association of Door-to-Door Municipalities that helped to spread this model across Catalonia; in 2019, more than 200 municipalities had adopted it.[21]

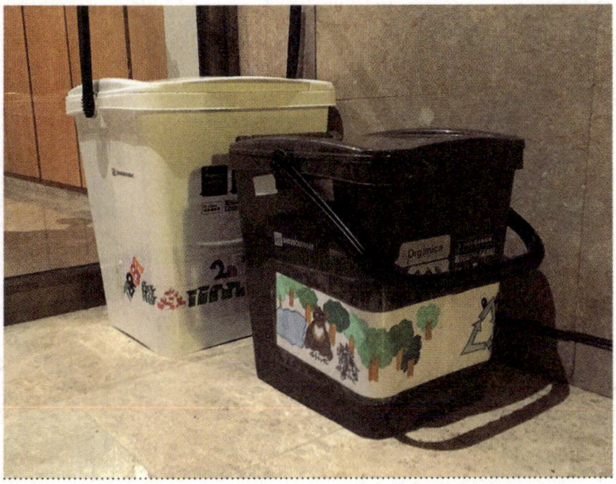

Rubbish bins for Door-to-Door waste collection.
Picture: Marta Vila

In 2009, BCNecologia delivered the first viability study on the implementation of this type of model in the municipality of Sant Just Desvern, though the project never came to fruition.

PALLARS SOBIRÀ: A LEADING COUNTY IN WASTE COLLECTION AND MANAGEMENT

As part of the European project SCOW (Selective Collection of the Organic Waste in tourist areas and valorisation in farm composting plants), subsidised by the ENPI-CBC-MED Mediterranean cooperation programme, a proposal for a model of high-quality, low-cost organic waste collection and recycling with simple technology was made for regions with areas popular with tourists and agricultural activity. The aim was to close the organic resource cycle with quality collection at the source and a sustainable, innovative, local waste treatment system at small, decentralised compost plants, mainly located on agricultural land, near to biodegradable waste production areas.

As a result, for the first time in Catalonia, a county – Pallars Sobirà, a tourist area which had fallen behind with its sep-

21 Giró, Francesc. "Recollida selectiva: per a què?", in *Jornada Prevenció i Gestió de Residus Municipals: cap al 2030*, Barcelona, October 2, 2019.

arate waste collection, with all the waste management difficulties that entails – implemented a door-to-door collection model in all of the valleys' settlements, including organic waste separation (which, until that point, had only been trialled in Llavorsí). Then, one of Catalonia's first small, decentralised compost plants was built, thus closing the organic matter cycle in the county. As a result, Pallars became a leader in separate waste collection in Catalonia and a role model for county waste management, as well as producing high-quality, useful compost to be applied to the county's soil. Furthermore, this move boosted the economy and generated jobs, both in the collection and treatment service and in environmental education, implementation inspection and monitoring activities.

As part of the project, similar systems were put in place across the Mediterranean basin, in Italy, Malta, Israel and Palestine, among other countries.

THE COMPOSTING PLANT IN SORT:
A SIMPLE, SMALL AND VERY MANAGEABLE PLANT

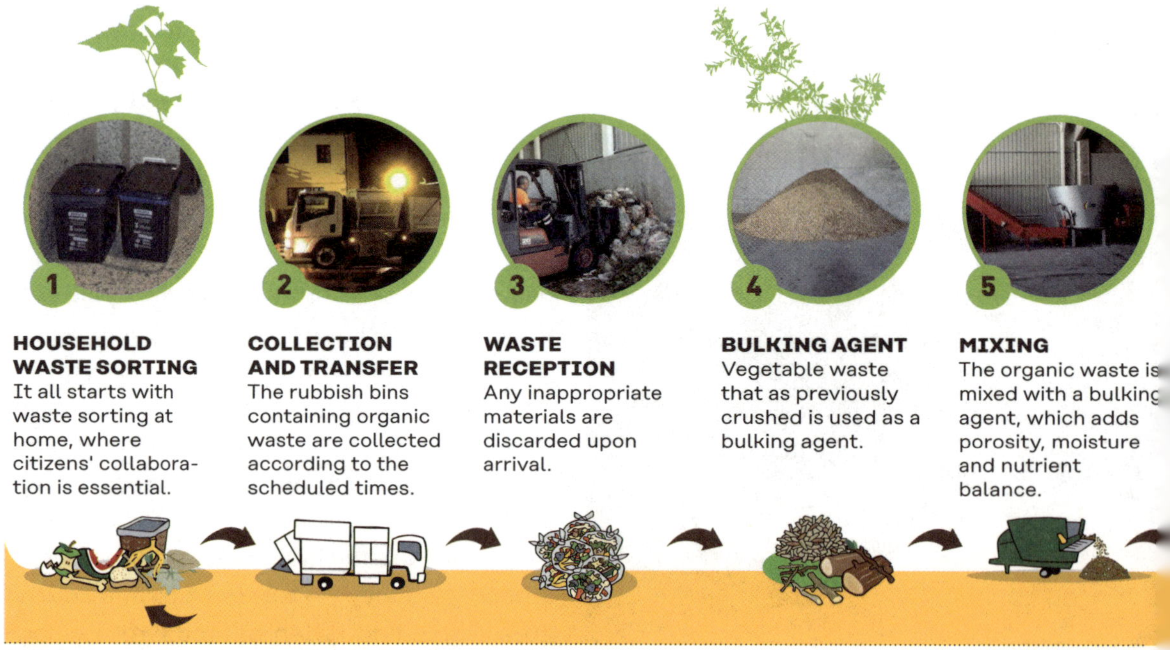

SORT. Completing the organic waste cycle in Pallars Sobirà.
Source: SCOW project (2013–2015)

NEW MUNICIPAL WASTE MODELS

In recent years, the gradual increase in the waste tax, new European regulations and new waste plans have made the need to innovate in municipal waste management models even more urgent. As a result of the targets set to separate the different recoverable waste fractions and minimise the amount of non-recoverable waste as much as possible, when reviewing contracts for waste collection and street cleaning services, many municipalities have opted to carry out viability studies for new models based on the individualisation and co-responsibility of waste generators. To this end, BCNecologia has taken part in design studies for door-to-door collection and locked containers with user identification scenarios; in technical, economic and environmental viability studies; and in the preparation of technical specifications documents for Sant Just Desvern (2017), Arenys de Mar (2017), Molins de Rei (2019), Santa Maria de Palautordera (2019), Mataró (2019) and various municipalities in Extremadura (2017–2018).

DOOR-TO-DOOR WASTE COLLECTION:
A KEY PART OF THE PROCESS

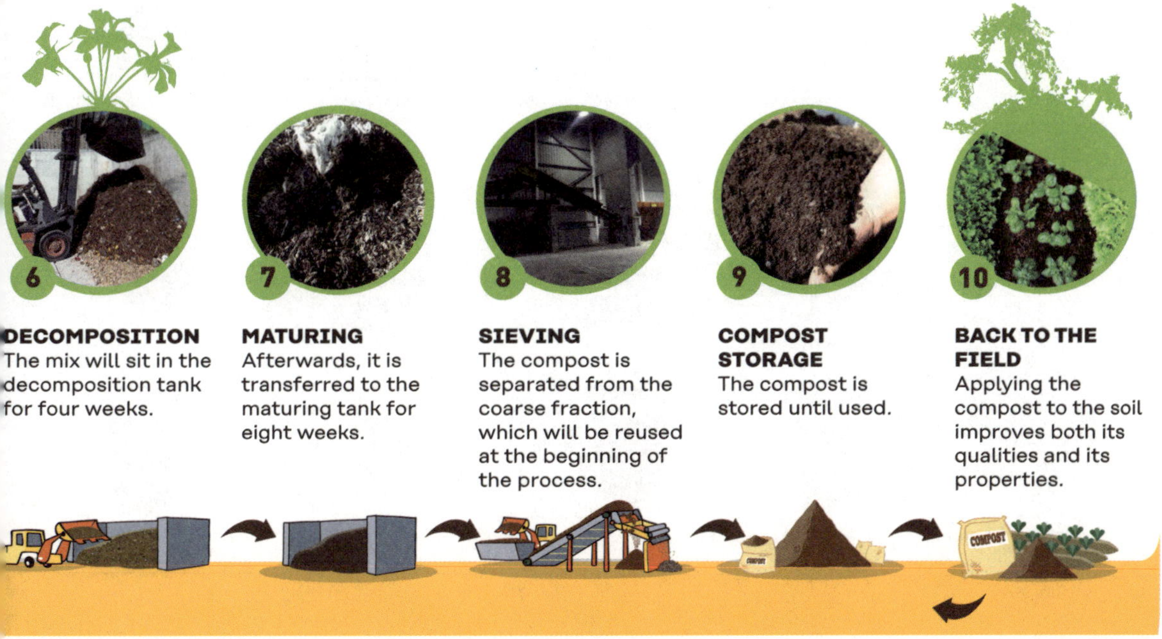

SANT JUST DESVERN AND MATARÓ

The Sant Just Desvern and Mataró cases are especially interesting. Following the viability study, the Agency also worked on the process to decide on models, the preparation of technical specifications for the new contracts deploying the new models, and the definition of complementary tools – especially for communication and implementing and monitoring new technologies – that can produce better results.

In both cases, individualisation was incorporated as a cornerstone of co-responsibility, accompanied by monitoring and a new, more transparent, flexible, dynamic and, above all, two-way relationship with users. For domestic users in Sant Just Desvern, locked containers with user identification have been proposed. This will make

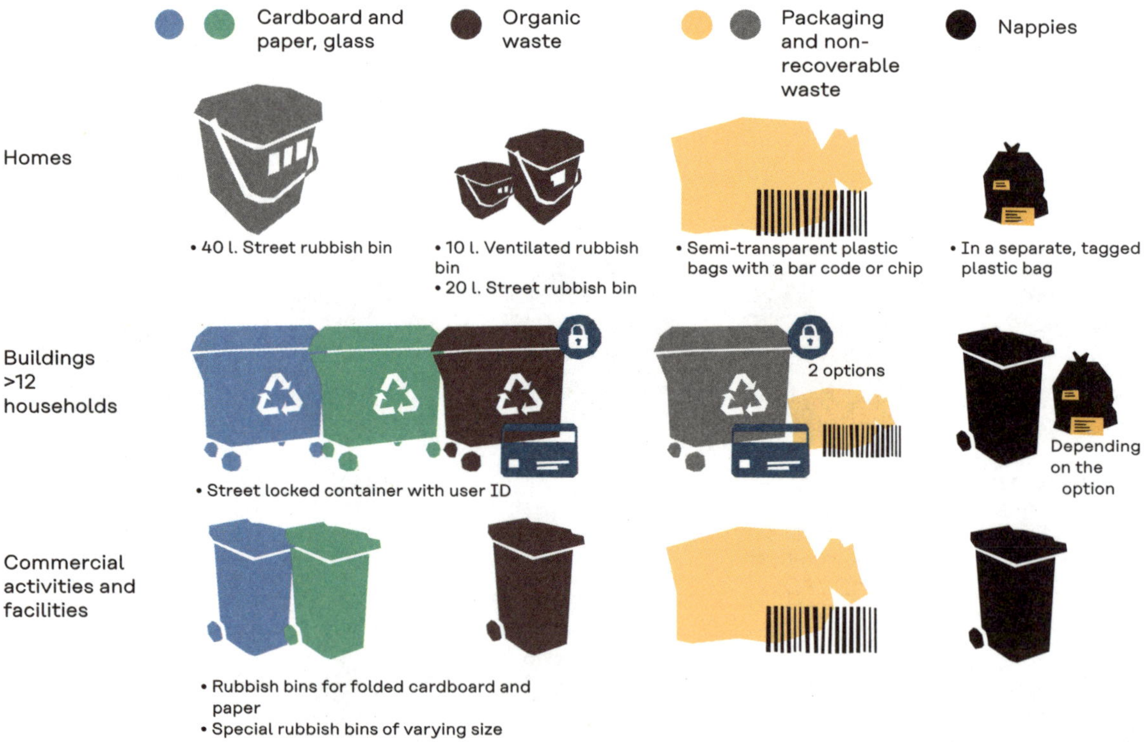

MOLINS DE REI. 2019. Innovative separate waste collection models.
Source: BCNecologia

it the first metropolitan municipality to have 100% of its non-recoverable and organic waste containers locked. As for Mataró, a series of pioneering territorial units have been defined. Three complementary models will be implemented in them: door-to-door (mixed, with locked containers for some high-density buildings), containers with electronic locks and user identification, and mobile separate collection areas (or emerging platforms), with electronic locks for all fractions.

In both Sant Just Desvern and Mataró, commercial door-to-door collection has been introduced to a certain degree. Through observation of how the system is used, the service can be monitored more carefully, and activities' contributions to the public system or authorised private managers can be controlled and traced.

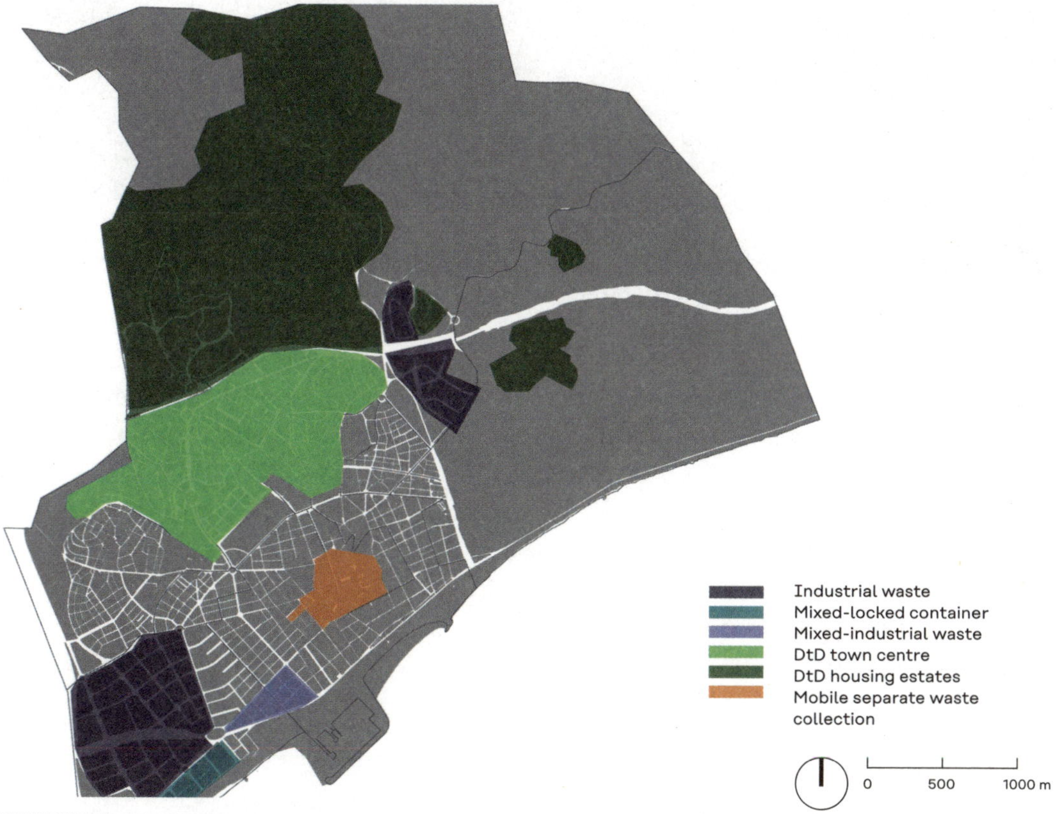

MATARÓ. 2019–2021. Zoning of the new innovative separate waste collection models.
Source: BCNecologia

BARCELONA. Organic waste sorting (lateral opening).
Picture: Marta Torrent

At the same time, more personalised user communication systems are being established, with payment for generation and participation.

These changes will generate a qualitative boost in the public's and businesses' co-responsibility and participation in waste management. This is thanks to the incorporation of new forms of collection that combine different models optimally to achieve separate waste collection quality goals, in tandem with waste prevention and circular economy strategies.

Conclusions

The increasingly challenging material recovery targets set by regulations to work towards a circular economy have given rise to the inclusion of new elements in waste management models. These new elements – essentially based on user proximity, individualisation and removal of anonymity – accompanied by fairer pricing, must act effectively as catalysts for substantial improvements in the quality and quantity of separate waste collection.

The Urban Ecology Agency of Barcelona has worked actively to configure new models and promote essential changes, through both the generation and the practical application of new instruments, with a holistic, comprehensive perspective, in city and public service strategies.

What is more, participation in European projects has enabled the Agency to learn from other experiences and to build a network of contacts and shared knowledge with technicians from other countries, thus enriching its work even more. Supporting and accompanying municipal bodies, in a kind of coaching role, in decision-making and the implementation of these new models has also been a crucial task throughout these years. Ideas have given way to action, and new follow-up, monitoring and participation elements have been incorporated into these transformation processes.

WASTE PREVENTION

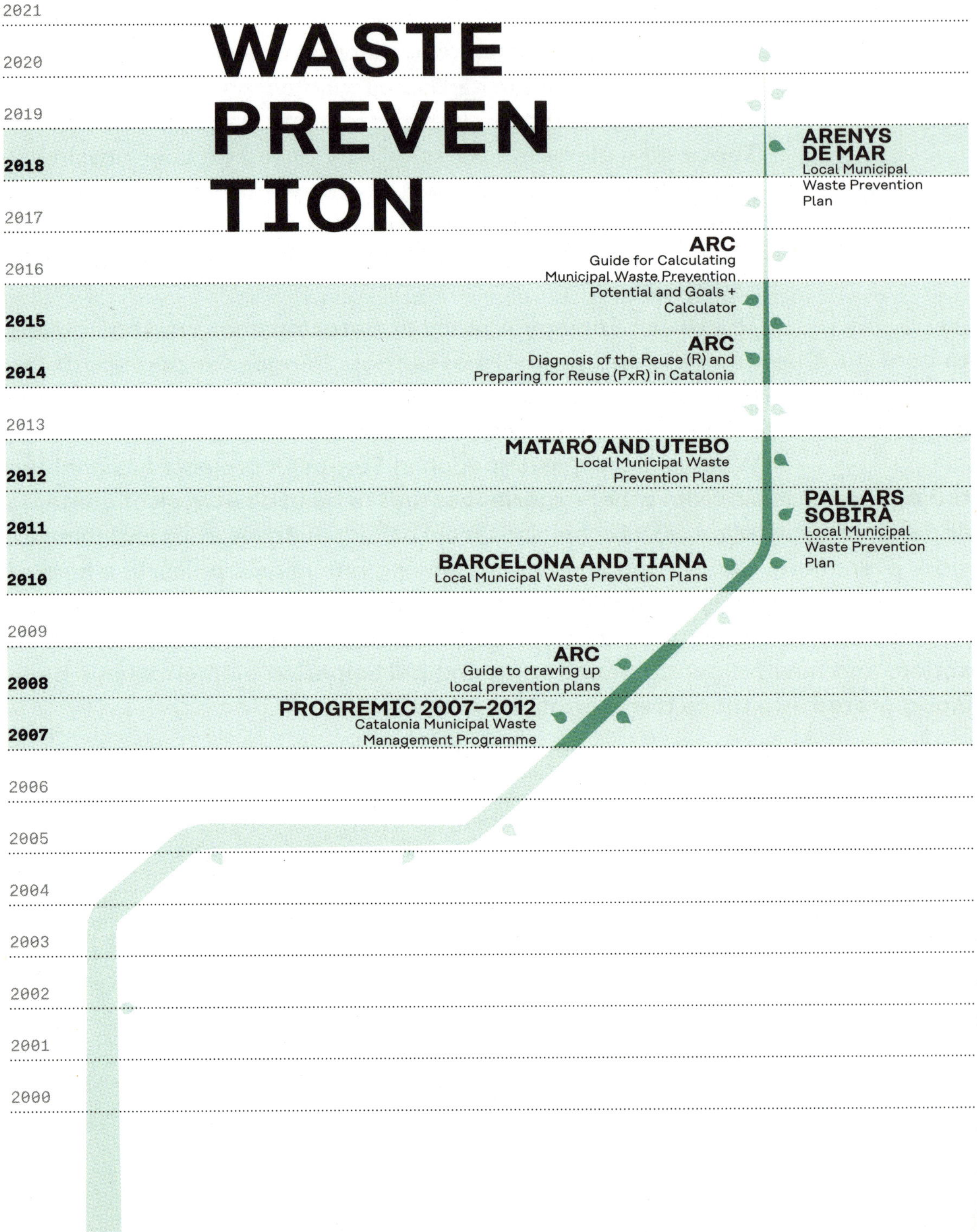

Waste prevention is the first priority of waste management, according to Directive 2008/98/EC of the European Parliament and of the Council, of 19 November 2008, on waste and repealing certain directives. This Directive requires Member States to adopt waste prevention plans and programmes, among other measures.

The Agency has driven and carried out a host of waste prevention studies, with a view to acquiring more knowledge of the field and diagnosing the state of reuse and preparing for reuse centres in Catalonia.

In 2008, upon request from the Waste Agency of Catalonia (ARC), the *Guide for the Preparation of Local Municipal Waste Prevention Plans*,[22] was drawn up: an important document in helping local organisations to put together waste prevention plans. The Guide is a response to the need to develop a medium-term and long-term waste prevention strategy, as indicated by the Catalonia Municipal Waste Management Programme (PROGREMIC) 2007–2012. Most of the plans created subsequently have followed this methodology.

Another commission from the ARC involved developing a new *Methodological Guide for Calculating Municipal Waste Prevention Potential and Goals*,[23] to facilitate goal calculation. Once quantitative prevention data linked to specific strategies was gathered, the *Prevention Calculator*,[24] was published. This online tool enabled local and wider-area organisations to calculate the possible results of applying local prevention plans in a much more real, harmonised way.

The Agency has also helped to draw up local prevention plans in Barcelona (2010), Tiana (2010), Pallars Sobirà (2011), Mataró (2011–2012), Utebo (2013) and Arenys de Mar (2018). Furthermore, it has worked on projects relating to the fight against food waste, such as the Study on Improving Use of Food Surplus in the Distribution and Restaurant Sectors in Cornellà de Llobregat, carried out in 2013.

22 Waste Agency of Catalonia. *Guide for the Preparation of Local Municipal Waste Prevention Plans.* Barcelona: Waste Agency of Catalonia (ARC), 2008.

23 Waste Agency of Catalonia. *Methodological Guide for Calculating Municipal Waste Prevention Potential and Goals.* Barcelona: Waste Agency of Catalonia (ARC), 2015.

24 Waste Agency of Catalonia. *Prevention Calculator.* Barcelona: Waste Agency of Catalonia (ARC), 2015. www.calculadoraprevencio.cat

PREVENTION AND PREPARATION FOR REUSE

Despite sitting at the top of the waste management hierarchy, waste prevention and preparing for reuse tend to be forgotten when it comes to generating knowledge and establishing real, viable medium- and long-term strategies.

Over the years, BCNecologia has worked on both aspects, collaborating on diagnoses in the sphere of reuse and developing then applying planning tools for local organisations.

In the Diagnosis of the Reuse and Preparing for Reuse Situation in Catalonia, published in 2014, one undoubtedly complex goal set was to quantify the amount of products and waste that could be reused or prepared for reuse in the conditions at the time in Catalonia. In addition, the Diagnosis aimed to find out what reuse (R), repair and preparing for reuse (PxR) activities were taking place in Catalonia and elsewhere, as well as assessing existing limitations and proposing ideas for expanding these pathways in the future.

There is a wide range of R and PxR pathways available, including rubbish tips, barter markets, second-hand markets and shops, virtual second-hand selling spaces, exchanges and donations among networks of friends and family, and charity donations, among others. This makes it difficult to generate reliable figures to quantify the phenomenon of reuse, especially when the recirculated items are not considered waste. Therefore, the quantitative analysis of these elements was limited to just some of these pathways, and a methodology to allow for future monitoring was determined. Some of the tasks carried out led the Agency to establish common, harmonised monitoring methodologies, which have been used subsequently to assess the impact of waste prevention initiatives, such as the launch of barter markets during the European Week for Waste Reduction.

THE STATE OF REUSE CENTRES IN CATALONIA

A diagnosis of the state of reuse centres in Catalonia has also recently been made (2020), as part of the European project Subtract (included in the Interreg programme).

The aim of this project is to improve R and PxR centres' economic sustainability and competitiveness through eco-innovative solutions that make them more functional, attractive, and economically and environmentally sustainable, while offering stable jobs, especially for groups with the least access to the job market. The diagnosis is one of the products of the project's first phase and will be used as a basis upon which members can continue to learn and exchange experiences. This process will culminate in the approval of a specific action plan for

BARCELONA. Bulky waste with a great reuse potential left on the street.
Picture: Paola de Grenet

improving R and PxR and the environmental sustainability and competitiveness of R and PxR centres.

PLANNING PREVENTION STRATEGIES

Planning waste prevention strategies is not an easy task, as it requires profound changes to traditional production, consumption and resource management practices. What is more, it necessitates maximum involvement from all stakeholders: governments, businesses, shops, associations, administrations, etc. The municipal administration is a key player in waste planning and management, but its powers are limited when it comes to prevention. Nonetheless, it must act as a facilitator and promote coordinated action between the various agents involved, with each making continual progress on their own level. To achieve this, it must plan and apply a medium-term and long-term strategy that raises stakeholders' awareness and ensures that they participate, in order to meet the waste reduction goals set. A key tool in this process is the local municipal waste prevention plan (PLP).

LOCAL WASTE PREVENTION PLANS

To promote the implementation of these local strategies, the Agency created the *Guide for the Preparation of Local Municipal Waste Prevention Plans,*[25] for the ARC, which it used to draw up one of the instruments included in PROGREMIC 2007–2012, within the waste prevention sub-programme.

Following this methodology, the first local waste prevention plans were put in place: in the city of Barcelona and the municipality of Tiana in 2010, in Pallars Sobirà in 2011 (the first county-wide plan), in Mataró in 2012, and in Arenys de Mar in 2018.

QUANTIFICATION OF PREVENTION

When these first plans were prepared, it became clear that it was important to set prevention goals deriving from the planned initiatives. From this process emerged the need to agree upon a common calculation methodology and terminology and to build a database of the results produced by initiatives in other regions as reference values. The aim of this was to collectively improve the definition of prevention on a local scale, while making it possible to compare different local strategies. As a response to this need, in 2013, the ARC asked BCNecologia to develop a support tool to calculate municipal waste prevention potential and goals. In the end, two different documents were created and published: the *Methodological Guide for Calculating Municipal Waste Prevention Potential and Goals,*[26] and the *Prevention Calculator.*[27]

It is worth nothing that quantifying prevention – in terms of both setting goals and assessing results – is a complex and relatively new requirement in waste management. Both the Guide and the Calculator were a first step in this direction and have been used widely for putting together local prevention plans in municipalities across Catalonia.

THE METHODOLOGICAL GUIDE FOR CALCULATING MUNICIPAL WASTE PREVENTION POTENTIAL AND GOALS

The guide includes recommendations regarding how to prepare the plan diagnosis with a view to obtaining certain basic parameters or data to be used to calculate potential and, later, goals. It

25 Waste Agency of Catalonia. *Guide for the Preparation of Local Municipal Waste Prevention Plans. Op. cit.*

26 Waste Agency of Catalonia. *Methodological Guide for Calculating Municipal Waste Prevention Potential and Goals. Op. cit.*

27 Waste Agency of Catalonia. *Prevention Calculator. Op.cit.*

also determines the calculation method or formula to use to establish the expected reduction potential and goals. In addition, it gathers data on various quantifiable initiatives, extracted from other experiences or studies (potential, goals, participation), and defines criteria to assess the qualitative impact of the reduction. Finally, it establishes the results indicators needed in the monitoring phase to calculate the real tons of waste saved and provides methodological indications for obtaining these values.

Food waste.
Picture: Marta Torrent

THE PREVENTION CALCULATOR

This is an online calculation tool (www.calculadoraprevencio.cat) that establishes the basic variables or data (through the entry of municipal data) for different initiatives, the reference waste reduction factors according to the type of initiative and for each waste stream, and the formulas that link these basic variables and reduction factors. It also calculates the amount of waste not generated.

Furthermore, it offers a summary table with the sum of the reductions according to waste stream and provides calculation formulas to determine the financial savings made by waste prevention through each municipality's management and the initial information (costs and municipal revenue).

Containers for second-hand clothes collection.
Picture: Paola de Grenet

COMMUNICATION OF WASTE PREVENTION

The Agency has also designed and developed waste prevention campaigns, though they are discussed in more detail in the chapter on waste management instruments. For example, in 2003, the 'Sant Andreu: Reduce Your Waste' campaign was launched in this district of Barcelona, with successful involvement from shops, organisations, schools and the public. In 2011, another campaign was launched for Mataró City Council, aimed at the general public, schools and municipal facilities. In Arenys de Mar, alongside the presentation of the municipality's Prevention Plan, various practical campaigns were carried out in 2018 to help residents and shops to reduce their packaging and food waste.

Conclusions

Prevention and preparing for reuse are two main areas of waste management strategies that, despite being high up the priority hierarchy, still tend to be neglected day to day in many municipalities.

Limited powers, or simply technical limitations, mean that, in cases like that of the Deposit-Return System (DRS), there is no point in implementing certain initiatives in small geographical areas. The fact that the collection service requires significant dedication and time from municipal technicians does not help the issue. This makes it even more urgent and useful to develop local assistance tools to find the options with the most prevention potential or with the most social impact.

Medium-term and long-term strategic planning thus becomes even more crucial, in order to drive effective, synergic local initiatives that lead to a real reduction in waste generation and a change in stakeholders' knowledge of and attitude towards prevention. With this in mind, the *Guide for the Preparation of Local Waste Prevention Plans*,[28] and the subsequent *Methodological Guide for Calculating Municipal Waste Prevention Potential and Goals*,[29] which led to the publication of the Calculator, were a real turning point for local and wider-area administrations in their prevention and PxR strategies.

Increasing awareness of the fight against food waste, a new understanding of rubbish tips as resource centres, and the need for public administrations to lead by example are just some of the catalysts helping to improve and spread these strategies.

28 Waste Agency of Catalonia. *Guide for the Preparation of Local Municipal Waste Prevention Plans. Op. cit.*

29 Waste Agency of Catalonia. *Methodological Guide for Calculating Municipal Waste Prevention Potential and Goals. Op. cit.*

WASTE MANAGEMENT PLANS AND PROGRAMMES

2021
2020
2019
2018
2017
2016
2015
2014
2013
2012
2011

2010

PGRUG 2010–2020
Galicia Urban Waste Management Programme

2009
2008

2007

PROGREMIC 2007–2012
Catalonia Municipal Waste Management Programme

2006
2005
2004
2003
2002
2001
2000

Over the past few decades, waste management has been a central part of environmental management. In the last ten years, perspectives have changed, and the focus has shifted from end-of-stream waste management to resource management with an emphasis on circularity and sustainability in general.

Waste management planning has clearly been influenced by the various directives and communications issued by the European Union. Furthermore, two highly relevant measures have been implemented in Catalonia: it became compulsory to collect organic waste separately (Law 6/1993, of 15 July, on waste regulation) and a landfill and waste incineration tax was passed, gradually increasing to reach almost €50/t in 2020.

On top of these incentives in Catalonia, recent times have been shaped by the definition of a waste management hierarchy, with the promotion of prevention and preparation for reuse above recycling and materials recovery, and by the transition from a linear to a circular economy (*COM 2014,*[30] *COM 2015,*[31] *EU Circular Economy Action Plan, 2020*). This transition has focused on reducing resource extraction and use, maximising resource circularity, working towards a decarbonised economy, protecting soil and creating jobs.

With these changes as a backdrop, BCNecologia has implemented two waste management plans (Catalonia 2007–2012 and Galicia 2010–2020), as well as participating in the development, design and redefinition of various studies associated with this planning process. A consistent systemic approach has been adopted in the definition of these strategies, both from a metabolic standpoint and from the perspective of the different needs, agents and keys to success involved in ensuring the goals set are achieved. BCNecologia's most significant projects include PROGREMIC 2007–2012, the Study on the Average Bin in Catalonia, the Study on Future Waste Tax Application Scenarios and the Galicia Urban Waste Management Programme (PGRUG) 2010–2020.

30 European Commission. *COM(2014) Towards a circular economy: A zero waste programme for Europe*. Brussels, European Commission, 2014.

31 European Commission. *COM(2015) Closing the loop - An EU action plan for the Circular Economy*. Brussels, European Commission, 2015.

PROGREMIC 2007–2012: A PROGRAMME FOR THE PEOPLE

In order to define the Catalonia Municipal Waste Management Programme (PROGREMIC 2007–2012), first, the waste management goals and criteria that would govern Catalonia in this new period were established. Specifically, these included goals to encourage sustainable consumption and to reduce waste generation; to minimise packaging and related waste, plastic bags (with specific targets) and paper; to implement the separate collection of organic waste all over Catalonia and treatment to make quality compost; to promote new reclamation strategies for paper, packaging, glass and other waste fractions, which were the subject of special attention; and to process residual waste before final disposal, among other aims.

The Programme also considered the technical, legal, organisational, economic and awareness-raising instruments needed to fulfil these new aims. In this area, care was taken to coordinate the Programme's contents with the Waste Treatment Infrastructure Sector Plan, which was drawn up and integrated in parallel, especially in terms of residual waste, organic waste, packaging and bulky waste.

In addition, the Programme incorporated a new perspective to be imposed on the usual implementation and monitoring of the waste hierarchy. This new approach was based on the crucial role people played in the decision-making and strategy-executing processes in the PROGREMIC programme, whether individually as generators of waste (as citizens) or within organisations that managed and made decisions regarding collection services, treatment plants, etc. A multidimensional matrix thus emerged, with three axes: waste management hierarchy, flow of resources and priorities for action (citizens, organisation and infrastructure).

At the same time, the Programme's Environmental Sustainability Report (ISA) was written up, mainly based on the assessment of the different management scenarios proposed through the SIMUR programme.

THE GALICIA URBAN WASTE MANAGEMENT PROGRAMME (PGRUG), ORGANIC WASTE AND IMPROVED TERRITORIAL ORGANISATION AS CORNERSTONES

Shortly afterwards, work began on the PGRUG 2010–2020, which updated a diagnosis of the state of urban waste management in Galicia made a few years before and developed new, strategic lines of action for Galicia, promoting new collection models and the inclusion of organic waste as a key element.

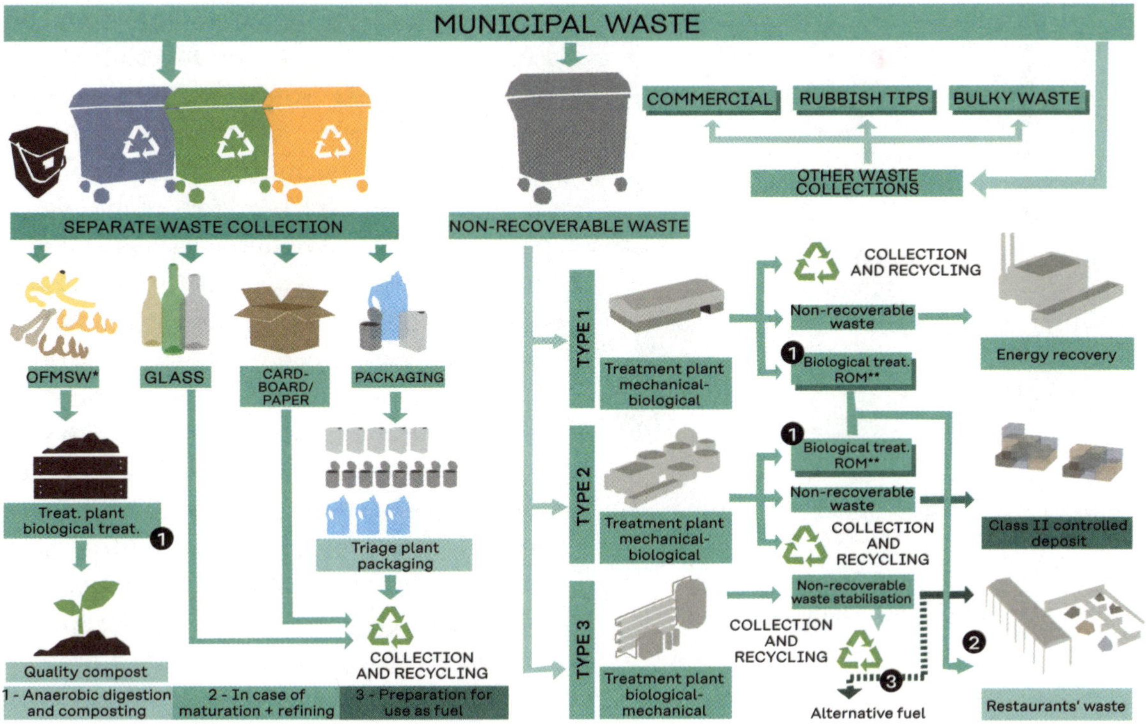

* Organic Fraction of Municipal Solid Waste
** Residual Organic Matter

Diagram of the municipal waste management in Catalonia.
Infrastructure Territorial Plan by Sectors 2007–2012.
Source: Scheme made by BCNecologia basing on PROGREMIC (ARC)

In parallel, the various documents needed in the PGRUG environmental assessment process were drawn up, in accordance with the guidelines established by the Autonomous Government of Galicia (Xunta). These included the Environmental Sustainability Report, the Response Document to Claims Made, the Introduction of Amendments to the PGRUG, and the Environmental Report.

OTHER INSTRUMENTS AS A CATALYST FOR IMPROVING WASTE MANAGEMENT MODELS

Generally, environmental policies include a mixture of complementary measures involving regulatory, economic, organisational and communication instruments. Together, they make up a puzzle in which every piece is essential in order to put to-

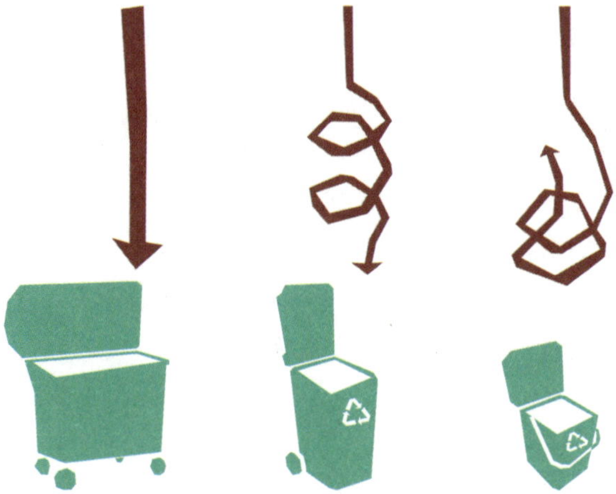

From a linear to a circular economy.
Source: BCNecologia

gether the picture we are aiming for: waste management that is as compatible as possible with the environmental hierarchy and principles of the circular economy. For these reasons, the Agency has also prioritised the study and definition of instruments that help to implement this planning strategy.

Economic instruments are especially significant, as they provide funds to pay for waste management initiatives and influence 'economic awareness'. In recent decades, even in the waste management sector, the use of economic instruments has become widespread. In 2004, Catalonia introduced a landfill tax (later extended to incineration), the funds from which are entirely dedicated to waste management initiatives. In particular, at least 50% of this income is required by law to be used for organic waste treatment. Two complementary studies on this tax were carried out, the first analysing its evolution and effectiveness, and the second exploring proposals and solutions for the future to improve the application of the tax and its distribution. The aim was to discourage the management strategies that recovered the least waste and to incentivise the ones that gathered the most waste, and of the best quality, for sorting. This way, enough income was generated to fund waste infrastructures and to provide financial support for local entities, which was used for specific purposes.

At the same time, the idea was for municipalities to plan their future strategies with the amounts to pay or receive in each scenario in mind, with enough time for those municipalities the furthest behind to adapt their strategies and establish a progressive tax model.

Conclusions

Good planning is essential to ensure waste prevention, sorting, recovery and other targets can be met.

The Agency's involvement in this area in various periods has made a real difference to the work carried out over recent years.

In all cases, great professionals have worked side by side in a participative environment that includes both stakeholders and experts in the debating and idea-forming processes. The result has been an enriching undertaking in which the ideas gathered and decisions made have led to the creation of practical yet ambitious documents.

It has been challenging to influence this high level of planning while combining the integration of more holistic, systemic goals with the use of practical tools that suit the reality of every context and time period and consider the host of technical, economic, organisation, communication and participation variables that make a waste programme viable. For instance, municipalities have been set a challenge for the first time that is undoubtedly tough, given their day-to-day activities: to strengthen local organisations with a view to moving towards achieving the targets set across the board by Europe.

This has led to progress in resource management in each of the territories affected and has greatly contributed to the knowledge acquired and generated by the Agency's technical team.

WASTE MANAGEMENT INSTRUMENTS

2021

2020

2019

2018

2017

2016
WASTE4THINK
H2020
Life Cycle Thinking

2015

2014

2013
MAGRAMA
Guide to implementing biowaste collection

2012

2011

2010

2009

2008
ARC
Guide to drawing up local prevention plans

2007

2006

2005

2004
SIMUR
Modelling waste management in the Barcelona Metropolitan Area

PREMIÀ DE MAR
Implementation campaign for organic waste collection

2003

2002

2001
BARCELONA
Implementation campaign for separate organic waste collection

2000

From its beginnings, in waste management and other areas, the Urban Ecology Agency of Barcelona has focused on the development of tools that help public administrations to define and apply strategies that make progress towards sustainability and, specifically, a circular economy. Within the framework of urban metabolism, a systemic approach has been key.

The viewpoint afforded by the field of ecology is part of the Agency's DNA and has permeated all of its activities, especially tasks related to urban metabolism and, in particular, those carried out by the Waste and Material Cycle Area. Clear examples of this are the development of the Urban Modelling System Applied to Waste (SIMUR), which assesses waste management models from a life cycle perspective, and the training and support given to councils and other local administrations regarding their waste model.

Other instruments, apart from the SIMUR, include the methodology designed to carry out organic waste collection or waste prevention campaigns, the ICT tools used as part of the Horizon 2020 Waste4Think and LIFE ReThinkWaste projects – which make the most of *big data* to improve both management and communication with users/generators – and the participation tools developed to reform the governance systems in place for diagnosing and defining street cleaning and municipal waste collection models.

Furthermore, to support public administrations in the process of designing and implementing their strategies, specific content and methodologies have been created to facilitate change and the transition to these new models. Throughout its years of activity, the work done by the Waste and Material Cycle Area of the Urban Ecology Agency of Barcelona has entailed putting on participation sessions to define roadmaps (alongside stakeholders, municipal technical staff and politicians), generating and promoting content on web portals, organising walking routes with service users, and much more.

ENVIRONMENTAL EDUCATION: A KEY ELEMENT FOR INDIVIDUAL AND COLLECTIVE CHANGE

One of the main sets of tools developed initially was that of environmental communication and education campaigns. This was one of the Agency's first commissions from Barcelona City Council, which, in 2001, was just starting to introduce the separate collection of organic waste in the city. In collaboration with the Ecology and Alternative Projects Centre (CEPA), an intensive campaign methodology was developed, with initiatives for the general public, schools, neighbourhood organisations, industries, etc. The main dissemination actions were accompanied by a

BARCELONA. SANT ANDREU, HORTA AND NOU BARRIS. 2001–2002. The Barni comic.
Campaign for the implementation of organic waste collection.
Source: BCNecologia and Albert Escoda

host of other activities: street cats taught children about various aspects of waste management, a comic told the story of Barni and his adventures with his friends, and a cartoon film was even made.

The first campaign was carried out in the neighbourhood of El Congrès, and 95% of the households surveyed declared that they had received the information put across. It was rolled out for over two years until it reached more than 125,000 households in the districts of Sant Andreu (where one of the city's first waste prevention campaigns took place), Nou Barris and Horta-Guinardó. All the campaigns were carried out in close collaboration with each neighbourhood's communication services and were met with support and excellent results.

SIMUR: A TOOL FOR THE DECISION-MAKING PROCESS

In these early years, the Agency also worked on the development of its own software, called SIMUR, the germ of which was the environmental impact analysis work done ad hoc for the Metropolitan Municipal Waste Management Programme (PMGRM) from 1997 to 2006. SIMUR models a particular municipality's waste management and generates an environmental analysis (mass balance, energy balance, emissions and costs). This way, results from different years can be compared, the municipality's overall progress can be determined, and results for possible new, alternative models can be calculated.

Its main characteristics are as follows:

- It is an innovative waste management tool.
- It can be applied to any waste management model, as it incorporates a variety of management options.
- It can evaluate a current management model using real data and identify management stages that could be modified for better environmental performance, as well as assessing the potential results.
- It can assess hypothetical management scenarios, incorporate standard data and design a future management model that takes all possible environmental advantages into account.

SIMUR has multiple functions:

- It generates an exhaustive analysis of the results of a waste management system in terms of mass balance, energy balance, environmental impacts and costs.
- It calculates indicators like the gross and net amounts of sorted waste, materials recovered, energy efficiency, greenhouse gas emissions, etc.
- It monitors any changes in the collection system.
- It compares different management systems with ease, thanks to a common analysis language and methodology.

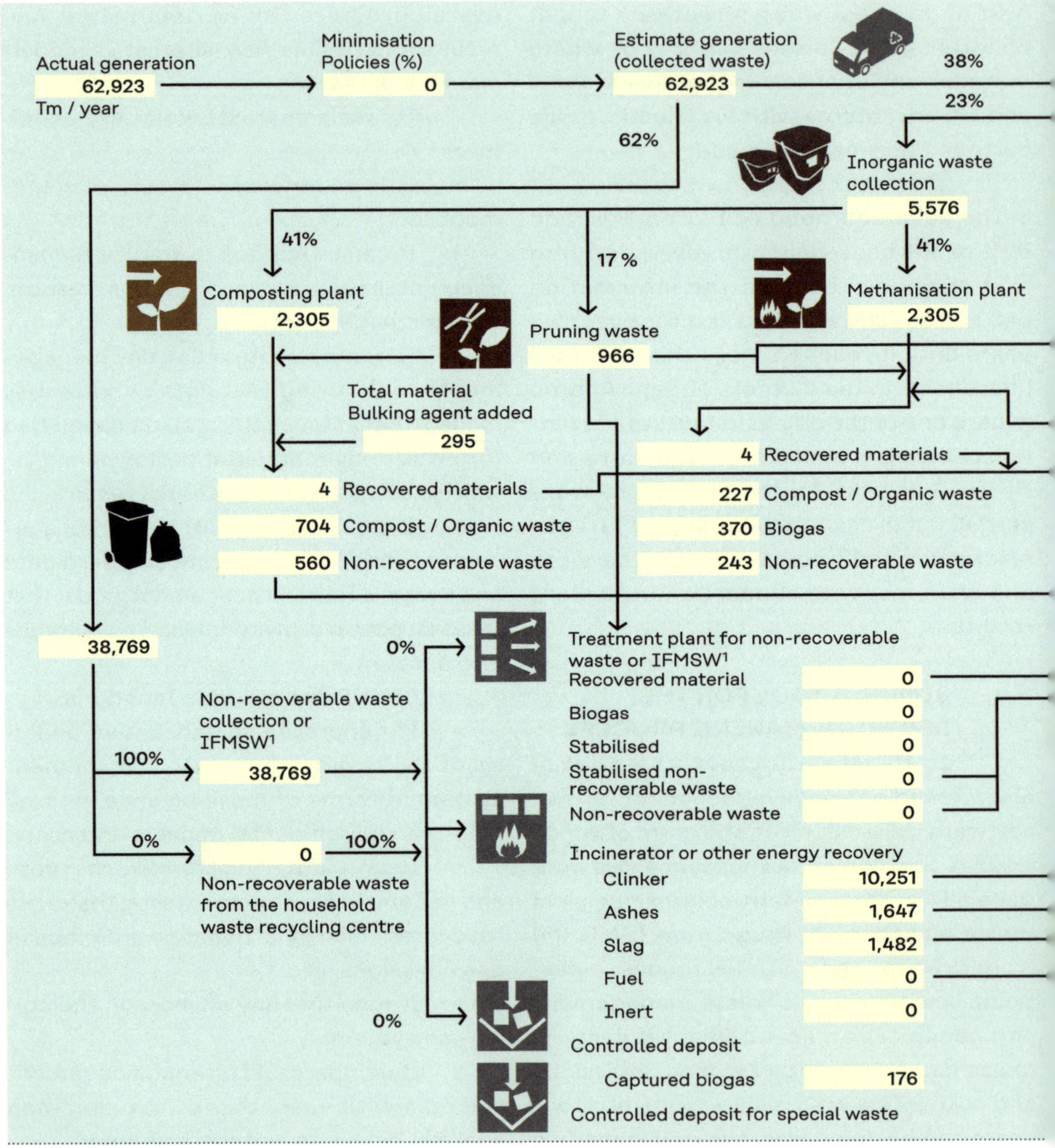

SIMUR. 2007. Diagram of the process of the Urban Waste Management Model Simulator process.
Main waste flows and indicators.
Source: BCNecologia

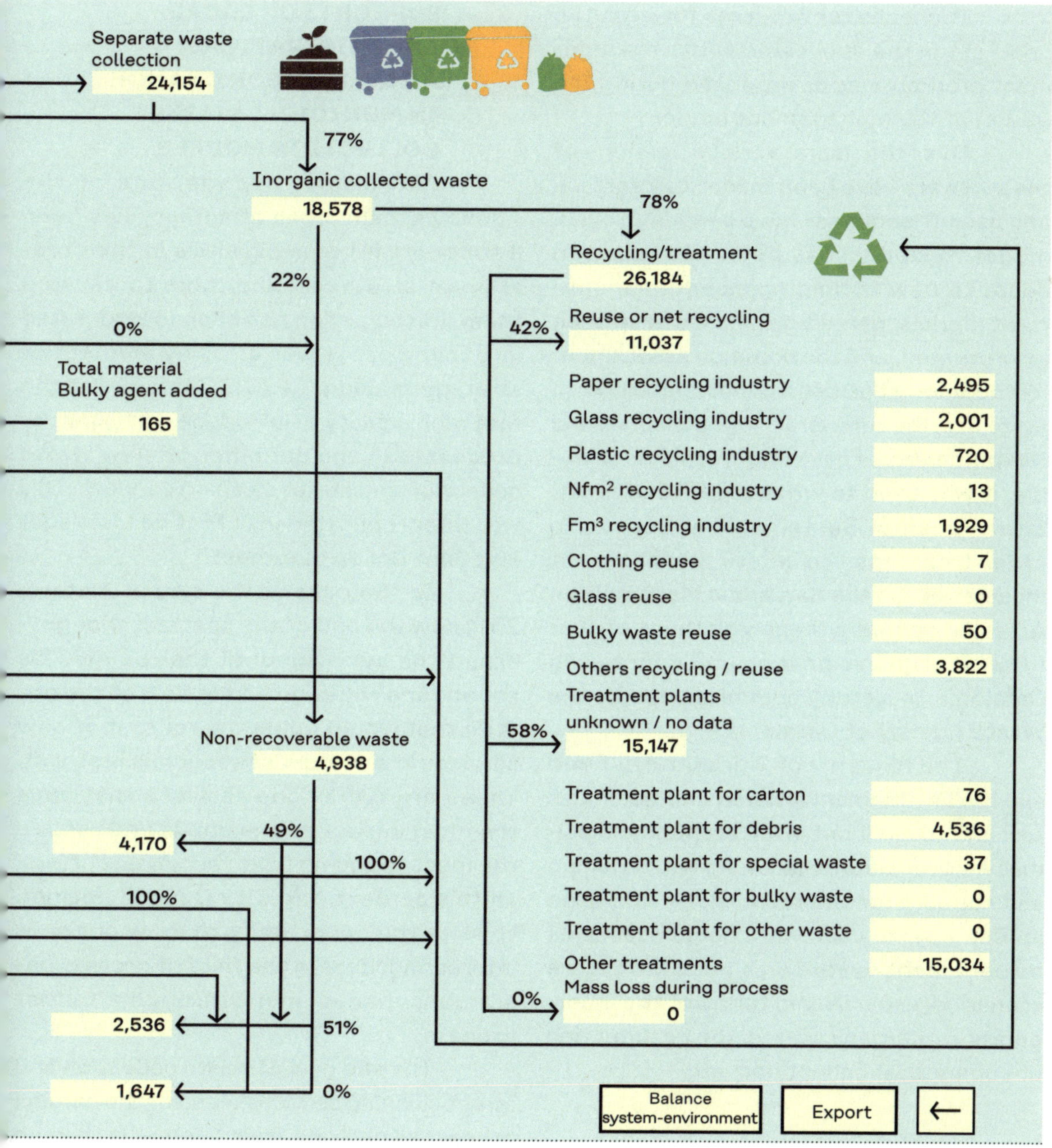

1 IFMSW: Inorganic Fraction of Municipal Solid Waste
2 Nfm: Non-Ferrous Metal
3 Fm: Ferrous Metal

- It checks for progress towards the goals set in the applicable waste management programmes or proposed during the design of the management model.

Over the years, various versions of the software have been made: its interface and user-friendliness have been improved, model flexibility has been increased to adapt to new technologies and management models, default databases have been incorporated, and the common assessment methodology has been consolidated. With every use, the software's functionalities and reference values have improved. For example, it was used to write the PROGREMIC Environmental Sustainability Report, in order to assess the waste management models used in the Barcelona Metropolitan Area and compare them with those of over fifty other municipalities and counties in Catalonia, in a study commissioned by the Waste Agency of Catalonia.

The Ministry of Agriculture, Food and the Environment showed interest in this tool and rolled it out in different municipalities all over Catalonia, along with training and support for the technicians who used it. This way, the software could assess its management systems or possible future scenarios, especially in terms of the incorporation of organic waste, the introduction of commercial collections, etc.

SUPPORT FOR LOCAL ADMINISTRATIONS: A CATALYST FOR CHANGE IN MUNICIPAL WASTE COLLECTION MODELS

In the last decade, one of the Agency's main areas of activity has been its support for municipalities in their creation of strategies and tools to develop them. Participation has been incorporated into many processes as a key element of strategy-making. In 2015, Mataró was the first municipality to introduce participatory processes in the definition of new waste collection and street cleaning services. This was later replicated in El Prat de Llobregat and Sant Boi de Llobregat.

In the case of the city of Mataró, 2014 saw the end of the contract that governed the services until that point. This called for a redesign and review of the criteria that would guide the roll-out of new services in a context of economic restraint. These are two of the services that have the most impact on the public and require the most spending from municipal coffers. In this context, the City Council decided to seize the opportunity to draw out new, interesting ideas in the field of professional public management through a tender process.

The end goal of waste collection and street cleaning services – and of the parallel processes deriving from them – is to keep

Participatory processes have been key in the definition of new waste collection and street cleaning services.
Picture: Shutterstock (blvdone)

the public space in excellent condition and to collect a large amount of high-quality waste sorted at the source, not to mention to encourage waste prevention as a priority strategy. The Council, the public (individuals and organisations) and businesses must all be involved in the process towards achieving these common goals. The public can become an active agent in these services – in terms of their own behaviour or encouraging good habits among neighbours – but the Administration must lead by example, facilitating coordination between the relevant departments, the circulation of information, and coordinated, agile decision-making.

STAKEHOLDERS' PARTICIPATION IN CHANGE AND THE DECISION-MAKING PROCESS FOR NEW COLLECTION MODELS

Within this frame of reference, in Mataró, the goal was to develop a new waste collection and street cleaning model with

MATARÓ. Street cleaning services.
Picture: Mataró City Council

a whole-city perspective. It needed to involve the public from the beginning, keep costs down, offer continual flexibility and improvements, ensure maximum resource efficiency, and adapt to the city's needs and changes. Another aim was to integrate environmental criteria and contractor co-responsibility with the implementation of a new kind of relationship between the Council, businesses and the public.

With all this in mind, a participatory methodology was developed to boost the public's knowledge, awareness and involvement in cleaning and waste collection in the city. BCNecologia worked in collaboration with Spora Sinergies, which designed how this process would be implemented alongside the City Council's Citizen Participation Service. Awareness of residents' main concerns was combined with data gathered in the technical report, so that the new services could fulfil both technical requirements and the needs expressed by the city's residents.

First, with a view to strengthening the technical analysis and supporting the decision-making process in the design of the new cleaning and collection services, a participatory diagnosis was made. This provided a much clearer, more comprehensive view of the aspects residents approved of and those that they would improve, in terms of both cleaning and waste collection. They highlighted over 2,000 different points in the city for special attention, for one reason or another.

In the second phase, feedback sessions were carried out to prioritise the aspects that concerned the public the most and basic criteria to govern the technical design and conditions of the new contract were established and reflected in the tender specifications as essential technical requirements.

Conclusions

One of the Agency's key areas of activity has been the development of tools that help to achieve waste prevention and sorting goals, especially those set for bodies with ultimate powers: local administrations. New governance models, in which environmental education and active participation from the public are essential for progress, have been one of the areas in which the Urban Ecology Agency of Barcelona has innovated and stood out.

Meanwhile, it is important to note SIMUR's potential in terms of decision-making, or simply understanding the environmental impact associated with any given model. SIMUR is a way of harmonising and simplifying the calculation of environmental impact from a life cycle perspective. Furthermore, it is a usable, friendly tool for technicians specialising in waste management, and probably one of the few that deals with municipal waste collection models in such detail. Indeed, it has been used to calculate some model results indicators, agreed upon by stakeholders, differentiating between gross and net amounts of sorted waste and identifying the first recycling destination.

All in all, the wide range of tools and projects developed by the Agency is a clear sign of the broad, systemic approach it has taken in resource management to work towards a circular economy.

BCNECOLOGIA: TWENTY YEARS OF MAKING CITIES MORE SUSTAINABLE

Salvador Rueda

'BCNecologia has envisioned and promoted links between ecology and urbanism, systemic thinking and cross-discipline work. The Agency, and especially Salvador Rueda, have maintained a key philosophy and theoretical framework: the superblock concept, and more broadly, the model of Barcelona as a compact, complex, Mediterranean city'.

BETTINA SCHAEFER
Architect. Public Space Project Coordinator 2002–2006.
BCNecologia.

BACKGROUND

The idea of creating a public institution like BCNecologia emerged in late 1980 – over forty years ago now – when preparations were being made for the first Urban Ecology Conference in Spain. The event took place in Sant Adrià de Besòs in February 1981, when I was at the head of the municipality's Environmental Department. Later, the year 1995 saw the publication of *Urban Ecology. Barcelona and its Metropolitan Region as Reference Points*,[32] a book that would mark the beginning of the Agency's theoretical journey.

When formalising the statutes for the new organisation in 2000, I decided to create a public consortium, rather than a private entity. Information tends to be an Achilles' heel for urban ecology projects, and the public sector could offer the databases needed for the purposes of an agency like BCNecologia and its work. The creation of the Urban Ecology Agency of Barcelona as a public consortium was made possible by Antoni Morral, the Environment Representative at Barcelona Provincial Council, and Xavier Casas, the First Deputy Mayor at Barcelona City Council.

THE CITY AS AN ECOSYSTEM

Ecology is the study of ecosystems. The Agency was founded on the scientific principles of academic ecology, which considers cities to be ecosystems.

Urban ecosystems are special systems – the most complex structures created by humankind – in which the main figures are people. In my eyes, the little progress made in the quest to find regularities that make urban ecology a science is related to the development of humankind's intentions. They create what we call culture – an information package that distinguishes humans from other species – and go beyond the intentions deriving from the information

32 Rueda, Salvador. *Ecologia urbana. Barcelona i la seva regió metropolitana com a referents*. Barcelona: Beta Editorial, 1995.

contained in the genetic package, which mainly focuses on survival. Part of the associations made between components of the urban system are connected to interests and power relations that change over time. That is why it is difficult to find certain regularities. Though BCNecologia has made steps to uncover regularities in urban systems, I am sure that the biggest step forward will come when someone defines the laws of power, just as progress has accelerated in the world of physics since the laws of thermodynamics were established. In fact, if power determines the behaviour of another person or thing, then power is to society what energy is to physics. Progress made in 'sociodynamics', which will likely become part of a general theory of urban complexity, must lead us to new scenarios with a greater capacity for foresight that will help us to redirect current uncertainties with a more scientific basis.

Despite the shortcomings of urban ecology in terms of specific knowledge of urban systems, the Agency has intentionally developed its work with a cross-discipline approach, which allows for the creation of comprehensive, systemic models, by using certain laws of nature and putting people at the heart of all proposals. Following these laws of nature leads to an approach that, by attempting to reduce the impacts and uncertainties caused by the functioning and organisation of urban systems, flies in the face of the status quo and capitalist principles, whose competitive strategy is largely based on growing consumption of natural resources and simplification of support systems.

OUR PROJECTS TO DATE

Within this context, BCNecologia has never allowed any natural or legal person to interfere in the development of the projects it has carried out over its twenty-year history. It has never been a cog in the machine of any institution, ideology or party. Or of any private interest. In most cases, BCNecologia's proposals have sought strategy and added value – through models for change and interventions that require little effort for major urban changes – by incorporating the aforementioned intentions and rejecting most projects put forward by organisations and companies with an 'orthodox' approach to reality, which is incompatible with urban ecology principles. This key part of the Agency's DNA has made us a leading, independent centre for research on the national and international scene and has pushed us to define a theoretical framework that has fuelled and been fuelled by a host of applied research projects. This work has given rise to a systemic approach to reality, a specific methodology, a broad suite of software, and a training programme that has offered practical experience (in real projects, where interns have been part of the Agency team) of the branches of urban planning and transformation in different cities and metropolises.

In recent years, after the financial crisis, contributions from the entities in the consortium have made up around 15% of BCNecologia's budget. The Agency has earned the rest of its income by working on urban ecology projects for cities all over the world.

I believe this was the smartest idea approved by some (but not all, unfortunately) of the political components of the consortium: they understood that the progress made in terms of theoretical, methodological and instrumental framework through BCNecologia's projects in other cities and with other institutions would provide a tried and tested basis for transforming the urban systems overseen by the organisations in the consortium. In other words, an outside party funded the applied research that would then be used in Barcelona.

the Urban Ecology Agency of Barcelona has always been a legal person with a wealth of knowledge and a team that, at different points in its history, has been made up of forty professionals from over fifteen academic disciplines working together with the integrated, holistic approach characteristic of urban ecology. The results produced in the vast majority of projects are down to excellent teamwork, with experts from more than ten academic specialities following a systemic, integrated model.

As an epilogue, I would like to offer a personal summary of some of the most iconic projects brought to life by the BCNecologia team, as they give an overview of the progress made in urban ecology as a discipline for the planning and transformation of urban systems.

The Agency's most comprehensive projects include the **strategic urban sustainability plans**, which provide an integrated blueprint of lines of action for each urban sector: urbanism, mobility, public space, housing, biodiversity, economic development, metabolism and social cohesion. These plans will likely replace the current general plans for urban planning in the near future. Perhaps one of the most complex plans put together by BCNecologia was the Revitalisation Plan for the Historic Centre of Quito. The starting conditions were so unfavourable that, at the beginning, it seemed almost impossible to design a plausible sustainability scenario. The result was a ray of hope for the regeneration of an area that was vulnerable in many ways: indeed, it was neglected, congested, polluted and unsafe. A similar proposal, but with a radically different starting point, was the Strategic Sustainability Plan for San Sebastián.

One day, around ten years ago now, the Head of Strategy for Telefónica in Catalonia came to see me. He asked if I could plan a sustainable city. I said I could plan a *more* sustainable one. 'And could you replicate it?', he asked. I said I had no idea how to. 'Well', he said, 'in China, 500 cities with more than a million inhabitants are set to be built in the coming years. Shall we make them sustainable?' After that conversation and finding out that the population of Africa would grow by around two billion in just three decades – and wondering how the cities to house these people would be planned, whether they would be unliveable and unsustainable like some cities today – we started to work on a methodology to replicate a sustainable city model. We created the **Ecosystemic Urbanism Certificate**, commissioned by the Ministry of Development. The Ministry named the document the *Guía Metodológica para los Sistemas de Auditoría, Certificación o Acreditación de la Calidad y Sostenibilidad en el Medio Urbano* (*Methodological Guide for Quality and Sustainability Auditing, Certification and Accreditation Systems in the Urban Environment*). The guide has become one of the key documents in the formulation of the Spanish urban agenda.

Over time, BCNecologia pieced together theoretical and methodological elements to create a new, comprehensive urban planning and transformation instrument[33] that could tackle the major challenges faced by cities in the early twenty-first century: **ecosystemic urbanism.**[34, 35, 36] This new urbanism is an instrument comprising fifteen principles 5 (see pages 34–35) that regenerates existing urban systems – an urgent task, as their organisation and way of functioning are at the root of the current unsustainable scenario – and designs new urban developments by fleshing out the urban model of a city that is compact in its morphology, complex in its organisation, metabolically efficient and socially cohesive. This model, which I proposed in the late 1980s, has been adopted by UN-Habitat and the Spanish Ministry for Transport and the Urban Agenda, as reflected in the new global and Spanish urban agendas.[37] The system of indicators assesses the degree to which each of the principles is fulfilled and evaluates the analysed or planned system's level of compactness, complexity, efficiency and cohesion. Basically, it indicates how sustainable an urban system is. The system of indicators was most recently used to analyse Ildefons Cerdà's nineteenth-century plan for Barcelona.[38] We simulated it as though it were implemented with current automotive, solar energy and other technologies, which enabled us to assess how ecological it would have been. We also simulated the plan in a superblock scenario.

33 Rueda, Salvador [*et al.*]. *Libro Verde de Sostenibilidad Urbana y Local en la Era de la Información. [Green Paper on Urban and Local Sustainability in the Information Age]*. Madrid: Ministry of Agriculture, Food and Environment. General Technical Secretariat. Publications Centre, 2012.

34 Rueda, Salvador. «El urbanismo ecosistémico» [Ecosystemic urbanism]. *Ciudad y territorio - Estudios Territoriales (CyTET)*, num. 202, («La Agenda Urbana Española»), p. 723–752, 2019.

35 Rueda, Salvador. *El urbanismo ecosistémico [Ecosystemic urbanism]*. Barcelona: Urban Ecology Agency of Barcelona, 2018.

36 Rueda [*et al.*]. *El urbanismo ecológico. Su aplicación en el diseño de un ecobarrio en Figueres. Op. cit.*

37 Rueda. *Barcelona, a compact and complex mediterranean city. A more sustainable vision for the future. Op. cit.*

38 Rueda, Salvador. *Regenerando el Plan Cerdà. De la manzana de Cerdà a las supermanzanas del urbanismo sistémico. [Regenerating the Cerdà Plan. From Cerdà's Block to the Ecosystemic Urbanism Superblock]*. Barcelona: Agbar, 2020.

Ecosystemic urbanism focuses on three levels: roofs, ground level and underground. This is the only way of including all the variables that must be planned. Each level must have enough room for the elements that constitute this new form of urbanism. The regulatory framework must be changed so that this new, sustainability-oriented approach to urban transformation becomes the standard and, ultimately, a legal requirement.

This type of urbanism is better known now that many architecture and engineering schools have included it in their syllabus. Referenced publications and lectures given all over the world have contributed to the concept's expansion. The *Charter for the Ecosystemic Planning of Cities and Metropolises*[39] was the last document the Agency published digitally. I wrote the first version, but noted urbanists have now participated in putting together some sections, so now it belongs to everyone. It aims to provide key methodological elements to be applied to any regeneration or new urban development process. The Charter is designed to be a practical document that makes the precepts included in the urban agenda a reality.

Superblocks[40, 41] were first proposed 33 years ago now, to make sure 75% of public space in Barcelona was quieter than 65 decibels – the upper limit of acceptable noise, exceeded by over 50% of the city at the time. To make sure the noise level on half of the city's streets was acceptable, the mobility model needed to be changed, as urban noise is mainly generated by motor vehicle traffic. In other words, the modal split had to be altered and public space normally dedicated to motorised mobility needed to be freed up for other urban uses and functions. The first superblock was implemented in the La Ribera neighbourhood in 1993. The next two were designed by BCNecologia as part of the Gràcia District Mobility Plan in 2005. In same year, the Agency formulated the Vitoria-Gasteiz Sustainable Mobility and Public Space Plan, which was based on superblocks. Other cities in Spain and further afield were given superblocks in the following years, including El

39 Rueda. *Carta para la planificación ecosistémica de ciudades y metrópolis. Op. cit.*

40 Rueda, Salvador. «Les superilles per al disseny de noves ciutats i la renovació de les existents: el cas de Barcelona». [Superblocks as a tool for new city planning and urban renewal: the case of Barcelona]. *Papers magazine: Regió Metropolitana de Barcelona: Territori, estratègies, planejament* («Nous reptes en la mobilitat quotidiana. Polítiques públiques per a un model més equitatiu i sostenible») [on line], num. 59, p. 78–93. Barcelona: Institut d'Estudis Regionals i Metropolitans de Barcelona, 2017.

Prat de Llobregat, Córdoba, A Coruña, San Sebastián, Quito, Buenos Aires... and Barcelona, in 2015. The superblock is an urban cell measuring 400x400 metres that calms traffic and can be applied to most urban fabrics with a wide range of morphologies. After almost thirty years in existence, superblocks have emerged as a basic element of mobility and public space models in any city. The superblock is the most efficient urban cell and frees up 70% of the public space in a city for citizens' uses and rights while reducing the number of vehicles on the road by less than 15%. The perimeter of each superblock makes up the network reserved for cars, as well as buses and bicycles if the street is wide enough. Meanwhile, pedestrians have priority in the spaces within the superblock, where the speed limit is set at 10 km/h. Cars cannot pass through them. At this speed, the streets become more like squares, where, as well as the right to movement (walking is a mode of transport), all other citizens' rights can be exercised, including leisure, exchange, culture and democratic expression. When this much space is freed up, the city can be renaturalised, cars can be replaced by vegetation, and a new urban green network can be created. Energy consumption, air pollution, greenhouse gas emissions and noise can be reduced, and 667 premature deaths in Barcelona can be avoided each year.[42] The superblock-based mobility plans for Vitoria-Gasteiz and the Catalan capital set a target percentage for motor vehicle reduction (26% and 21%, respectively) to remain below the agreed level of CO_2 emissions and under the air pollutant immission levels set by the EU.

This urban model has evolved and gone from being a cell to reduce noise in the public space to the basis for a mobility and public space model in any city. And this evolution is not over yet. One of the features of ecosystems is their scalability, so one might wonder what the smallest possible urban system looks like. We have discovered that the minimum urban ecosystem that integrates the fifteen principles of ecosystemic urbanism coincides with the characteristics of the superblock archetype, which makes this the

41 Rueda, Salvador [*et al.*]. «Superblocks for the Design of New Cities and Renovation of Existing Ones: Barcelona's Case». In: Nieuwenhuijsen, Mark; Khries, Haneen (eds.). *Integrating Human Health into Urban and Transport Planning*. (p. 135–153). Switzerland: Springer Nature, 2019.

42 Mueller, N. [*et al.*]. *Changing the Urban Design of Cities for Health. The Superblock Model. Environmental International.* Elsevier, Ltd., 2019. Several members of BCNecologia team participated in this research.

building block of the urban planning model,[43] acting like a fractal within urban systems.

In 2002, I was part of the Advisory Board for TMB (Barcelona Metropolitan Transport), and we were tasked with redesigning the **new bus network for Barcelona**. I believed the network should be orthogonal – the most efficient structure in urban systems – and should run along the perimeters of the superblocks in order to guarantee the new system's operational speed. Public transport is the fairest mode of transport, in terms of access to the city. For BCNecologia, it sits in second place in the hierarchy of modes of transport, and not third, like in most other sustainable urban mobility plans (PMUS). The basic components for the design were psychological: the average wait time needed to be around two minutes, as users' mental clock starts to tick from two minutes onwards (they do not feel like they are waiting when the wait is less than two minutes), and the maximum journey time needed to be under 35 minutes, because otherwise, people would choose another mode of transport (usually the car). With this new system, which has maintained the same number of buses, service frequency has been improved to around four minutes, with an average wait time of two minutes, across the network (down from an average frequency of nearly fifteen minutes). Thanks to the new network, 60% of Barcelona residents can get to any point in the municipality by bus in less than 35 minutes. Everyone has access to the same bus service, whether they live in the city centre or on the outskirts. Connectedness has also improved, and 99% of the population (30,000 more inhabitants) now live within 300 metres of a bus stop. A similar improvement has been made to connectivity: ten million hours of travel are saved each year. It is important to note that, though the network was designed in 2002, ten more years passed before the first five routes started to be implemented. The final push to launch the orthogonal network in Barcelona was given by the **new bus network in Vitoria-Gasteiz**, which was put into service overnight in October 2009 as part of the PMUS the Agency designed for

43 Rueda. *Carta para la planificación ecosistémica de ciudades y metrópolis. Op. cit.*

the Basque capital. The results were spectacular. By 2012, the number of public transport users had risen from 14 million to 24 million. In Barcelona, the number of people using the TMB bus service increased by 12% in just five months when the new orthogonal network was implemented.

BCNecologia has continued to redesign public transport networks in Córdoba, A Coruña, Ferrol and Quito. The project in the Ecuadorian capital was undoubtedly the most complex of them all, with a network of 3,300 buses (for comparison, the TMB fleet is made up of just over 800 vehicles), a metro system and urban settlements of various morphologies and typologies.

A turning point in the design of our **system of urban indicators** was the project commissioned by Seville City Council to flesh out the Special Sustainability Indicators Plan, which was included in the city's General Plan for Urban Planning (PGOU). This Special Plan was to inform all developments in the PGOU. For this reason, any aspects of the system that did not align with the Special Sustainability Indicators Plan had to be modified. This Special Plan was the Trojan horse that would make urban planning more sustainable. Including a Special Sustainability Indicators Plan, like the one designed by BCNecologia, in every PGOU would be a real coup for urban sustainability in our cities. Later on, the system of indicators was included in the PGOU for the cities of Vitoria-Gasteiz and Bilbao and in the Strategic Plan for San Sebastián.

Within this system, there are indicators that evaluate the **Public Space Liveability Index**. These are nine variables that determine the degree of comfort (noise, air quality and thermal comfort), attractiveness (proximity to basic services, diversity of legal persons and amount of urban greenery) and ergonomics (accessibility, space dedicated to cars and other uses, and building height to street width ratio) that control the area's other variables, much like the control exercised by natural ecosystems in their development towards maturity. As the ecosystem reaches the climax stage, it gains more control over factors like moisture, temperature and sunlight, thus increasing its biodiversity.

BCNecologia has developed the theoretical and instrumental framework to measure **urban complexity,** using information theory. To this end, a dictionary for reading the city was formulated. It contained over 2,000 ideograms – similar to Chinese or Japanese characters – that expressed the diversity of legal persons included in the Statistical Classification of Economic Activities in the European Community. This measurement reveals how mixed the uses of a certain area are, how information is organised in each urban fabric and the area's degree of centrality. An analysis of Barcelona's urban complexity justified the decision to make La Sagrera the city's next central station, over Sants, which was the option put forward by the old Ministry of Development.

Measuring urban complexity is especially important when comparing urban fabrics and territories, and when assessing the development of a single urban fabric over time.

Focusing on knowledge-dense activities within this measurement system can determine a city's level of **urban intelligence**, as these activities hold the useful information in urban systems.

The Agency was commissioned by the Barcelona Metropolitan Area (AMB) to put together a **Water Plan for the Barcelona Metropolitan Region (RMB)**. The aim was to establish the key elements in guaranteeing the water supply and its quality in a more sustainable way, with climate change in mind, while replenishing bodies of water. If the water quality improved sufficiently, people would no longer have to lug around large bottles of drinking water. Water is probably the most restricting factor on the organisation of the RMB. It is a fundamental aspect that defines its carrying capacity. Out of all the infrastructural proposals put forward – including using and replenishing the Besòs and Llobregat aquifers, reclaiming wastewater, desalinating water from the Llobregat River, changing the focal point for supply water treatment, and using the Abrera pipe intensively – I would like to highlight the proposal to transfer water from the Urgell Canal to the Llosa del Cavall reservoir (Cardener).

The project was designed to ensure a supply guarantee of over 95%. What could, or can, justify the transfer of water when it was not and is still not politically correct?

The Urgell Canal transports just over 600 hm^3 of water annually (yearly water consumption in the RMB is less than 600 hm^3) to irrigate 70,000 ha of land. This equates to 9,000 m^3/ha (rice can be grown with 11,000 m^3). An analysis of this wastage, carried out in collaboration with the Government of Catalonia's Department of Agriculture, Livestock and Fishing, concluded that between 80 and 120 hm^3 could be saved each year. The RMB needed an average of 20 hm^3 yearly to guarantee its water supply, though this figure fluctuated from year to year. At the same time, if required, up to 60 hm^3 of reclaimed water could be transferred from the El Prat de Llobregat waste water treatment plant to the Canal (water that was perfectly suitable for irrigation purposes). The Government of Catalonia rejected this proposal because it was 'politically incorrect' and opted to build a desalination plant in El Prat: a facility that, at full capacity, would consume as much energy as a new city with 250,000 inhabitants, like Badalona. It is no wonder that it is operating at the minimum possible capacity for maintenance purposes.

In the same vein, but on a different project, a comprehensive management solution was designed for natural and reclaimed water resources in the municipalities of Viladecans, Gavà and Castelldefels. It consisted of a synergistic combination of cutting-edge technologies, social initiatives and management strategies to facilitate internal **water self-sufficiency** (11 hm^3), on a sustainable basis, while promoting the replenishment of the Llobregat delta aquifers.

In 2009, Vitoria-Gasteiz tasked BCNecologia with formulating a Plan to Manage Energy and Combat Climate Change. The proposal created an **energy self-sufficiency scenario** for the city (excluding industry) and its *surrounding area*: in this case, the province of Araba. At the same time, a combination of energy consumption reduction initiatives, the use of renewable sources and CO_2 capture through carbon sinks resulted in a **carbon-neutral scenario**. The implementation of the Plan included the construction of a facility to use straw for energy. The significant investments made were wasted when the new People's Party government and Minister of Industry, Energy and Tourism, José Manuel Soria, changed the rules of the game. Sustainable energy management was tossed aside, and has still not fully recovered. A similar exercise was designed for San Sebastián, with a proposal that achieved energy self-sufficiency by using renewable energy and created a carbon-neutral scenario.

One of the systems designed by BCNecologia to achieve energy self-sufficiency in urban systems is the **Heating and Domestic Hot Water System (SCACS)**, which combines solar energy, seasonal thermal storage tanks and heat pumps. This system achieves energy self-sufficiency for heating and domestic hot water, with energy performance of between 600% and 800% (1 kWe of electricity gives 6–8 kWt of heat), while heat pump heating systems offer performance of between 150% (with conventional heat pumps) and 300% (with inverter heat pumps).

I led the formulation of the first **Catalonia Municipal Waste Management Programme** in 1993, and the first AMB Municipal Waste Management Plan in 1997. From the year 2000 onwards, BCNecologia was tasked with reviewing both of these plans and designing others for Galicia and various municipalities. The first plans contained a significant infrastructure component and set the management directions that have been followed ever since. The idea of closing material cycles is included in all plans designed by the Agency. These plans were therefore the first that would later give meaning to the proposals framed in the context of the circular economy. The subsequent plans focused on people and their behaviour as active agents in domestic waste management and the circular economy, as well as opening up lines of applied research within all waste flow management models in order to minimise, reuse and recycle waste.

To define **Barcelona's main green corridors**, BCNecologia developed a methodology that assessed each urban fabric's impedance (or resistance) to one of these corridors passing through the city without interruption. This methodology can be used to define urban planning strategies to reduce the high morphological and structural pressure indices of urban fabrics, to make progress in urban renaturalisation and, therefore, to reach the city's equilibrium point. The whole city's calibrated, corrected compactness was calculated in order to define Barcelona's green corridors.

The corridors proposed by the Agency are included in the Strategic Urban Greenery and Biodiversity Plan for Barcelona, and more could be added following the implementation of more superblocks in the city. A calculation of the calibrated, corrected compactness of the city after the application of superblocks shows that its urban fabrics' impedance is reduced, as 70% of the public space currently dedicated to motorised mobility is freed up.

One of the green corridors emerging from the implementation of superblocks stretches from the Besòs River to La Barceloneta beach, passing through five urban parks: Besòs River Park (Sant Adrià de Besòs), El Poblenou Central Park, El Nord Park, La Ciutadella Park and La Catalana Park. The axes that connect them are Carrer de Cristòbal de Moura, which is forty metres wide along some stretches, Carrer de Pere IV and Carrer dels Almogàvers, until it reaches Passeig de Lluís Companys. A footbridge would cross the Ronda Litoral ring road and join La Ciutadella Park to La Barceloneta.

The push to renaturalise the city also included a green roof project. Some of the green roofs suggested have now been made a reality.

The Biotop project aimed to **regenerate Barcelona's seabed** by creating a barrier made from rough material in the shape of a rocky reefs. The rough texture of the material creates a bigger surface area, thus encouraging marine life to thrive. The regeneration speed facilitated by this system in an area as damaged as the seabed off the Barcelona coast is significantly faster than it would be if nothing were done. But regenerating the seabed was not the project's only goal: the other, and the more significant justification for the proposal, was to turn the area from the breakwater to the mouth of the Besòs River (10 km^2) into the twelfth district of Barcelona (the eleventh being Sarajevo), similar in size to any other district in the city. This seaside district would host leisure functions and uses, including fishing, diving, water sports, food and drink, etc. It would regenerate and, if necessary, promote activity on the sea front. The creation of the seaside district – including its uses and services, like waste collection – would probably need to be governed by municipal by-laws. The proximity of such a large leisure area would also reduce the pressure on vulnerable, ecologically valuable areas like the Medes Islands and other protected coastal zones exerted by Barcelona residents who dive, fish and practise water sports.

Barcelona City Council has embarked on an iconic project known as the '**social superblock**'. The decentralised deployment of social services through territorial units of similar dimensions to superblocks would make the most of institutional resources, as well as efforts made by organisations and volunteers, to serve the people. The care programme for elderly people is especially noteworthy. A shortage of care homes for elderly people can be solved through home care provided by decentralised social services teams, located less than five minutes from anyone in this age group. Elderly people often do not want to go to a home, as they see it as a sign that they do not have long left to live. In fact, elderly people live an average of thirty months once they enter a care home. It can be unbearable to see fellow residents dying, reminding them that they could be next. With this project, they can live at home and go for a walk – with or without company – on the streets of their superblock. They can say hello to the neighbours they have known for years and go shopping in their usual shops, with the help of the City Council's social teams and volunteers, and with all the support that would be provided by a home. All in all, this is a project that, once again, puts people at the centre of the planning process.

BCNecologia was commissioned by Barcelona City Council to carry out multiple factor analysis work to determine the most efficient way to accommodate the decentralised social services teams, taking superblocks and other territorial and management variables into account.

By way of **conclusion**, I must say that we have had the privilege of working at the highest level and with new planning and management instruments on projects linked to strategic plans, urban planning, public space, mobility, economic development, biodiversity, energy, waste, water, housing and social cohesion. We have built a real institution to train new professionals and disseminated the knowledge we have acquired through nine books and over fifty articles in national and international journals. And all in twenty very fruitful years.

PUBLICATIONS

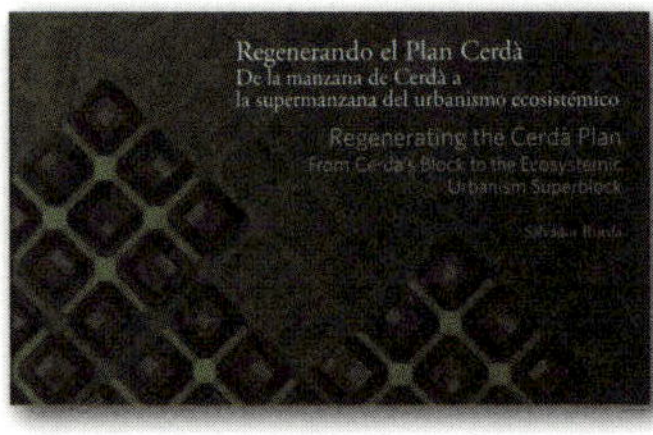

A

B

C

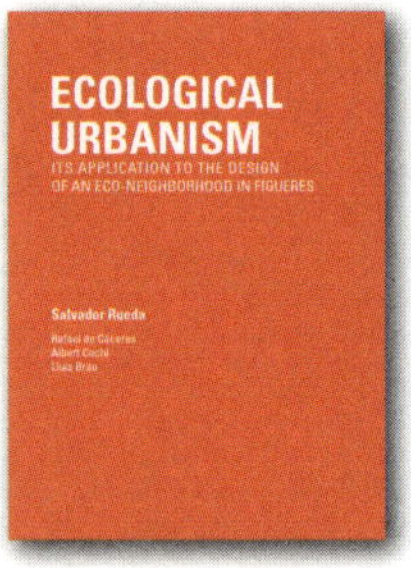

D

E

F

G

H

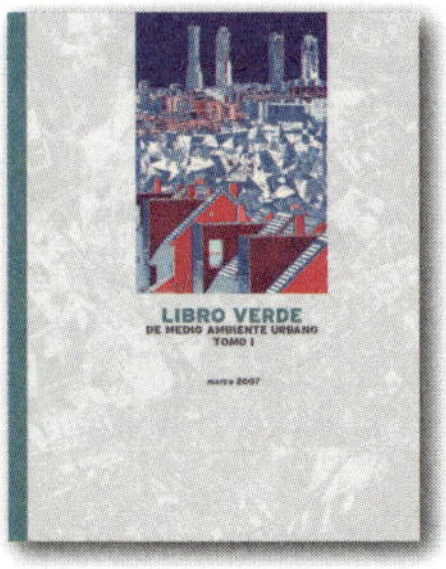

I (Vol. I)

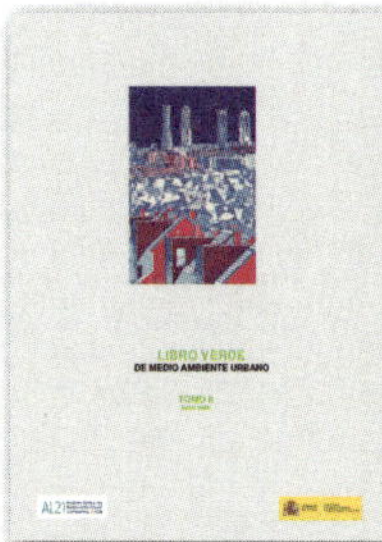

I (Vol II)

J

K

L

Publications in which BCNecologia has participated as an author

A **Rueda**, Salvador. *Regenerando el Plan Cerdà. De la manzana de Cerdà a la supermanzana del urbanismo ecosistémico*. Barcelona: Agbar, 2020.

B **Rueda**, Salvador. *Barcelona, ciudad mediterránea, compacta y compleja. Una visión de futuro más sostenible.* Barcelona: Ajuntament de Barcelona. Sector de Manteniment i Serveis. Direcció d'Educació Ambiental i Participació, 2007.

C **Rueda**, Salvador. *Barcelona, ciutat mediterrània, compacta i complexa. Una visió de futur més sostenible.* Barcelona: Ajuntament de Barcelona. Sector de Manteniment i Serveis. Direcció d'Educació Ambiental i Participació, 2002.

Publications in which BCNecologia has participated as a co-author

D **Rueda**, Salvador. [*et al.*] *Ecological Urbanism. Its application to the design of an eco-neighborhood in Figueres.* Barcelona: Agència d'Ecologia Urbana de Barcelona, 2014.

E **Rueda**, Salvador. [*et al.*] *Libro Verde de Sostenibilidad Urbana y Local en la Era de la Información*. Madrid: Ministerio de Agricultura, Alimentación y Medio Ambiente. Secretaría General Técnica. Centro de Publicaciones, 2012.

F **Rueda**, Salvador. *Guía Metodológica para los Sistemas de Auditoría, Certificación o Acreditación de la Calidad y Sostenibilidad en el Medio Urbano.* Madrid: Ministerio de Fomento. Dirección General de Arquitectura, Vivienda y Suelo. Secretaría General Técnica. Centro de Publicaciones, 2012.

G **Rueda**, Salvador. [*et al.*] *El urbanismo ecológico. Su aplicación en el diseño de un ecobarrio en Figueres*. Barcelona: Agència d'Ecologia Urbana de Barcelona, 2012.

H **Ministerio de Medio Ambiente, y Medio Rural y Marino**. Dirección General de Calidad y Evaluación Ambiental; Ministerio de Fomento. Secretaría de Estado de Vivienda y Actuaciones Urbanas. *Estrategia Española de Sostenibilidad Urbana (EESUL).* Madrid: Gobierno de España. Ministerio de Medio Ambiente, y Medio Rural y Marino, Ministerio de Fomento, 2011.

I **Rueda**, Salvador. [*et al.*] *Libro Verde de Medio Ambiente Urbano*. Madrid: Ministerio de Medio Ambiente y Medio Rural y Marino. Dirección General de Calidad y Evaluación Ambiental. (Vol. I, 2007; Vol. II, 2009).

J **Ministerio de Medio Ambiente; Red de Redes de Desarrollo Local Sostenible.** *Estrategia de Medio Ambiente Urbano (EMAU).* Madrid: Ministerio de Medio Ambiente. Secretaría General Técnica. Centro de Publicaciones, 2006.

Publications for internal use written by BCNecologia

K **Rueda**, Salvador. *Certificado del urbanismo ecosistémico*. Barcelona: Agència d'Ecologia Urbana de Barcelona, 2018.

L **Rueda**, Salvador. [*et al.*] *El urbanismo ecosistémico. Su aplicación en el diseño de un ecobarrio en Figueres*. Barcelona: Agència d'Ecologia Urbana de Barcelona, 2018.

BIBLIOGRAPHY

Barcelona City Council. *Guide to Living Terraces and Roofs*. Barcelona: Urban Ecology Area. Barcelona City Council, 2015.

CONAMA. *Global Change Spain 2020/50 Cities Programme. Towards a Pact between Spanish Cities Faced with Global Change.* Madrid: CONAMA, 2009.

European Commission. *COM(2014) Towards a circular economy: A zero waste programme for Europe*. Brussels, European Commission, 2014.

— *COM(2015) Closing the loop - An EU action plan for the Circular Economy.* Brussels, European Commission, 2015.

European Environment Agency. *Air quality in Europe – 2018 report.* Copenhagen: European Environment Agency, 2018.

Giró, Francesc. "Recollida selectiva: per a què?", in *Jornada Prevenció i Gestió de Residus Municipals: cap al 2030*, Barcelona, October 2, 2019.

Ministry of Agriculture, Food and Environment. *Guide to Implementing Separate Organic Waste Collection and Treatment. Municipal Management of Biodegradable Waste.* Madrid. Ministry of Agriculture, Food and Environment (MAGRAMA), 2013.

Ministry of Environment. Network of Local Sustainable Development Networks. *Urban Environment Strategy (EMAU).* Madrid: Ministry of the Environment. General Technical Secretariat. Publications Centre, 2006.

— *Spanish Strategy for Climate Change and Clean Energy, Horizon 2007–2012–2020.* Madrid: Ministry of Environment, 2007.

— *Spanish Sustainable Development Strategy (EEDS).* Madrid, Ministry of Environment, 2007.

Ministry of the Environment, Rural and Marine Affairs. General Directorate of Quality and Environmental Assessment; Ministry of Public Works and Transport. Secretariat of State's Housing and Urban Actions. *Spanish Urban and Local Sustainability Strategy (EESUL).* Madrid: Government of Spain: Ministry of the Environment, Rural and Marine Affairs, Ministry of Public Works and Transport, 2011.

Mueller, N. [*et al.*]. *Changing the Urban Design of Cities for Health. The Superblock Model. Environmental International.* Elsevier, Ltd., 2019. Several members of BCNecologia team participated in this research.

Rueda, Salvador. *Ecologia urbana. Barcelona i la seva regió metropolitana com a referents [Urban Ecology. Barcelona and its Metropolitan Region as Reference Points].* Barcelona: Beta Editorial, 1995.

— *Barcelona, a compact and complex mediterranean city. A more sustainable vision for the future*. Barcelona: Barcelona City Council. Maintenance and Services Sector. Environmental Education and Participation, 2007. (Catalan version, 2002; English/Spanish version, 2007).

— *Guía Metodológica para los Sistemas de Auditoría, Certificación o Acreditación de la Calidad y Sostenibilidad en el Medio Urbano [Methodological Guide for Quality and Sustainability Auditing, Certification and Accreditation in the Urban Environment].* Madrid: Ministry of Development. General Directorate for Architecture, Housing and Land. General Technical Secretariat. Publications Centre, 2012.

— «Les superilles per al disseny de noves ciutats i la renovació de les existents: el cas de Barcelona». [Superblocks as a tool for new city planning and urban renewal: the case of Barcelona]. *Papers magazine: Regió Metropolitana de Barcelona: Territori, estratègies, planejament* («Nous reptes en la mobilitat quotidiana. Polítiques públiques per a un model més equitatiu i sostenible») [on line], num. 59, p. 78–93. Barcelona: Barcelona Institute of Regional and Metropolitan Studies, 2017.

— *Carta para la planificación ecosistémica de ciudades y metrópolis [Charter for the Ecosystemic Planning of Cities and Metropolises]*, 2018. Digital edition available until 2019.

— *El urbanismo ecosistémico [Ecosystemic urbanism]*. Barcelona: Urban Ecology Agency of Barcelona, 2018.

— «El urbanismo ecosistémico» [Ecosystemic urbanism]. *Ciudad y territorio - Estudios Territoriales (CyTET)*, num. 202, («La Agenda Urbana Española»), p. 723–752, 2019.

— *Regenerando el Plan Cerdà. De la manzana de Cerdà a las supermanzanas del urbanismo sistémico. [Regenerating the Cerdà Plan. From Cerdà's Block to the Ecosystemic Urbanism Superblock].* Barcelona: Agbar, 2020.

Rueda, Salvador *[et al.]. El urbanismo ecológico. Su aplicación en el diseño de un ecobarrio en Figueres. [Ecological Urbanism. Its application in the design of an eco-neighbourhood in Figueres].* Barcelona: Urban Ecology Agency of Barcelona, 2012.

— *Libro Verde de Sostenibilidad Urbana y Local en la Era de la Información. [Green Paper on Urban and Local Sustainability in the Information Age].* Madrid: Ministry of Agriculture, Food and Environment. General Technical Secretariat. Publications Centre, 2012.

— «Superblocks for the Design of New Cities and Renovation of Existing Ones: Barcelona's Case». In: Nieuwenhuijsen, Mark; Khries, Haneen (eds.). *Integrating Human Health into Urban and Transport Planning*. (p. 135–153). Switzerland: Springer Nature, 2019.

UN. Kyoto Protocol - United Nations Framework Convention on Climate Change (United Nations, 1998).

— *2030 Agenda for Sustainable Development*. United Nations General Assembly, 25 September 2015.

Waste Agency of Catalonia. *Guide for the Preparation of Local Municipal Waste Prevention Plans*. Barcelona: Waste Agency of Catalonia (ARC), 2008.

— *Prevention Calculator*. Barcelona: Waste Agency of Catalonia (ARC), 2015. www.calculadoraprevencio.cat

— *Methodological Guide for Calculating Municipal Waste Prevention Potential and Goals*. Barcelona: Waste Agency of Catalonia (ARC), 2015.

Wurman, R. S.; Passonneau, J. R. *Urban Atlas: 20 American Cities*. Cambridge: MIT Press, 1966.

ABBREVIATIONS AND ACRONYMS

ACA Catalan Water Agency

AMB Barcelona Metropolitan Area

ARC Waste Agency of Catalonia

AUCORSA Autobuses de Córdoba, S.A.

BCNecologia Urban Ecology Agency of Barcelona

BEI Smart Electric Bus

BLUENE Interreg Med Programme Marine energy from the Mediterranean

BR Barcelona Regional. Agència de Desenvolupament Urbà, S.A.

BRT Bus Rapid Transit System

CAP Primary Healthcare Centre

CAT-MED MED European project. Change Mediterranean Metropolises Around Time

CCMRR Citizens' Centre for Waste Prevention and Recycling (BCNecologia)

CEA Environmental Studies Centre (Vitoria City Council)

CEPA Ecology and Alternative Projects Centre

CETICA The Eco-Techno-Logical City: New Construction Models for a Sustainable Urban Habitat

CHESS SETUP Horizon 2020 European Project. Combined Heat Supply System by using Solar Energy and heaT pUmPs

CIEMAT Centre for Energy, Environmental and Technological Research

CiU Convergència i Unió (political party)

CLABSA Clavegueram de Barcelona, S.A.

CONAMA National Environment Congress

CTIC Information and Communication Technology Centre

CTPA Corporation of Architectural Design Workshops

DFA Araba Provincial Council

DHW Domestic hot water

DMQ Metropolitan District of Quito

DNA Deoxyribonucleic Acid

DRS Deposit-Return System

DtD Door-to-door system

EDAR Waste Water Treatment Plant

EEDS Spanish Sustainable Development Strategy

EESUL Spanish Strategy on Local Urban Sustainability

ELECTRIFIC Horizon 2020 European Project. Smart, Green and Integrated Transport

ELIPTIC Horizon 2020 European Project. Electrification of Public Transport in Cities

EMAU Urban Environment Strategy

EMSHTR Metropolitan Water Services and Waste Treatment Entity

EMT Metropolitan Transport Authority

EPSA Andalusian Public Land Company

ERDF European Regional Development Fund

ETSAV Vallès School of Architecture (Polytechnic University of Catalonia)

EU European Union

EUSKOTREN Eusko Trenbideak. Ferrocarriles Vascos, S.A.

EV Electric Vehicle

Fm Ferrous Metal

GHG Greenhouse gas emissions

GIPSA Provincial Real Estate Management (Seville Provincial Council)

GIS Geographic Information Systems

IAG Overall Accessibility Index

ICAEN Catalan Energy Institute

ICTs Information and Communication Technologies

IFMSW Inorganic Fraction of Municipal Solid Waste

IGME Geological and Mining Institute of Spain

ISA Environmental Sustainability Report

ISGLOBAL Barcelona Global Health Institute

L/U Loading and Unloading

LEZ Low Emission Zone

LIMA Low Impact Mediterranean Architecture

LSA Large Seassonal Accumulator

MaaS Mobility as a Service

MAGRAMA Ministry of Agriculture, Food and the Environment

MSW Municipal Solid Waste

NDVI Normalized Difference Vegetation Index

Nfm Non-Ferrous Metal

OEUF Office de l'Éclectisme Urbain et Fonctionnel (Vancouver, Canada)

OFMSW Organic Fraction of Municipal Solid Waste

PAAC Pet Rescue Park

PAES Sustainable Energy Action Plan

PAMQA Air Quality Improvement Action Plan

PEIN Plan for Spaces of Natural Interest

PGOU General Plan for Urban Planning

PGRUG Galicia Urban Waste Management Programme

PHN Spanish National Water Plan

PLP Local Municipal Waste Prevention Plans

PMEP Mobility and the Public Space

PMGRM Metropolitan Municipal Waste Management Programme

PMSEP Mobility and the Public Space Plan

PMTPC A Coruña Metropolitan Public Transport Plan

PMU Urban Mobility Plan

PMUS Sustainable Urban Mobility Plan

PMV Personal Mobility Vehicles

POL Galician Coastal Management Plan

PRM Persons with Reduced Mobility

PRS Noise Reduction Plan

PSARU Urban Wastewater Treatment Plan

PVT Photovoltaic/thermal hybrid solar panels

R and PxR Reuse (R), repair and preparing for reuse (PxR)

RENFE National Network of Spanish Railways

REthinkWASTE LIFE European Project. Rethinking municipal tariff systems to improve urban waste governance

RMB Barcelona Metropolitan Region

ROM Residual Organic Material

RUS Residuos Urbanos Sólidos

SAD Home Care Service

SCACS Heating and Domestic Hot Water System

SCARP School of Community and Regional Planning (UBC)

SCEWC Smart City Expo World Congress

SCOW ENPI-CBCMED European Project. Selective Collection of the Organic Waste in tourist areas and valorisation in farm composting plants

SDGs Sustainable Development Goals

SEEDS Social Ecological Economic Development Studies

SIMUA Urban Water Information and Modelling System

SIMUE Ecosystemic Urbanism Information and Modelling System

SIMUQA Urban Air Quality Information and Modelling System

SIMUR Urban Waste Information and Modelling System

SME Small and medium-sized enterprise

SPA Special Protection Area for Wild Birds

SUBTRACT Interreg European Project. Sustainable Reuse Centres

THA Historical Territory of Araba

TMB Barcelona Metropolitan Transport

TUVISA Transportes Urbanos de Vitoria-Gasteiz, S.A.

UAB Universitat Autònoma de Barcelona

UBC University of British Columbia

UdC University of A Coruña

UFD Urban Freight Distribution

UIA Urban Innovative Actions

UIC International University of Catalonia

UN United Nations

UNESCO United Nations Educational, Scientific and Cultural Organization

UN-Habitat United Nations Human Settlements Programme

UPC Polytechnic University of Catalonia

VILAWATT European Project. Urban Innovative Actions

VIMCORSA Viviendas Municipales de Córdoba, S.A.

VIMED Viladecans Mediterrània

Waste4Think Horizon 2020 European Project. Moving towards life cycle thinking by integrating advanced waste management systems

WFD EU Water Framework Directive

WHO World Health Organisation

XVPCA Air Pollution Monitoring and Prevention Network

ZeEUS Zero Emission Urban Bus System

PROJECT TEAM

URBAN SUSTAINABILITY INDICATORS

METHODOLOGICAL GUIDE TO THE SYSTEM OF INDICATORS

→ Page 62

2007. Special urbanistic activity indicators plan in the new PGOU for Seville

Team: Salvador Rueda, Berta Cormenzana, David Andrés, Jennifer Coronado, Cynthia Echave, Manuel García, Cristian Gesell, Elisabet López, Julià Massó, Moisès Morató, Gemma Nohales, Adrià Ortiz, Joan Palou, Anabel Rubio, Mercè Taberna, Gemma Salvador, Mercedes Vidal, Marta Vila and Yuji Yoshimura.

Contributors: Albert Cuchí, Architect and Senior Lecturer at the Polytechnic University of Catalonia, and Jaume Terradas, Professor of Ecology at the Universitat Autònoma de Barcelona.

Bodies: Seville City Council. Urban Planning Department. Coordination: José Antonio García Cebrián and Josefa García-Jaén.

2010. CETICA. The Eco-Techno-Logical City: New Construction Models for a Sustainable Urban Habitat (2007–2010)

Team: Salvador Rueda, Francisco Cárdenas, Cynthia Echave, Marta Vila, Mercedes Vidal, Berta Cormenzana and Elisabet López.

Bodies: TECTUM Ingeniería. Coordination: Constantino Hurtado and Elena Prieto.

Ecosistema Urbano Arquitectos. Coordination: Belinda Tato.

Collaborating companies: Arcelor España (empresa líder del projecte); Acciona Infraestructuras; Gas Natural; Sistemas Avanzados de Tecnología; Grupo Temer; Grupo Ingeteam; Modultec Modular Systems; Ideas en Metal; Ecosistema Urbano Arquitectos; Tectum Ingeniería, and Asociación para la Promoción Técnica del Acero.

Collaborating research centres: LABEIN; Centro Tecnológico de Materiales; Fatronik; Fundación Centro Tecnológico de la Información y la Comunicación (CTIC); Centro de Investigaciones Energéticas, Medioambientales y Tecnológicas (CIEMAT); Universitat Politècnica de Catalunya; Centro Nacional de Energías Renovables; Universidad Pública de Navarra; Instituto Nacional del Carbón; Universidad de Oviedo; Fundación Agustín de Betancourt; Centro de Investigaciones Técnicas, and Universidad Politécnica de Madrid.

2012. Methodological Guide for Quality and Sustainability Auditing, Certification and Accreditation in the Urban Environment

Team: Salvador Rueda, Francisco Cárdenas, Berta Cormenzana, Mercedes Vidal, Jordi Abadal, David Andrés, Vanesa Benítez, Gabriela Berrocal, Marta Blanco, Elisenda Comas, Cristina Cosma, Cynthia Echave, Manuel García, Cristian Gesell, Elisabet López, Montse Masanas, Moisès Morató, Marta Pascual, Carlos Sánchez, Ferran Sanchis and Marta Vila.

Bodies: commissioned by the General Directorate of Land and Urban Policies. Directorate-General for Land and Urban Policies. Ministry of Development. Government of Spain.

Coordination: María Dolores Aguado. Technical team: Luis Miguel Rodríguez and Eduardo de Santiago.

APPLYING THE SYSTEM OF INDICATORS TO REGIONS AND CITIES

→ Page 72

2007. Sustainability Strategy for Donostia-San Sebastián

Team: Salvador Rueda, Elisabet López, Mercedes Vidal, David Andrés, Anna Bacardit, Marta Blanco, Berta Cormenzana, Jennifer Coronado, Anabela Fernandes, Manuel García, Cristian Gesell, Susana Gomes, Roser Masjuan, Carmen Maté, Moisès Morató, Gemma Nohales, Adrià Ortiz, Albert Punsola and Ferran Sanchis.

Bodies: San Sebastián City Council.

2008. Special Environmental Sustainability Indicators Plan for the neighbourhood of Altza (San Sebastián)

Team: Salvador Rueda, Elisabet López, Mercedes Vidal, David Andrés, Cristian Gesell, Susana Gomes, Adrià Ortiz, Gemma Salvador, Ferran Sanchis and Lüder Thienken.

Bodies: San Sebastián City Council.

2009. Vitoria-Gasteiz Urban Sustainability Indicators Plan

Team: Salvador Rueda, Berta Cormenzana, Carmen Maté, Jordi Abadal, David Andrés, Marta Blanco, Cynthia Echave, Manuel García, Cristian Gesell, Árua Ibrahim, Elisabet López, Montse Masanas, Marta Pascual, Xavi Pont, Ferran Sanchis, Mercedes Vidal and Marta Vila.

Bodies: Vitoria-Gasteiz City Council. Environment Department. Coordination: Miguel Virizuela, Andrés Alonso, Alfredo Bengoa, Juan Carlos Escudero and Luis Mendizábal.

2011. Instruments for dynamic territorial management and the application of the Coastal Management Plan (POL)

Team: Salvador Rueda, Francisco Cárdenas, Annabel Subías, Marta Blanco, José Cárdenas, Manuel García, Elisabet López, Montse Masanas, Alba Miró, Mariona Morera, Norma Rey and Marta Vila.

Bodies: Autonomous Government of Galicia. Eixoecologia (Atlantic Axis urban ecology agency) Coordination: Manuel Borobio, Melania Payán, Concha Alonso, José Turrado and Nacho Varela.

2013. Measurement of urban sustainability in Bilbao and its neighbourhoods

Team: Salvador Rueda, Berta Cormenzana, Elisabet López, Mercedes Vidal, Moisès Morató, Jordi Abadal, David Andrés, Marta Blanco, Cristina Cosma, Cynthia Echave, Manuel García, Cristian Gesell, Jesús Pla, Norma Rey and Ferran Sanchis.

Bodies: Bilbao City Council. Office of the General Plan for Urban Planning. Coordination: Mauro José Valdivielso and Susana Ruiz.

2019. Analysis and creation of urban planning indicators in Sant Feliu de Llobregat

Team: Salvador Rueda, Berta Cormenzana, Natalia Alvaredo, Andrea Cappai, Neus Ayza, Cynthia Echave, Erundina González, Elisabet López, Gemma Mas and Carolina Mejías.

Bodies: Sant Feliu de Llobregat City Council. Technical Office for Moving the Railway Underground. Urban Transformation. Coordination: Albert Ferrer.

APPLYING THE SYSTEM OF INDICATORS TO URBAN PROJECTS

→ Page 88

2008. Consultation for the implementation of environmental sustainability indicators in sectors SUS-DBP-03 and SUS-DBP-04, Cortijo de Cuarto, as part of the General Plan for Urban Planning for Seville

Team: Salvador Rueda, Berta Cormenzana, Cynthia Echave, David Andrés, Anna Bacardit, Jennifer Coronado, Manuel García, Elisabet López, Moisès Morató, María Salas Mendoza, Sergio Rodríguez, Gemma Salvador, Ferran Sanchis, Pablo Sendra, Manuel Sierra, Mercedes Vidal and Marta Vila.

Bodies: EPSA (Andalusian Public Land Company). Autonomous Community of Andalusia.

GIPSA (Provincial Real Estate Management). Seville Provincial Council.

2010. Formulation of the criteria for urban planning for the Llevant Sector in Figueres

Team: Salvador Rueda, Cynthia Echave, Berta Cormenzana, Jordi Abadal, Marta Blanco, Francisco Cárdenas, Cristina Cosma, David Andrés, Manuel García, Cristian Gesell, Alice Lancien, Montse Masanas, Carmen Maté, Moisès Morató, Gemma Nohales, Marta Pascual, Joan Palou, Carlos Sánchez, Ferran Sanchis, Laura Silva, Marta Vila, Mercedes Vidal and Núria Vilajuana.

Bodies: Codirection: Albert Cuchí (Escola Tècnica Superior d'Arquitectura del Vallès - ETSAV, UPC), Rafael de Cáceres (Estudi d'Arquitectura), Lluís Brau (Nova Gestió, urbanisme i arquitectura).

Government of Catalonia. Environment and Housing Department. Housing Department

Figueres City Council.

Contributors: ETSAV (Fabián López, Gerardo Wadel, Kim Arcas, Marina Casals and David Motos); Estudi d'Arquitectura Rafael de Cáceres (Xavier de Cáceres, Albert Aragall and Silvia Necchi); Nova Gestió, urbanisme i arquitectura (Manuel Fernández and Andrea Fernàndez).

2010. Sustainability audit of the study on urban regeneration alternatives for the Plaza de Santa Bárbara area (Vitoria-Gasteiz)

Team: Salvador Rueda, Berta Cormenzana, Carmen Maté, Jordi Abadal, David Andrés, Marta Blanco, Cristina Cosma, Cynthia Echave, Ferran Sanchis, Manuel García, Cristian Gesell, Elisabet López, Montse Masanas, Alba Meya, Marta Pascual, Carlos Sánchez and Mercedes Vidal.

Bodies: Vitoria-Gasteiz City Council. Urban Planning Department. Coordination: Ana Oregi.

2010. Sustainability audit of the study on urban regeneration alternatives for the Los Herrán area (Vitoria-Gasteiz)

Team: Salvador Rueda, Berta Cormenzana, Carmen Maté, Jordi Abadal, David Andrés, Marta Blanco, Cristina Cosma, Cynthia Echave, Ferran Sanchis, Manuel García, Cristian Gesell, Elisabet López, Montse Masanas, Alba Meya, Marta Pascual, Carlos Sánchez and Mercedes Vidal.

Bodies: Vitoria-Gasteiz City Council. Urban Planning Department. Coordination: Ana Oregi.

2012. Master Plan for Fonsès Eco-neighbourhood (Villeneuve-Tolosane, France)

Team: Salvador Rueda, Cynthia Echave, Jordi Abadal, Berta Cormenzana, Cristina Cosma, Cristian Gesell, Carmen Maté, Moisès Morató, Ferran Sanchis and Marta Vila.

Bodies: Editorial team: Jornet-Llop-Pastor SLP, Arquitectes (Sebastià Jornet, Carles Llop and Joan Enric Pastor i Fernández) and Forgas Arquitectes SLP (Joan Forgas and Dolors Ylla-Català).

Contributors: Anjoyi Beltrando, Arquitectes (Tomoko Anjoyi and Yannick Beltrando); Factors de Paisatge (Manel Colomines and Camila Acosta); Dopec SL BET (Norbert Torres, Juan Cayuela and Narcís Julià); Intra SL (Jordi Parés, Albert Oromí and Xavier Bach), and Promo Assessors Consultors, SAP (Miquel Morell and Agustí Jover).

2017. Ecosystemic report. Review of indicators of the existing UBC

Campus fabric (Vancouver, Canada)

Team: Salvador Rueda, Berta Cormenzana, Cynthia Echave, Asier Eguilaz, Elisabet López and Ferran Sanchis.

Bodies: Coordination: Daniel Pearl. Associate Architect, Co-founder of OEUF (Office de l'Éclectisme Urbain et Fonctionnel).

2018. Stadium Road Neighbourhood. Report 2 Comparative analysis of two options (Vancouver, Canada)

Team: Salvador Rueda, Berta Cormenzana, Natalia Alvaredo, Neus Ayza, Cynthia Echave, Asier Eguilaz and Elisabet López.

Bodies: Coordination: Daniel Pearl. Associate Architect, Co-founder of OEUF (Office de l'Éclectisme Urbain et Fonctionnel).

AUTOMATION TOOLS

→ Page 100

2009. SIMUA. Urban Water Information and Modelling System

Team: Salvador Rueda, Manuel García, Carlos Sánchez, Sofía Nadime and Greta Gogiel.

Bodies: Urban Ecology Agency of Barcelona.

2010. SIMUQA. Urban Air Quality Information and Modelling System

Team: Salvador Rueda, Francisco Cárdenas, David Andrés and Ferran Fàbregas.

Bodies: Urban Ecology Agency of Barcelona.

2012. SIMUR. Urban Waste Information and Modelling System. User manual

Team: Salvador Rueda, Marta Vila, Gemma Nohales and Miguel Ángel Pérez.

Bodies: Urban Ecology Agency of Barcelona.

2015. Methodological Guide for Calculating Municipal Waste Prevention Potential and Goals.

Team: Salvador Rueda, Marta Vila, Jordi Abadal, Montse Masanas, Gemma Nohales and Laia Riera.

Bodies: Waste Agency of Catalonia (ARC).

Team: Alfred Vara and Elena Bagaria.

2015. SIMUE. Ecosystemic Urbanism Information and Modelling System. Application of Ecosystemic Urbanism Certificate indicators. User manual.

Team: Salvador Rueda and Berta Cormenzana.

Bodies: Urban Ecology Agency of Barcelona.

2019. LUPA

Team: Salvador Rueda and Berta Cormenzana.

Bodies: Urban Ecology Agency of Barcelona.

URBAN REGENERATION STRATEGIES

BARCELONA'S SUPERBLOCKS: THE BASIC UNIT OF ECOSYSTEMIC URBANISM

→ Page 118

2005. Pilot superblocks in Vila de Gràcia

Team: Salvador Rueda, Bettina Schaefer, Francesc Magrinyà, Francisco Cárdenas, Julià Massó, Jordi Selfa, Josep López, Robert Colombo, Ana Jacas, Moisès Morató, Sergio Oliete, Adrià Ortiz, Joan Palou, Ona Riera, Alberto Rodríguez, Jordi Romero, Anabel Rubio and Núria Vilajuana.

2006. Superblock study in the district of Sants-Montjuïc

Team: Salvador Rueda, Bettina Schaefer, Elisabet López, Adrià Ortiz, Berta Cormenzana, Cynthia Echave, Manuel García, Cristian Gesell, Irene Luna, Julià Massó, Moisès Morató, Jennifer Ortega, Ona Riera, Anabel Rubio, Gemma Salvador, Mercè Taberna and Núria Vilajuana.

2012. Superblock study in the district of Sarrià-Sant Gervasi

Team: Salvador Rueda, Cynthia Echave, Jordi Abadal, David Andrés, Berta Cormenzana, Cristian Gesell, Erundina González, Antonio Herrero, Elisabet López, Montserrat Luque, Moisès Morató, Xavier Pont, Carmen Maté, Norma Rey, Ferran Sanchis, Annabel Subías, Mercedes Vidal and Marta Vila.

2013. Superblock plan in the district of Les Corts

Team: Salvador Rueda, Cynthia Echave, Jordi Abadal, David Andrés, Berta Cormenzana, Cristina Cosma, Cristian Gesell, Elisabet López, Xavier Pont, Norma Rey, Ferran Sanchis, Annabel Subías, Mercedes Vidal, Marta Vila and Verónica Villalba.

2014. Diagnosis and proposals. 'Promoting superblocks' Programme

Team: Salvador Rueda, Cynthia Echave, Jordi Abadal, David Andrés, Berta Cormenzana, Alessandra Curreli, Cristian Gesell, Erundina González, Elisabet López, Carmen Maté, Moisès Morató, Joan Palou, Xavier Pont, Norma Rey, Ona Riera, Ferran Sanchis, Annabel Subías, Mercedes Vidal and Marta Vila.

2014. Superblock plan in the district of Sant Martí

Team: Salvador Rueda, Cynthia Echave, Berta Cormenzana, Jordi Abadal, David Andrés, Irene Capdevila, Alessandra Curreli, Linda Danefelde, Asier Eguilaz, Cristian Gesell, Agnese Jenina, Elisabet López, Moisès Morató, Xavier Pont, Ona Riera, Martín Sabbatini, Ferran Sanchis, Annabel Subías, Arnolds Timofejevs and Simone Trevisan.

2016. Pilot Superblock in Poblenou

Team: Salvador Rueda, Berta Cormenzana, David Andrés, Neus Ayza, Asier Eguilaz, Erundina González, Elisabet López, Ona Riera and Ferran Sanchis.

2016–2020. Analysis of indicators in the pilot areas

Team: Salvador Rueda, Berta Cormenzana, Cynthia Echave, Natalia Alvaredo, David Andrés, Irene Capdevila, Erundina González, Elisabet López, Norma Rey,

Ona Riera, Ferran Sanchis and Annabel Subías.

2019. Social superblocks

Team: Salvador Rueda, Berta Cormenzana, Natalia Alvaredo and Mercedes Vidal.

Bodies:
Barcelona City Council. Barcelona Mobility Department (2012–2020); Barcelona Environmental Services Department (2003–2006); Gràcia District (2003–2007); Sants-Montjuïc District (2004–2005); Sarrià-Sant Gervasi District (2012); Les Corts District (2012–2013); Barcelona d'Infraestructures Municipals SA (2013); Sant Martí District (2014–2015); Urban Planning Department. Urban Habitat (2011–2015); Barcelona Urban Ecology and Mobility Area (2015–2020); Barcelona Social Rights Area (2019–2020).

SUPERBLOCKS IN THE BASQUE COUNTRY

→ Page 128

2007. Strategic Sustainability Plan for Donostia-San Sebastián

Team: Salvador Rueda, Elisabet López, Mercedes Vidal, David Andrés, Anna Bacardit, Marta Blanco, Berta Cormenzana, Jennifer Coronado, Anabela Fernandes, Manuel García, Cristian Gesell, Susana Gomes, Roser Masjuan, Carmen Maté, Moisès Morató, Gemma Nohales, Adrià Ortiz, Albert Punsola and Ferran Sanchis.

Bodies: San Sebastián City Council.

2010. 'Central Superblock'. Pilot Area Implementation Study. Vitoria-Gasteiz Sustainable Mobility and Public Space Plan

Team: Salvador Rueda, Cynthia Echave, Carmen Maté, David Andrés, Berta Cormenzana, Cristina Cosma, Cristian Gesell, Árua Ibrahim, Roser Masjuan, Juan Pablo Olavarrieta, Joan Palou, Xavier Pont, Ferran Sanchis and Mercedes Vidal.

Bodies: Vitoria-Gasteiz City Council. Environment Department.

Management: Miguel Virizuela and Mónica Ibarrondo.

Coordination: Juan Carlos Escudero.

Contributors: Eduardo Rojo, Marian Mesanza, Luis Mendizábal and Asier Sarasua.

2010. Plan to Combat Climate Change in Vitoria-Gasteiz (2010–2020)

Team: Salvador Rueda, David Andrés, Carmen Maté, Jordi Abadal, Marta Blanco, Edaimon DeJuan, Manuel García, Árua Ibrahim, Montse Masanas, Roser Masjuan, Moisès Morató, Gemma Nohales, Marta Pascual, Carlos Sánchez and Marta Vila.

Bodies: Vitoria-Gasteiz City Council. Environment Department. Institutional leadership: Miguel Virizuela and Andrés Alonso.

Coordination: Iñaki Arriba.

Contributors: Eduardo Rojo, Marian Mesanza, Luis Mendizábal and Asier Sarasua.

2012. Superblock Master Plan in Vitoria-Gasteiz Mobility and Public Space Plan

Team: Salvador Rueda, Cynthia Echave, Carmen Maté, Jordi Abadal, David Andrés, Berta Cormenzana, Cristina Cosma, Ferran Fàbregas, Cristian Gesell, Erundina González, Elisabet López, Juan Pablo Olivarreta, Xavier Pont, Ferran Sanchis and Mercedes Vidal.

Special contribution: Rafael de Cáceres.

Bodies: Vitoria-Gasteiz City Council. Environment Department. Management: Miguel Virizuela and Mónica Ibarrondo.

Coordination: Juan Carlos Escudero and Eduardo Rojo.

2015. Urban Feasibility Analysis for the Application of the Superblock Model in Bilbao

Team: Salvador Rueda, Cynthia Echave, Berta Cormenzana, Asier Eguilaz, Erundina González, Ona Riera and Sascha Huditz.

Bodies: Bilbao City Council. Urban Planning Area.

SUPERBLOCKS AROUND THE WORLD

→ Page 142

2010. CAT-MED. Change Mediterranean Metropolises Around Time

Team: Salvador Rueda, Francisco Cárdenas and Mercedes Vidal.

Bodies: Leader: OMAU (Urban Environment Observatory of Malaga City Council). Team: Pedro Marín, Sandra Marín and Rafael Báez.

Project partners: FIVEC (Valencia City Council Foundation for Urban Innovation and the Knowledge Society); Seville City Council (Seville Global: Comprehensive Urban Development Agency); The Pays d'Aix Community (CPA); Marseille City Council; Genoa City Council; Turin City Council; Rome City Council; Athens City Council; Thessaloniki City Council and Mediterranean Institute (Marseille).

2015. Revitalisation Plan for the Historic Centre of Quito (HCQ)

Team: Salvador Rueda, Cynthia Echave, Jordi Abadal, David Andrés, Francisco Cárdenas, Elisenda Comas, Berta Cormenzana, Alessandra Curreli, Asier Eguilaz, Matilde Escobar, Ferran Fàbregas, Cristian Gesell, Erundina González, Elisabet López, Carmen Maté, Moisès Morató, Joan Palou, Xavier Pont, Norma Rey, Ona Riera, Ferran Sanchis, Annabel Subías, Simone Trevisan, Mercedes Vidal, Marta Vila and Núria Vilajuana.

Technical Coordination: José María Sáez.

Bodies: Quito Metropolitan District. Metropolitan Heritage Institute. Department for Territory, Habitat and Housing.

Field work team: Byron Pérez, Belén Quillupangui, Christian Cerón, Isaac Flores, Isabel Nuñez, Nataly Moreno, Pablo Sandoval, Reinaldo Espinoza and Jeanine Serrano.

2018. Action Plan for the Articulation of Planning and Management Instruments in Old Havana with ecosystemic urbanism principles

Team: Salvador Rueda, Berta Cormenzana, David Andrés, Ander Bilbao, Irene Capdevila, Cynthia Echave, Asier Eguilaz, Erundina González, Elisabet López, Mikel Monclús, Moisès Morató, Xavier Pont, Norma Rey, Ona Riera, María Amaya Saade, Ferran Sanchis, Annabel Subías, Marta Vila and Arturo Vegas.

Bodies: Barcelona City Council. Department for Global Justice and International Cooperation.

Master Plan for the Comprehensive Revitalisation of Old Havana. Havana City Historian's Office.

Team: Patrícia Rodríguez, Juan Carlos Bresó and Kiovet Sánchez.

2018. Study on the Application of the Superblock Model to Four Areas of Buenos Aires

Team: Salvador Rueda, Cynthia Echave, Natalia Alvaredo, Neus Ayza, Erundina González, Elisabet López, Ferran Sanchis, Francesco Mitolo, Mireia Ferrer, Nicolás Silva and Eduardo Velez.

Bodies: Buenos Aires City Government Ministry of the Environment and Public Space.

Team: Pablo Guiraldes, Jimena Rodríguez and Augusto Tovar.

SUPERBLOCKS AND URBAN LIVEABILITY

→ Page. 152

2007. Sustainable Mobility and Public Space (PMSEP) Vitoria-Gasteiz

Team: Salvador Rueda, Cynthia Echave, Joan Palou, David Andrés, Berta Cormenzana, Jennifer Coronado, Cristian Gesell, Erundina González, Elisabet López, Julià Massó, Moisès Morató, Xavier Pont, Albert Punsola, Anabel Rubio, Gemma Salvador, Ferran Sanchis, Mercè Taberna, Mercedes Vidal, Yuji Yoshimura, Esteve Codina (UPC) and Lídia Montero (UPC).

Bodies: commissioned by Vitoria-Gasteiz City Council. Coordination: Jorge Ozcariz.

Team: Environmental Studies Centre - CEA (Luis Andrés Orive, Mónica Ibarrondo, Juan Carlos Escudero, Roberto González, Asier Sarasua, Esther Albaina and Iñaki Álvarez); TUVISA - Transportes Urbanos de Vitoria-Gasteiz, SA (Javier Latorre); Mayor's Office (Iñigo Bilbao); Economic Promotion (Moisés Guridi and Maite de Juan); Technology Management and Citizens' Advice (Begoña Orcasitas, Amaia Mujika, Luis Mendizábal, Ana Bazterrika and Laura Garrido); Strategic Planning (Juan Castro); Local Police (Luis Cid and José Antonio Ferreiro); Presidency (José Luis Pérez and Juan Carlos Alonso); Urbanism (Antón Sáez de Santamaría, Iñaki Sagardoy, Aitziber Elorrieta, Alfredo Bengoa, Juan Carrascal, Elsa Larrea and David García); Environment (Carmen Calles, Eduardo Rojo, Iñaki Arriba and Marisol Monte).

2009. Public space liveability study in the districts of Sants-Montjuïc, Eixample, Gràcia and Nou Barris

Team: Salvador Rueda, Cynthia Echave, Berta Cormenzana, David Andrés, Cristina Cosma, Cristian Gesell, Erundina González, Ana Mourão, Mercedes Vidal and Adriana Zaragoza.

Bodies: Barcelona City Council. Environment Department.

2010. Ecological urbanism. Plan for Urban Planning in the Llevant Sector of Figueres

Team: Salvador Rueda, Cynthia Echave, Berta Cormenzana, Jordi Abadal, Marta Blanco, Francisco Cárdenas, Cristina Cosma, David Andrés, Manuel García, Cristian Gesell, Alice Lancien, Montse Masanas, Carmen Maté, Moisès Morató, Gemma Nohales, Marta Pascual, Joan Palou, Carlos Sánchez, Ferran Sanchis, Laura Silva, Marta Vila, Mercedes Vidal and Núria Vilajuana.

Bodies: commissioned by the Government of Catalonia (Environment and Housing Department, Housing Department) and Figueres City Council.

Codirection: Albert Cuchí (Escola Tècnica Superior d'Arquitectura del Vallès - ETSAV, UPC), Rafael de Cáceres (Estudi d'Arquitectura), Lluís Brau (Nova Gestió, urbanisme i arquitectura).

Contributors: ETSAV (Fabián López, Gerardo Wadel, Kim Arcas, Marina Casals and David Motos); Estudi d'Arquitectura Rafael de Cáceres (Xavier de Cáceres, Albert Aragall and Silvia Necchi); Nova Gestió, urbanisme i arquitectura (Manuel Fernández and Andrea Fernàndez).

2015. Neighbourhood of Ciudad Jardín Urban Regeneration Plan in Córdoba

Team: Salvador Rueda, Cynthia Echave, Jordi Abadal, David Andrés, Berta Cormenzana, Alessandra Curreli, Asier Eguilaz, Rafael Garrido, Elisabet López, Moisès Morató, Xavier Pont, Ona Riera, Ferran Sanchis and Annabel Subías.

Bodies: Viviendas Municipales de Córdoba, SA. (VIMCORSA).

2019. Social superblocks

Team: Salvador Rueda, Berta Cormenzana, Natalia Alvaredo and Mercedes Vidal.

Bodies: Barcelona City Council. Social Rights Area.

MOBILITY AND PUBLIC SPACE

A MORE SUSTAINABLE MOBILITY AND PUBLIC SPACE MODEL FOR BARCELONA

→ Page 174

2003. Gràcia Mobility and Public Space Plan

Team: Salvador Rueda, Bettina Schaefer, Francesc Magrinyà, Francisco Cárdenas, Julià Massó, Jordi Selfa, Josep López, Robert Colombo, Ana Jacas, Moisès Morató, Sergio Oliete, Adrià Ortiz, Joan Palou, Ona Riera, Alberto Rodríguez, Jordi Romero, Anabel Rubio and Núria Vilajuana.

Bodies: Barcelona City Council. Gràcia District.

Contributors: Esther García, Pere Camps, Joan Ramón Farré, Raúl de Toro, Gerard Cuevas, Santiago Fernández, Ana Martí, José Manuel Murillo, Maria del Mar Reventós, Felipe Riquer and Núria Vives.

2012. Barcelona Urban Mobility Plan (PMU) 2013–2018

Team: Salvador Rueda, Joan Palou, Annabel Subías, David Andrés, Irene Capdevila, Berta Cormenzana, Asier Eguilaz, Elisabet López, Moisès Morató, Xavier Pont, Ona Riera, Ferran Sanchis and Norma Rey.

Bodies: Barcelona City Council. Ecology, Urbanism and Mobility Area. Mobility Services Department.

Contributors: Adrià Gomila, Carlos López and Isabel Montané.

2016. Barcelona Sustainable Urban Mobility Plan (PMUS) 2019–2024

Team: Salvador Rueda, Xavier Pont, Joan Palou, Xavier Guarderas, Berta Cormenzana, Haritz Ferrando, Elisabet López, Norma Rey, Ferran Sanchis and Rodrigo Vargas.

Bodies: Barcelona City Council. Mobility and Infrastructures Office. Urban Ecology. Mobility Services Department.

Contributors: Adrià Gomila, Carlos López, Eugeni Rico and Ángel López.

SUSTAINABLE MOBILITY AND PUBLIC SPACE IN VITORIA-GASTEIZ

→ Page 188

2007. Sustainable Mobility and Public Space (PMSEP) Vitoria-Gasteiz

Team: Salvador Rueda, Cynthia Echave, Joan Palou, David Andrés, Berta Cormenzana, Jennifer Coronado, Cristian Gesell, Erundina González, Elisabet López, Julià Massó, Moisès Morató, Xavier Pont, Albert Punsola, Anabel Rubio, Gemma Salvador, Ferran Sanchis, Mercè Taberna, Mercedes Vidal, Yuji Yoshimura, Esteve Codina (UPC) and Lídia Montero (UPC).

Bodies: Vitoria-Gasteiz City Council. Coordination: Jorge Ozcariz.

Team: Environmental Studies Centre - CEA (Luis Andrés Orive, Mónica Ibarrondo, Juan Carlos Escudero, Roberto González, Asier Sarasua, Esther Albaina and Iñaki Álvarez); TUVISA - Transportes Urbanos de Vitoria-Gasteiz, SA (Javier Latorre); Mayor's Office (Iñigo Bilbao); Economic Promotion (Moisés Guridi and Maite de Juan); Technology Management and Citizens' Advice (Begoña Orcasitas, Amaia Mujika, Luis Mendizábal, Ana Bazterrika and Laura Garrido); Strategic Planning (Juan Castro); Local Police (Luis Cid and José Antonio Ferreiro); Presidency (José Luis Pérez and Juan Carlos Alonso); Urbanism (Antón Sáez de Santamaría, Iñaki Sagardoy, Aitziber Elorrieta, Alfredo Bengoa, Juan Carrascal, Elsa Larrea and David García); Environment (Carmen Calles, Eduardo Rojo, Iñaki Arriba and Marisol Monte).

2010. Public Transport Master Plan for the Historical Territory of Araba

Team: Salvador Rueda, Ona Riera, Joan Palou, Elisabet Badia, Vanesa Benítez, Elisenda Comas, Elisabet López, Roser Masjuan, Xavier Pont, Albert Punsola, Carlos Sánchez, Ferran Sanchis, Alba Rey and Mercè Taberna.

Bodies: Araba Provincial Council.

Team: Luis Zarrabeitia, Javier de Andrés, Emilio de Francisco, Pedro José García, Unai Grajales, Ane Miren Arrieta and Ángel Martínez de Antoñana.

2010. Technical support in the process of implementing, promoting and disseminating the Intercity Transport Master Plan for the Historical Territory of Araba

Team: Salvador Rueda, Joan Palou and Edaimon DeJuan.

Bodies: Araba Provincial Council. Transport and Mobility Services.

Team: Ane Miren Arrieta and Ángel Martínez de Antoñana.

2011. Pedestrian Mobility and Public Space Design Criteria Master Plan

Team: Salvador Rueda, Carmen Maté, Cristina Cosma, Cynthia Echave, Cristian Gesell, Elisabet López, Erundina González, Ferran Sanchis, Irene Roade, José Cárdenas, Juan Pablo Olivarreta, Lizeth Sánchez, Montse Masanas, Marta Pascual and Marta Vila.

Special contribution: Rafael de Cáceres.

Bodies: Vitoria-Gasteiz City Council. Environment Department.

Team: Eduardo Rojo, Juan Carlos Escudero and Mónica Ibarrondo.

2011. Vitoria-Gasteiz Mobility Plan for industrial estates

Team: Salvador Rueda, Carmen Maté, Ona Riera, Erundina González, Norma Rey, Eduardo Montoya, Tine Vleugels and Esteve Codina (UPC).

Bodies: Araba Provincial Council.

Team: Alicia Ruiz de Infante, Juan Ramírez López, Emilio de Francisco, Ane Miren Arrieta and Ángel Martínez de Antoñana.

2011. School mobility and other discretionary services in Vitoria-Gasteiz

Team: Salvador Rueda, Xavier Pont, Carmen Maté, Erundina González, Víctor Magdaleno, Norma Rey, Ona Riera and Annabel Subías.

Bodies: Vitoria-Gasteiz City Council. Co-director: Mónica Ibarrondo.

Team: Juan Carlos Escudero, Jesús Marcos, Jesús M. Mesanza and Iñaki Sagardoy.

2013. The Intra-County Mobility Plan for the Historical Territory of Araba. Proposal to implement a demand-responsive transport management system

Team: Salvador Rueda, Carmen Maté, Ona Riera, Ferran Fàbregas, Erundina González, Eduardo Montoya and Tine Vleugels.

Bodies: Araba Provincial Council.

Team: Alicia Ruiz de Infante, Juan Ramírez López, Emilio de Francisco, Ane Miren Arrieta and Ángel Martínez de Antoñana.

2013. Study on the sizing and basic design of the demand-responsive transport management system in the Historical Territory of Araba

Team: Salvador Rueda, Ona Riera, Ferran Fàbregas, Moisès Morató and Joan Palou.

Bodies: Araba Provincial Council. Public Works and Transport Department. Transport and Mobility Services.

Team: Alicia Ruiz de Infante, Juan Ramírez López and Ángel Martínez de Antoñana.

2015. Territorial Sectoral Plan for Cycle Lanes and Green Routes in Araba

Team: Salvador Rueda, Carmen Maté, Ona Riera, Elisenda Comas, Joan Palou and Annabel Subías.

Bodies: commissioned by LKS, Ingeniería, S. Coop. Coordination: José Luis Azkarate.

Araba Provincial Council.

2017. Extension of the study on the sizing and basic design of the demand-responsive transport management system in the Historical Territory of Araba

Team: Salvador Rueda, Ona Riera, Joan Palou, Ferran Fàbregas and Moisès Morató.

Bodies: Araba Provincial Council. Department of Road Infrastructures and Mobility. Transport and Mobility Services.

Team: Jesús María López Ubierna, M. Ángeles Gutiérrez Ondarza, Estíbaliz Ruiz de Eguino and Ángel Martínez de Antoñana.

2018. Sustainable Mobility and Public Space (PMSEP) Vitoria-Gasteiz (2020–2030)

Team: Salvador Rueda, Joan Palou, Xavier Pont, Xavier Guarderas, Natàlia Alvaredo, Berta Cormenzana, Cynthia Echave, Haritz Ferrando, Erundina González, Elisabet López, Ferran Sanchis and Norma Rey.

Bodies: Vitoria-Gasteiz City Council. Coordination: Juan Carlos Escudero.

Team: Centro de Estudios Ambientales - CEA (Luis Andrés Orive, Roberto González and Asier Sarasua); TUVISA -Transportes Urbanos de Vitoria-Gasteiz, SA (Javier Latorre); Mobility (Iñaki Sagardoy and David García); Environment (Eduardo Rojo).

Contributors: Jorge Ozcariz (OMV).

2018. Comprehensive Electric Mobility Plan for the Basque Country

Team: Salvador Rueda, Ona Riera, David Andrés, Erundina González, Moisès Morató, Annabel Subías and Antonio Tobella.

Bodies: commissioned by Edenway, SL.

Basque Government. Department of Economic Development and Infrastructures. Energy Agency of the Basque Government.

OTHER SUPERBLOCK-BASED MOBILITY PLANS

→ Page 200

2005. El Prat de Llobregat Sustainable Mobility and Public Space Plan

Team: Salvador Rueda, Bettina Schaefer, Mercè Taberna, Moisès Morató, Adrià Ortiz and Ona Riera.

Bodies: El Prat de Llobregat City Council. Mobility Services.

2006. Environmental analysis of the present and future of the public space and mobility in the municipality of Viladecans

Team: Salvador Rueda, Cynthia Echave, Julià Massó, Héctor Becerra, Berta Cormenzana, Jennifer Coronado, Manuel García, Cristian Gesell, Laura Latora, Elisabet López, Irene Luna, Moisès Morató, Joan Palou, Ona Riera, Anabel Rubio, Mercè Taberna and Mercedes Vidal.

Bodies: Viladecans City Council. Municipal Technical Services.

Coordination: Municipal company Viladecans Mediterrània (VIMED).

2009. Concello de Ferrol Mobility and Public Space Plan

Team: Salvador Rueda, Xavier Pont, David Andrés, Meritxell Batalla, Joan Palou, Ona Riera, Anabel Rubio, Marta Sas, Pablo Sendra and Ana Ybran.

Contributors: Esteve Codina (UPC) and Aresta Ingeniería (Maria Ramos and Cecilia Luaces).

Bodies: Ferrol City Council.

Coordination: Councillor's Office for Mobility and Accessibility (Gerardo López Castrillón).

Contributors: Sport and Citizen Participation Area; Urbanism, Environment, Mobility and Accessibility Area; Housing, Heritage Economic Promotion, and Business, Administrative Modernisation and Tourism Promotion Area; Culture, Education and Universities Area; Social Welfare, Women's and Young People's Area, and Citizen Safety Area.

Other contributors: Autonomous Government of Galicia (Department for Territorial Policy, Public Works and Transport); residents' associations; Ferrol Cyclists' Club; Critical Mass Cyclists' Association; Tranvias de Ferrol, SA; Rialsa (Monbus) and Arriva Noroeste.

2009. Lugo Mobility and Public Space Plan

Team: Salvador Rueda, Adrià Ortiz, Elisabet López, David Andrés, Meritxell Batalla, Joao Caxias, Jordina Guillamet, Judit Monlleó, Xavier Pont, Norma Rey, Anabel Rubio, Mireia Ruiz, Ferran Sanchis, Marta Sas, Annabel Subías and Ana Ybran.

Bodies: Lugo City Council. Councillor's Office for Mobility and Transport.

2011. A Coruña Mobility and Public Space Plan

Team: Salvador Rueda, Francisco Cárdenas, Xavier Pont, David Andrés, Natalia Aravena, Elisabet Badia, Cynthia Echave, Mónica Galindo, Erundina González, Irene Lanau, Elisabet López, Víctor Magdaleno, Alba Rey, Norma Rey, Carlos Sánchez, Annabel Subías, Mercedes Vidal, Camila Wollmann and Adriana Zaragoza.

Bodies: A Coruña City Council. Coordination: Management of the Environment, Sustainability and Mobility Area.

Contributors: Environment, Sustainability and Mobility Area; Citizen Safety and Traffic Area; Urbanism Area and Planning Area.

2014. Córdoba Sustainable Mobility and Public Space Plan

Team: Salvador Rueda, Xavier Pont, Annabel Subías, Jordi Abadal, David Andrés, Sergio Cadenas, Berta Cormenzana, Cynthia Echave, Javier Fernández, Cristian Gesell, Erundina González, Joan Palou, Ferran Sanchis, Maitena Vega and Mercedes Vidal.

Bodies: Coordination: Autobuses de Córdoba, SA (AUCORSA); Delegation for Mobility, Accessibility and Transport.

Contributors: Córdoba City Council. Urban Planning Department and Viviendas Municipales de Córdoba, SA (VIMCORSA).

2017. A Coruña Metropolitan Public Transport Plan (PMTPC)

Team: Salvador Rueda, Xavier Pont, Xavier Guarderas, David Andrés, Francisco Cárdenas, Elisenda Comas, Berta Cormenzana, Cynthia Echave, Erundina González, Gemma Latorre, Elisabet López, Mikel Monclús, Moisès Morató, Joan Palou, Norma Rey, Ona Riera, Ferran Sanchis, Annabel Subías and Antonio Tobella.

Bodies: A Coruña City Council. Department for Sustainable Mobility. Urban Mobility Services.

2018. A Coruña Transport Network Integration Plan

Team: Salvador Rueda, Xavier Pont, Francisco Cárdenas, Elisenda Comas, Berta Cormenzana, Cynthia Echave, Asier Eguilaz, Haritz Ferrando, Susanna García, Erundina González, Xavier Guarderas, Gemma Latorre, Elisabet López, Moisès Morató, Gemma Nohales, Joan Palou, Ferran Sanchis and Antonio Tobella.

Bodies: A Coruña City Council. Coordination: Department for Sustainable Mobility. Urban Mobility Services.

ORTHOGONAL PUBLIC TRANSPORT NETWORKS AND SUPERBLOCKS

→ Page 214

2004–2005–2013. Barcelona's orthogonal bus network and further studies

Team: Salvador Rueda, Francesc Magrinyà, Mercè Taberna, Adrià Ortiz, Xavier Pont, Joan Palou, Jordi Abadal, David Andrés, Anna Bacardit, Rocío Cabezas, Miguel Cañedo, Francisco Cárdenas, Edaimon Dejuan, Cynthia Echave, Elisabet López, Julià Massó, Moisès Morató, Sergio Oliete, Jennifer Ortega, Marta Pascual, Anabel Rubio, Òscar Sbert, Bettina Schaefer, Ferran Sanchis, Carla Sospedra, Mercedes Vidal, Núria Vilajuana and Yuji Yoshimura.

Bodies: Barcelona Metropolitan Transport (TMB) Team: Jacint Soler, Lluís Peláez, Josep Mension, Josep Maria Armengol, Ramon Lupiáñez, Ramon Ballesteros, Francesc González, Isabel Criado, Judit Reviejo and Juan Carlos Fernández.

Mobility Services Department at Barcelona City Council, Metropolitan Transport Authority (EMT); Ministry for the Environment.

2005. El Prat de Llobregat Sustainable Mobility and Public Space Plan

Team: Salvador Rueda, Bettina Schaefer, Mercè Taberna, Moisès Morató, Adrià Ortiz and Ona Riera.

Bodies: El Prat de Llobregat City Council. Mobility Services.

2006. Environmental analysis of the present and future of the public space and mobility in the municipality of Viladecans

Team: Salvador Rueda, Cynthia Echave, Julià Massó, Héctor Becerra, Berta Cormenzana, Jennifer Coronado, Manuel García, Cristian Gesell, Laura Latora, Elisabet López, Irene Luna, Moisès Morató, Joan Palou, Ona Riera, Anabel Rubio, Mercè Taberna and Mercedes Vidal.

Bodies: Viladecans City Council. Municipal Technical Services.

Coordination: Municipal company Viladecans Mediterrània (VIMED).

2009. Vitoria-Gasteiz orthogonal bus network

Team: Salvador Rueda, Joan Palou and Xavier Pont.

Bodies: Vitoria-Gasteiz City Council.

Coordination: Javier Latorre (TUVISA - Transportes Urbanos de Vitoria-Gasteiz, SA).

2009. Concello de Ferrol Mobility and Public Space Plan

Team: Salvador Rueda, Xavier Pont, David Andrés, Meritxell Batalla, Joan Palou, Ona Riera, Anabel Rubio, Marta Sas, Pablo Sendra and Ana Ybran.

Contributors: Esteve Codina (UPC) and Aresta Ingeniería (Maria Ramos and Cecilia Luaces).

Bodies: Ferrol City Council. Coordination: Councillor's Office for Mobility and Accessibility (Gerardo López Castrillón).

Contributors: Sport and Citizen Participation Area; Urbanism, Environment, Mobility and Accessibility Area; Housing, Heritage Economic Promotion, and Business, Administrative Modernisation and Tourism Promotion Area; Culture, Education and Universities Area; Social Welfare, Women's and Young People's Area, and Citizen Safety Area.

Other contributors: Autonomous Government of Galicia (Department for Territorial Policy, Public Works and Transport); residents' associations; Ferrol Cyclists' Club; Critical Mass Cyclists' Association; Tranvias de Ferrol, SA; Rialsa (Monbus) and Arriva Noroeste.

2009. Lugo Mobility and Public Space Plan

Team: Salvador Rueda, Adrià Ortiz, Elisabet López, David Andrés, Meritxell Batalla, Joao Caxias, Jordina Guillamet, Judit Monlleó, Xavier Pont, Norma Rey, Anabel Rubio, Mireia Ruiz, Ferran Sanchis, Marta Sas, Annabel Subías and Ana Ybran.

Bodies: Lugo City Council.

Councillor's Office for Mobility and Transport.

2011. A Coruña Mobility and Public Space Plan

Team: Salvador Rueda, Francisco Cárdenas, Xavier Pont, David Andrés, Natalia Aravena, Elisabet Badia, Cynthia Echave, Mónica Galindo, Erundina González, Irene Lanau, Elisabet López, Víctor Magdaleno, Alba Rey, Norma Rey, Carlos Sánchez, Annabel Subías, Mercedes Vidal, Camila Wollmann and Adriana Zaragoza.

Bodies: A Coruña City Council. Coordination: Management of the Environment, Sustainability and Mobility Area.

Contributors: Environment, Sustainability and Mobility Area; Citizen Safety and Traffic Area; Urbanism Area and Planning Area.

2014. Córdoba Sustainable Mobility and Public Space Plan

Team: Salvador Rueda, Xavier Pont, Annabel Subías, Jordi Abadal, David Andrés, Sergio Cadenas, Berta Cormenzana, Cynthia Echave, Javier Fernández, Cristian Gesell, Erundina González, Joan Palou, Ferran Sanchis, Maitena Vega and Mercedes Vidal.

Bodies: Coordination: Autobuses de Córdoba, SA (AUCORSA); Delegation for Mobility, Accessibility and Transport.

Contributors: Córdoba City Council. Urban Planning Department and Viviendas Municipales de Córdoba, SA. (VIMCORSA).

2016. Restructuration of the public transport network in the Metropolitan District of Quito

Team: Salvador Rueda, Xavier Guarderas, Xavier Pont, Francisco Cárdenas, Elisenda Comas, Joan Palou, David Andrés, Irene Capdevila, Andrea Cappai, Berta Cormenzana, Asier Eguilaz, Elisabet López, Moisès Morató, Annabel Subías, Ferran Sanchis, Norma Rey, Ona Riera and Antonio Tobella.

Bodies: Quito Metropolitan District. Technical Services.

Contributors: José María Saez and AOC Ingeniería.

2018. Review of the Vitoria-Gasteiz Sustainable Mobility and Public Space Plan

Team: Salvador Rueda, Joan Palou, Xavier Pont and Rodrigo Vargas.

Bodies: Vitoria-Gasteiz City Council. Urban Planning Department. Planning and Urban Management Service. Office for the Revision of the General Plan for Urban Planning.

Contributors: Javier Latorre (TUVISA - Transportes Urbanos de Vitoria-Gasteiz, SA).

ENVIRONMENT

WATER CYCLE MANAGEMENT

→ Page 236

2002. Water Balance of the Barcelona Metropolitan Area Assessment of water systems and demand management

Team: Salvador Rueda, Francisco Cárdenas and Núria Vilajuana.

Bodies: Barcelona Metropolitan Area. Environment Entity.

2004. Aquatic Systems Conservation and Water Demand Management Programme in the RMB

Team: Salvador Rueda, Francisco Cárdenas, Cristina Castillo, Josep Esquerrà, Antonio Esteban, Xavier Flotats, Manuel García, Tiphaine Lebreton, Moisès Morató, Laia Núñez, Miguel Ángel Pérez, Oriol Porcel, Mariona Prat, Ona Riera, Bettina Schaefer, Mercedes Vidal and Núria Vilajuana.

Bodies: commissioned by the Barcelona Metropolitan Area (AMB) Environment Entity.

Contributors: EMSHTR (Carles Conill, Martín Gullón, Antonio Palacios and Esther Suárez); APSA (Francisco Alcalá, Aure García and Jordi Miró); CDC Besòs (Josep Arràez and Manel Isnard); Catalan Water Agency (Gabriel Borràs, Sebastià Datzira, Francesc Farreras, Josep Maria Niñerola, Josep M. Puigdengoles, José Miguel Diéguez and Andreu Manzano), Depurbaix, SA (Joan Comte and Tomás Cazurra); Barcelona City Council (Ramon Arandes); CLABSA (Mònica Enrich); Consorci Alba-Ter (Dolors Roset); Regsega, SA (Jaume Cortasa); Institut d'Estudis Territorials (Xavier Abadia); UAB. Geography Department (David Saurí), and CCP (Lluís Graus).

2010. Ecosystemic Urbanism Plan for Urban Planning in the Llevant Sector of Figueres

Team: Salvador Rueda, Cynthia Echave, Berta Cormenzana, Jordi Abadal, Marta Blanco, Francisco Cárdenas, Cristina Cosma, David Andrés, Manuel García, Cristian Gesell, Alice Lancien, Montse Masanas, Carmen Maté, Moisès Morató, Gemma Nohales, Marta Pascual, Joan Palou, Carlos Sánchez, Ferran Sanchis, Laura Silva, Marta Vila, Mercedes Vidal and Núria Vilajuana.

Bodies: commissioned by the Government of Catalonia (Environment and Housing Department, Housing Department) and Figueres City Council.

Codirection: Albert Cuchí (Escola Tècnica Superior d'Arquitectura del Vallès - ETSAV, UPC), Rafael de Cáceres (Estudi d'Arquitectura) and Lluís Brau (Nova Gestió, urbanisme i arquitectura).

Contributors: ETSAV (Fabián López, Gerardo Wadel, Kim Arcas, Marina Casals and David Motos); Estudi d'Arquitectura Rafael de Cáceres (Xavier de Cáceres, Albert Aragall and Silvia Necchi) and Nova Gestió, urbanisme i arquitectura (Manuel Fernández and Andrea Fernàndez).

EFFICIENCY AND ENERGY TRANSITION

→ Page 248

2010. SCACS. Heating and Domestic Hot Water System

Team: Salvador Rueda and Moisès Morató.

Bodies: Urban Ecology Agency of Barcelona.

2014. BLUENE. Blue energy in Mediterranean Europe

Team: Salvador Rueda, Francisco Cárdenas and Jordi Abadal.

MED European programme. Project partners: CoNISMa-National Inter-University Consortium for Marine Sciences (Roma, Italy); Zadar County Development Agency-ZADRA NOVA (Croatia) and Hellenic Centre for Marine Research (Greece).

2016. Vilawatt

Team: Salvador Rueda, Sergio Sánchez, Elisabet López, Moisès Morató, Jordi Abadal, Mikel Monclús, Arnau Alarcón, Natalia Alvaredo, Ander Bilbao, Asier Eguilaz and Norma Rey.

Project leader: Viladecans City Council.

Contributors: Ubiquat Technologies SL; ICAEN (Catalan Energy Institute); LIMA (Low Impact Mediterranean Architecture) Association; Círculo Gespromat, SL; EGM Energy Efficiency; VIGEM; MED European programme. Viladecans Mediterránea (VIMED) and Cíclica SCCL.

2016. Chess Setup

Team: Salvador Rueda, Moisès Morató, Jordi Abadal, Mikel Monclús, Sergio Sánchez, Ander Bilbao, Arnau Alarcón and Antonio Tobella.

Project leader: BCNecologia.

Contributors: University of Ulster and Electric Corby (UK); Wandsronk Architektuur (Netherlands); Eurogrant GmbH (Germany); Edenway SAS (France); Lavola; Wattia-Innova; Veolia, and Sant Cugat del Vallès City Council.

2016. Electrific

Team: Salvador Rueda, Sergio Sánchez, Javier Guarderas, Irene Capdevila, Asier Eguilaz, Susanna Garcia, Moisès Morató, Ona Riera, Annabel Subías and Antonio Tobella.

Project leader: Gfi NV (Heverlee, Belgium).

Project partners: BCNecologia; Energis (Belgium); Czech Technical University Czech Technical University in Prague and E-ŠUMAVA. CZ (Czech Republic); Has.to.be GmbH (Radstadt, Austria), and Bayernwerk; Deggendorf Institute of Technology (DHT); University of Mannheim; University of Passau, and E-WALD GmbH (Technologie Campus Teicnach) (Germany).

2017. ZeEUS (Zero Emission Urban Bus System, 2015–2018). Operability of the new electric bus routes in Barcelona: the case of the H16

Team: Salvador Rueda, Moisès Morató, Antonio Tobella, Irene Capdevila, Erundina González and Roger Liarte.

Commissioned by Barcelona Metropolitan Transport (TMB).

2018. Eliptic (Electrification of Public Transport in Cities, 2017–2018). Dynamic simulation for the new TMB V13 electric bus route

Team: Salvador Rueda, Moisès Morató, Antonio Tobella.

Commissioned by Barcelona Metropolitan Transport (TMB).

CLIMATE CHANGE ADAPTATION AND MITIGATION

→ Page 264

2009. Development of methodological and instrumental resources and the creation of Local Climate Change Strategies

Team: Salvador Rueda, Carmen Maté, Jordi Abadal, David Andrés, Vanesa Benítez, Marta Blanco, Edaimon DeJuan, Matilde Escobar, Manuel García, Erundina González, Árua Ibrahim, Montse Masanas, Moisès Morató, Sofia Nadime, Gemma Nohales, Marta Pascual, Miguel Ángel Pérez, Carlos Sánchez, Pau Santacana and Marta Vila.

Bodies: commissioned by Fundación Biodiversidad.

2009. Plan to Combat Climate Change in Vitoria-Gasteiz (2010–2020)

Team: Salvador Rueda, David Andrés, Carmen Maté, Jordi Abadal, Marta Blanco, Edaimon DeJuan, Manuel García, Árua Ibrahim, Montse Masanas, Roser Masjuan, Moisès Morató, Gemma Nohales, Marta Pascual, Carlos Sánchez and Marta Vila.

Bodies: Vitoria-Gasteiz City Council. Environment Department. Management: Miguel Virizuela and Andrés Alonso. Coordination: Iñaki Arriba.

Contributors: Eduardo Rojo, Marian Mesanza, Luis Mendizábal and Asier Sarasua.

2010. Vitoria-Gasteiz: a Carbon-Neutral City (scenario 2020–2050)

Team: Salvador Rueda, Carmen Maté, Jordi Abadal, Carlos Sánchez, David Andrés, Edaimon DeJuan, Gemma Nohales, Joan Palou, Marta Blanco, Marta Pascual, Marta Vila, Manuel García, Moisès Morató, Montse Masanas and Roser Masjuan.

Bodies: Vitoria-Gasteiz City Council. Environment Department. Management: Miguel Virizuela.

Coordination: Andrés Alonso and Iñaki Arriba.

AIR QUALITY IMPROVEMENT PLANS

→ Page 276

2013. Badalona Air Quality Improvement Action Plan (2008–2015)

Team: Salvador Rueda, Francisco Cárdenas, David Andrés, Jordi Abadal, Edaimon DeJuan, Elisabet López and Verónica Villalba.

Bodies: Barcelona Provincial Council. Environmental Diagnosis and Control Section. Coordination: Maria Llorens.

Badalona City Council. Urban Ecology Department. Coordination: Josep Montes.

2014. Terrassa Air Quality Improvement Plan (2015–2020)

Team: Salvador Rueda, Francisco Cárdenas, David Andrés, Jordi Abadal, Elisabet López and Manuela Sanfelix.

Bodies: Barcelona Provincial Council. Environmental Diagnosis and Control Section. Coordination: Maria Llorens and David Casabona.

Terrassa City Council. Environment

and Sustainability Department. Coordination: Marc Cadevall, Josep Latorre, Laia Font, Susi López, Betina Verger, Pau Vilaplana, Iñigo Fages, Albert Marín, Jesús Romero, Francesc Pruñonosa, Pere Puigdomenech, Xavier Massallé, Roser Guardiola, Eduardo Sebastián, Maria Vicenta Villar, Jose Luís Fernández, Salvador Pérez, Begoña Linuesa and Ana Maria López.

2016. County-wide Air Quality Improvement Action Plan in Vallès Oriental

Team: Salvador Rueda, Francisco Cárdenas and David Andrés.

Bodies: Barcelona Provincial Council. Environmental Diagnosis and Control Section. Coordination: Maria Llorens and David Casabona.

Government of Catalonia. Department for the Prevention and Control of Air Pollution. Coordination: Isabel Hernández and Susana Gil.

Vallès Oriental County Council. Coordination: Jaume Viure.

Municipal Councils of Canovelles (Marga Giralt); Granollers (Marta Chillida); La Llagosta (Sergi Moreno); La Roca del Vallès (Santi Raimí); Les Franqueses del Vallès (Maria Mercè Miquel); Lliçà de Vall (Jofre Campdepadrós); Martorelles (Mercè Raïch); Mollet del Vallès (Josep Maria Mompín); Montmeló (Jordi Bartrolí); Montornès del Vallès (José Manuel Pérez); Parets del Vallès (Joan Carles Millet) and Sant Fost de Campsentelles (Xavier Martí).

2016. Santa Coloma de Gramenet Air Quality Improvement Action Plan (2008–2020)

Team: Salvador Rueda, Francisco Cárdenas, David Andrés, Jordi Abadal, Elisabet López and Manuela Sanfelix.

Bodies: Barcelona Provincial Council. Environmental Diagnosis and Control Section. Coordination: Maria Llorens and David Casabona.

Santa Coloma de Gramenet City Council. Coordination: Francesc Bernet, Amparo Benjumea, Isabel Garcia, Miquel Roig, Glòria Tormo, Antoni Herraez, Rafael Vela and Marina Ollé.

2016. L'Hospitalet de Llobregat Air Quality Improvement Action Plan (2008–2015–2020)

Team: Salvador Rueda, Francisco Cárdenas and David Andrés.

Bodies: Barcelona Provincial Council. Environmental Diagnosis and Control Section. Coordination: Maria Llorens and David Casabona.

L'Hospitalet de Llobregat City Council. Coordination: Manuel de Zarobe.

Government of Catalonia. Air Monitoring and Control Service. Coordination: Susana Gil.

2017. Sabadell 2022. PAMQA. Air Quality Improvement Action Plans

Team: Salvador Rueda, Francisco Cárdenas, David Andrés, Alba Bravo and Mireia Martínez.

Bodies: Barcelona Provincial Council. Environmental Diagnosis and Control Section. Coordination: Maria Llorens and David Casabona.

Government of Catalonia. Technical Office for Air Quality Improvement Plans. General Directorate for Environmental Quality. Coordination: Susana Gil.

Sabadell City Council. Coordination: Jaume Enciso. Rosa Martínez, Adam Bonnin, Núria Centelles, Jose Luis Baron and Teresa Corbella.

ISGLOBAL. Coordination: Jordi Sunyer, Maribel Casas, Antonia Valenín and Marta Cirach.

2019. County-wide Air Quality Improvement Plan for 13 municipalities of the Baix Llobregat (2019–2025)

Team: Salvador Rueda, Francisco Cárdenas and Haritz Ferrando.

Bodies: Barcelona Provincial Council. Environmental Diagnosis and Control Section. Coordination: Maria Llorens and David Casabona.

Government of Catalonia. Technical Office for Air Quality Improvement Plans. General Directorate for Environmental Quality. Coordination: Susana Gil.

Barcelona Metropolitan Area. Coordination: Elena Veza.

Municipal Councils of Castellbisbal (Enrico Martinell, Lluís Vaquero and Bibiana Catalán); Cervelló (Rubén Domínguez); Corbera de Llobregat (Xavi Miquel and Anna Arcalís); Papiol (Joan Borràs, Albert Querol and Judit Solana); la Palma de Cervelló (Maria Rosa Martín); Martorell (Elisabet Ferrer and Joan Casademont); Molins de Rei (Josep Raventós and Patrícia Viñals); Pallejà (Sònia Cano); Sant Andreu de la Barca (Rubén Castro and Rosa Maria Asensio); Sant Climent de Llobregat (Marc Martínez); Sant Feliu de Llobregat (Manel Leiva and Jordi Pedrol); Sant Vicenç dels Horts (coordination: Alejandro Aparicio, Ramon Montaña and Albert Sanz) and Torrelles de Llobregat (Jaume Macià).

2020. Formulation of the update to the Air Quality Improvement Plan for Badalona

Team: Josep Bohigas, Francisco Cárdenas and Haritz Ferrando.

Bodies: Barcelona Provincial Council. Environmental Diagnosis and Control Section. Coordination: Maria Llorens.

Badalona City Council. Coordination: Josep Montes, Marisa Forcadell and Josep Amador.

2020. Formulation of the Air Quality Improvement Action Plan for Cerdanyola del Vallès

Team: Josep Bohigas, Francisco Cárdenas and Haritz Ferrando.

Bodies: Barcelona Provincial Council. Environmental Diagnosis and Control Section. Coordination: Maria Llorens.

Cerdanyola del Vallès City Council. Coordination: Elena Martí and Àngel Reyes.

URBAN BIODIVERSITY AND GREEN NETWORK IN BARCELONA

→ Page 286

2006. Strategic Plan for Open Spaces in Barcelona. Definition of Urban Green Corridors

Team: Salvador Rueda, Cynthia Echave, Bettina Schaefer, Berta

Cormenzana, Cristian Gesell, Gabriel Lanfranchi, Elisabet López, Jennifer Ortega, Adrià Ortiz, Ona Riera, Anabel Rubio, Gemma Salvador, Mercè Taberna and Mercedes Vidal.

Bodies: Barcelona City Council. Environment Department.

Team: Txema Castiella, Teresa Franquesa, Margarita Parés and Maria Alba Fransi.

2009. Sustainability Report for the Pet Rescue Park (PAAC)

Team: Salvador Rueda and Carmen Maté.

Bodies: Barcelona City Council. Environment Office.

Collaboration: various entities relating to animal protection.

2010. Green roofs and walls in Barcelona. Study on existing roofs, their potential and implementation strategies

Team: Salvador Rueda, Carmen Maté, Cynthia Echave, Manuel García, Cristian Gesell, Erundina González, Judit Monlleó, Moisès Morató, Marta Pascual, Alba Rey, Norma Rey, Verónica Siguero and Núria Vilajuana.

Bodies: Contributors: Intemper; Zinco; Burés; Vivers Ter and Planning Department in the Environment Area, Barcelona City Council.

2011. Model for the Study of the Economic and Energy Costs of Maintaining and Conserving Parks, Gardens and Urban Trees

Team: Salvador Rueda, Carmen Maté, Cristian Gesell, Jordi Abadal, Marta Blanco, Cynthia Echave, Matilde Escobar, Manuel García, Erundina González, Alícia Grima, Clara Montaner, Norma Rey and Carlos Sánchez.

Bodies: commissioned by Fundación Biodiversidad.

Contributors: Municipal Councils of Bilbao, Collbató, Premià de Mar, Vitoria-Gasteiz, and Barcelona Parks and Gardens Department.

CIRCULAR ECONOMY

INNOVATIVE SEPARATE WASTE COLLECTION MODELS

→ Page 306

2005. Technical Consultation and Preparation of the Waste Management and Street Cleaning Programme for Mataró, with development of the technical specification for the new contract

Team: Salvador Rueda, Marta Vila and Gemma Nohales.

Bodies: Mataró City Council.

2009. Design studies for door-to-door collection and the preparation of technical specifications documents for street cleaning and municipal waste collection in Just Desvern

Team: Salvador Rueda, Marta Vila and Gemma Nohales.

Bodies: Sant Just Desvern City Council.

LOVIC: Vicens Garcés.

2010. Guide to implementing separate waste collection and managing municipal organic waste. MAGRAMA (2010–2013)

Team: Salvador Rueda, Gemma Nohales, Marta Vila, Alícia Grima and Montse Masanas.

Bodies: MAGRAMA. Management: Ana Rodríguez and Margarita Ruiz.

Contributors: Raquel Gómez (MAGRAMA); Inés Iribarren (IGME); Dr. Florian Amlinger (Compost-Consulting & Development, Austria); Ignasi Puig and Marta Jofra (ENT Environment & Management); Francesc Giró (Waste Agency of Catalonia); Josep Muñoz (APPLUS AGROAMBIENTAL); Joaquín Moreno (University of Almeria, coordinator of the Spanish Composting Network), and Montserrat Soliva.

2012. SCOW (Selective Collection of the Organic Waste in Tourist Areas and Valorisation in Farm Composting Plants)

Team: Salvador Rueda, Marta Vila and Gemma Nohales.

Bodies: Pallars Sobirà County Council.

Spora: Laia Valenzuela.

2017. DtD viability study and locked containers in Sant Just Desvern

Team: Salvador Rueda, Marta Vila and Gemma Nohales.

Bodies: Sant Just Desvern City Council.

2017. Consultation for and development of the new Comprehensive Waste Management Plan for Extremadura (2017–2022)

Team: Salvador Rueda and Marta Vila.

Bodies: Autonomous Government of Extremadura.

2019. New waste and street cleaning contract for Mataró

Team: Salvador Rueda, Marta Vila and Gemma Nohales.

Bodies: Mataró City Council.

2019. Door-to-door collection model implementation study in Santa Maria de Palautordera

Team: Salvador Rueda and Marta Vila.

Bodies: Santa Maria de Palautordera Town Council.

Entorna3: Alícia Grima and Lluna López.

2019. Campaign and waste management improvement in Molins de Rei

Team: Salvador Rueda and Marta Vila.

Bodies: Molins de Rei Town Council.

WASTE PREVENTION

→ Page 316

2003. Environmental education campaign for organic waste collection in Sant Andreu

Team: Salvador Rueda and Marta Vila.

Bodies: Barcelona City Council. Sant Andreu District.

2008. Guide for the Preparation of Local Municipal Waste Prevention Plans

Team: Salvador Rueda, Marta Vila and Gemma Nohales.

Bodies: Waste Agency of Catalonia (ARC). Coordination: Pilar Chiva, Elena Bagaria and Alfred Vara.

2010. Barcelona Waste Prevention Plan

Team: Salvador Rueda, Marta Vila, Gemma Nohales and Montse Masanas.

Bodies: Barcelona City Council. Coordination: Carles Vázquez and Helena Barracó.

2010. Tiana Municipal Waste Prevention Plan

Team: Salvador Rueda, Marta Vila, Gemma Nohales, Alícia Grima and Montse Masanas.

Bodies: Tiana Town Council. Coordination: Olga Llobet.

2011. Pallars Sobirà County Plan for Municipal Waste Prevention

Team: Salvador Rueda, Marta Vila and Alicia Grima.

Bodies: Pallars Sobirà County Council. Coordination: Marc Sans.

2013. Mataró Municipal Waste Prevention Plan

Team: Salvador Rueda and Marta Vila.

Bodies: Mataró City Council. Coordination: Albert Galan.

2013. Study on improving use of food surplus in the distribution and restaurant sectors in Cornellà de Llobregat

Team: Salvador Rueda, Marta Vila, Alícia Grima and Lluna López.

Bodies: Cornellà de Llobregat Town Council.

2014. Diagnosis of the Reuse and Preparing for Reuse Situation in Catalonia (2012–2013)_R and PxR

Team: Salvador Rueda, Marta Vila, Alícia Grima and Norma Rey.

Bodies: Waste Agency of Catalonia (ARC). Coordination: Elena Bagaria and Alfred Vara.

2014. Utebo Municipal Waste Prevention Plan 2014–2019

Team: Salvador Rueda, Marta Vila and Teresa Rivero.

Bodies: Utebo Town Council. Coordination: Rubén Estévez and Ignacio Laseo.

2015. Methodological Guide for Calculating Waste Prevention Potential and Goals + Prevention Calculator

Team: Salvador Rueda, Marta Vila, Gemma Nohales, Montse Masanas and Ferran Fàbregas.

Bodies: Waste Agency of Catalonia (ARC). Coordination: Elena Bagaria and Alfred Vara.

2018. Arenys de Mar Waste Prevention Plan

Team: Salvador Rueda, Marta Vila, Gemma Nohales and Norma Rey.

Bodies: Arenys de Mar Town Council. Coordination: Laia Martin, Jordi Simó and Inés Malleu.

2020. SUBTRACT (Sustainable Reuse Centres) Diagnosis

Team: Salvador Rueda, Marta Vila and Montse Aulinas.

Bodies: Entorna3. Coordination: Alícia Grima, Lluna López and Alex Rollán.

Waste Agency of Catalonia (ARC). Coordination: Elena Bagaria and Alfred Vara.

WASTE MANAGEMENT PLANS AND PROGRAMMES

→ Page 324

2007–2012. Diagnosis and Formulation of the Catalonia Municipal Waste Management Programme (PROGREMIC)

Team: Salvador Rueda and Marta Vila.

Bodies: Waste Agency of Catalonia (ARC). Coordination: Josep Simó, Pilar Chiva and Teresa Guerrero.

2007. Procedures, methodology and initial results of the calculation of the composition of waste generation in Catalonia (average bin)

Team: Salvador Rueda, Marta Vila and Gemma Nohales.

Bodies: Waste Agency of Catalonia (ARC).

2008. Environmental Sustainability Report (ISA) of the new Catalonia Municipal Waste Management Programme (PROGREMIC) 2007–2012

Team: Salvador Rueda and Marta Vila.

Bodies: Waste Agency of Catalonia (ARC).

2009. Galicia Urban Waste Management Programme 2010–2020 (PGRUG) and Strategic environmental assessment

Team: Salvador Rueda, Marta Vila and Gemma Nohales.

Bodies: Ministry of the Environment and Sustainable Development. General Directorate for Environmental Quality and Assessment. Autonomous Government of Galicia.

2012. Study on future waste tax application scenarios

Team: Salvador Rueda, Marta Vila and Gemma Nohales.

Bodies: Waste Agency of Catalonia (ARC).

WASTE MANAGEMENT INSTRUMENTS

→ Page 330

2001–2004. Implementation campaign for separate organic waste collection in Barcelona

Team: Salvador Rueda and Marta Vila.

Bodies: Barcelona City Council.

2003. Modelling the waste management in the Barcelona Metropolitan Area (SIMUR v1)

Team: Salvador Rueda, Marta Vila and Gemma Nohales.

Bodies: Municipal Councils: El Prat de Llobregat, Sant Adrià de Besòs and Molins de Rei.

2004. Implementation campaign for organic waste collection in Premià de Mar

Team: Salvador Rueda and Marta Vila.

Bodies: Premià de Mar Town Council.

2006. Implementation campaign for separate organic waste collection in Mataró

Team: Salvador Rueda, Marta Vila, Irene Luna and Alícia Grima.

Bodies: Mataró City Council.

2008. SIMUR v2 programming and pilot test

Team: Salvador Rueda, Marta Vila, Gemma Nohales, Miguel Ángel Pérez, Alícia Grima and Montse Masanas.

Bodies: Waste Agency of Catalonia (ARC).

2009. Campaigns to bolster the implementation of separate organic waste collection in Mataró

Team: Salvador Rueda, Marta Vila, Irene Luna and Alícia Grima.

Bodies: Mataró City Council.

2010. Design and launch of the PROGREMIC portal

Team: Salvador Rueda, Marta Vila, Gemma Nohales and Alícia Grima.

Bodies: Waste Agency of Catalonia (ARC).

2013. Promotion of the PROGREMIC portal

Team: Salvador Rueda, Marta Vila, Gemma Nohales and Alícia Grima.

Bodies: Waste Agency of Catalonia (ARC).

2013. Participatory design for the new waste collection and street cleaning services in Mataró

Team: Salvador Rueda, Marta Vila and Gemma Nohales.

Bodies: LOVIC, Spora Sinergies and Mataró City Council.

2016. Participation and communication campaign for a change in the municipal waste management model in Sant Boi de Llobregat

Team: Salvador Rueda, Marta Vila, Erundina González and Norma Rey.

Bodies: Sant Boi de Llobregat Town Council.

2016. Waste4Think: Moving towards Life Cycle Thinking by Integrating Advanced Waste Management Systems. Programa H2020

Team: Salvador Rueda, Marta Vila, Gemma Nohales, Alexandra Farbiarz and Meritxell Casellas.

European project. Project leader: Fundación Deusto.

Partners from Spain, Greece, Denmark, Italy, Portugal and Germany.

Pilot locations: Zamudio (Spain); Halandri (Greece); Seveso (Italy), and Cascais (Portugal).

2017. Public participatory diagnosis for the new waste collection and street cleaning contract in El Prat de Llobregat

Team: Salvador Rueda, Marta Vila, Erundina González, Norma Rey and Ferran Sanchis.

Bodies: Spora Sinergies and El Prat de Llobregat City Council.

2020. LIFE REthinkWASTE (Sant Just Desvern and 2.0 LCA)

Team: Salvador Rueda, Marta Vila and Montse Aulinas.

Bodies: European project. Project leader: Etra (Veneto, Italy).

Partners from Italy and Belgium, Waste Agency of Catalonia (ARC) and Sant Just Desvern Town Council.

THEMATIC INDEX

A

B

C

D

E

N

O

P

Q

R

S

T

U

V

W

Z

BCNECOLOGIA
20 YEARS OF THE URBAN ECOLOGY AGENCY OF BARCELONA

EDITED BY
Barcelona City Council
BCNecologia
Barcelona Regional

AJUNTAMENT DE BARCELONA

EDITORIAL AND PUBLISHING COUNCIL OF THE CITY OF BARCELONA
Jordi Martí Grau, Joan Subirats Humet, Marc Andreu Acebal, Gemma Arau Ceballos, Águeda Bañón Pérez, Marta Clari Padrós, Núria Costa Galobart, Laura Pérez Castaño, Jordi Rabassa Massons, Joan Ramón Riera Alemany, Pilar Roca Viola, Edgar Rovira Sebastià and Anna Giralt Brunet.

HEAD OF COMMUNICATIONS
Águeda Bañón

HEAD OF PUBLISHING SERVICES
Núria Costa

CHIEF EDITOR
Oriol Guiu

PRODUCTION
Maribel Baños

DISTRIBUTION
M. Àngels Alonso

The Publishing Services Department of the City of Barcelona
Passeig de la Zona Franca, 66
08038 Barcelona
Tel. 93 402 31 31
barcelona.cat/barcelonallibres

DISTRIBUTION IN THE UNITED STATES

Arquine
Amsterdam, 163 A
Colonia Hipódromo
06100 Ciudad de México
www.arquine.com

Artbook D.A.P.
www.artbook.com

PUBLICATION

HEAD OF PUBLICATION
Josep Bohigas

EDITORIAL COORDINATION
Susanna G. Larios

COORDINATION AND TECHNICAL REVIEW
Cynthia Echave
Berta Cormenzana
Mercedes Vidal

EDITING
Núria Vilajuana

TEXT AUTHORS
Natalia Alvaredo, Montse Aulinas, Berta Cormenzana, Cynthia Echave, Haritz Ferrando, Susanna G. Larios, Erundina González, Francisco Xavier Guarderas, Elisabet López, Moisès Morató, Sergio Sánchez, Ferran Sanchis, Norma Rey, Joan Palou, Xavier Pont, Antonio Tobella, Rodrigo Vargas, Mercedes Vidal, Marta Vila and Núria Vilajuana.

PROOFREADING AND TRANSLATION
T&S
OLISTIS SCCL

GRAPHIC DESIGN
Spread: Tomoko Sakamoto - David Lorente

PHOTOGRAPHY
Chapter opening pages and superblocks
Marta Torrent

ILLUSTRATIONS
Berta Cormenzana, Cynthia Echave, Albert Escoda, Francisco Xavier Guarderas, Moisès Morató i Rodrigo Vargas.

PRINTING
Gràfiques Ortells, Barcelona

Printed on ecologic paper, Munken Print White 90g

ADMINISTRATION
Maria Vila d'Abadal

Barcelona Regional
Carrer 60, 25–27
Edifici Z. 2a planta
Sector A. Zona Franca
08040 Barcelona
www.bcnregional.com

ACKNOWLEDGMENTS
To all the team at BCNecologia and Barcelona Regional.

Municipal Councils of Barcelona, Córdoba, Mataró, Sant Cugat del Vallès, Terrassa and Vitoria-Gasteiz.

ISBN: 978-607-9489-87-8
Barcelona, July 2021

ALSO AVAILABLE:
Spanish edition: *BCNecologia. 20 años de la Agencia de Ecología Urbana de Barcelona.*
ISBN: 978-607-9489-86-1

Catalan edition: *BCNecologia. 20 anys de l'Agència d'Ecologia Urbana de Barcelona.*
ISBN: 978-84-9156-337-2

Urban Ecology Agency of Barcelona (BCNecologia) was founded on 5 June 2000 by ecologist Salvador Rueda as a public consortium made up of Barcelona City Council, Barcelona Metropolitan Area and Barcelona Provincial Council. Rueda was the director of the Agency from then until 2019, when he retired and was succeeded by architect Josep Bohigas, who was also director of Barcelona Regional (BR). In September 2020, the BCNecologia team joined Barcelona Regional.

Within Barcelona Regional – the city's public entity for strategic planning, urbanism and infrastructures, created in 1993 – the BCNecologia team continues to play its part in the process of making cities more sustainable.

THE AGENCY'S TEAM

BCNecologia has been driven by an extensive team of expert professionals, mainly from the areas of environmental science; civil, industrial, structural, forest and hydraulic engineering; architecture; geography; biology; physics; journalism; information technology; law; economics; and chemistry. Experts in the sciences make up 74.1% of the team, while 25.9% have a humanities background.

Throughout the Agency's history, the team has been made up of mainly women (58%), who have occupied all kinds of posts – from technician to decision-making roles – in various areas.

The human team behind BCNecologia has fluctuated in number between 20 and 40, even exceeding this figure on occasion, during awareness-raising campaigns. In general, the team has always been compact and organised into different areas of knowledge. The Agency gradually consolidated these areas into the spheres of mobility, urbanism and the public space, energy, water cycle management, waste management, and noise and air pollution.

In broad strokes, the typical profile of someone who has worked at the Urban Ecology Agency of Barcelona over the years would be that of a **woman aged around 30 with scientific training**.

THE AGENCY IN FIGURES

GENDER
(%)

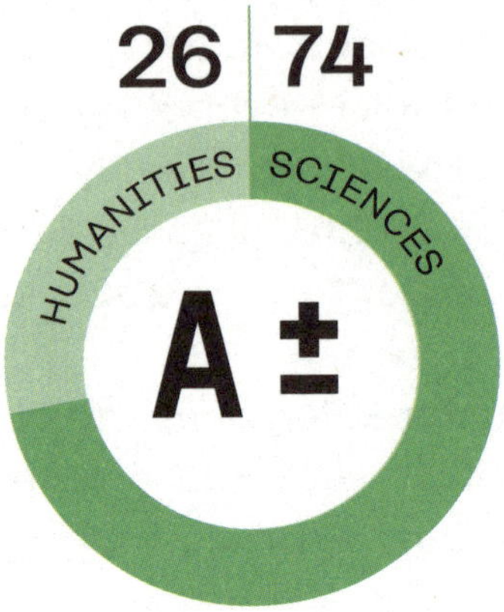

STUDIES
(%)

ORIGIN
(%)

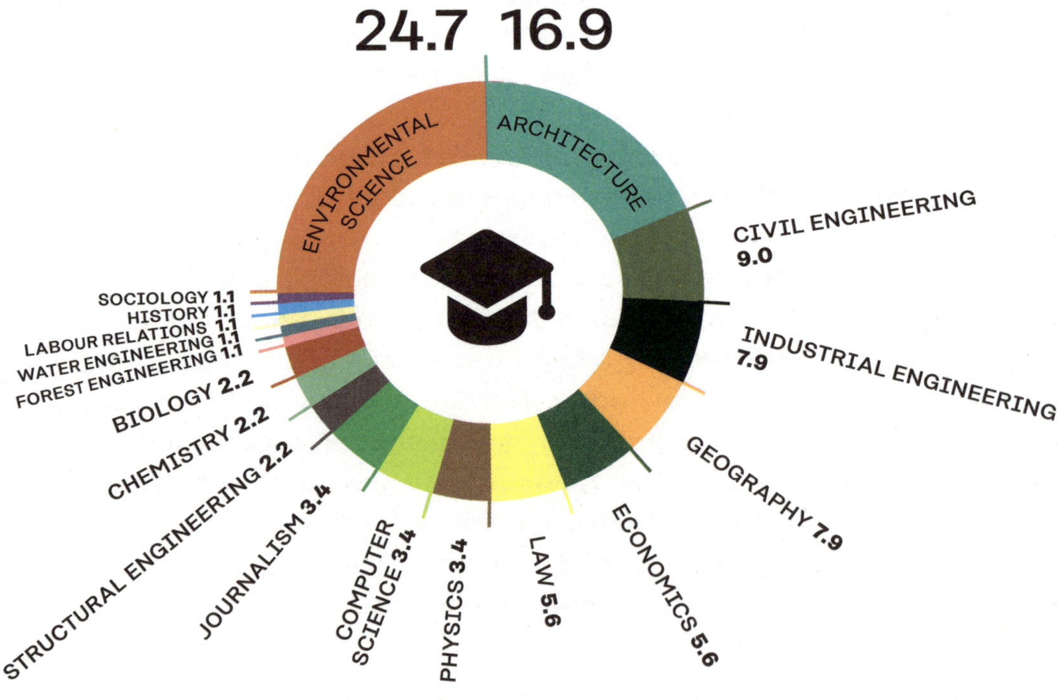

PROFESSIONAL SPECIALITY
(%)